# Advances in Predictive, Preventive and Personalised Medicine

Volume 18

R. Andrew Tasker, University of Prince Edward Island, Charlottetown, PE, Canada

Christine Nardini, University of Bologna and Verona, Cryolab and Diatheva, Italy
Laboratory Medicine, Karolinska Institute, Stockholm, Sweden

Lotfi Chaari, Higher Institute of Computer Science and Multimedia of Sfax
Sakiet Ezzit, Tunisia

Jiri Polivka Jr., Department of Histology and Embryology, Biomedical Centre
Faculty of Medicine in Plzeň, Plzeň, Czech Republic

Silvia Mandel, University of Haifa, Haifa, Israel

Carl Erb, Private Institute of Applied Ophthalmology, Berlin, Germany

Wei Wang, School of Medical and Health Sciences, Edith Cowan University,
Perth, WA, Australia

What this book series is about... Current healthcare: What is behind the issue? For many acute and chronic disorders, the current healthcare outcomes are considered as being inadequate: global figures cry for preventive measures and personalised treatments. In fact, severe chronic pathologies such as cardiovascular disorders, diabetes and cancer are treated after onset of the disease, frequently at near end-stages. Pessimistic prognosis considers pandemic scenario for type 2 diabetes mellitus, neurodegenerative disorders and some types of cancer over the next 10-20 years followed by the economic disaster of healthcare systems in a global scale. Advanced healthcare tailored to the person: What is beyond the issue? Advanced healthcare promotes the paradigm change from delayed interventional to predictive medicine tailored to the person, from reactive to preventive medicine and from disease to wellness. The innovative Predictive, Preventive and Personalised Medicine (PPPM) is emerging as the focal point of efforts in healthcare aimed at curbing the prevalence of both communicable and non-communicable diseases such as diabetes, cardiovascular diseases, chronic respiratory diseases, cancer and dental pathologies. The cost-effective management of diseases and the critical role of PPPM in modernisation of healthcare have been acknowledged as priorities by global and regional organizations and health-related institutions such as the Organisation of United Nations, the European Union and The National Institutes of Health. Why integrative medical approach by PPPM as the medicine of the future? PPPM is the new integrative concept in healthcare sector that enables to predict individual predisposition before onset of the disease, to provide targeted preventive measures and create personalised treatment algorithms tailored to the person. The expected outcomes are conducive to more effective population screening, prevention early in childhood, identification of persons at-risk, stratification of patients for the optimal therapy planning, prediction and reduction of adverse drug-drug or drug-disease interactions relying on emerging technologies, such as pharmacogenetics, pathology-specific molecular patters, sub/cellular imaging, disease modelling, individual patient profiles, etc. Integrative approach by PPPM is considered as the medicine of the future. Being at the forefront of the global efforts, The European Association for Predictive, Preventive and Personalised Medicine (EPMA, http://www.epmanet.eu/) promotes the integrative concept of PPPM among healthcare stakeholders, governmental institutions, educators, funding bodies, patient organisations and in the public domain. Current Book Series, published by Springer in collaboration with EPMA, overview multidisciplinary aspects of advanced bio/medical approaches and innovative technologies. Integration of individual professional groups into the overall concept of PPPM is a particular advantage of this book series. Expert recommendations focus on the cost-effective management tailored to the person in health and disease. Innovative strategies are considered for standardisation of healthcare services. New guidelines are proposed for medical ethics, treatment of rare diseases, innovative approaches to early and predictive diagnostics, patient stratification and targeted prevention in healthy individuals, persons at-risk, individual patient groups, sub/populations, institutions, healthcare economy and marketing.

Wei Wang
Editor

# All Around Suboptimal Health

## Advanced Approaches by Predictive, Preventive and Personalised Medicine for Healthy Populations

Springer

*Editor*
Wei Wang
Centre for Precision Health
Edith Cowan University
Perth, Australia

ISSN 2211-3495 ISSN 2211-3509 (electronic)
Advances in Predictive, Preventive and Personalised Medicine

ISBN 978-3-031-46890-2 ISBN 978-3-031-46891-9 (eBook)
https://doi.org/10.1007/978-3-031-46891-9



This Springer imprint is published by the registered company Springer Nature Switzerland AG
The registered company address is: Gewerbestrasse 11, 6330 Cham, Switzerland

Printed on acid-free paper

# Contents

# Editors

## About the Book Series Editor

**Olga Golubnitschaja** Department of Radiology, Medical Faculty, Rheinische Friedrich-Wilhelms-Universität, Bonn, Germany, has studied journalism, biotechnology and medicine and has been awarded research fellowships in Austria, Russia, the UK, Germany, the Netherlands and Switzerland (early and predictive diagnostics in paediatrics, neurosciences and cancer). She is the author of more than 400 well-cited international publications (research and review articles, position papers, books and book contributions) in the innovative field of predictive, preventive and personalised medicine (PPPM) with the main research focus on pre- and perinatal diagnostics, diagnostics of cardiovascular disease and neurodegenerative pathologies, predictive diagnostics in cancer and diabetes. She has been awarded National and International Fellowship of the Alexander von Humboldt Foundation and Highest Prize in Medicine and Eiselsberg Prize in Austria. Since 2009, Dr. Golubnitschaja is the Secretary General of the European Association for Predictive, Preventive and Personalised Medicine (EPMA, Brussels) networking over 50 countries worldwide (www.epmanet.eu), Series Editor of Advances in Predictive, Preventive and Personalised Medicine (Springer Nature), Volume Editor of Predictive Diagnostics and Personalised Treatment: Dream or Reality (Nova Science Publishers, New York 2009) and Co-editor of Personalisierte Medizin (Health Academy, Dresden 2010). She is the European Representative in the EDR Network at the National Institutes of Health, USA (http://edrn.nci.nih.gov/). She is a regular reviewer for over 30 clinical and scientific journals and serves as a grant reviewer for national (ministries of health in several European countries) and international funding bodies. Since 2007 until now, she has been working as the European Commission evaluation expert for FP7, Horizon

2020, IMI-1 (Innovative Medical Initiatives) and IMI-2. From 2010 to 2013, she was involved in creating the PPPM-related contents for the European Programme 'Horizon 2020'. Currently, Dr. Golubnitschaja is Vice-Chair of the Evaluation Panel for Marie Curie Mobility Actions at the European Commission in Brussels.

# About the Volume Editor

**Wei Wang** MD, PhD, FFPH, FRSB, FRSM, is Pro-Vice-Chancellor (China) at Edith Cowan University (ECU), Australia. He is also Professor of Public Health in the Centre for Precision Health ECU, Australia, and Chief Scientist, Institute of Glycome Studies, Shantou University Medical College (SUMC), China.

Prior to joining ECU, Professor Wang was Vice Director of Research at Peking University-Hong Kong University of Sciences & Technology Medical Centre in Shenzhen, Vice Dean of School of Life Science, University of Chinese Academy of Sciences, and Dean of School of Public Health and Family Medicine, Capital Medical University, Beijing, China, and Professor, Public Health, Edith Cowan University, Australia.

He has had an interest in forensic medicine and global health for almost 30 years. In addition to his role as Professor in the School of Medical and Health Sciences at ECU, Professor Wang is also the Chief Scientist, Institute of Glycome Studies, SUMC, China, Adjunct Professor, School of Public Health, Shandong First Medical University (SFMU), China, and Director of the Beijing Municipal Key Laboratory-Centre of Excellence on Clinical Epidemiology, Capital Medical University (CMU), China.

His contributions to medical science include service as an executive member of the International Society of Translational Medicine, Membership of the Standing Committee of the International Association of Physiological Anthropology and Membership of the Expert Panel advising the WHO on its 'Grand Challenges in Genomics for Public Health in Developing Countries'. He was also a steering committee member of the OECD initiative on Public Health Genomics.

Professor Wang was the Foundation Chief Editor of the *Journal of Family Medicine and Community Health* (BMJ). Currently, he is Associate Editor of *EPMA Journal* (Springer), and regional editor of *Journal of Global Health* (University of Edinburgh Press), *OMICS: A Journal of Integrative Biology* (Mary Ann Liebert), *Journal of Human Hypertension* (Nature Publishing Group), *Clinical and Translational Medicine* (Wiley), *Engineering* (*CAE-Elsevier*), and *PloS ONE* (PLoS).

Professor Wang holds the degrees of Doctor of Medicine from China Medical University and Doctor of Philosophy from Oita Medical University, Japan.

Professor Wang's principal interests are in human genetics and global health, where he is a specialist in medical genetics, glycomics, population health, suboptimal health, and paternity testing. He has published over 300 scientific papers in prestigious journals including *Science*, *Nature Genetics*, and *The Lancet*.

# Suboptimal Health Management in the Framework of PPP Medicine

**Wei Wang, Vincenzo Costigliola, and Olga Golubnitschaja**

W. Wang (✉)
First Affiliated Hospital, Shantou University Medical College, Shantou, China

Beijing Key Laboratory of Clinical Epidemiology, Capital Medical University, Beijing, China

School of Public Health, Shandong First Medical University and Shandong Academy of Medical Sciences, Jinan, China

Centre for Precision Health, Edith Cowan University, Perth, Australia

Suboptimal Health Study Consortium, Kumasi, Ghana

Suboptimal Health Study Consortium, Perth, Australia

Suboptimal Health Study Consortium, Beijing, China

Suboptimal Health Study Consortium, Bonn, Germany

European Association for Predictive, Preventive and Personalised Medicine, EPMA, Brussels, Belgium
e-mail: wei.wang@ecu.edu.au

V. Costigliola
European Association for Predictive, Preventive and Personalised Medicine, EPMA, Brussels, Belgium

European Medical Association, EMA, Brussels, Belgium
e-mail: vincenzo@emanet.org

O. Golubnitschaja (✉)
Suboptimal Health Study Consortium, Bonn, Germany

European Association for Predictive, Preventive and Personalised Medicine, EPMA, Brussels, Belgium

3P Medicine Research Unit, University Hospital, Rheinische Friedrich-Wilhelms Universität Bonn, Bonn, Germany
e-mail: olga.golubnitschaja@ukbonn.de


W. Wang (ed.), *All Around Suboptimal Health*, Advances in Predictive, Preventive and Personalised Medicine 18,
https://doi.org/10.1007/978-3-031-46891-9_1

## Abbreviations

| | |
|---|---|
| CTD | Connective tissues dysfunction |
| EPMA | European Association for Predictive, Preventive and Personalised Medicine |
| ET-1 | Endothelin-1 |
| FS | Flammer syndrome |
| GAH | Gestational arterial hypertension |
| GD | Gestational diabetes |
| PE | Preeclampsia |
| PPPM/3PM | Predictive, preventive and personalised medicine |
| SH | Suboptimal health |

## 1 Suboptimal Health (SH) Definition

Suboptimal health (SH) can be easily defined as the reversible phase of the health-to-disease transition. Consequently, the time-frame between the SH condition onset and related clinically manifested disorder is the operational window to protect the affected person against the disease which he/she is predisposed to [1].

## 2 Cost-Effective Prevention of Persons in SH Conditions from the Health-to-Disease Transition Is One of the Highest Priorities of PPP Medicine Concepts in Primary and Secondary Care

Prevention of people from the health-to-disease transition is a highly comprehensive approach based on predictive diagnostics and intervention tailored to the individualised health. Cost-effectiveness inversely correlates with the suboptimal severity grade and level of care. Consequently, PPPM management of subtle health alterations in primary care is the most cost-effective approach compared to irreversible health-to-disease transition and disease progression (secondary care). Contextually, major efforts have to be dedicated to the population screening focused on early stages of SH conditions, precisive diagnosis followed by the targeted individualised prevention. Corresponding paradigm shift from delayed-reactive medical services to advanced PPPM approach in biomedical sciences and daily practice is propagated by the EPMA (European Association for Predictive, Preventive and Personalised Medicine) (https://www.epmanet.eu) who is considered the world leader in PPPM [2].

PPPM research and implementation rely on a robust conceptual and technological innovation including multi-professional expertise (researchers, caregivers, educators, technologists, policy-makers, diagnostic and pharmaceutical industry), application of artificial intelligence in medicine, education provided to professionals and general population, active involvement of patient organisation and affected individuals into the doctor–patient collaborative process (participatory medicine), amongst others. This can be exemplified by the newly proposed mitochondrial health quality check-up.

## 3 A Holistic Approach by the Mitochondrial Health Quality Check-Up (MHQC)

An evident reciprocity between mitochondrial and organismal health status is clearly reflected in the health-to-disease transition and systemic damage. Therefore, a routine non-invasive mitochondrial health quality control test is strongly recommended as the holistic predictive diagnostics to benefit both primary and secondary care. With the highest priority, MHQC is proposed to implement for the pre-pregnancy check-up, health-to-disease transition check-up, accompanying diagnostics in sport medicine and coached body exercise, physiotherapeutic and well-being services, and therapy efficacy monitoring for personalised treatments, e.g. in chrono- and sleep-medicine, chronic fatigue and burnout syndrome, mood disorders and systemic impairments, amongst others [3, 4].

## 4 Microbiome-Related Health-Maintaining Technologies in PPPM

Microbiome-related health-maintaining technologies is a promising PPPM approach in SH as reviewed by the recently released book "Microbiome in 3P Medicine Strategies – The First Exploitation Guide" [5]. Microbiome demonstrates holistic effects on human health, i.e.: a multi-functional interplay between the individual health status and microbiome profile composed of microflora on skin, in nasal/oral cavities, in airways, and also in gastro-intestinal and urogenital tracts. The microbiota colonisation starts at birth in humans, demonstrating two levels, i.e., local and global ones, of the immune response. Microbiota composition is a modifiable risk factor that can be modulated being therefore an attractive target for overall SH management.

## 5 Needs of Young Populations Are in Focus of SH Concepts in PPPM

In order to be effective for healthcare systems, PPPM approach has to be implemented early in life of each individual. Per accumulated scientific evidence, health condition of the mother and offspring to great extent is created during the pregnancy because of highly increased haemodynamic stress which mother is exposed to. In case of maternal sub-optimal health that is usually overlooked in pre pregnancy period, progressive abnormalities will get progressed and visible during pregnancy and post-partum. Following the principles of PPPM, advanced screening programmes applied to young populations as well as timely companion diagnoses during pregnancy have been promoted by the EPMA expert working group in the area of PPPM in youth [6] to early diagnose and cost-effectively prevent post-partum health risks of the mother and child. Great clinical utility of the proposed PPPM concept has been recently demonstrated as summarised in Fig. 1.

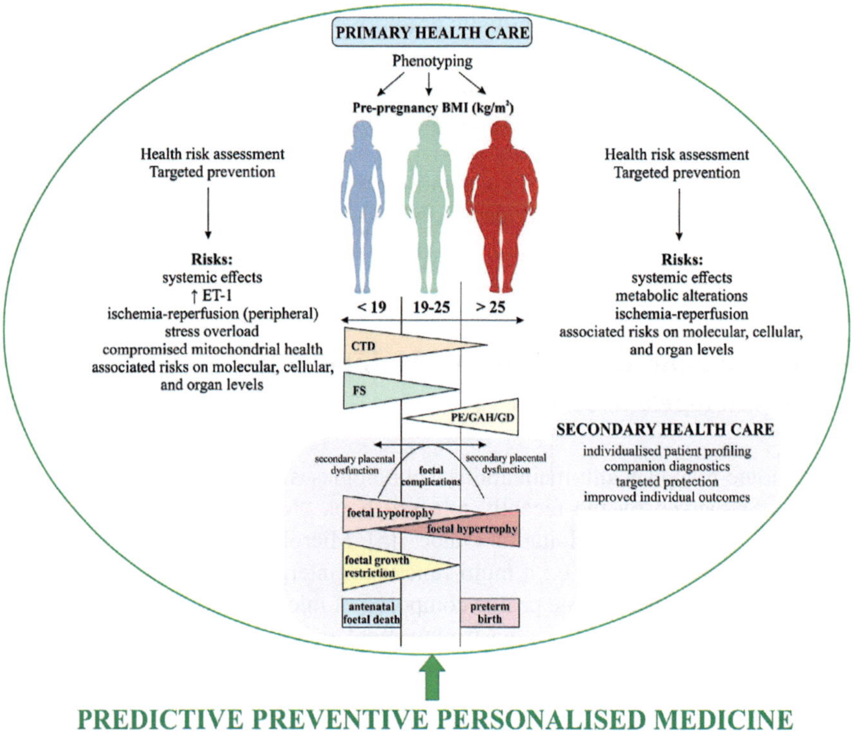


**Fig. 1** PPPM approach proposed by the EPMA expert group revealed the susceptible pregnancy-related health risks to mother and child; proposed screening programme based on phenotyping of the mother prior to pregnancy, precisive health risk assessment and individual tailored protective and mitigating measures for primary and secondary care. *Abbreviations*: *CTD* connective tissues dysfunction, *ET-1* enddothelin-1, *FS* Flammer syndrome, *GAH* gestational arterial hypertension, *GD* gestational diabetes, *PE* preeclampsia. Image is adapted from Youth [6]

## 6 Who Are the Beneficiaries of SH-Innovation in the Framework of PPPM?

The joint position paper released by the EPMA J. in 2021 on behalf of the Suboptimal Health Study Consortium and European Association for Predictive, Preventive and Personalised Medicine [1] stated that below listed medical fields might strongly benefit from the scientific promotion and practical implementation of the SH-related innovation in the framework of PPPM:

- Mental health and physical vitality at any age.
- Reproductive health.
- Planned pregnancies.
- Chrono- and sleep-medicine.
- Sport medicine and coached body exercises.
- Periodontal health.
- Longevity and anti-ageing medicine.
- Disease pre-stages.
- Anti-stress programmes.
- Protection of populations against communicable and non-communicable disorders.

## References

1. Wang W, Yan Y, Guo Z, Hou H, Garcia M, Tan X, Anto EO, Mahara G, Zheng Y, Li B, Wang Y, Guo X, Golubnitschaja O (2021) All Around Suboptimal Health. A joint position paper of the Suboptimal Health Study Consortium and European Association for Predictive, Preventive and Personalised Medicine. EPMA J 12(4):1–31. https://doi.org/10.1007/s13167-021-00253-2
2. Golubnitschaja O, Baban B, Boniolo G, Wang W, Bubnov R, Kapalla M, Krapfenbauer K, Mozaffari M, Costigliola V (2016) Medicine in the early twenty-first century: paradigm and anticipation – EPMA position paper 2016. EPMA J 7:23. https://doi.org/10.1186/s13167-016-0072-4
3. Koklesova L, Mazurakova A, Samec M, Kudela E, Biringer K, Kubatka P, Golubnitschaja O (2022) Mitochondrial health quality control: measurements and interpretation in the framework of predictive, preventive, and personalized medicine. EPMA J 13:177–193. https://doi.org/10.1007/s13167-022-00281-6
4. Golubnitschaja O (2023) What is the routine mitochondrial health check-up good for? In: Podbielska H, Kapalla M (eds) A holistic approach in the framework of 3P medicine. Book-chapter in the book-volume "Predictive, preventive and personalised medicine: from bench to bedside", Book Series "Advances in Predictive, Preventive and Personalised Medicine". Spinger. https://doi.org/10.1007/978-3-031-19564-8
5. Golubnitschaja O (2023) In: Boyko N, Golubnitschaja O (eds) Microbiome in 3P medicine strategies – the first exploitation guide, Hardcover ISBN: 978-3-031-19563-1; eBook ISBN: 978-3-031-19564-8 in the book series "Advances in Predictive, Preventive and Personalised Medicine". Springer. https://doi.org/10.1007/978-3-031-19564-8
6. Evsevieva M, Sergeeva O, Mazurakova A, Koklesova L, Prokhorenko-Kolomoytseva I, Shchetinin E, Birkenbihl C, Costigliola V, Kubatka P, Golubnitschaja O (2022) Pre-pregnancy check-up of maternal vascular status and associated phenotype is crucial for the health of mother and offspring. EPMA J 13(3):351–366. https://doi.org/10.1007/s13167-022-00294-1

# Definition of Suboptimal Health

**Haifeng Hou and Wei Wang**

## Abbreviations

| | |
|---|---|
| ASCVD | Atherosclerotic cardiovascular diseases |
| CFIDS | Chronic fatigue immune dysfunction syndrome |
| CFS | Chronic fatigue syndrome |
| CVH | Cardiovascular health |

H. Hou
School of Public Health, Shandong First Medical University and Shandong Academy of Medical Sciences, Jinan, China

Tai'an, China

Centre for Precision Health, Edith Cowan University, Perth, Australia

W. Wang (✉)
First Affiliated Hospital, Shantou University Medical College, Shantou, China

Beijing Key Laboratory of Clinical Epidemiology, Capital Medical University, Beijing, China

Jinan, China

Centre for Precision Health, Edith Cowan University, Perth, Australia

Suboptimal Health Study Consortium, Kumasi, Ghana

Suboptimal Health Study Consortium, Perth, Australia

Suboptimal Health Study Consortium, Beijing, China

Suboptimal Health Study Consortium, Bonn, Germany

European Association for Predictive, Preventive and Personalised Medicine, EPMA, Brussels, Belgium
e-mail: wei.wang@ecu.edu.au


W. Wang (ed.), *All Around Suboptimal Health*, Advances in Predictive, Preventive and Personalised Medicine 18,
https://doi.org/10.1007/978-3-031-46891-9_2

| | |
|---|---|
| HELLP | Haemolysis elevated liver enzymes and low platelet count |
| ME | Myalgic encephalomyelitis |
| NCDs | Non-communicable chronic diseases |
| NO | Nitric oxide |
| PE | Preeclampsia |
| PVFS | Post-viral fatigue syndrome |
| RA | Rheumatoid arthritis |
| SHS | Suboptimal health status |
| SHSQ-25 | Suboptimal Health Status Questionnaire-25 |
| SLE | Systemic lupus erythematosus |
| TL | Telomere length |
| UMS | Unexplained medical syndrome |
| VD | Vaginal dryness |

## 1 Definition of Suboptimal Health

SHS is intermediate condition between optimal health and diseases. SHS is commonly characterised by reversible loss of vitality, decline of physiological function and less capacity for self-adaptation. Individual with SHS suffers from self-perceived general weakness, low energy or health complaints but does not match any criteria of diseases, which increase the predispositions to physical or psychological disorders. It is demonstrated that a variety of non-communicable chronic diseases (NCDs) have a reversible period of SHS prior to specific pathological disorders [1].

Different from either early stage or preclinical period of diseases, SHS is defined as a period preceding the occurrence of diagnosable manifestations of diseases. Individuals in this pre-disease stage are healthy who cannot be diagnosed as any of the specific virtual diseases. In contrast, individuals in preclinical period of specific disease usually have the specific signs or indications of the disease and need to be treated with targeted therapies that contribute to prevent or delay the process of the disease. By reference to the guideline of PPPM, persons with SHS are considered to require nonspecific health promotion management, including physical activities, prudent dietary practices, quitting smoking and psychological counselling, which lead to reversion of health status, and reduction of likelihood of disease. However, compared with commonly-recognized pre-disease, the features of SHS make it feasible to identify the persons who suffer from SHS. In addition, the well recognition of SHS may motivate the specific preventive approaches to prevent SHS-related diseases.

Even though SHS is common, only 23% of SHS are reported to seek immediate medical services [2], and approximately 80% of them showed no improvements in health condition within 6 months [3]. Therefore, it is urgently needed to call for concerted efforts and positive contributions to the timely detection of persons with SHS, which are advocated by the professionals of PPP medicine [4].

## 2 Examples of SHS-Associated Disease and Dysfunctions

Since early diagnosis, accompanied with targeted intervention is crucial for the prevention and control of NCDs, it is demanded for clinic practitioners to shift their perspective from clinical intervention for diagnosable disease to the priority of identifying persons at SHS stage [5]. However, it is difficult, at present, to discriminate those with SHS from generally apparent healthy individuals, due to the variety of health-related perceptions, and heterogeneous somatic complaints. Commonly, five domains are of interest for screening SHS-associated problems: fatigue, cardiovascular system, digestive tract, immune system and mental state (Fig. 1).

**Fig. 1** Suboptimal health status is instrumental for health care of non-communicable diseases. The figure is adapted from Ref. [6]

The key role of SHS in the pathogenesis and progression of health damages or dysfunctions has been investigated. The findings on SHS-associated diseases and dysfunctions offer a window opportunity to reserve the progression of damages to the health.

## 2.1 Cardiovascular System

SHS is associated with poor cardiovascular health (CVH) metrics that consist of high blood pressure, dyslipidaemia and hyperglycaemia, smoking, overweight, lack of physical activity and irregular diet [7]. Multi-ethnicities studies also confirmed that SHS is closely correlated to hypertension, hyperglycaemia and dyslipidaemia [4, 8]. A Russian study revealed that endothelial function is associated not only with overall SHS, but also with individual sub-domains of SHS, including fatigue, mental and cardiovascular system [9]. With regard to behavioural factors, SHS is attributable to cigarette smoking, irregular breakfast, lack of physical activity and alcohol consumption [4, 10]. Therefore, SHS can be used as one of the behavioural candidates for indicating a healthy lifestyle. Meal composition and timing can influence metabolic patterns that may lead to the occurrence of SHS. Skipping breakfast reduces insulin sensitivity, resulting from pre-loading and distortion of energy metabolism [11]. The improved belief and practice of healthy breakfast behaviours will consequently lead to the improvement of health conditions.

## 2.2 Immune System and Reproductive Health

Pregnant women in SHS are exposed to abnormal elevation of oxidative stress and unbalance of pro- and anti-angiogenic growth stimulators [12]. After a 20-week follow-up of normotensive pregnant women in Ghana, persons in the condition of SHS suffered a significantly higher incidence of preeclampsia (PE) and other related adverse pregnancy complications, including intrauterine growth restriction, stillbirth, haemolysis elevated liver enzymes and low platelet count (HELLP) syndrome, acute kidney injury and dyslipidaemia [5]. HELLP syndrome is featured by microangiopathic anaemia, thrombocytopenia and periportal hepatic necrosis, which is one of the causes of eclampsia-associated health disorders during pregnancy [13]. Hepatic involvement in preeclampsia is attributed to the precipitation of fibrin within liver periportal areas and vasospasm, which result in liver cell necrosis and lobular ischemia [14]. The association between SHS and preeclampsia-coexisting HELLP syndrome might also result from mental health indicators. In addition, SHS has a causal relationship with vascular endothelium dysfunction [9], which may also contribute to understanding the relationship between SHS and PE. Endothelial dysfunction is closely related to placental hypoxia, nitric oxide (NO) deficiency and oxidative stress that are induced by poor extravillous trophoblast cell invasion and lack of maternal artery remodelling [15]. Another facet needs to be explained is maternal psychosocial stress since psychosocial stress and fatigue are the SHS-specific syndromes [16]. Vaginal dryness (VD), resulting from hormonal regulation changes in women during the climacteric period, is also considered as a syndrome of SHS [17].

Besides, individuals in different levels of SHS have diversity of IgG N-glycosylation traits, an important post-translation modification of IgG [18]. Glycosylation affects more than 90% of mammalian proteins and enables them normal structure and a variety of biological functions. N-linked glycans modulate the function of IgG between anti-inflammatory and pro-inflammatory and influence the development of not only inflammatory diseases but also chronic and autoimmune diseases, including cardiovascular diseases, systemic lupus erythematosus (SLE), rheumatoid arthritis (RA), dyslipidaemia, diabetes, Alzheimer and Parkinson's disease [19]. This enables IgG N-glycans to precisely predict and early diagnose these diseases.

## 2.3 *Fatigue and Labour Efficiency*

Employees exposed to psychosocial work hazards (e.g., insecurity, workplace justice) or psychosocial stress (e.g., high demands at work, interpersonal relations and leadership) were in poor health status and predisposed to SHS [20, 21]. The frequencies of sickness absence are associated with the prevalence of chronic conditions during occupation, and the future adverse health outcomes after retirement. A prospective study conducted in a large sample size population demonstrated a long-term association between sickness absence and subsequent SHS, in which workers exposed to more sickness absences were observed of increased risk for SHS over a 14-year follow-up [22, 23]. In addition, individuals with SHS experienced much more non-permanent employment [24].

Objective health measures have been investigated on SHS. For example, telomere, consisting of repetitive sequences at the ends of chromosomes, plays a crucial role in maintaining genomic integrity. Telomere length (TL) is shorter in patients with age-related chronic diseases, including diabetes, cardiovascular diseases, impaired immune function and certain types of cancer [25]. Compared to individuals with ideal health, shorter TL was observed in persons with SHS [25]. Consistently, longer TL has been found in those with better self-reported health conditions [26]. Healthy centenarians have been found to have relatively higher TL compared with those with poorer healthy conditions in a North American study [27]. This partly results from the positive association between TL and CVH parameters. In addition, shorter TL is associated with unhealthy lifestyle, which is also an important contributor to SHS [28].

## 2.4 *Digestive Tract and Metabolites*

In spite of the lack of an explicit mechanism, the intestinal microbiota is reported to be associated with SHS, and individuals with SHS have alterations of intestinal microbiota composition compared to those in ideal health conditions [29]. In addition, plasma metabolites in SHS are predominantly different from those with ideal health, including sphingomyelin, sphinganine, sphingosine, pregnenolone, progesterone and bilirubin [30]. As reported, overexpression of sphingomyelin synthase-2 increases plasma sphingomyelin and then aggravates atherosclerosis in animal experiments [31]. Furthermore, a decrease in atherosclerotic lesions and inflammatory disorder has been observed in the mice model of sphingomyelin synthase-2 deficiency [32]. As such, sphingomyelin synthase-2 is a potential therapeutic target for atherosclerotic cardiovascular diseases (ASCVD). The finding on sphingomyelin also evidences that sphingomyelin is associated with the phenotypes of the cardiovascular system in SHS individuals, which provided a new target for the personalised prevention of cardiovascular diseases.

Loss of amino acid, identified by amino acid excretion has been found in persons under one subtype of SHS, i.e., long-term fatigue [33]. A negative nitrogen balance induces the development of sub-optimal haemoglobin production that results in fatigue. Consequently, the particular group of people more susceptible to histidine loss need to supplement appropriate proteins. Early studies carried out in breast cancer radiotherapy patients showed that women who suffered from more fatigue had higher levels of urinary histidine excretion [34].

## 2.5 *Mental Status and Neurological Dysfunctions*

Complaint of psychological or mental health is one of the important domains of SHS. As such, studies have investigated the association of psychological and mental symptoms with SHS [35]. It is notable that adolescents with SHS have an increased incidence of self-reported suicidal ideation during a one-year follow-up [36], suggesting more studies on SHS amongst adolescents than expected.

The association between SHS and cognitive impairment was analysed in middle-aged and older Chinese populations, among whom SHS is observed to be linked to the decrease of cognitive function [37]. SHS and other multifactorial risk factors (e.g., genetic predisposition, toxic chemical, endogenous and exogenous stress, systemic ischemia-reperfusion and mitochondrial vulnerability) are involved in neurodegenerative processes, which result in multiple neurological symptoms and irreversible impairment of nervous systems [38–40].

## 3 Summary/Outlook

SHS, by reference to its apparent features and implications, is understood as closely associated with a range of health outcomes, i.e., unexplained medical syndrome (UMS), chronic fatigue syndrome (CFS), myalgic encephalomyelitis (ME), post-viral fatigue syndrome (PVFS) and chronic fatigue immune dysfunction syndrome (CFIDS) [41]. More studies are advocated to elucidate the key role of SHS in the development of NCDs, by which targeted healthcare services can be developed to improve optimal well-being.

## References


1. Golubnitschaja O (2019) Flammer syndrome:advances in predictive, preventive and personalised medicine, Book Series "Advances in Predictive, Preventive and Personalised Medicine". Spinger. https://doi.org/10.1007/978-3-030-13550-8
2. Shin S, Oh H, Kang M, Park M, Koh BH, Hwang M (2019) Feasibility and effectiveness assessment of a mobile application for subhealth management: study protocol for a randomized controlled trial. Medicine 98(21):e15704. https://doi.org/10.1097/md.0000000000015704
3. Lee J, Dong SO, Lee Y, Kim SH, Lee S (2014) Recognition of and interventions for Mibyeong (subhealth) in South Korea: a national web-based survey of Korean medicine practitioners. Integr Med Res 3(2):60–66. https://doi.org/10.1016/j.imr.2013.09.001
4. Yan YX, Dong J, Liu YQ, Yang XH, Li M, Shia G, Wang W (2012) Association of suboptimal health status and cardiovascular risk factors in urban Chinese workers. J Urban Health 89(2):329–338. https://doi.org/10.1007/s11524-011-9636-8
5. Anto EO, Roberts P, Coall D, Turpin CA, Adua E, Wang Y, Wang W (2019) Integration of suboptimal health status evaluation as a criterion for prediction of preeclampsia is strongly recommended for healthcare management in pregnancy: a prospective cohort study in a Ghanaian population. EPMA J 10(3):211–226. https://doi.org/10.1007/s13167-019-00183-0
6. Wang W, Yan Y, Guo Z, Hou H, Garcia M, Tan X, Anto EO, Mahara G, Zheng Y, Li B, Kang T, Zhong Z, Wang Y, Guo X, Golubnitschaja O, Suboptimal Health Study C, European Association for Predictive P, Personalised M (2021) All around suboptimal health - a joint position paper of the suboptimal health study consortium and European Association for Predictive, preventive and personalised medicine. EPMA J 12:403–433. https://doi.org/10.1007/s13167-021-00253-2
7. Wang Y, Liu X, Qiu J, Wang H, Liu D, Zhao Z, Song M, Song Q, Wang X, Zhou Y, Wang W (2017) Association between ideal cardiovascular health metrics and suboptimal health status in Chinese population. Sci Rep 7(1):14975. https://doi.org/10.1038/s41598-017-15101-5
8. Adua E, Roberts P, Wang W (2017) Incorporation of suboptimal health status as a potential risk assessment for type II diabetes mellitus: a case-control study in a Ghanaian population. EPMA J 8(4):345–355. https://doi.org/10.1007/s13167-017-0119-1
9. Kupaev V, Borisov O, Marutina E, Yan YX, Wang W (2016) Integration of suboptimal health status and endothelial dysfunction as a new aspect for risk evaluation of cardiovascular disease. EPMA J 7(1):19. https://doi.org/10.1186/s13167-016-0068-0
10. Chen J, Cheng J, Liu Y, Tang Y, Sun X, Wang T, Xiao Y, Li F, Xiang L, Jiang P, Wu S, Wu L, Luo R, Zhao X (2014) Associations between breakfast eating habits and health-promoting lifestyle, suboptimal health status in southern China: a population based, cross sectional study. J Transl Med 12:348. https://doi.org/10.1186/s12967-014-0348-1

11. Astbury NM, Taylor MA, Macdonald IA (2011) Breakfast consumption affects appetite, energy intake, and the metabolic and endocrine responses to foods consumed later in the day in male habitual breakfast eaters. J Nutr 141(7):1381–1389. https://doi.org/10.3945/jn.110.128645
12. Anto EO, Roberts P, Coall DA, Adua E, Turpin CA, Tawiah A, Wang Y, Wang W (2020) Suboptimal health pregnant women are associated with increased oxidative stress and unbalanced pro- and antiangiogenic growth mediators: a cross-sectional study in a Ghanaian population. Free Radic Res 54(1):27–42. https://doi.org/10.1080/10715762.2019.1685668
13. Delahaije D, Dirksen C, Peeters L, Smits L (2012) PP105. Mental health problems following preeclampsia or HELLP syndrome: do we have a case? A systematic review. Pregn Hypertens 2(3):296. https://doi.org/10.1016/j.preghy.2012.04.216
14. Alese MO, Moodley J, Naicker T (2021) Preeclampsia and HELLP syndrome, the role of the liver. J Maternal Fetal Neonatal Med 34(1):117–123. https://doi.org/10.1080/14767058.2019.1572737
15. Anto EO, Roberts P, Turpin CA, Wang W (2018) Oxidative stress as a key signaling pathway in placental angiogenesis changes in preeclampsia: updates in pathogenesis, novel biomarkers and therapeutics. Curr Pharmacogen Personal Med 16(3):167–181. https://doi.org/10.2174/1875692117666181207120011
16. Valsamakis G, Kanaka-Gantenbein C, Malamitsi-Puchner A, Mastorakos G (2006) Causes of intrauterine growth restriction and the postnatal development of the metabolic syndrome. Ann N Y Acad Sci 1092:138–147. https://doi.org/10.1196/annals.1365.012
17. Goncharenko V, Bubnov R, Polivka J Jr, Zubor P, Biringer K, Bielik T, Kuhn W, Golubnitschaja O (2019) Vaginal dryness: individualised patient profiles, risks and mitigating measures. EPMA J 10(1):73–79. https://doi.org/10.1007/s13167-019-00164-3
18. Adua E, Memarian E, Russell A, Trbojević-Akmačić I, Gudelj I, Jurić J, Roberts P, Lauc G, Wang W (2019) Utilization of N-glycosylation profiles as risk stratification biomarkers for suboptimal health status and metabolic syndrome in a Ghanaian population. Biomark Med 13(15):1273–1287. https://doi.org/10.2217/bmm-2019-0005
19. Hou H, Xu X, Sun F, Zhang X, Dong H, Wang L, Ge S, An K, Sun Q, Li Y, Cao W, Song M, Hu S, Xing W, Wang W, Li D, Wang Y (2019) Hyperuricemia is associated with immunoglobulin G N-glycosylation: a community-based study of glycan biomarkers. Omics 23(12):660–667. https://doi.org/10.1089/omi.2019.0004
20. Hsu SH, Chen DR, Cheng Y, Su TC (2016) Association of psychosocial work hazards with depression and suboptimal health in executive employees. J Occup Environ Med 58(7):728–736. https://doi.org/10.1097/jom.0000000000000760
21. Yan YX, Dong J, Liu YQ, Zhang J, Song MS, He Y, Wang W (2015) Association of suboptimal health status with psychosocial stress, plasma cortisol and mRNA expression of glucocorticoid receptor α/β in lymphocyte. Stress (Amsterdam, Netherlands) 18(1):29–34. https://doi.org/10.3109/10253890.2014.999233
22. Vahtera J, Westerlund H, Ferrie JE, Head J, Melchior M, Singh-Manoux A, Zins M, Goldberg M, Alexanderson K, Kivimäki M (2010) All-cause and diagnosis-specific sickness absence as a predictor of sustained suboptimal health: a 14-year follow-up in the GAZEL cohort. J Epidemiol Community Health 64(4):311–317. https://doi.org/10.1136/jech.2008.083923
23. Ferrie JE, Kivimäki M, Westerlund H, Head J, Melchior M, Singh-Manoux A, Zins M, Goldberg M, Alexanderson K, Vahtera J (2011) Differences in the association between sickness absence and long-term sub-optimal health by occupational position: a 14-year follow-up in the GAZEL cohort. Occup Environ Med 68(10):729–733. https://doi.org/10.1136/oem.2010.060210
24. Virtanen P, Janlert U, Hammarström A (2013) Suboptimal health as a predictor of non-permanent employment in middle age: a 12-year follow-up study of the northern Swedish cohort. Int Arch Occup Environ Health 86(2):139–145. https://doi.org/10.1007/s00420-011-0695-7
25. Alzain MA, Asweto CO, Zhang J, Fang H, Zhao Z, Guo X, Song M, Zhou Y, Chang N, Wang Y, Wang W (2017) Telomere length and accelerated biological aging in the China suboptimal health cohort: a case-control study. Omics 21(6):333–339. https://doi.org/10.1089/omi.2017.0050

26. Njajou OT, Hsueh WC, Blackburn EH, Newman AB, Wu SH, Li R, Simonsick EM, Harris TM, Cummings SR, Cawthon RM (2009) Association between telomere length, specific causes of death, and years of healthy life in health, aging, and body composition, a population-based cohort study. J Gerontol A Biol Sci Med Sci 64(8):860–864. https://doi.org/10.1093/gerona/glp061
27. Peng H, Mete M, Desale S, Fretts AM, Cole SA, Best LG, Lin J, Blackburn E, Lee ET, Howard BV, Zhao J (2017) Leukocyte telomere length and ideal cardiovascular health in American Indians: the strong heart family study. Eur J Epidemiol 32(1):67–75. https://doi.org/10.1007/s10654-016-0199-6
28. Sun Q, Shi L, Prescott J, Chiuve SE, Hu FB, De Vivo I, Stampfer MJ, Franks PW, Manson JE, Rexrode KM (2012) Healthy lifestyle and leukocyte telomere length in U.S. women. PLoS One 7(5):e38374. https://doi.org/10.1371/journal.pone.0038374
29. Sun Q, Xu X, Zhang J, Sun M, Tian Q, Li Q, Cao W, Zhang X, Wang H, Liu J, Zhang J, Meng X, Wu L, Song M, Liu H, Wang W, Wang Y (2020) Association of suboptimal health status with intestinal microbiota in Chinese youths. J Cell Mol Med 24(2):1837–1847. https://doi.org/10.1111/jcmm.14880
30. Wang H, Tian Q, Zhang J, Liu H, Zhang X, Cao W, Zhang J, Anto EO, Li X, Wang X, Liu D, Zheng Y, Guo Z, Wu L, Song M, Wang Y, Wang W (2020) Population-based case-control study revealed metabolomic biomarkers of suboptimal health status in Chinese population-potential utility for innovative approach by predictive, preventive, and personalized medicine. EPMA J 11(2):147–160. https://doi.org/10.1007/s13167-020-00200-7
31. Zhao YR, Dong JB, Li Y, Wu MP (2012) Sphingomyelin synthase 2 over-expression induces expression of aortic inflammatory biomarkers and decreases circulating EPCs in ApoE KO mice. Life Sci 90(21–22):867–873. https://doi.org/10.1016/j.lfs.2012.04.003
32. Liu J, Huan C, Chakraborty M, Zhang H, Lu D, Kuo MS, Cao G, Jiang XC (2009) Macrophage sphingomyelin synthase 2 deficiency decreases atherosclerosis in mice. Circ Res 105(3):295–303. https://doi.org/10.1161/circresaha.109.194613
33. Dunstan RH, Sparkes DL, Macdonald MM, De Jonge XJ, Dascombe BJ, Gottfries J, Gottfries CG, Roberts TK (2017) Diverse characteristics of the urinary excretion of amino acids in humans and the use of amino acid supplementation to reduce fatigue and sub-health in adults. Nutr J 16(1):19. https://doi.org/10.1186/s12937-017-0240-y
34. Hugh Dunstan R, Sparkes DL, Macdonald MM, Roberts TK, Wratten C, Kumar MB, Baines S, Denham JW, Gallagher SA, Rothkirch T (2011) Altered amino acid homeostasis and the development of fatigue by breast cancer radiotherapy patients: a pilot study. Clin Biochem 44(2–3):208–215. https://doi.org/10.1016/j.clinbiochem.2010.10.002
35. Hou H, Feng X, Li Y, Meng Z, Guo D, Wang F, Guo Z, Zheng Y, Peng Z, Zhang W, Li D, Ding G, Wang W (2018) Suboptimal health status and psychological symptoms among Chinese college students: a perspective of predictive, preventive and personalised health. EPMA J 9(4):367–377. https://doi.org/10.1007/s13167-018-0148-4
36. Tu C, Huang Z, Fu L, Fang Y, Wang J, Guo T, Li M, Hao J, Tao F (2012) Predictors of suicidal ideation with sub-optimal health status and anxiety symptom among Chinese adolescents. J Trop Pediatr 58(4):314–319. https://doi.org/10.1093/tropej/fmr090
37. Ding G, Zhao X, Wang Y, Song D, Chen D, Deng Y, Xing W, Dong H, Zhou Y, Li D, Hou H (2020) Evaluation of the relationship between cognitive impairment and suboptimal health status in a northern Chinese population: a cross-sectional study. J Glob Health 10(1):010804. https://doi.org/10.7189/jogh.10.010804
38. Chen AX, Conti TF, Hom GL, Greenlee TE, Raimondi R, Briskin IN, Rich CA, Kampani R, Engel R, Sharma S, Talcott KE, Singh RP (2021) Functional imaging of mitochondria in retinal diseases using flavoprotein fluorescence. Eye (Lond) 35(1):74–92. https://doi.org/10.1038/s41433-020-1110-y
39. Polivka J Jr, Polivka J, Pesta M, Rohan V, Celedova L, Mahajani S, Topolcan O, Golubnitschaja O (2019) Risks associated with the stroke predisposition at young age: facts and hypotheses in

light of individualized predictive and preventive approach. EPMA J 10(1):81–99. https://doi.org/10.1007/s13167-019-00162-5
40. Koklesova L, Samec M, Liskova A, Zhai K, Büsselberg D, Giordano FA, Kubatka P, Golunitschaja O (2021) Mitochondrial impairments in aetiopathology of multifactorial diseases: common origin but individual outcomes in context of 3P medicine. EPMA J 12(1):1–14. https://doi.org/10.1007/s13167-021-00237-2
41. Wang W, Russell A, Yan Y (2014) Traditional Chinese medicine and new concepts of predictive, preventive and personalized medicine in diagnosis and treatment of suboptimal health. EPMA J 5(1):4. https://doi.org/10.1186/1878-5085-5-4

# Mitochondrion: The Subordinated Partner Who Agreed to Come Short But Insists in Healthy Life

**Olga Golubnitschaja**

## Abbreviations

| | |
|---|---|
| ADP | Adenosine diphosphate |
| ATP | Adenosine triphosphate |
| BHI | Bio-energetic health index |
| $CO_2$ | Carbon dioxide |
| CoA | Coenzyme A |
| CoQ | Coenzyme Q |
| Cyt c | Cytochrome c |
| ETC | Electron transport chain |
| $FADH_2$ | Flavin adenine dinukleotide |
| GTP | Guanosine triphosphate |
| MHI | Mitochondrial health index |
| mtDNA | Mitochondrial DNA |
| NADH | Nicotinamide adenine dinucleotide |
| OXPHOS | Oxidative phosphorylation |
| TCA | Tricarboxylic acid |

O. Golubnitschaja (✉)
3P Medicine Research Unit, University Hospital, Rheinische Friedrich-Wilhelms Universität Bonn, Bonn, Germany

European Association for Predictive, Preventive and Personalised Medicine, Brussels, Belgium
e-mail: olga.golubnitschaja@ukbonn.de



W. Wang (ed.), *All Around Suboptimal Health*, Advances in Predictive, Preventive and Personalised Medicine 18,
https://doi.org/10.1007/978-3-031-46891-9_3

# 1 Preamble

About two billion years ago in the Earth history, that time, the archaea in a sequence first instead of to combat, started to tolerate some types of invaded bacteria and stepwise learned to adapt them and at the end subordinated them taking advantage of their properties and abilities such as an effective production of heating and energy resources and well-developed sensors towards good versus bad quality of life. By this long way of coming together into business, the unique form of cooperation between eukaryotes and their intimate partner, the mitochondria, had been created.

Although became subordinated by eukaryotes, mitochondria maintain a certain level of their independence, e.g., by possessing own genetic information (mtDNA) for replication and highly dynamic homeostasis (fission, fusion, mitophagy) that enables healthy mitochondria to effectively react towards changing environmental conditions and to remain within their comfort zone despite appearing health risks. Certainly, both partners, mitochondria and human cells, have their interests in common to protect the quality of life. Contextually, they learned to cooperate together on minimising health risks by utilising a spectrum of properties both complementary possess. However, under critical conditions such as toxic environments, from both partners, the subordinated mitochondrion is exactly the partner who always comes short. It is an intention that both partners apparently agreed on with correspondingly well-elaborated synergies. To this end, in contrast to chrDNA that is well protected against stressors, mtDNA remains fully unprotected being therefore the primary target of the damage. Under stress conditions, mitochondria operate via their highly dynamic homeostasis and react promptly towards injury by increased mitophagy (mitochondrial autophagy resulting in mtDNA fragmentation and cell-free nucleic acids), which has a dual function in both—mitochondrial health itself and health of the human body as the cooperation partner, namely:

1. To remove damaged mitochondria which will get substituted by a renewed mitochondrial population later on (the rejuvenation process) and
2. To send warning signals to all systems of the human body for a prompt induction of adaptive mechanisms aimed at increasing the level of systemic protection such as activated anti-oxidant defence and repair machinery.

Only very sick cells are not able to follow the warning signals distributed systemically by mitophagy being, therefore, resistant against cooperation with mitochondria. In particularly severe cases, this results in so-called "vicious circle" characterised by increasingly uncontrolled production of ROS and diminished energy supply—both highly relevant to strongly compromised mitochondrial health, dysfunctional repair machinery and cell populations at organismal level as summarised by Fig. 1.

The phenomenon of "vicious circle" is well-described for compromised mitochondrial health, reduced population of functional mitochondrial and mitochondrial

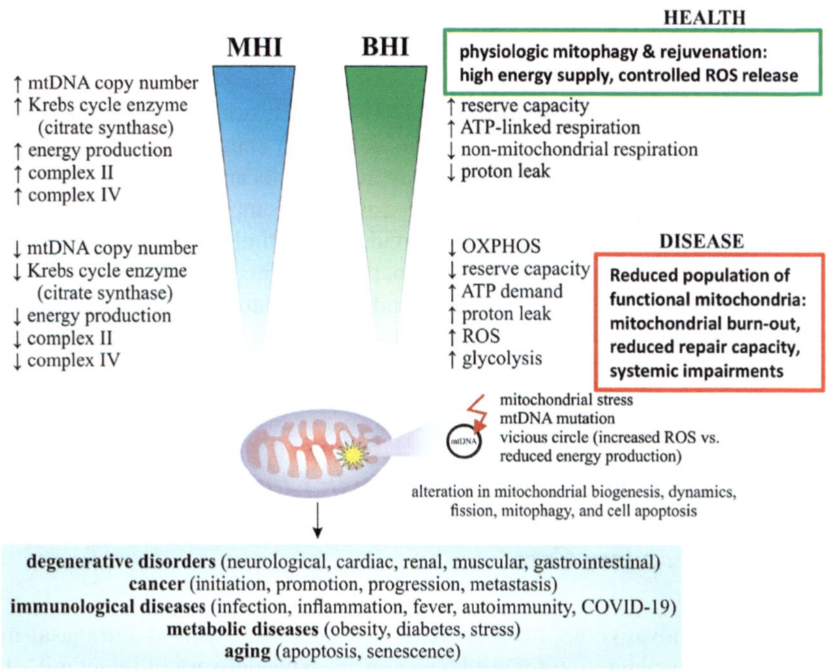


**Fig. 1** The complexity of MitochondiralHealth Index (MHI) and Bioenergetic Health Index (BHI) is illustrated for both—physiologic processes and transition from health-to-disease to be predicted and cost-effectively prevented in primary care; these concepts are promoted by EPMA, Brussels; the image is adapted from Ref. [1]

burn-out leading to reduced repair capacity and systemic impairments per evidence involved in the manifestation of severe pathologies such as progressive Alzheimer's disease and metastatic breast cancer [1, 2]. Acting as effectors and targets of injury, mitochondria are considered a novel hub for resuscitation from cardiac arrest and effective cardio-protection against myocardial infarction, sudden heart attack and arrhythmias [3–7].

Above summarised abilities and functions of mitochondria and synergies in their cooperation with human cells create a spectrum of instruments to be used for predictive diagnostics, targeted prevention and personalisation of treatment algorithms for the paradigm shift from reactive medicine to PPPM promoted by the European Association for Predictive Preventive and Personalised Medicine (EPMA, Brussels) [8]. The prominent examples are presented below to demonstrate the clinical relevance of the mitochondrial medicine and to highlight its essential involvement into protection against health-to-disease transition in suboptimal health conditions relevant for both primary and secondary care.

## 2 To Maintain and Enhance the Population of Functional Mitochondria Is the Highest Priority

How to reach this highly ambitious goal? The issue is not as simple as just an antioxidant intake to mitigate mitochondrial "corrosion" caused by the ROS release as the high costs we have to pay for the way human cells and mitochondria agreed to go together for the energy supply. The measures are complex and focused on beneficial systemic effects considering individually optimised lifestyle, appropriate behavioural and dietary habits, rejuvenation of mitochondrial populations and multi-modal anti-stress programme including respiratory and physical exercises, high quality of sleep, vitamin and nutrient supplements, physio-therapy and meditation, amongst others.

### *2.1 Mitochondrial Transplantation in Clinically Manifested Disorders May Significantly Improve Individual Outcomes in Secondary Care*

There are innovative approaches under consideration such as intranasal mitochondrial transplantation focused on a non-invasive delivery of intact mitochondria to human cells affected by quantitative and qualitative mitochondrial deficits [9]. This research area is motivated by growing evidence on enriching populations of functional mitochondria as the central target in the treatment of devastating neurological and neurodegenerative pathologies such as Parkinson's disease. Indeed, the feasibility of the mitochondrial internalisation has been demonstrated in pre-clinical study sets bypassing the blood–brain barrier and improving overall disease manifestation parameters measured. Promising results by mitochondrial transplantation have been demonstrated also for antitumour approach, including improved mitochondrial dynamics and mitigated chemo-resistance in breast cancer cells [10]. This area clearly demonstrates that maintaining and enhancing populations of functional mitochondria is the highest priority in treatment of severe pathologies being therefore highly relevant for improving individual outcomes in the secondary care, when mitochondrial health is compromised and associated pathologies are clinically manifested. However, for the paradigm shift from reactive to predictive, preventive and personalised medicine, a cost-effective protection on individuals against the health-to-disease transition utilising the protection of mitochondrial health and maintaining their functional populations, is highly attractive and realistic as demonstrated below.

## 2.2 *Targeted Application of the Phyto-Medical Approach Is Highly Attractive for Maintaining Functional Mitochondrial Populations in Primary Care: Clinically Relevant Examples*

There is well-justified multi-professional interest in nutraceutical substances as dietary supplements to protect individuals against clinically manifested disorders with a great cost-efficacy of corresponding treatments. In the context of mitochondrial health, below we exemplify clinically relevant nutraceutical substances.

### 2.2.1 *Acetyl-L-carnitine (ALC)*

*Acetyl-L-carnitine (ALC)* is a well-tolerated nutraceutical substance. In general, carnitine profiling is a useful diagnostic and prognostic tool under neuropathological and altered metabolic conditions such as diabetes mellitus with neurodegenerative complications [11] ,neurotoxicity and mental disorders [12]. ALC demonstrates beneficial effects on the ageing brain and in overall protection against stress-related disorders, and strengthens antidepressant mechanisms including aspects of serotonergic, noradrenergic and GABA neurotransmission. L-carnitine (biologically active stereoisomer) transports long-chain fatty acids from cytoplasm to mitochondria for the energy production (the beta-oxidation pathway via acetyl-CoA formation) and removes short- and medium-chain fatty acids preventing their accumulation in mitochondria. ALC acts as the "mitochondrial nutrient" by reversing stress- and age-related mitochondrial dysfunction and mitigating inadequate reactions of aged and impaired mitochondrial populations.

### 2.2.2 Quercetin

Anti-ageing and rejuvenating effects of quercetin have been demonstrated in many pre-clinical studies [13]. Quercetin and its derivatives act as a proteasome activator with anti-oxidant properties strongly influencing cellular lifespan, survival and viability of human fibroblasts: Significant rejuvenating effects and improved homeostasis have been observed on senescent fibroblasts. The mechanism underlying rejuvenation effects by quercetin is linked to restoring physiologic levels of mitophagy and mitochondrial health quality control (the Sirt1-agonist function), resulting in renewing functional populations of mitochondria [2]. Positive effects of quercetin supplementation were demonstrated for the reproductive medicine, namely the sperm motility, plasma membrane integrity, viability, and overall parameters of the mitochondrial health were significantly improved [14].

### 2.2.3 Resveratrol

Both *resveratrol and metformin* act as the AMPK-activators and have been proposed for supporting compensatory mechanisms of targeted treatments that prompt mitochondria to enhance ATP production by overexpressed anti-oxidants and respiratory complex subunits [2]. Resveratrol (3,4′,5-trihydroxystilbene; $C_{14}H_{12}O_3$) is a common bioactive constituent found in grapes, berries, peanuts and wines and demonstrated to improve mitochondrial function under both in vitro and in vivo conditions. The positive effects of this natural polyphenolic phytoalexin are evident for mitochondrial populations with its strong anti-inflammatory, anti-apoptotic and anticancer capacity [15, 16]. Resveratrol is of great pharmacological value being a systemic multi-functional gene-expression modulator that stimulates mitochondria biogenesis via gene-regulating effects including protein deacetylase sirtuin 1 and the nuclear factor-E2-related factor-2 pathways and reduces mitochondrial superoxide generation within the pathway of endothelial nitric oxide-synthase.

### 2.2.4 Melatonin

The reciprocity has been demonstrated between mitochondrial functionality and melatonin metabolism. The melatonin–mitochondria axis effectively attenuates adverse systemic effects such as pro-inflammatory and carcinogenic processes [17]. Remarkable cardio-protective properties of melatonin are linked to maintaining mitochondrion bio-energetic homeostasis [18]. Consequently, the chronotherapeutic approach restoring nocturnal melatonin production and/or dietary melatonin supplementation is strongly recommended for shift work as the circadian misalignment to prevent systemic mitochondrial dysfunction-associated damage [19]. In preclinical studies, melatonin treatment has been demonstrated as highly beneficial for the amelioration of ageing-related impairments in mitochondrial function [20].

### 2.2.5 Allicin

Allicin (S-allyl prop-2-ene-1-sulfinothiolate) is the main bioactive compound of garlic (Allium sativum) demonstrating clinically relevant properties including immune-modulatory, anti-stress and anti-inflammatory, anti-biotic/parasitic, anti-cancer as well as cardio- and neuro-protective activities. The cornerstone of corresponding protection mechanisms is the promotion of mitochondrial homeostasis (fusion) and function via NRF2 and HSP70 pathways as reviewed by Mocayar Marón et al. [21].

# 3 Cardio-Respiratory Fitness (CRF) Linked to the Mitochondrial Health Is a Crucial Biomarker for the Health Risk Assessment in Primary Care

CRF indexes an individual capacity of two synergic systems, namely the circulatory and respiratory ones to supply $O_2$ to mitochondrial populations in human skeletal muscles for the concomitant energy production during physical exercises. This biomarker is crucial for the health risk assessment as stated by several professional organisations in the area [22]. It is believed that only 40% of US American youth demonstrate physiological values of CRF influenced by non-modifiable and modifiable factors. The latter consider inadequate dietary habits as a strong risk factor of CRF being directly linked to mitochondrial health and functionality. To this end, the nutritional contribution to the CRF quality is rooted in the efficiency of mitochondrial energetics, and optimal dietary patterns rich in polyphenols and omega-3-fatty acids promote both—an appropriate mitochondrial bioenergetics and physiologic CRF values.

# 4 Multi-Modal Life-Style Intervention for Well-Functional Mitochondria

From the above-listed facts, it is getting clear that for maintaining well-functional mitochondrial populations, a multi-modal lifestyle intervention is essential in both health and disease. This statement is well-justified by CRF in primary care to prevent health-to-disease transition as well as in secondary care to stabilise the health of affected individuals. To this end, specifically, the multi-modal lifestyle approach focused on mitochondrial health and functionality restoration has been proven as particularly promising for treating severe systemic disabilities such as progressive multiple sclerosis that remains uncurable and demands an innovative concepts' development [23]. Below a spectrum of methods is considered to promote the concept of innovative multi-modal lifestyle intervention taking advantage of unique properties of mitochondria.

## *4.1 Coached Respiratory and Physical Exercise*

Exercise intervention is the cornerstone in maintaining, enriching and rejuvenation of mitochondrial populations, disease prevention and treatment including respiratory, cardio-cerebral-vascular, nervous, immune, motor and digestive metabolic systems [24]. Specifically, mitochondrial respiratory capacity is the metabolic biomarker, indicating health stability in a holistic way [25]. Preclinical studies demonstrated distinguishable mitochondrial phenotypes specific for sedentary *versus* exercise-trained animals [26]. Whereas in the exercise-train animals, exercise protects cardiac mitochondria against ischaemia-reperfusion injury, in untrained animals, the long-lasting exercise causes ROS overproduction, mitochondrial stress and increased level of damaged mitochondrial subpopulation that altogether mimics ischaemia-reperfusion injury [27]. The exercise-induced fatigue linked to transient mitochondrial damage in acute high-intensity exercise is described for athletes followed by initiating exercise-induced mitochondrial adaptation [28]. Furthermore, several research groups involved in the field emphasise that the type of exercise is decisive for the successful treatment of pathologies. Therefore, the critical role of individually couched physical activities and sport exercises is concluded for both—healthy lifestyles and disease treatments. Finally, an individualised post-exercise approach is essential to be kept in mind. To this end, specifically, the *massage therapy* in physical rehabilitation is strongly recommended: per evidence, massage mitigates cellular and mitochondrial stress resulting from myofiber injury by promoting mitochondrial biogenesis and reducing inflammation [29]. Moreover, *manual acupuncture and electro-acupuncture* can protect cells from injury related to acute and intensive sport activities maintaining mitochondrial populations at high level and thereby mitigating exercise-induced fatigue and prolonging the working time of muscles, preventing skeletal muscle cells from the acute damage [30].

## *4.2 Acupuncture*

Beneficial health effects of manual acupuncture and electro-acupuncture, per evidence, function via increasing the mitochondrial population mass in both healthy and diseased individuals [31]. High level of clinical utility of the approach has been demonstrated in rehabilitation and sport medicine [30], improved neurological outcomes in the ischaemic stroke and intracranial haemorrage, myocardial and cerebral ischaemia-reperfusion, dementia of Alzheimer's and non-Alzheimer's type [32–37].

## *4.3 Electromagnetic Stimulation: Promotor or Antagonist?*

Accumulated scientific evidence demonstrates mitochondrial oscillation that is distinguishable between healthy conditions and disorders [38]. To this end, specifically under metabolic stress perturbing ROS generation against scavenging capacity, the mitochondrial network changes the frequency/amplitude oscillation mode resulting in the energy dissipation. This leads to depolarization and suppression of the electrical excitability/$Ca^{2+}$ handling—the main attributes of cardiac cells the functionality of which is hampered in this way as reflected, for example, by fatal arrhythmias. Due to the high physiologic utility of the fine oscillation, mitochondrial health and functionality are highly sensitive to electro-magnetic environmental noises. For example, the impacts of different music types on the mitochondrial function are significant ranging from evidently beneficial effects (increased ATP production, anti-oxidant and -stress protection) to significantly harmful ones including the ROS overproduction and mitochondrial stress, causing the reduced cell viability [39]. Contextually, extremely low-frequency pulses of faint magnetic field (which is weaker than the geomagnetic field) have been proposed to treat ageing mitochondrial population for neuro- and cardio-protection of affected individuals. The underlying mechanism is the induced mitophagy by inhibiting the electron flux in the ECT complex II, translocating PARKIN and PINK1 to the mitochondria and recruiting LC3-II [40]. The induced mitophagy restarts the PGC-1-alpha-medicated mitochondrial biogenesis rejuvenating mitochondrial population.

## 5 Concluding Remarks

Keeping in mind the reciprocity of mitochondrial and human cells partnering and consequent interdependencies, interests of both sides should be thoroughly considered when choosing for most suitable

- Life-style options
- Dietary and behavioural habits
- Vitamins and supplements intake
- Health-supportive therapies
- Medications and
- Treatment algorithms tailored to the individualised patient profile.

Figure 2 illustrates the mitochondrial health index and mitophagy as the predictive and prognostic biomarker-panel and powerful diagnostic tools. Specifically, mitophagy is considered highly instrumental for health risk assessment and therapy monitoring as well as effective target for treatment of sub-optimal health conditions [2].

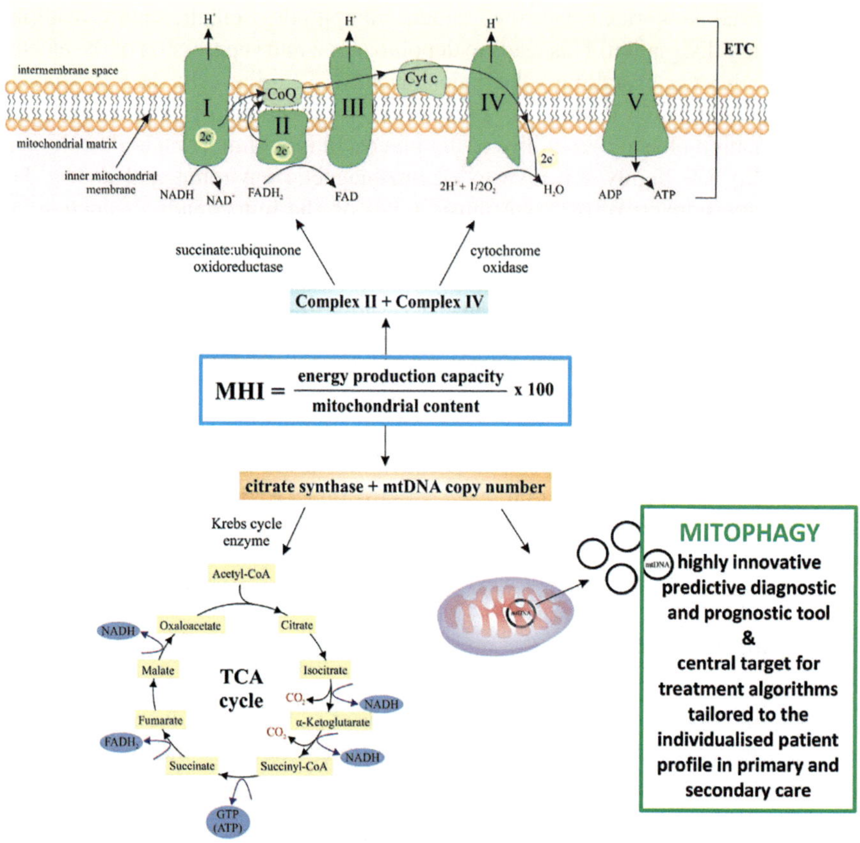


**Fig. 2** Mitochondrial Health Index (MHI) and mitophagy as the predictive and prognostics biomarker-panel and powerful diagnostic tools; specifically, mitophagy is considered highly innovative and effective target for treatment of sub-optimal health conditions; ETC and TCA enzymes are specified in the figure; the image is adapted from Ref. [1]

## References


1. Koklesova L, Mazurakova A, Samec M, Kudela E, Biringer K, Kubatka P, Golubnitschaja O (2022) Mitochondrial health quality control: measurements and interpretation in the framework of predictive, preventive, and personalized medicine. EPMA J 13(2):177–193. https://doi.org/10.1007/s13167-022-00281-6
2. Golubnitschaja O (2023). What is the routine mitochondrial health check-up good for? A holistic approach in the framework of 3P medicine. Book chapter in "Predictive, Preventive, and Personalised Medicine: From Bench to Bedside", Podbielska H, Kapalla M (eds), Springer. https://doi.org/10.1007/978-3-031-34884-6
3. Ayoub IM, Radhakrishnan J, Gazmuri RJ (2008) Targeting mitochondria for resuscitation from cardiac arrest. Crit Care Med 36(11 Suppl):S440–S446. https://doi.org/10.1097/ccm.0b013e31818a89f4

4. Donnino MW, Liu X, Andersen LW, Rittenberger JC, Abella BS, Gaieski DF, Ornato JP, Gazmuri RJ, Grossestreuer AV, Cocchi MN, Abbate A, Uber A, Clore J, Peberdy MA, Callaway CW, National Post Arrest Research Consortium (NPARC) Investigators (2017) Characterization of mitochondrial injury after cardiac arrest (COMICA). Resuscitation 113:56–62. https://doi.org/10.1016/j.resuscitation.2016.12.029
5. Patil KD, Halperin HR, Becker LB (2015) Cardiac arrest: resuscitation and reperfusion. Circ Res 116(12):2041–2049. https://doi.org/10.1161/CIRCRESAHA.116.304495
6. Ramachandra CJA, Hernandez-Resendiz S, Crespo-Avilan GE, Lin YH, Hausenloy DJ (2020) Mitochondria in acute myocardial infarction and cardioprotection. EBioMedicine 57:102884. https://doi.org/10.1016/j.ebiom.2020.102884
7. Yang KC, Bonini MG, Dudley SC Jr (2014) Mitochondria and arrhythmias. Free Radic Biol Med 71:351–361. https://doi.org/10.1016/j.freeradbiomed.2014.03.033
8. Golubnitschaja O, Baban B, Boniolo G, Wang W, Bubnov R, Kapalla M, Krapfenbauer K, Mozaffari M, Costigliola V (2016) Medicine in the early twenty-first century: paradigm and anticipation – EPMA position paper 2016. EPMA J 7:23. https://doi.org/10.1186/s13167-016-0072-4
9. Chang JC, Chao YC, Chang HS, Wu YL, Chang HJ, Lin YS, Cheng WL, Lin TT, Liu CS (2021) Intranasal delivery of mitochondria for treatment of Parkinson's disease model rats lesioned with 6-hydroxydopamine. Sci Rep 11(1):10597. https://doi.org/10.1038/s41598-021-90094-w
10. Chang JC, Chang HS, Wu YC, Cheng WL, Lin TT, Chang HJ, Kuo SJ, Chen ST, Liu CS (2019) Mitochondrial transplantation regulates antitumour activity, chemoresistance and mitochondrial dynamics in breast cancer. J Exp Clin Cancer Res 38(1):30. https://doi.org/10.1186/s13046-019-1028-z
11. Kropp M, De Clerck E, Vo TKS, Thumann G, Costigliola V, Golubnitschaja O (2023) Short communication: unique metabolic signature of proliferative retinopathy in the tear fluid of diabetic patients with comorbidities - preliminary data for PPPM validation. EPMA J 14(1):43–51. https://doi.org/10.1007/s13167-023-00318-4
12. Traina G (2016) The neurobiology of acetyl-L-carnitine. Front Biosci (Landmark Ed) 21(7):1314–1329. https://doi.org/10.2741/4459
13. Chondrogianni N, Kapeta S, Chinou I, Vassilatou K, Papassideri I, Gonos ES (2010) Anti-ageing and rejuvenating effects of quercetin. Exp Gerontol 45(10):763–771. https://doi.org/10.1016/j.exger.2010.07.001
14. Rakha BA, Qurrat-Ul-Ain, Ansari MS, Akhter S, Akhter A, Awan MA, Santiago-Moreno J (2020) Effect of quercetin on oxidative stress, mitochondrial activity, and quality of Indian red jungle fowl (*Gallus gallus murgha*) sperm. J Biopreserv Biobank 18(4):311–320. https://doi.org/10.1089/bio.2020.0007
15. Jardim FR, de Rossi FT, Nascimento MX, da Silva Barros RG, Borges PA, Prescilio IC, de Oliveira MR (2018) Resveratrol and brain mitochondria: a review. Mol Neurobiol 55(3):2085–2101. https://doi.org/10.1007/s12035-017-0448-z
16. Xia N, Daiber A, Förstermann U, Li H (2017) Antioxidant effects of resveratrol in the cardiovascular system. Br J Pharmacol 174(12):1633–1646. https://doi.org/10.1111/bph.13492
17. Slominski AT, Zmijewski MA, Semak I, Kim TK, Janjetovic Z, Slominski RM, Zmijewski JW (2017) Melatonin, mitochondria, and the skin. Cell Mol Life Sci 74(21):3913–3925. https://doi.org/10.1007/s00018-017-2617-7
18. Arinno A, Maneechote C, Khuanjing T, Ongnok B, Prathumsap N, Chunchai T, Arunsak B, Kerdphoo S, Shinlapawittayatorn K, Chattipakorn SC, Chattipakorn N (2021) Cardioprotective effects of melatonin and metformin against doxorubicin-induced cardiotoxicity in rats are through preserving mitochondrial function and dynamics. Biochem Pharmacol 192:114743. https://doi.org/10.1016/j.bcp.2021.114743
19. Munmun F, Witt-Enderby PA (2021) Melatonin effects on bone: implications for use as a therapy for managing bone loss. J Pineal Res 71(1):e12749. https://doi.org/10.1111/jpi.12749
20. Ahluwalia A, Patel K, Hoa N, Brzozowska I, Jones MK, Tarnawski AS (2021) Melatonin ameliorates aging-related impaired angiogenesis in gastric endothelial cells via local actions

on mitochondria and VEGF-survivin signaling. Am J Physiol Gastrointest Liver Physiol 321(6):G682–G689. https://doi.org/10.1152/ajpgi.00101.2021
21. Mocayar Marón FJ, Camargo AB, Manucha W (2020) Allicin pharmacology: common molecular mechanisms against neuroinflammation and cardiovascular diseases. Life Sci 249:117513. https://doi.org/10.1016/j.lfs.2020.117513
22. Raghuveer G, Hartz J, Lubans DR, Takken T, Wiltz JL, Mietus-Snyder M, Perak AM, Baker-Smith C, Pietris N, Edwards NM, American Heart Association Young Hearts Athero (2020) Hypertension and Obesity in the Young Committee of the Council on Lifelong Congenital Heart Disease and Heart Health in the Young. Cardiorespiratory Fitness in Youth: An Important Marker of Health: A Scientific Statement From the American Heart Association. Circulation 142(7):e101–e118. https://doi.org/10.1161/CIR.0000000000000866
23. Bisht B, Darling WG, White EC, White KA, Shivapour ET, Zimmerman MB, Wahls TL (2017) Effects of a multimodal intervention on gait and balance of subjects with progressive multiple sclerosis: a prospective longitudinal pilot study. Degener Neurol Neuromuscul Dis 7:79–93. https://doi.org/10.2147/DNND.S128872
24. Guo S, Huang Y, Zhang Y, Huang H, Hong S, Liu T (2020) Impacts of exercise interventions on different diseases and organ functions in mice. J Sport Health Sci 9(1):53–73. https://doi.org/10.1016/j.jshs.2019.07.004
25. Krako Jakovljevic N, Pavlovic K, Jotic A, Lalic K, Stoiljkovic M, Lukic L, Milicic T, Macesic M, Stanarcic Gajovic J, Lalic NM (2021) Targeting mitochondria in diabetes. Int J Mol Sci 22(12):6642
26. Lee Y, Min K, Talbert EE, Kavazis AN, Smuder AJ, Willis WT, Powers SK (2012) Exercise protects cardiac mitochondria against ischemia-reperfusion injury. Med Sci Sports Exerc 44(3):397–405. https://doi.org/10.1249/MSS.0b013e318231c037
27. Di Meo S, Venditti P (2001) Mitochondria in exercise-induced oxidative stress. Biol Signals Recept 10(1–2):125–140. https://doi.org/10.1159/000046880
28. Layec G, Blain GM, Rossman MJ, Park SY, Hart CR, Trinity JD, Gifford JR, Sidhu SK, Weavil JC, Hureau TJ, Amann M, Richardson RS (2018) Acute high-intensity exercise impairs skeletal muscle respiratory capacity. Med Sci Sports Exerc 50(12):2409–2417. https://doi.org/10.1249/MSS.0000000000001735
29. Crane JD, Ogborn DI, Cupido C, Melov S, Hubbard A, Bourgeois JM, Tarnopolsky MA (2012) Massage therapy attenuates inflammatory signaling after exercise-induced muscle damage. Sci Transl Med 4(119):119ra13. https://doi.org/10.1126/scitranslmed.3002882
30. Gao M, Yang HY, Liu TY, Kuai L (2005) Effects of manual acupuncture and electro-acupuncture on mitochondria of skeletal muscle cells in rats of acute swimming exercise. Zhongguo Zhen Jiu 25(6):421–424
31. Lee YM, Choi DH, Park JH, Cheon MW, Kim JG, Kim JS, Choi T, Kim HR, Youn D (2023) The effects of manual acupuncture on mitochondrial fusion and fission gene expression in rat spleen. J Acupunct Meridian Stud 16(2):49–55. https://doi.org/10.51507/j.jams.2023.16.2.49
32. Li MY, Dai XH, Yu XP, Zou W, Teng W, Liu P, Yu XY, An Q, Wen X (2022) Scalp acupuncture protects against neuronal ferroptosis by activating the p62-Keap1-Nrf2 pathway in rat models of intracranial haemorrhage. J Mol Neurosci 72(1):82–96. https://doi.org/10.1007/s12031-021-01890-y
33. Wang H, Chen S, Zhang Y, Xu H, Sun H (2019) Electroacupuncture ameliorates neuronal injury by Pink1/Parkin-mediated mitophagy clearance in cerebral ischemia-reperfusion. Nitric Oxide 91:23–34. https://doi.org/10.1016/j.niox.2019.07.004
34. Jiang YH, He JK, Li R, Chen ZH, Jia BH (2022) Mechanisms of acupuncture in improving Alzheimer's disease caused by mitochondrial damage. Chin J Integr Med 28(3):272–280. https://doi.org/10.1007/s11655-022-3511-6
35. Xiao Y, Chen W, Zhong Z, Ding L, Bai H, Chen H, Zhang H, Gu Y, Lu S (2020) Electroacupuncture preconditioning attenuates myocardial ischemia-reperfusion injury by inhibiting mitophagy mediated by the mTORC1-ULK1-FUNDC1 pathway. Biomed Pharmacother 127:110148. https://doi.org/10.1016/j.biopha.2020.110148

36. Li H, Liu Y, Lin LT, Wang XR, Du SQ, Yan CQ, He T, Yang JW, Liu CZ (2016) Acupuncture reversed hippocampal mitochondrial dysfunction in vascular dementia rats. Neurochem Int 92:35–42. https://doi.org/10.1016/j.neuint.2015.12.001
37. Jittiwat J (2017) Laser acupuncture at GV20 improves brain damage and oxidative stress in animal model of focal ischemic stroke. J Acupunct Meridian Stud 10(5):324–330. https://doi.org/10.1016/j.jams.2017.08.003
38. Aon MA, Cortassa S, O'Rourke B (2008) Mitochondrial oscillations in physiology and pathophysiology. Adv Exp Med Biol 641:98–117. https://doi.org/10.1007/978-0-387-09794-7_8
39. Feng Q, Wang L, Chen Y, Teng J, Li M, Cai Z, Niu X, Rein G, Yang Q, Shao X, Zhang C, Bai X (2022) Effects of different music on HEK293T cell growth and mitochondrial functions. Explore (NY) 18(6):670–675. https://doi.org/10.1016/j.explore.2022.01.002
40. Toda T, Ito M, Takeda JI, Masuda A, Mino H, Hattori N, Mohri K, Ohno K (2022) Extremely low-frequency pulses of faint magnetic field induce mitophagy to rejuvenate mitochondria. Commun Biol 5(1):453. https://doi.org/10.1038/s42003-022-03389-7

# Suboptimal Health and the Economic Impact to Healthcare from the Perspective of PPP Medicine

**Monique Garcia and Wei Wang**

## Abbreviations

| | |
|---|---|
| CVD | Cardiovascular disease |
| HPA | Hypothalamic-pituitary-adrenal axis |
| PPPM/3PM | Predictive, preventive, and personalised medicine |
| SAM | Sympatho-adrenomedullary axis |
| SH | Suboptimal health |
| SHSQ-25 | Suboptimal health status questionnaire-25 |
| T2DM | Type 2 diabetes mellitus |
| WHO | World Health Organisation |

M. Garcia
Centre for Precision Health, Edith Cowan University, Perth Australia, Joondalup, WA, Australia

W. Wang (✉)
First Affiliated Hospital, Shantou University Medical College, Shantou, China

Beijing Key Laboratory of Clinical Epidemiology, Capital Medical University, Beijing, China

School of Public Health, Shandong First Medical University and Shandong Academy of Medical Sciences, Jinan, China

Centre for Precision Health, Edith Cowan University, Perth, Australia

Suboptimal Health Study Consortium, Kumasi, Ghana

Suboptimal Health Study Consortium, Perth, Australia

Suboptimal Health Study Consortium, Beijing, China

Suboptimal Health Study Consortium, Bonn, Germany

European Association for Predictive, Preventive and Personalised Medicine, EPMA, Brussels, Belgium
e-mail: wei.wang@ecu.edu.au


W. Wang (ed.), *All Around Suboptimal Health*, Advances in Predictive, Preventive and Personalised Medicine 18,
https://doi.org/10.1007/978-3-031-46891-9_4

## 1 Suboptimal Health (SH) Definition

The definition of "health" according to the World Health Organisation (WHO) is "a state of complete physical, mental, and social well-being and not merely the absence of disease or infirmity" [1]. Suboptimal Health (SH) is considered to be an intermediate state between health and disease, identified through the self-reporting of general malaise and ambiguous health complaints in the absence of a diagnosable condition [2]. It is when a person moves away from ideal health, and towards chronic disease. SH is a "reversible, subclinical stage of pre-chronic disease" [2].

## 2 A Paradigm Shift

SH shifts the paradigm from reactive to proactive healthcare by providing a unique window of opportunity to prevent chronic disease [3]. Chronic diseases are an international issue and a serious threat to human health, defined as diseases of long duration, slow progression, and are the major cause of adult morbidity and mortality in the world (WHO). Each year, chronic diseases account for 71% of total global deaths and kill more than 41 million people. Cardiovascular disease (CVD), cancer, respiratory disease and type 2 diabetes mellitus (T2DM) are responsible for over 80% of all chronic disease-related deaths [4]. Globally, CVD remains the leading cause of death, causing 30% of all deaths and about 50% of all chronic diseases [4].

## 3 Reactive Healthcare

The current biomedical model of health has been reactive in its response to managing chronic diseases, typically initiating treatments only after the clinical manifestation of disease [3]. The impact of chronic diseases on both healthcare and economies is enormous. A recent economic study forecasted an increase of 22% in total global cost for CVD from 2010 (US$863 billion) to 2030 (US$1044 billion) [4]. Similar predictions were made for other chronic diseases including cancer, mental disorders, T2DM and chronic obstructive pulmonary disease (COPD). Another economic report measured the "value of lost output" from cancer, CVD, respiratory disease, T2DM and mental disorders, and estimated the total cost from 2011 to 2030 to be US$ 47 trillion [4]. For context, the entire economic output for Europe in 2016 amounted to $17.8 trillion [4].

## 4 Proactive Healthcare

Disease prevention strategies are highly effective tools for the reduction of chronic diseases and the promotion of better health [5]. Whilst the literature clearly articulates the obvious benefits of primary prevention, including millions of lives saved, and indeed billions of dollars saved, investment in such strategies remains dismally low, with most nations spending approximately 2–4% of total health sector budgets on disease prevention programs [6, 4]. Effective disease prevention measures, including screening tools for the detection of SHS, that can markedly decrease their economic impact on health systems, should be explored [4]. Considering the WHO's recent recommendations calling for empirical, low-cost disease prevention strategies, SH should be given urgent priority [6].

SH has a proactive approach to healthcare by predicting a person's risk of developing certain chronic diseases, an outcome shared by predictive, preventive and personalised medicine (PPPM) [1, 6, 7]. The conceptual framework of PPPM lies in its ability to predict an individual's predisposition to disease before its onset, followed by the timely delivery of personalised, disease prevention and treatment strategies [6]. In line with PPPM, SH allows a window of opportunity for disease prevention by initiating targeted interventions in at-risk individuals before the onset of clinical symptoms, altering the course of disease trajectories, and potentially preventing the disease from occurring altogether [7]. SH's unique capacity to prevent disease also confers economic benefits, directing funding and resources to exactly where it is needed [7]. At a time when global healthcare is overcome by the perpetual growing burden of chronic diseases, SH, with all its potential, should be adopted as the new gold standard in the fight against chronic diseases from the perspective of PPPM.

## 5 Theoretical Background of SH—Stress

SH was first identified as a public health challenge in China, with its prevalence expected to escalate worldwide. Stress has been identified as a key contributing factor to SH. With our increasingly chaotic lifestyles, societal changes, social media use and work pressures, the stress-related disease epidemic has become an important public health issue [2].

## 6 The Human Stress Response

The human stress response is an evolutionarily conserved, dynamic process that aims to overcome a stressor (a real or perceived threat), promote survival and restore homeostasis [3]. The role of the two major components involved in the stress response—the sympatho-adrenomedullary (SAM) axis and hypothalamic-pituitary-adrenal (HPA) axis, respectively, is well documented [3, 8].

## *6.1 SAM Axis*

The SAM axis responds to both physical and psychological stressors by mounting a rapid, short-term, physiological response [9]. This is achieved via the release of catecholamine-filled vesicles (epinephrine and norepinephrine) from chromaffin cells within the adrenal glands [3, 8–10]. Catecholamines travel in the bloodstream and prepare the body for "fight or flight", activating the sympathetic nervous system by targeting alpha- and beta-adrenergic receptors [3, 8–10]. This induces physiological changes in blood vessels, smooth muscles, organs and glands. The effects of SAM axis activation include an increase in blood pressure, maintained alertness, increased contractility of the cardiac muscle, elevated heart rate, pupil dilation, pilo-erection, heightened blood glucose levels via gluconeogenesis and glycogenolysis, lipolysis, relaxation of smooth muscles in the gastrointestinal and urinary tracts, as well as the bronchioles (resulting in increased oxygen consumption), elevated respiratory rate, thermoregulation, decreased insulin secretion, and the inhibition of mast cells and basophils [3, 8–10].

## *6.2 HPA Axis*

The HPA axis also responds to both physical and psychological stressors, but via a slower, more protracted pathway than the SAM axis [3, 8–10]. The HPA axis produces and releases cortisol, the main glucocorticoid hormone in humans. The function of the HPA axis is to quickly mobilise energy stores and improve the chances of survival (e.g., running away from a lion). Under normal conditions, cortisol is secreted in a pulsatile fashion with higher levels observed upon waking, followed by a gradual decline to basal levels at night [3]. Cortisol follows a circadian pattern and is controlled by the suprachiasmatic nucleus that communicates with the paraventricular nucleus (PVN) in the hypothalamus [3]. Corticotropic releasing hormone (CRH) and vasopressin (VP) are released into the hypophyseal portal system to the pituitary gland, where corticotropes subsequently release adrenocorticotropic releasing hormone (ACTH). ACTH travels to the adrenal cortex via the systemic circulation, activating the production of cortisol [3]. Cortisol is transported back to the systemic circulation where it exerts its effects on target tissues. As a steroid hormone synthesised from cholesterol, cortisol crosses cell membranes and binds to receptors in the cytoplasm, with the cortisol–receptor complex then crossing the nuclear membrane to affect gene transcription [9]. The effect of cortisol includes increased blood glucose to the brain, increased gluconeogenesis and decreased glycogen synthesis in the liver, decreased glucose uptake and increased protein degradation in the muscles, increased lipolysis in adipose tissue, suppression of B cells antibody production and decreased migration of neutrophils in the immune system, and decreased insulin secretion and increased glucagon secretion in the pancreas [10]. Finally, the presence of cortisol augments the function of catecholamines [3, 8–10].

# 7 Acute Stress Versus Chronic Stress

During acute stress, the SAM axis is activated within seconds, expeditiously releasing catecholamines epinephrine and nor-epinephrine [9]. This is followed by recruitment of the HPA axis, with peak cortisol levels observed 15–20 min after the initial onset of stress [3]. Once the stressor has passed, negative feedback loops restore homeostasis, and hormone levels return to basal levels [3]. During chronic stress, however, these processes become maladaptive, and cortisol levels remain elevated [3]. In chronic stress, hypothalamic activation of the pituitary switches from CRH to vasopressin, decreasing the metabolism of cortisol [3]. Elevated cortisol levels and long-term cortisol exposure result, which are toxic to the human body and lead to chronic disease [3]. Our health is influenced by multiple factors including genetics, access to quality healthcare services and exposure to "upstream" risk factors [4]. Risk factors include health behaviours such as diet/physical activity, environmental factors such as our work environments, as well as socioeconomic, demographic and cultural factors [4]. Chronic diseases arise from a combination of modifiable (such as poor diet) and non-modifiable risk factors (such as genetic make-up) [4]. Modifiable risk factors can lead to chronic diseases through both classical risk factors—including obesity, high blood glucose levels, blood pressure and cholesterol, and through non-classical risk factors such as chronic stress [4]. SHS is associated with both classical (direct) and non-classical (indirect) modifiable risk factors of chronic disease, including CVD and T2DM [11, 15].

# 8 Development of an Instrument for Measuring SH

In response to the stress-related disease epidemic and SH, researchers sought to develop a screening tool that could effectively measure SHS [2].

## *8.1 Study 1: Questionnaire Development*

Stress was identified as a major aspect leading to poor health by all participants involved in the focus group discussions [2]. The initial questionnaire consisted of 42 items; 37 statements (describing health complaints caused by stress) resulted from focus group discussions; 7 items were derived from a questionnaire study of SHS and 9 items were derived from the Cornell Medical Index [2]. The questionnaire was approved for content validity by 4 clinicians, followed by a pilot study being conducted at three hospitals, with the questionnaire distributed to 30 individuals [2]. These individuals had numerous health complaints yet were otherwise free from disease. The results were reviewed, and the questionnaire was consolidated, consisting of a 25-item questionnaire related to SHS. Known as the SHSQ-25, the 25 items were categorised into 5 subscales measuring health across domains. These included fatigue (9 items), mental status (7 items), immune system (3 items), digestive tract (3 items) and the cardiovascular system (3 items) [2].

### 8.2 *Study 2: Validity of the SHSQ-25*

A total of 2799 participants completed the SHSQ-25 questionnaire, with all participants also undergoing physical examination. Participants were asked to rate each item on the SHSQ-25, according to how often they have felt that way over the last 3 months [2]. Raw scores of 1–5 on the questionnaire will be recorded as 0–4. An individual's total suboptimal health score is calculated by adding the ratings from all items together [2]. The SHSQ-25 score ranges numerically from 0 to 100, with 0 indicating optimal health, and 100 indicating the poorest health. The cut-off value for SHS was initially determined using the median score of all participants surveyed;, however, more recently, the SHS cut-off value has been determined using a one-tailed 90% upper limit of SHSQ-25 scores, improving accuracy [2]. The SHSQ-25 showed good test–retest reliability and internal consistency. Confirmatory factor analysis showed a reasonable fit of the data to the multidimensional structure of the questionnaire. It was also found the SHSQ-25 had a discriminative ability between individuals with good health and those with suboptimal health [2]. Convergent validity showed the scores for SHS and stress to be statistically significant (Pearson's $r = 0.57$, $p = <0.001$). The SHSQ-25 was established as a valid, subjective health measure for the detection of SHS.

## 9 SH Is Associated with Objective Biomarkers

The SHSQ-25 has leverage over existing screening tools by virtue of its simplicity—it is quick and easy to use [7]. What makes the SH truly unique, however, is its inclusion of, and association with, objective biomarkers [7]. Since its inception in 2009, the majority of SHSQ-25 studies have sought to investigate the association between the SH and objective biomarkers (Fig. 1). The linkage of subjective and objective markers is not dissimilar to the approach of integrative medicine—where traditional eastern (subjective) meets modern western (objective) medicine [7]. Indeed, closing the gap between traditional and modern medicine is the goal of SH, with the hybridised mind-body approach combining the advantages of both disciplines to improve patient outcomes [7]. The inclusion of subjective and objective biomarkers demonstrates that SH is associated with chronic diseases.

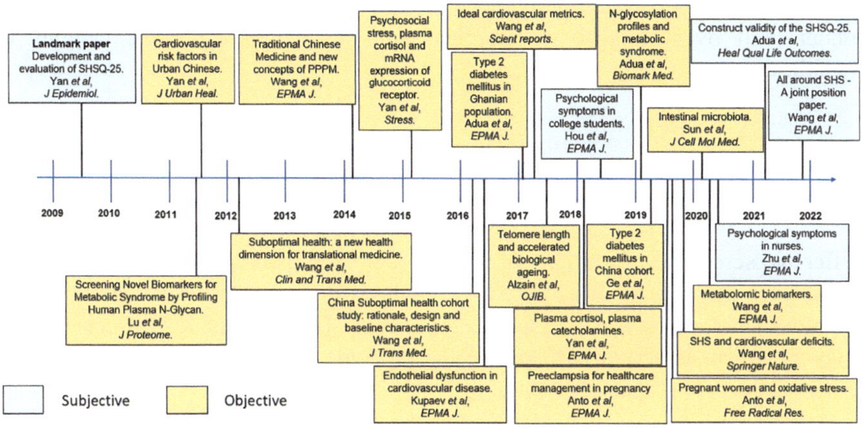


**Fig. 1** SH research timeline

## 10 SH Confers a Significant Economic Benefit to Healthcare Systems

SH confers substantial economic benefits to healthcare by discriminating between individuals at high versus low risk: avoiding under- and over-diagnosis. Previous investigations have demonstrated that SH can distinguish between at-risk individuals for T2DM, and that high systolic and diastolic blood pressure were statistically associated with SH. Another study discovered that the risk of T2DM development increased as the SH performance of the affected person increased. Another study found that SH is associated with chronic stress, with SH individuals having higher levels of both psychosocial stress and cortisol than those with optimal health. Furthermore, SH stratified individuals into high- and low-risk groups for CVD, showing that high SH scores were associated with classical risk factors (including high cholesterol and endothelial dysfunction) and certain health metrics (such as smoking and sedentary behaviour) of CVD, whereas low SH scores were associated with ideal CVD metrics (such as ideal dietary intake and never smoked), acting as an independent protection factor for SHS.

## 11 The Under- and Over-Diagnosis of Disease

The under- and over-diagnosis of chronic diseases only serve to contribute to the significant economic burdens of healthcare [12]. Underdiagnosis is defined as "the failure to recognize or correctly diagnose a disease or condition especially in a significant proportion of patients" [17]. Overdiagnosis occurs when a person is diagnosed with, and treated for, a disease that wouldn't have ordinarily led to clinical symptoms or complications, with the effects of treatments outweighing any possible benefits [12, 13]. This chapter uses a series of case studies to illustrate how

SH discriminates between individuals at high versus low risk: circumventing the under- and over-diagnosis of disease, with substantial economic benefits to healthcare.

# 12 Underdiagnosis

Effective screening of chronic diseases is key to PPPMs mission to reduce their prevalence [6]. Early detection of diseases affords timely interventions to be employed and can reduce long-term complications [14]. A reliable, low-cost screening instrument is urgent [2]. Among the new approaches of screening tools, the SHSQ-25 deserves special attention [2].

## 12.1 *Case Study One: Suboptimal Health Is Associated with Psychological Symptoms*

A recent study investigated the prevalence of SH and its correlation with psychological symptoms along with SH-related risk factors [20]. A total of 4119 undergraduate students were recruited for the study from two universities. Participants were evaluated for SH using the SHSQ-25, and psychological states using the Symptom Checklist (SCL-90) [20]. The SCL-90 is a 90-item scale measuring somatic and psychological symptoms. The 90 items are categorised into 10 domains, such as somatisation and depression. Participants were asked to rate how they've been feeling over the past week. Participants who score 160 or above are considered to exhibit psychological symptoms. Students completed the two questionnaires that took under 30 min to complete [20]. The results found college students had an SH prevalence of 21% [20]. Furthermore, participants with SH also had higher SCL-90 scores (159.0 (quartile 135.0—190.0)) than healthy participants (108.00 (quartile 98.0–126.0)), showing that SH participants experienced more psychological problems than healthy students [20]. Further analysis showed a high correlation between SH scores and SCL-90 scores, with somatisation, obsessive-compulsive, interpersonal sensitivity, depression and sleep and diet problems being the key factors positively associated with SH [20]. Specifically, female students, sophomore students, medical students and students from rural regions were all identified as vulnerable subpopulations who were at the highest risk of SH and psychological problems [20]. This research highlighted the utility of the SHSQ-25 in conjunction with the SCL-90 to identify students with SH and psychological problems who are at risk of developing disease [20].

## 12.2 Case Study Two: Integration of Suboptimal Health Evaluation as a Criterion for Prediction of Preeclampsia

This study sought to understand the utility and applicability of the SHS-25 for the screening and prediction of normotensive pregnant women (NTN-PW) at risk of developing preeclampsia (PE) in Ghana [14]. A condition that develops exclusively in pregnancy, PE is diagnosed by the presence of proteinuria and hypertension from 20 weeks gestation in pregnant women who have otherwise been normotensive [21]. The prospective study recruited 593 normotensive, healthy, pregnant females aged between 18 and 45 years. Participants underwent a physical examination and assessment by an obstetric specialist prior to inclusion in the study. Participants then underwent a baseline examination at 10–20 weeks gestation to measure their general health [14]. Data collected included the SHSQ-25 subjective health measure, sociodemographic and obstetric information, and clinical assessment. The clinical assessment included blood pressure (mmHg) measurements, BMI and presence of proteinuria (via urine reagent dipstick). Clinical assessment was measured at three separate points: baseline, 21–31 weeks, and again at 32–42 weeks. A total of 498 pregnant women returned at delivery, with 301 women presenting as normotensive and without proteinuria (NTN-PW) (controls), and 197 presenting with PE (cases). A total of 49.8% (248/498) of pregnant women were found to have SH at baseline, whilst 50.2% (250/498) of pregnant women had optimal health. Of the 248 women who had high SH at baseline, 61.7% (153/248) progressed to PE (95 did not). Of the 250 women who had optimal health at baseline, 17.6% (44/250) progressed to PE (206 did not). It was also found that the incidence of PE increased as the individual SH domain scores increased. Normotensive pregnant women with high SH at baseline were found to be at four-fold increased odds of developing PE, demonstrating a significant, independent association between SH and PE. This study showed the versatility and applicability of employing the SHSQ-25 as an independent risk stratification tool for the detection of pregnancy-related health problems, such as PE. The SHSQ-25 has the potential to circumvent underdiagnosis of adverse pregnancy outcomes in women in developing countries such as Ghana, with a significant economic impact to healthcare.

## 12.3 Case Study Three: SH and Metabolomic Biomarkers

This case–control investigation sought to identify metabolic biomarkers for the detection of SH [22]. Metabolites are intermediate or end products of metabolism essential for cellular functions [23]. Metabolites mirror genome encoding, environmental modifications and downstream cellular processing, providing valuable insights into the functions of biological systems and aiding in the diagnosis of chronic diseases via metabolic signatures [24]. Therefore, the authors of this study hypothesised that the metabolic signatures in participants with SH might be altered [22]. Participants included Chinese undergraduate students between the ages of 18–20 years who were free from disease from the province of Shandong [22]. Participants completed the SHSQ-25 at baseline, and again after 3 months. Lifestyle data, anthropometric measurements and blood samples for biochemical analysis were collected [22]. Individuals with an SH score of >35 were included as cases, while individuals with an SH score of <35 were included as age- and sex-matched controls. The results showed that 24 metabolites were significantly different between participants with SH and participants with optimal health [22]. Further analysis revealed that three metabolic pathways were specifically involved: taurine metabolism, sphingolipid metabolism and steroid hormone biosynthesis [22]. Four metabolites were able to be used as predictive biomarkers to discriminate between participants with SH and participants with optimal health (sensitivity of 94.0%, specificity of 90.0% and an AUC of 0.977). These results demonstrated that metabolic biomarkers had a high predictive power for detecting SHS [22]. The SHSQ-25 could be used in population-level screening strategies, with the ability to early detect SH-related metabolic changes, thereby avoiding the underdiagnosis with a significant economic impact to healthcare.

These case studies serve as powerful examples of how SH avoids the underdiagnosis of chronic diseases [11, 14, 22]. Detection of SH, via the SHSQ-25, has particular relevance in developing countries. Indeed, screening for SH at a population level would circumvent the inherent economic barriers that result in a lack of laboratory tests and treatments, facilitating PPPM, and thus leading to substantial benefits to healthcare [14].

## 13 Overdiagnosis

Overdiagnosis can have significant consequences for not only individuals, but also for adding to the cost burden of healthcare systems; persons are subjected to potentially unnecessary diagnostic tests, procedures, and treatments, and expensive healthcare resources and time are wasted that would be better spent treating or preventing genuine illness [12]. Overdiagnosis costs billions of dollars from healthcare systems annually with approximately $200 billion wasted on unnecessary procedures and treatments in the United States every year [12]. Overdiagnosis assumes that diagnosis will confer no benefit [25]. SH, however, assumes diagnosis confers a benefit. Detection of SH in the first instance provides patient stratification through the prediction of a person's predisposition to disease, allowing clinicians the unique opportunity to prescribe personalised treatment algorithms [15]. Detection of SH effectively circumvents overdiagnosis. We evidence this in the case series below.

## 13.1 Case Study Four: SH Is Associated with Intestinal Microbiota

Past investigations have demonstrated intestinal microbiota to be linked with specific chronic diseases and have found disturbances in the microbiota of individuals with certain chronic diseases [16]. This case–control study sought to explore the relationship between SH and intestinal microbiota [15]. Participants completed the SHSQ-25 at baseline, and again after 3 months. Individuals with an SH score of >35 were included as cases, and individuals with an SH score of <35 were included as age- and sex-matched controls. Faecal sample collection was performed using a specimen collection kit, and bacterial DNA was extracted using a TIANGEN kit [15]. The results found diversity of the intestinal microbiota in participants with SH was statistically higher than in participants with optimal health [15]. This evidences that intestinal microbiota disturbances are associated with SH [15]. This could provide additional diagnostic tests in the future, thereby avoiding the overdiagnosis of chronic disease from the perspective of PPPM, having a significant economic impact on healthcare.

## 13.2 Case Study Five: Suboptimal Health and Endothelial Dysfunction as a New Aspect for Risk Evaluation of Cardiovascular Disease

In the context of cardiovascular disease, chronic stress not only directly affects the vessel wall by increasing heart rate and blood pressure, but also causes endothelial dysfunction, a factor known to trigger the development of atherosclerosis.

A recent cross-sectional study ($n = 459$) explored cardiovascular risk assessment using an integrated approach by combining SH evaluation with indicators of endothelial dysfunction [17]. All participants completed the SHSQ-25 questionnaire, physical examination and laboratory measures (including lipid profile). Arterial stiffness and endothelial dysfunction were determined using standard brachial plethysmography. The results found SH is associated with endothelial dysfunction [17]. The index of endothelial function was found to significantly correlate with the overall performance of suboptimal health ($r = -0.31$, $p < 0.05$), as well as with individual sub-scales of the questionnaire SHSQ-25: fatigue ($r = -0.36$, $p < 0.05$), the cardiovascular system ($r = -0.36$, $p < 0.05$), and mental ($r = -0.29$, $p < 0.05$) [17]. There was a significant correlation between SH scores, risk factors for the cardiovascular system, and indicators of endothelial dysfunction ($p < 0.001$), demonstrating that even at a suboptimal health stage, an association between vascular wall stiffness and several traditional determinants (age, body mass index, blood pressure) of cardiovascular disease (CVD) was present [17]. The group with risk factors for CVD had significantly higher levels of systolic blood pressure, diastolic blood pressure, body mass index, smoking index, total cholesterol, triglycerides and low-density lipoprotein cholesterol, confirming SH is associated with risk factors of CVD. The study concluded that the assessment of SH, taken together with the evaluation of endothelial dysfunction, enables the identification of the risk of developing CVD [17].

## 13.3 Case Study Six: SH Is Associated with Shortened Relative Telomere Length

A retrospective case–control study ($n = 294$ cases; $n = 294$ controls) investigated the association between SH and telomere length (TL) [18]. Participants, who were otherwise free from disease, completed the SHSQ-25 as part of a community survey. A quantitative polymerase chain reaction (PCR) then measured each participant's relative telomere length (RTL) [19]. Telomeres, made of nucleoproteins, are the capped ends of chromosomes protecting chromosomal degradation [20]. With each cell division, telomeres progressively shorten, eventually resulting in cell senescence [21]. Telomere shortening can be accelerated by external factors, including psychological stress [20]. Shorter telomere lengths are associated with chronic disease, whereas longer telomere lengths are linked to better health [20]. It has been postulated that telomere erosion is both modifiable and independent of chronological age [22]. The results of the study showed that individuals with SH had shorter telomeres compared to individuals with optimal health. SH was found to be significantly associated with shorter RTL ($p = <0.005$) [19]. Furthermore, lack of physical activities in males, oversleeping (>9 h per night) in females and memory loss were all associated with shorter RTL [19]. The SHSQ-25 offers an excellent alternative to measuring RTL in low- to middle-income countries where there is a lack of laboratory-based resources to investigate RTL [19]. These findings also have important implications for disadvantaged populations in society who are known to suffer from higher levels of stress. For example, one study investigated the mean telomere length in healthy premenopausal mothers who had either a healthy child (controls) or a child who was chronically ill (carers) [23]. The results found that chronic, psychological stress was significantly associated with shorter telomere length [23]. Alarmingly, the telomeres in mothers who had the highest levels of stress were shorter by approximately one decade of ageing when compared to the telomeres in mothers who had low stress [23]. These findings were validated in a larger study that found the RTL in caregivers with the highest levels of stress had the shortest telomeres that corresponded to an excess of 10–15 years of additional ageing [24]. The association of SH and psychological symptoms in carers should be explored in future research studies to better understand the influence of the caregiving role on SH. Moreover, the SHSQ-25, and its applicability in assessing biological ageing, could be a cost-effective screening tool for carers at the population level to avoid overdiagnosis.

Here we evidence, through a series of case studies, how SH avoids overdiagnosis of chronic diseases, through the effective stratification of individuals into high- and low-risk groups [15, 17]. Distinguishing between individuals at high and low risk allows for the prescription of personalised treatment algorithms in the primary care setting, allocating valuable resources to where they are most effective.

Primary prevention strategies have been shown to be highly cost-effective in healthcare systems [4]. A recent study found that investment in collaborative care that sought to address psychological stress with depression risk and anxiety conditions (that has been associated with diabetes and CVD) found the investment to be a cost-saving initiative, with a positive return on investment of $1.52 for every $1 dollar invested [7]. The cost-effectiveness of primary prevention is greatly improved when the strategy has the capacity to a) discriminate between high- and low-risk populations, and b) target the treatments towards individuals most at risk [4, 6].

In an ideal setting, detection of SH, via the SHSQ-25 should direct people to have their health (clinical/biomarkers) investigated by their doctor. Indeed, an individual with SH may have an undiagnosed disease that requires intervention. This proactive approach to healthcare has the potential to not only change the trajectory of disease but to also have substantial economic benefits for healthcare. SH has the hallmarks of a first-line screening tool for chronic diseases. SH and its vital role in the prediction and prevention of chronic diseases must be considered.

## 14 Expert Recommendations

Future studies from diverse populations are needed to identify SH in individuals at risk of developing chronic diseases. Assessment of SH in disadvantaged populations that are at greater risk of developing chronic diseases should explored, for example, informal unpaid carers, who are known to experience significantly higher levels of psychological distress than the general population. Such studies would have great significance for women's health, considering the overwhelming majority of carers are female.

## 15 Conclusions

SH offers a significant economic impact to healthcare by identifying and stratifying persons at high versus low risk, thus avoiding the under- and over-diagnosis of chronic diseases [4, 3]. The utilisation of SH enables targeted interventions to be aimed specifically at persons at risk of developing chronic diseases, directing valuable resources to where they are actually needed. At a time where healthcare systems worldwide are being overwhelmed by the perpetual growth of chronic diseases, failure to adopt SH will only serve to contribute to economic disaster. This is especially urgent considering the calls from multiple leading healthcare sectors for the adoption of cost-effective, evidence-based disease prevention strategies to alleviate the burden of chronic diseases. This book chapter evidences SH as the new gold standard in the global fight against chronic diseases from the perspective of PPPM.

## References

1. WHO https://www.who.int/en/news-room/fact-sheets/detail/noncommunicable-diseases
2. Yan YX, Liu YQ, Li M, Hu PF, Guo AM, Yang XH, Qiu JJ, Yang SS, Shen J, Zhang LP, Wang W (2009) Development and evaluation of a questionnaire for measuring suboptimal health status in urban Chinese. J Epidemiol 19(6):333–341. https://doi.org/10.2188/jea.je20080086
3. Golubnitschaja O, Baban b, Boniolo G, Wang W, Bubnov R, Kapalla M, Krapfenbauer K, Mozaffari MS, Vincenzo Costigliola V (2016) Medicine in the early twenty-first century: paradigm and anticipation - EPMA position paper. EPMA J 7(1):23
4. World Health Organization (2018) Regional Office for Europe, European Observatory on Health Systems and Policies & McDaid, David Using economic evidence to help make the case for investing in health promotion and disease prevention. World Health Organization. Regional Office for Europe. https://apps.who.int/iris/handle/10665/331981
5. World Health Organisation—Global Action Plan for the Prevention and Control of NCDs 2013–2020 https://www.who.int/publications/i/item/9789241506236
6. Golubnitschaja O, Kinkorova J, Costigliola V (2014) Predictive, preventive and personalised medicine as the hardcore of 'horizon 2020': EPMA position paper. EPMA J 5(1):6–6
7. Wang W, Yan Y, Guo Z, Hou H, Garcia M, Tan X, Anto EO, Mahara G, Zheng Y, Li B, Kang T, Zhong Z, Wang Y, Guo X, Golubnitschaja O, Suboptimal Health Study Consortium and European Association for Predictive, Preventive and Personalised Medicine (2021) All around suboptimal health - a joint position paper of the Suboptimal Health Study Consortium and European Association for Predictive, Preventive and Personalised Medicine. EPMA J 12(4):403–433. https://doi.org/10.1007/s13167-021-00253-2
8. Godoy LD, Rossignoli MT, Delfino-Pereira P, Garcia-Cairasco N, de Lima Umeoka EH (2018) A comprehensive overview on stress neurobiology: basic concepts and clinical implications. Front Behav Neurosci 12:127. https://doi.org/10.3389/fnbeh.2018.00127
9. Thau L, Gandhi J, Sharma S (2022) Physiology, cortisol. In: StatPearls. StatPearls Publishing, Treasure Island, FL
10. Paravati S, Rosani A, Warrington SJ (2022) Physiology, catecholamines. In: StatPearls. StatPearls Publishing, Treasure Island, FL
11. Wang Y, Ge S, Yan Y, Wang A , ZhaoZ, Yu X, Qiu J, Alzain MA, Wang H, Fang HH, Gao Q, Song MS, Jie Zhang J, Zhou Y, Wang W (2016) China suboptimal health cohort study: rationale, design and baseline characteristics. J Transl Med 14:291. https://doi.org/10.1186/s12967-016-1046-y
12. Moynihan R, Doust J, Henry D (2012) Preventing overdiagnosis: how to stop harming the healthy. BMJ 2012:344
13. Doust J, Glasziou P (2013) Is the problem that everything is a diagnosis? Aust Fam Physician 42(12):856–859
14. Anto EO, Roberts P, Coall D, Turpin CA, Adua E, Wang Y, Wang W (2019) Integration of suboptimal health status evaluation as a criterion for prediction of preeclampsia is strongly recommended for healthcare management in pregnancy: a prospective cohort study in a Ghanaian population. EPMA J 10(3):211–226. https://doi.org/10.1007/s13167-019-00183-0

15. Wang W, Russell AC, Yan Y (2014) Traditional Chinese medicine and new concepts of predictive, preventive and personalized medicine in diagnosis and treatment of suboptimal health. EPMA J 5(4):1–9
16. Jonsson AL, Bäckhed F (2016) Role of gut microbiota in atherosclerosis. Nat Rev Cardiol 14(2):79–87. https://doi.org/10.1038/nrcardio.2016.183
17. McDaid D, Park A, Knapp M (2017) Commissioning cost-effective services for promotion of mental health and wellbeing and prevention of mental ill-health. Public Health England, London
18. Anto EO, Roberts P, Coall DA, Adua E, Turpin CA, Tawiah A, Wang Y, Wang W (2020) Suboptimal health pregnant women are associated with increased oxidative stress and unbalanced pro- and antiangiogenic growth mediators: a cross-sectional study in a Ghanaian population. Free Radic Res 54(1):27–42. https://doi.org/10.1080/10715762.2019.1685668
19. Alzain MA, Asweto CO, Zhang J, Fang H, Zhao Z, Guo X, Song M, Zhou Y, Chang N, Wang Y, Wang W (2017) Telomere length and accelerated biological aging in the China suboptimal health cohort: a case-control study. Omics 21(6):333–339. https://doi.org/10.1089/omi.2017.0050
20. O'Callaghan NJ, Fenech M (2011) A quantitative PCR method for measuring absolute telomere length. Biol Proced Online 13:3. https://doi.org/10.1186/1480-9222-13-3
21. Hsieh AYY, Sabert S, Ajaykumar A, Hukezalie K, Gadawski I, Sattha B, Côté HCF (2016) Optimization of a relative telomere length assay by monochromatic multiplex real-time quantitative PCR on the LightCycler 480: sources of variability and quality control considerations. J Mol Diagn 18(3):425–437. https://doi.org/10.1016/j.jmoldx.2016.01.004
22. Crous-Bou M, Fung TT, Prescott J, Julin B, Du M, Sun Q, Rexrode KM, Hu FB, De Vivo I (2014) Mediterranean diet and telomere length in Nurses' health study: population-based cohort study. BMJ 349:g6674. https://doi.org/10.1136/bmj.g6674
23. Epel ES, Blackburn EH, Lin J, Dhabhar FS, Adler NE, Morrow JD, Cawthon RM (2004) Accelerated telomere shortening in response to life stress. Proc Natl Acad Sci 101(49):17312–17315. https://doi.org/10.1073/pnas.0407162101
24. Litzelman K, Witt WP, Gangnon RE, Nieto FJ, Engelman CD, Mailick MR, Skinner HG (2014) Association between informal caregiving and cellular aging in the survey of the health of Wisconsin: the role of caregiving characteristics, stress, and strain. Am J Epidemiol 179(11):1340–1352. https://doi.org/10.1093/aje/kwu066
25. Kupaev V, Borisov O, Marutina E, Yan YX, Wang W (2016) Integration of suboptimal health status and endothelial dysfunction as a new aspect for risk evaluation of cardiovascular disease. EPMA J 7(1):19. https://doi.org/10.1186/s13167-016-0068-0
26. WHO https://www.who.int/news-room/fact-sheets/detail/the-top-10-causes-of-death
27. Centres for Disease Control and Prevention (2017) National Diabetes Statistics Report. Atlanta, GA, U.S. Department of Health and Human Services
28. Lagraauw H, Kuiper J, Bot I (2015) Acute and chronic psychological stress as risk factors for cardiovascular disease: insights gained from epidemiological, clinical and experimental studies. Brain Behav Immun 50:18–30
29. Bamberger C, Bamberger A, de Castro M, Chrousos G (1995) Glucocorticoid receptor beta, a potential endogenous inhibitor of glucocorticoid action in humans. J Clin Invest 95(6):2435–2441
30. Dall T, Yang W (2019) The economic burden of elevated blood glucose levels in 2017: diagnosed and undiagnosed diabetes, gestational diabetes mellitus, and pre-diabetes. Diabetes Care 42:1661–1668
31. O'Connell J, Manson S (2019) Understanding the economic costs of diabetes and prediabetes and what we may learn about reducing the health and economic burden of these conditions. Diabetes Care 42(9):1609–1611
32. American Diabetes Association (2019) Classification and diagnosis of diabetes: standards of medical Care in Diabetes. Diabetes Care 42(1):13–28

33. Casagrande SS, Cowie CC, Genuth SM (2014) Self-reported prevalence of diabetes screening in the U.S., 2005–2010. Am J Prev Med 47(6):780–787. https://doi.org/10.1016/j.amepre.2014.07.039
34. Ge S, Xu X, Zhang J, Hou H, Wang H, Liu D, Zhang X, Song M, Li D, Zhou Y, Wang Y, Wang W (2019) Suboptimal health status as an independent risk factor for type 2 diabetes mellitus in a community-based cohort: the China suboptimal health cohort study. EPMA J 10(1):65–72. https://doi.org/10.1007/s13167-019-0159-9
35. Adua E, Memarian E, Russell A, Trbojević-Akmačić I, Gudelj I, Jurić J, Roberts P, Lauc G, Wang W (2019) Utilization of N-glycosylation profiles as risk stratification biomarkers for suboptimal health status and metabolic syndrome in a Ghanaian population. Biomark Med 13(15):1273–1287. https://doi.org/10.2217/bmm-2019-0005

# Tools of Predictive Diagnostics: Status Quo and Outlook

**Bo Li and Bingbing Li**

## Abbreviations

| | |
|---|---|
| AUC | The area under the receiver operating characteristic curve |
| CFS | Chronic fatigue syndrome |
| CI | Confidence interval |
| MSQA | The multidimensional sub-health questionnaire for adolescents |
| PPI | Protein–protein interaction |
| PPPM | Predictive, preventive, and personalised medicine |
| QOL | Quality of life |
| RTL | Relative telomere length |
| SHMS V1.0 | The sub-health measurement scale V1.0 |
| SHS | Suboptimal health status |
| SHSQ-25 | The suboptimal health status questionnaire-25 |
| SSS | The sub-health self assessment scale |
| T2DM | Type 2 diabetes mellitus |
| TGF-B1 | Transforming growth factor-β1 |
| WHO | The World Health Organisation |
| WHOQOL-100 | The WHO Quality of Life-100 |

B. Li (✉)
Institute of Chronic Disease Risks Assessment, School of Nursing and Health, Henan University, Kaifeng, China
e-mail: 10210022@vip.henu.edu.cn

B. Li
School of Nursing, Tongji Medical College, Huazhong University of Science and Technology, Wuhan, China



W. Wang (ed.), *All Around Suboptimal Health*, Advances in Predictive, Preventive and Personalised Medicine 18,
https://doi.org/10.1007/978-3-031-46891-9_5

# 1 Introduction

Suboptimal health status (SHS) refers to the intermediate state between health and disease [1]. It is regarded as a subclinical, reversible stage of chronic disease [2]. When a person is in SHS, no obvious or specific clinical manifestation can be observed, and neither relevant laboratory indexes are helpful, which makes SHS difficult to be assessed. SHS is mainly manifested as a variety of early stages of chronic health conditions. Therefore, the appropriate diagnostic tools are essential for the correct assessment and intervention of SHS and the maintenance of population health.

With the progress of SHS study, the work on SHS assessment and prediction tools has been carried out constantly, which provides the possibility to reveal SHS and explore the occurrence and development mechanism of SHS from different levels: tissue, gene, molecule and human as a whole.

# 2 The Status Quo of Predictive Diagnostic Instrument for Suboptimal Health

At present, the research on the subjective and objective assessments and quantitative diagnosis of SHS is still in its infancy. The predictive diagnostic tools for SHS mainly include subjective measures, i.e., health questionnaires and scales, and objective measures: laboratory-based biological, biochemical and molecular biology tests and big data analysis.

## *2.1 Subjective Health Assessment Measures*

### 2.1.1 Health-Related Quality of Life

Quality of life (QOL) has been widely used as a measure of health and functional status [3]. It includes many factors, such as individual's physical and psychological health status, independent levels, social relationships and so on [4]. The World Health Organisation (WHO) developed a questionnaire, named the WHO Quality of Life-100 (WHOQOL-100).

The WHOQOL-100 is a universal tool for assessing quality of life. It can be used for people with chronic diseases, people under stress and healthy people. It was developed in fifteen centers around the world [5]. It consists of six dimensions, including physiology, psychology, independence, social relations, environment and spiritual world, such as support, religion and personal belief [3]. After many verifications, the WHOQOL-100 showed enough reliability and is recognised by researchers. Facet reliability ranged from 0.43 for physical environment to 0.96 for activities of daily living [5]. The construct validity of the whole questionnaire and the dimensions was good. Reliability values for overall quality of life and overall health were 0.91 [5].

Based on WHOQOL-100, WHOQOL-Brief and WHOQOL-Old, special for health-related quality of life research of specific populations, are developed [6]. Because of its efficiency, WHOQOL-Brief is popular and has been applied in many researches. It consists of 26 items, which makes it convenient to use. Now, 15 international field centers have been committed to developing WHOQOL-Brief to obtain an effective tool to assess an individual's status cross-culturally [3]. The WHOQOL-Brief item scores for each dimension were very similar to the WHOQOL-100 scores, explaining approximately 95% of the variance in the total scores for the four domains (range 77–91%) [7]. Besides, the results of many studies show that the QOL of the elderly population has its own particularity and should be measured by a specific scale. For this reason, WHOQOL-OLD was developed by the WHOQOL group [8]. Questionnaires are available free to the community and researchers in the region. They are available in Portuguese at: *www.whoqolweb.com.br*. Previous research focused on generic quality-of-life issues has proven that WHOQOL-OLD has good psychometric properties [9]. Its reliability, validity and responsiveness make researchers confident that it can be widely used.

Health-related quality of life is a broad-ranging concept. This scale is applicable to a wide range of health-related states, and SHS is just one of them. In other words, this scale cannot accurately and adequately measure SHS. Therefore, research on suboptimal health needs specific tools.

## 2.2 *Suboptimal Health Status*

The suboptimal health status questionnaire-25 (SHSQ-25) has been developed to precisely measure suboptimal health status. The SHSQ-25 has been proven to be very effective in Africa, China and the Caucasus. It consists of 25 items in five dimensions: fatigue, cardiovascular, digestive, immune and mental status [10] (Fig. 1). A 5-point Likert scale is used to rate each item (from never or almost never to always). The total score ranges from 0 to 100, a high score indicating a poor health. Both healthcare and community settings can use the SHSQ-25. The SHSQ-25 could identify people who report being in poor health but who have not had a diagnosable illness in the last 3 months [11, 12]. The specific contents of SHSQ-25 are listed in Fig. 1.

The main advantage of the SHSQ-25 is that it is short and easy to answer. It is suitable not only for large population studies but also for routine health surveys [1]. To date, SHSQ-25 has been verified in a variety of populations, suggesting that it can be used as a practical SHS survey instrument for screening high-risk groups. Some previous studies found that SHS is a sensitive indicator for type 2 diabetes mellitus (T2DM) [13] and cardiovascular diseases [14].

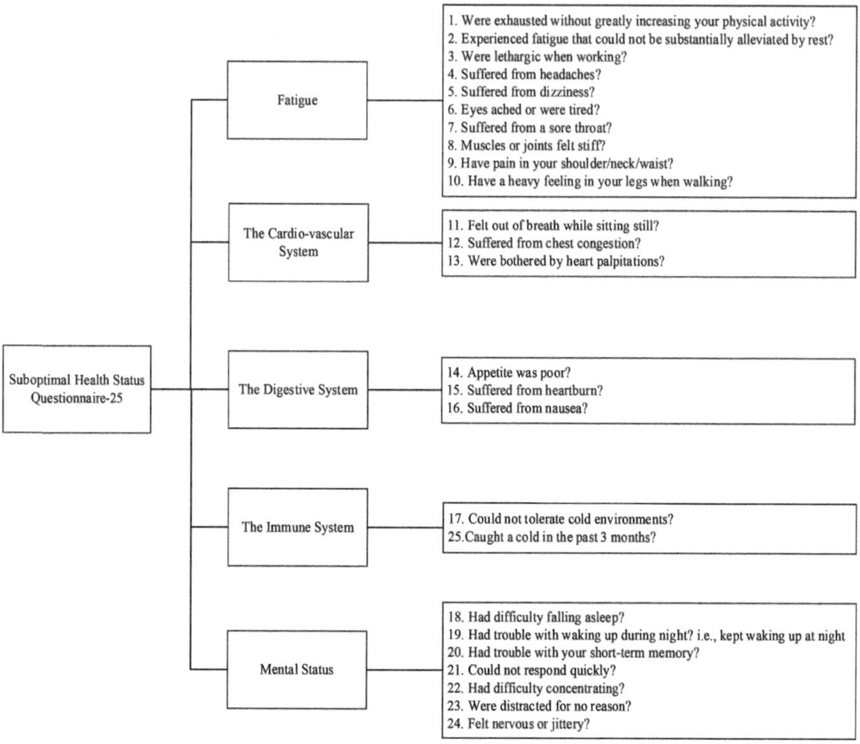


**Fig. 1** Items of the Suboptimal Health Status Questionnaire-25 [1, 2]

The SHSQ-25 has been used in different population. In a cohort study of pregnant women in Ghana, Anto et al. found that a high SHS score was associated with an increased incidence of pre-eclampsia [12]. Studies conducted among adult community residents suggested that SHS was a new independent risk factor for T2DM and associated with endothelial dysfunction [15]. SHS was also proven to be related to psychological health among nurses and college students. A study conducted in Chinese college students demonstrated that SHS was associated with psychological symptoms (e.g., somatisation, obsessive-compulsive, interpersonal sensitivity and depression) [16]. In another study, the prevalence of SHS was higher among nurses who had psychological symptoms such as depression and anxiety [17].

Although it cannot be used to diagnose diseases, SHSQ-25 can ring the alarm for us before the outbreak of diseases to carry out health interventions for people as early as possible. This is therefore a contribution to the reduction of the burden of disease [18]. In addition to the SHSQ-25, there are other tools used to assess SHS. For example, the Sub-Health Self Assessment Scale (SSS) is currently used in the field of Chinese medicine. In China, the SSS is used to assess the SHS of undergraduate students [19]. This scale contains 3 symptom dimensions, with 58 items corresponding to 10 factors (Fig. 2). The current research suggests that SSS has satisfactory sensibility, representation and internal consistency [19]. However, it has

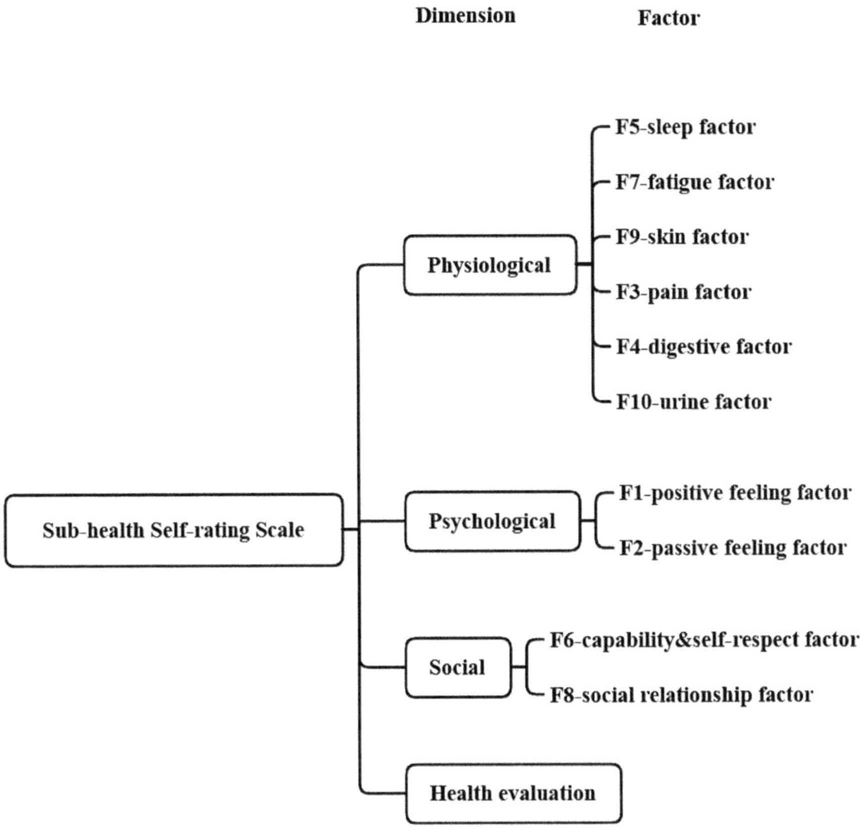


**Fig. 2** Theoretical framework for the Sub-Health Self-rating Scale (SSS) [19]

a limited scope of application and must be tested and improved by more practice, because it is a self-assessment scale applied in groups of students, and the survey is only conducted among a few schools.

## 2.3 *Sub-Health Measurement Scale V1.0*

The Sub-Health Measurement Scale V1.0 (SHMS V1.0) is developed among Chinese adults aged 18 years and over. The SHMS V1.0 consists of three subscales (physical, mental and social domains) with a total of 35 items. Cut-offs for suboptimal health were established among Chinese urban residents by age group [20]. The study using the SHMS V1.0 for the estimation of suboptimal health status has mainly focused on the relationship between the lifestyle and the SHS, and participants are limited among Chinese [21–25]. It is unknown whether it has good reliability and validity to be applied in different populations or ethnicities.

### 2.4 *The Multidimensional Sub-Health Questionnaire of Adolescent*

The Multidimensional Sub-Health Questionnaire for Adolescents (MSQA) has been used on a large scale with Chinese students over the past few years. The MSQA is a multidimensional, self-reporting screening tool developed in China that examines physical and psychological symptoms in adolescents. It contains 71 items: physical symptoms (32 items) and psychological symptoms (39 items) [26].

## 3 Objective Measures for SHS

Aided by rapid advances in biotechnology and the availability of mega-health databases, health professionals are well placed to raise the issues of genetics, environment and behaviour and to motivate the introduction of predictive, preventive and personalised Medicine (PPPM) into routine medical care [11]. Modern biochemical and molecular biological research provides new ideas and tools for assessing health status and predicting disease progress, which is of great significance for SHS research. Traditional Chinese medicine and digital biomarkers might provide a new vision for evaluating SHS. However, owing to the complexity, diversity and non-specificity of SHS symptoms, an index system for biochemically assessing SHS is still lacking. The good news is that some achievements have been obtained in laboratory experiments.

### 3.1 *Laboratory Examination*

#### 3.1.1 General Biological and Biochemical Indexes

Evidence from existing research showed that many biological and biochemical indexes have significant correlations with SHS, such as systolic blood pressure, diastolic blood pressure, total cholesterol and high-density lipoprotein cholesterol. In addition, studies have found that plasma glucose levels in men and triglyceride levels in women have an association with SHS [11]. SHS scores and serum cortisol levels were also significantly linearly correlated [11].

The SHSQ-25 has been found to be an accurate measure of chronic psychological distress. Plasma cortisol and glucocorticoid receptors are two important physiological mediators of psychological stress [27]. In this study, plasma cortisol levels and SHS score were significantly positively correlated, whereas glucocorticoid receptor mRNA expression in peripheral blood monocytes was negatively correlated with SHS score [27]. Another study also revealed that plasma cortisol detection played an important role in evaluating SHS [28].

A study of Ghanaian women found that oxidative stress was strongly associated with SHS. Endothelial dysfunction, a complication of oxidative stress, may also contribute to the development of SHS [29]. The association has also been verified in another Russian population-based study [14]. People scoring high on the SHS had significantly higher average levels of diastolic and systolic blood pressure, body mass index, triglycerides, total cholesterol and low-density lipoprotein cholesterol [14]. The combination of SHS and endothelial dysfunction provides a new opportunity to gain a comprehensive understanding of the relationship between subjective and objective health indicators. This suggests that SHS can be used to help screen for cardiovascular disease on a routine basis.

## 3.2 *Molecular Biological Measures*

The development of proteomics, glycogenomics and metabolomics makes it possible to research the physiological or pathological mechanism of SHS because SHS is a transitional stage from health to disease, which will inevitably be accompanied by changes at the biological and molecular level.

Proteomic studies have shown that many people with SHS have immune abnormalities that manifest clinically as cytokine-mediated immune responses with inflammatory consequences. In a controlled study, the Japanese patients, with chronic fatigue syndrome (CFS), were detected to reduce production of mRNA and transforming growth factor-β1 (TGF-B1) significantly [30]. Cytokine deficiency increases the risk of myalgia and muscle fatigue.

The analysis results using protein–protein interaction (PPI) network showed that10 hub genes (AMHR2, BMP10, BMPER, GJA1, KRT1, MT3, NTM, TWIST2, TUBB3 and TMEM98) were related to SHS. A transcriptomic prediction model can effectively discriminate SHS individuals from healthy individuals, its sensitivity was 83.3% with a 95% confidence interval (CI): 73.9–92.7%, and its specificity was 90.0% with 95% CI: 82.4–97.6%), and the area under the receiver operating characteristic curve (AUC) was 0.938 with 95% CI: 0.882–0.994 [31]. Therefore, two transcripts were selected in the model that was set up based on the candidate transcripts. It is shown below.

$$\text{Logit}\left(p = \text{SHS}\right) = 0.137 - 66.878 \times \left(\text{BMPER mRNA}\right) + 29.328 \times \left(\text{AMHR2 mRNA}\right)$$

The sensitivity of the model was 83.3% (95% CI: 73.9–92.7%). Its specificity was 90.0% (95% CI: 82.4–97.6%), and the AUC was 0.938 (95% CI: 0.882–0.994) [31].

In another report, SHS is positively correlated with the risk of developing metabolic syndrome. N-glycans have been found to be associated with the development

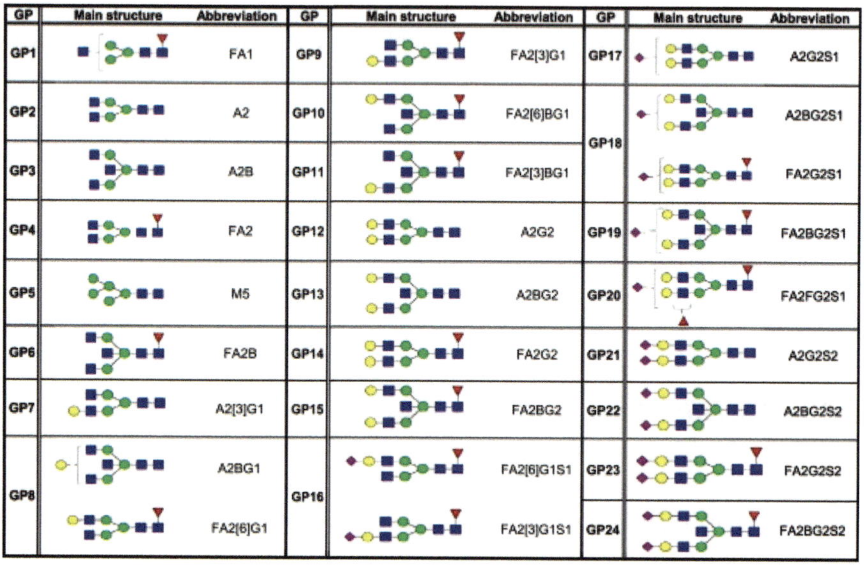


**Fig. 3** The 24 IgG glycan peaks as measured with ultra-performance liquid chromatography [33]. Shown is the structure of the main IgG glycan component(s)

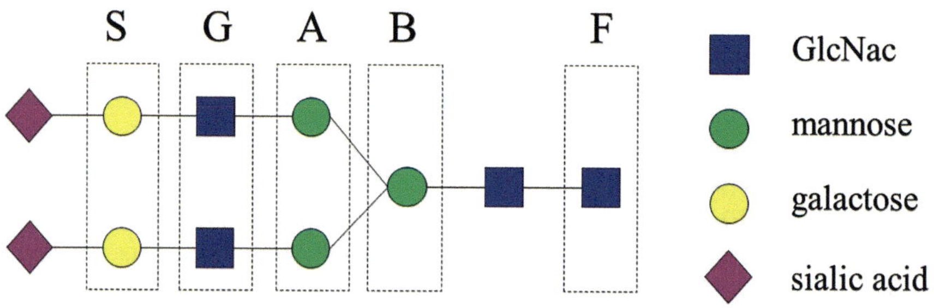


**Fig. 4** Structural abbreviations and structural schemes

of metabolic syndrome in studies related to suboptimal health and glycosomics [32]. The glycan peaks (GPs) of GP8 (FA2[6]G1), GP18 (FA2G2S1), GP21(FA2G2S2) and GP34 (A4G4S[3,3,6,]3) could be used to predict SHS and metabolic syndrome [32].

Figure 3 highlights glycomics as a diagnostic tool for SHS. Figure 4 shows the structural abbreviations (a) and structural schemes (b).

Metabonomics studies have shown that the clinical manifestation of CFS represents a highly coordinated hypometabolic response, demonstrating that Metabonomics could be used as a powerful method for the identification of biochemical differences between health and disease [33]. An experimental method combining four metabolic biomarkers (sphingomyelin, progesterone, bovine heparan sulphate and cervinyl carnitine) is able to distinguish people with SHS from healthy people; its sensitivity was 94.0% and its specificity was 90.0%, and the AUC was 0.977 [34]. Existing research suggests that metabolic disorders associated with SHS can be identified at an early stage. Therefore, from a PPPM perspective, the ability to identify SHS-related metabolites early may represent a window of opportunity to manage chronic disease [34].

Studies have shown a high turnover of collagen and non-myofibrillar proteins in the amino acid composition of women's urine, suggesting that analysis of amino acids in female urine may be a useful tool for assessing fatigue and suboptimal health when administering amino acid supplementation to individuals [35].

In addition to physiological and biological measures, short relative telomere length (RTL) has been reported to have a significant association with SHS. This suggests that the combination of subjective (SHS) and objective (RTL) measures of subjects could provide a new and more practical tool for healthy ageing research [10].

### *3.3 Digital Biomarkers*

A study of 200 Russian university students found that the vocal changes they made under stress could serve as an important biomarker for identifying SHS. Artificial intelligence using predictive machine learning models can automatically derive digital biomarkers based on the voice recordings of study participants, which could be a useful tool for identifying SHS [36]. This bodes well for the possibility of developing a method for the detection of SHS that is both convenient to use and non-invasive.

## 4 The Outlook of SHS Diagnostic Tools

The SHSQ-25 has been shown to have a wide range of applicability in previous studies, which means that the SHSQ-25 will be translated into other different languages and used by more researchers. To date, SHSQ-25 has had three language versions, Chinese, English and Russian. In the future, SHSQ-25 in more languages will be applied among different ethnic population.

Animal models are essential for SHS mechanistic studies. Although experiments have been performed on some animals, such as rats and mice, to establish animal models of SHS, they cannot completely simulate the human state [37, 38]. Even so, animal study provides more possibilities for us to deeply understand the mechanism of SHS, and it is helpful to establish an objective indicator system.

The current SHS evaluation criteria and thresholds are extrapolated from the range of clinical disease diagnoses. The reliability is uncertain and the scope of application is narrow. Therefore, only a single or a few indicators cannot reflect the real state of individual SHS. To solve this problem, we can carry out a large sample investigation or experiment, combine the scale investigation with experimental research, and find out the physiological and biochemical index spectrum corresponding to different subtypes of SHS, which might effectively improve the reliability and effectiveness of SHS diagnosis. In addition, according to the findings of our previous studies, the sensitive indicators might be different for people of different age and status, like pregnant women and general communities. The future studies could make an effort to explore the specific indicators in certain population to improve the recognising precision.

The molecular biology research on SHS has made remarkable achievements, but these researches rely heavily on laboratory detections, and some of them are not mature enough. Therefore, convenient, fast, efficient, sensitive and inexpensive practical tools need to be developed for future research and application [27, 28]. In the current diagnostic or screening technology, biodetection chips or kits have the advantages of high throughput, standardisation and practicality, and become the main development choice for SHS diagnosis in the future. N-glycans are involved in intracellular/extracellular interactions or signal transduction, cell adhesion, metastasis, cell–cell or molecular–cell interactions, inflammation and immune function, making them ideal dynamic biomarkers for monitoring physiological conditions. Thus, the N-glycan biochip can be used to help evaluate individual SHS. The advanced detection measurement based on glycomics is expected to develop into a powerful tool to evaluate objective indexes of SHS [39–43].

Based on the previous study, automated artificial intelligence (AI) analysis of voice recordings using predictive machine learning models can be effective in determining an individual's health status and can be used as potential digital biomarkers. In addition, analysis of disease-specific cell-free nucleic acid data (ccfDNA, ctDNA, mtDNA, miRNA) combined with metabolic patterns can be used for subsequent stratification and monitoring of individual SHS tests. This is a cost-effective application that allows for targeted prevention at the stage of reversible damage to health [36].

Future research on SHS needs to be conducted using a comprehensive paradigm with a large sample size. This should be a combination of qualitative and quantitative studies. As a consequence, massive data will be generated. If we include massive amounts of bioinformatics data, then the following requirement for technological development is that the revolutionary ability to process and analyse big data must be advanced (such as artificial intelligence).

## References

1. Wang W, Yan Y (2012) Suboptimal health: a new health dimension for translational medicine. Clin Transl Med 1(1):28. https://doi.org/10.1186/2001-1326-1-28
2. Yan Y-X, Liu Y-Q, Li M, Hu P-F, Guo A-M, Yang X-H, Qiu J-J, Yang S-S, Shen J, Zhang L-P, Wang W (2009) Development and evaluation of a questionnaire for measuring suboptimal health status in urban Chinese. J Epidemiol 19(6):333–341. https://doi.org/10.2188/jea.je20080086

3. Group TW (1998) The World Health Organization quality of life assessment (WHOQOL): development and general psychometric properties. Soc Sci Med 46(12):1569–1585. https://doi.org/10.1016/s0277-9536(98)00009-4
4. Group W (1995) The World Health Organization quality of life assessment (WHOQOL): position paper from the World Health Organization. Soc Sci Med 41(10):1403–1409. https://doi.org/10.1016/0277-9536(95)00112-k
5. De Vries J, Van Heck GL (1997) The World Health Organization Quality of Life Assessment Instrument (WHOQOL-100): validation study with the Dutch version. Eur J Psychol Assess 13(3):164–178. https://doi.org/10.1027/1015-5759.13.3.164
6. Casamali FFC, Schuch FB, Scortegagna SA, Legnani E, De Marchi ACB (2019) Accordance and reproducibility of the electronic version of the WHOQOL-BREF and WHOQOL-OLD questionnaires. Exp Gerontol 125:110683. https://doi.org/10.1016/j.exger.2019.110683
7. Skevington SM, Sartorius N, Amir M (2004) Developing methods for assessing quality of life in different cultural settings: the history of the WHOQOL instruments. Soc Psychiatry Psychiatr Epidemiol 39(1):1–8. https://doi.org/10.1007/s00127-004-0700-5
8. Melo RL, Silva Júnior EG, Souto RQ, Leão ÍS, Eulálio MD (2018) Psychometric properties of the complete version of the World Health Organization quality of life assessment (WHOQOL-OLD): reduced response scale. Psicol Reflex Crít 31(1):1–10. https://doi.org/10.1186/s41155-018-0084-1
9. Rowthorn MJ, Billington DR, Krägeloh CU, Landon J, Medvedev ON (2019) Development of a mental health recovery module for the WHOQOL. Qual Life Res 28(12):3363–3374. https://doi.org/10.1007/s11136-019-02265-y
10. Ali AM, Otieno AC, Jie Z, Honghong F, Zhongyao Z, Xiuhua G, Manshu S, Yong Z, Naibai C, Youxin W, Wei W (2017) Telomere length and accelerated biological aging in the China suboptimal health cohort: a case-control study. Omics 21(6):333–339. https://doi.org/10.1089/omi.2017.0050
11. Wang W, Russell A, Yan Y (2014) Traditional Chinese medicine and new concepts of predictive, preventive and personalized medicine in diagnosis and treatment of suboptimal health. EPMA J 5(1):4. https://doi.org/10.1186/1878-5085-5-4
12. Anto EO, Roberts P, Coall D, Turpin CA, Adua E, Wang Y, Wang W (2019) Integration of suboptimal health status evaluation as a criterion for prediction of preeclampsia is strongly recommended for healthcare management in pregnancy: a prospective cohort study in a Ghanaian population. EPMA J 10(3):211–226. https://doi.org/10.1007/s13167-019-00183-0
13. Adua E, Roberts P, Wang W (2017) Incorporation of suboptimal health status as a potential risk assessment for type II diabetes mellitus: a case-control study in a Ghanaian population. EPMA J 8(4):345–355. https://doi.org/10.1007/s13167-017-0119-1
14. Kupaev V, Borisov O, Marutina E, Yan YX, Wang W (2016) Integration of suboptimal health status and endothelial dysfunction as a new aspect for risk evaluation of cardiovascular disease. EPMA J 7(1):19. https://doi.org/10.1186/s13167-016-0068-0
15. Ge S, Xu X, Zhang J, Hou H, Wang H, Liu D, Zhang X, Song M, Li D, Zhou Y, Wang Y, Wang W (2019) Suboptimal health status as an independent risk factor for type 2 diabetes mellitus in a community-based cohort: the China suboptimal health cohort study. EPMA J 10(1):65–72. https://doi.org/10.1007/s13167-019-0159-9
16. Hou H, Feng X, Li Y, Meng Z, Guo D, Wang F, Guo Z, Zheng Y, Peng Z, Zhang W, Li D, Ding G, Wang W (2018) Suboptimal health status and psychological symptoms among Chinese college students: a perspective of predictive, preventive and personalised health. EPMA J 9(4):367–377. https://doi.org/10.1007/s13167-018-0148-4
17. Zhu J, Ying W, Zhang L, Peng G, Chen W, Anto EO, Wang X, Lu N, Gao S, Wu G, Yan J, Ye J, Wu S, Yu C, Yue M, Huang X, Xu N, Ying P, Chen Y, Tan X, Wang W (2020) Psychological symptoms in Chinese nurses may be associated with predisposition to chronic disease: a cross-sectional study of suboptimal health status. EPMA J 11(4):1–13. https://doi.org/10.1007/s13167-020-00225-y

18. Wang Y, Ge S, Yan Y, Wang A, Zhao Z, Yu X, Qiu J, Alzain MA, Wang H, Fang H, Gao Q, Song M, Zhang J, Zhou Y, Wang W (2016) China suboptimal health cohort study: rationale, design and baseline characteristics. J Transl Med 14(1):291. https://doi.org/10.1186/s12967-016-1046-y
19. Bi JL, Chen J, Sun XM, Nie XL, Liu YY, Luo R, Zhao XS (2019) The development and evaluation of a sub-health self-rating scale for university students in China. BMC Public Health 19(1):330. https://doi.org/10.1186/s12889-019-6650-3
20. Xu J, Xue Y, Liu G, Feng Y, Xu M, Xie J, Wang X, Chen X, Jiang L (2019) Establishment of the norms of sub-health measurement scale version 1.0 for Chinese urban residents. Nan Fang Yi Ke Da Xue Xue Bao 39(3):271–278. https://doi.org/10.12122/j.issn.1673-4254.2019.03.03
21. Xue Y, Liu G, Feng Y, Xu M, Jiang L, Lin Y, Xu J (2020) Mediating effect of health consciousness in the relationship of lifestyle and suboptimal health status: a cross-sectional study involving Chinese urban residents. BMJ Open 10(10):e039701. https://doi.org/10.1136/bmjopen-2020-039701
22. Wu S, Xuan Z, Li F, Xiao W, Fu X, Jiang P, Chen J, Xiang L, Liu Y, Nie X, Luo R, Sun X, Kwan H, Zhao X (2016) Work-recreation balance, health-promoting lifestyles and suboptimal health status in southern China: a cross-sectional study. Int J Environ Res Public Health 13(3):339. https://doi.org/10.3390/ijerph13030339
23. Bi J, Huang Y, Xiao Y, Cheng J, Li F, Wang T, Chen J, Wu L, Liu Y, Luo R, Zhao X (2014) Association of lifestyle factors and suboptimal health status: a cross-sectional study of Chinese students. BMJ Open 4(6):e005156. https://doi.org/10.1136/bmjopen-2014-005156
24. Chen J, Xiang H, Jiang P, Yu L, Jing Y, Li F, Wu S, Fu X, Liu Y, Kwan H, Luo R, Zhao X, Sun X (2017) The role of healthy lifestyle in the implementation of regressing suboptimal health status among college students in China: a nested case-control study. Int J Environ Res Public Health 14(3):240. https://doi.org/10.3390/ijerph14030240
25. Chen J, Cheng J, Liu Y, Tang Y, Sun X, Wang T, Xiao Y, Li F, Xiang L, Jiang P, Wu S, Wu L, Luo R, Zhao X (2014) Associations between breakfast eating habits and health-promoting lifestyle, suboptimal health status in southern China: a population based, cross sectional study. J Transl Med 12:348. https://doi.org/10.1186/s12967-014-0348-1
26. Cao H, Tao FB, Huang L, Wan YH, Sun Y, Su PY, Hao JH (2012) Situation of common psychosomatic symptom in adolescent and its influence on 6 months later suicide and self-injurious behavior. Zhonghua Yu Fang Yi Xue Za Zhi 46(3):202–208
27. Yan Y-X, Dong J, Liu Y-Q, Zhang J, Song M-S, He Y, Wang W (2015) Association of suboptimal health status with psychosocial stress, plasma cortisol and mRNA expression of glucocorticoid receptor α/β in lymphocyte. Stress (Amsterdam, Netherlands) 18(1):29–34. https://doi.org/10.3109/10253890.2014.999233
28. Yu-Xiang Y, Li-Juan W, Huan-Bo X, Shuo W, Jing D, Wei W (2018) Latent class analysis to evaluate performance of plasma cortisol, plasma catecholamines, and SHSQ-25 for early recognition of suboptimal health status. EPMA J 9(3):299–305. https://doi.org/10.1007/s13167-018-0144-8
29. Anto EO, Roberts P, Coall DA, Adua E, Turpin CA, Tawiah A, Wang Y, Wang W (2020) Suboptimal health pregnant women are associated with increased oxidative stress and unbalanced pro- and antiangiogenic growth mediators: a cross-sectional study in a Ghanaian population. Free Radic Res 54(1):27–42. https://doi.org/10.1080/10715762.2019.1685668
30. Tomoda A, Joudoi T, Rabab E-M, Matsumoto T, Park TH, Miike T (2005) Cytokine production and modulation: comparison of patients with chronic fatigue syndrome and normal controls. Psychiatry Res 134(1):101–104. https://doi.org/10.1016/j.psychres.2005.01.002
31. Wang H, Tian Q, Zhang J, Liu H, Zhang J, Cao W, Zhang X, Li X, Wu L, Song M (2021) Blood transcriptome profiling as potential biomarkers of suboptimal health status: potential utility of novel biomarkers for predictive, preventive, and personalized medicine strategy. EPMA J 12(2):103–115. https://doi.org/10.1007/s13167-021-00238-1
32. Adua E, Memarian E, Russell A, Trbojević-Akmačić I, Gudelj I, Jurić J, Roberts P, Lauc G, Wang W (2019) Utilization of N-glycosylation profiles as risk stratification biomarkers for

suboptimal health status and metabolic syndrome in a Ghanaian population. Biomark Med 13(15):1273–1287. https://doi.org/10.2217/bmm-2019-0005
33. Naviaux RK, Naviaux JC, Li K, Bright AT, Alaynick WA, Wang L, Baxter A, Nathan N, Anderson W, Gordon E (2016) Metabolic features of chronic fatigue syndrome. Proc Natl Acad Sci 113(46):E5472–E5480. https://doi.org/10.1073/pnas.1607571113
34. Wang H, Tian Q, Zhang J, Liu H, Zhang X, Cao W, Zhang J, Anto EO, Li X, Wang X (2020) Population-based case-control study revealed metabolomic biomarkers of suboptimal health status in Chinese population—potential utility for innovative approach by predictive, preventive, and personalized medicine. EPMA J 11(2):147–160. https://doi.org/10.1007/s13167-020-00200-7
35. Dunstan RH, Sparkes DL, Macdonald MM, De Jonge XJ, Dascombe BJ, Gottfries J, Gottfries CG, Roberts TK (2017) Diverse characteristics of the urinary excretion of amino acids in humans and the use of amino acid supplementation to reduce fatigue and sub-health in adults. Nutr J 16(1):19. https://doi.org/10.1186/s12937-017-0240-y
36. Kunin A, Sargheini N, Birkenbihl C, Moiseeva N, Fröhlich H, Golubnitschaja O (2020) Voice perturbations under the stress overload in young individuals: phenotyping and suboptimal health as predictors for cascading pathologies. EPMA J 11(4):1–11. https://doi.org/10.1007/s13167-020-00229-8
37. Yu Y, Yang S, Mao L-G, Liu C-M, Chen J, Hu Y-T, Gan L, Jiang T-T (2020) Identification of potential metabolic biomarkers in yin deficiency syndrome using LC-MS. Anat Rec 303(8):2121–2130. https://doi.org/10.1002/ar.24025
38. Zhao R, Cai Y, Shao X, Ma B (2015) Improving the activity of Lycium barbarum polysaccharide on sub-health mice. Food Funct 6(6):2033–2040. https://doi.org/10.1039/c4fo01108b
39. Gornik O, Wagner J, Pucic M, Knezevic A, Redzic I, Lauc G (2009) Stability of N-glycan profiles in human plasma. Glycobiology 19(12):1547–1553. https://doi.org/10.1093/glycob/cwp134
40. Kukuruzinska MA, Lennon K (1998) Protein N-glycosylation: molecular genetics and functional significance. Crit Rev Oral Biol Med 9(4):415–448. https://doi.org/10.1177/10454411980090040301
41. Dube DH, Bertozzi CR (2005) Glycans in cancer and inflammation. Potential for therapeutics and diagnostics. Nat Rev Drug Discov 4(6):477–488. https://doi.org/10.1038/nrd1751
42. Knezevic A, Polasek O, Gornik O, Rudan I, Campbell H, Hayward C, Wright A, Kolcic I, O'Donoghue N, Bones J, Rudd PM, Lauc G (2009) Variability, heritability and environmental determinants of human plasma N-Glycome. J Proteome Res 8(2):694–701. https://doi.org/10.1021/pr800737u
43. Lauc G, Zoldos V (2010) Protein glycosylation-an evolutionary crossroad between genes and environment. Mol BioSyst 6(12):2373–2379. https://doi.org/10.1039/c0mb00067a

# Risk Factors, Health Status, and Risk Groups in Suboptimal Health Condition

**Gehendra Mahara, Xuerui Tan, and Wei Wang**

## Abbreviations

| | |
|---|---|
| COPD | Chronic Obstructive Pulmonary Disease |
| CVD | Cardiovascular diseases |
| GBD | Global Burden of Diseases |

G. Mahara
Clinical Research Center, First Affiliated Hospital of Shantou University Medical College, Shantou, Guangdong, China

X. Tan (✉)
Department of Cardiovascular Medicine, First Affiliated Hospital of Shantou University Medical College, Shantou, Guangdong, China

W. Wang
First Affiliated Hospital, Shantou University Medical College, Shantou, China

Beijing Key Laboratory of Clinical Epidemiology, Capital Medical University, Beijing, China

School of Public Health, Shandong First Medical University and Shandong Academy of Medical Sciences, Jinan, China

Centre for Precision Health, Edith Cowan University, Perth, Australia

Suboptimal Health Study Consortium, Kumasi, Ghana

Suboptimal Health Study Consortium, Perth, Australia

Suboptimal Health Study Consortium, Beijing, China

Suboptimal Health Study Consortium, Bonn, Germany

European Association for Predictive, Preventive and Personalised Medicine, EPMA, Brussels, Belgium
e-mail: wei.wang@ecu.edu.au


W. Wang (ed.), *All Around Suboptimal Health*, Advances in Predictive, Preventive and Personalised Medicine 18,
https://doi.org/10.1007/978-3-031-46891-9_6

| | |
|---|---|
| LMIC | Low- and Middle-income Countries |
| NCD | Non-communicable diseases |
| PPPM | Predictive, Preventive, and Personalised Medicine |
| SHS | Suboptimal Health Status |
| WHO | World Health Organisation |

## 1 Intermediate State Between Health and Disease

A person's physical, psychological, and social stress can result in suboptimal health status, sometimes referred to as sub-health status (SHS), a transitional condition between health and illness with several adverse effects [1–3]. Its main underlying process is yet unknown [4]. However, physical, psychological, and social functions deteriorate due to the total coordination of the body's systems, including the neurological, endocrine, and immune systems, becoming unbalanced and dysfunctional, resulting in physical and psychological alterations. The body has not yet progressed to the illness stage [4–6].

Numerous chronic symptoms, including chronic fatigue, headaches, vertigo, unhappiness, anxiety, lack of hunger, sleeplessness, and functional problems, are experienced by people with SHS [3, 5, 7]. Similar to this, some organ systems, generalised discomfort, and functional abnormalities of many organ systems, such as the digestive, cardiovascular, pulmonary, and urinary systems, are connected to short- or long-term detrimental health effects [6, 7]. For instance, SHS contributes significantly to lower quality of life, frequent hospital visits, and expensive medical expenses [8, 9]. The afflicted continue to feel disappointed and unable to live normal lives because there are no obvious indications of any one disease [2–4]. Does the pathway to a chronic disease state appear to be shifting away from an optimal health status? Around the world, it is a difficult and real problem [10].

SHS seems to be common in China [6], and it has been steadily increasing in other nations [8, 11, 12]. The signs of SHS may be ignored worldwide, and many people are unaware that they have the condition [3]. SHS is displayed with various persons and organisations, including teachers, government employees, company owners, local citizens, healthcare professionals, and others [3, 5]. As a result, many academics and scientists worldwide have recently been concentrating on the age, sex, profession, topographical area, and behavior of people who are at higher threat of SHS. An individual health monitoring system inspired by the predictive, preventative, and personalised medicine (PPPM) technique, which is actively spreading throughout the world, is necessary to stop SHS from progressing to the state of chronic disease [13, 14].

## 2 Relationship Between SHS and Chronic Disorders

According to the WHO, non-communicable diseases (NCDs), often referred to as chronic disorders, kill 41 million people worldwide each year [15–19]. In addition, between the ages of 30 and 69, a productive age group, more than 15 million people die prematurely from NCD each year, with low- and middle-income countries (LMICs) accounting for 77% of deaths [15–19]. In addition, roughly 17.9 million people worldwide die each year from cardiovascular diseases (heart attacks and strokes), followed by cancer (9.3%), COPD (chronic obstructive pulmonary disease (COPD), and 1.5 million individuals with diabetes mellitus. Notably, these four illnesses account for more than 80% of NCD-related early mortality [15–19].

The risk factors for NCDs, like a bad diet, not being active, smoking, and drinking too much, are more common in young people, adults, and seniors [20, 21]. Similarly, young people, adults, and seniors are more susceptible to the influencing aspects leading to NCDs, such as poor diet, inactivity, smoking, and alcohol abuse [7, 9, 15–19]. On the other hand, SHS has been noted as a potential risk factor for various malignancies and metabolic diseases, as well as diabetes mellitus, heart disease, and stroke. It is recognised as a sub-clinical reversible stage of chronic diseases.

There is strong evidence that NCD risk factors include modifying personal behaviors like smoking, inactivity, poor diet, and excessive alcohol consumption. An estimated 7.2 million people die from smoking each year, followed by 4.1 million from eating too much salt, 3.3 million from drinking alcohol and developing cancer, and 1.6 million from not getting enough exercise [15–19]. As a result, WHO has set a target of reducing premature mortality brought on by NCDs by 2030 through a sustainable development agenda [15–19].

Examples of risk factors for chronic disease include socioeconomic status, degree of education, physical inactivity, salt consumption, blood pressure, cardiovascular indications, triglycerides, lipid, alcohol use, poor diet, etc. [2, 4, 22]. Similarly, SHS risk is directly correlated with smoking behaviors, physical activity, poor nutritional intake, insufficient sleep, and uncontrolled blood pressure [3, 4, 7, 23, 24]. These risk factors are connected to a person's lifestyle or behavior, and these unhealthy ways of living or behaviors significantly contribute to the rise in SHS [4, 20, 23].

The prevalence of chronic diseases such as cardiovascular diseases, hypertension, stroke, cancer, chronic obstructive pulmonary disease, and diabetes is rising as a result of modern lifestyles, higher work demands, and changes in diet and eating patterns [25]. Due to the preclinical and treatable stage of chronic diseases, SHS is crucial to the pathophysiology of these conditions [3]. SHS is diagnosed based on symptoms and biomarkers because the causes and mechanisms of the disease are yet unknown [26].

Along with the immune system [12, 27], neurological system [28], digestive system [29], and cardiovascular system [30], which are all parts of SHS [3, 7], intestinal microbiota also plays a crucial role in human health [31]. Emerging research supports the link between the intestinal microbiota and a number of disorders, including atherosclerosis [32], hypertension [33], diabetes [34], and immune deficiency syndromes [35].

## 3 Psychological Symptoms and Relationship with Chronic Diseases

Such professions affect SHS. Nursing is consistently regarded as one of the most stressful and demanding professions out of several. Working very long hours, work schedules, patient complaints, and low salaries are among the many workplace stressors that nurses frequently deal with [36]. Along with physical side-effects, including pain, weariness, reduced immunity, and other issues, such demanding work may severely influence mental health and quality of life, as well as physical side-effects, including pain, exhaustion, lowered immunity, and so forth [37].

There is evidence linking SHS to cognitive impairments [38], psychosocial stress [39], and mental health illnesses [40]. One of the four main elements impacting health, along with chemical, physical, and biological components, is referred to as a psychosocial or psychological factor(s) [41]. Health, both mental and physical, is getting more emphasis. According to recent epidemiological statistics [42, 43], between 35.8% and 61.7% of nurses experienced depressive symptoms. The two mental health conditions that are most common and have serious repercussions are depression and anxiety. As a result, it impacts how well society functions and how people live their lives and helps fuel social problems and economic losses [44–46].

Predictive, preventative, and customised medicine are replacing response treatment in the new, emerging medical paradigm (PPPM). It comprises medical care personalisation, preventive measures, and forecasting models for infectious diseases and catastrophic pandemics like COVID-19 [47]. It also covers chronic and noncommunicable diseases.

The ideal use of PPPM occupies a distinct market segment in healthcare. A few examples include a new level of professional interests, a new scale of knowledge integration, highly motivated technological innovation, highly motivated interdisciplinary and multidisciplinary cooperation, individualised care, predictive medicine, the new range of screening programs, targeted prevention, currently unmet needs of healthy subpopulations and patient cohorts, cost-effective medical services, and an optimised health care economy [48–50]. The ground-breaking PPPM is quickly becoming the focus of healthcare initiatives focused on reducing the prevalence of chronic diseases like cancer, diabetes, and cardiovascular disorders [51–53]. Cardiovascular illnesses, diabetes mellitus, oral drugs, lifelong health conditions, cancer therapy, and postoperative tumour assessment have all seen practical applications of PPPM ideas [54–56]. However, the study didn't fully explain how SHS affects nurses' mental health symptoms. Nursing staff's poor physical and mental health is caused by a long-term buildup of intangible workplace risks, even though it has a less immediate effect on their day-to-day work and activities. It affects people's general health [57]. Contrarily, good health makes it simpler to avoid errors in routine clinical practice because errors here can frustrate patients and possibly harm their prognosis.

In the framework of PPPM, the SHS concept is one of the creative alternatives [5, 57]. To stop or slow the progression of SHS before it reaches the disease level in nurses, targeted prevention and individualised treatment are needed. According to the PPPM model, screening the SHS population, figuring out disease risk forecasts, and then coming up with individualised interventions offer a window of opportunity to halt or delay the onset and progression of several diseases, significantly enhancing the model, which already has a medical component [58].

One of the unique solutions is the PPPM concept [5, 57]. To stop or slow down the progression of SHS into a disease state in nurses, it is important to use targeted preventive and specialist therapy. By screening the SHS population, figuring out who is most likely to get sick, and then making individualised interventions based on the PPPM model, there is a chance to avoid or delay the onset of several diseases. This significantly enhances the current medical model [58].

## 4 Lifestyle Factors and SHS

The most significant factor influencing human health is lifestyle [59–62]. Direct lifestyle factor correlations with physical, mental, and social SHS are weaker than indirect lifestyle factor correlations with physical, mental, and social SHS via health consciousness [6]. Furthermore, it has been demonstrated that physical, mental, and social SHS substantially correlate with health consciousness [63]. As a result, lifestyle variables such as drinking alcohol, skipping breakfast, eating an unbalanced diet, not exercising, and having sleep issues are significant risk factors for SHS [3, 64]. SHS is consistently linked to chronic disease risk factors and predisposed to the onset of these illnesses [53]. Therefore, people can be protected from chronic diseases by changing their bad lifestyle habits.

A person's capacity to sustain their energy balance over time is impacted by various lifestyle choices, such as how much sleep they get can affect their energy intake, energy output, or both [65, 66]. The amount of sleep that people get is crucial to their metabolism. Several causes include lifestyle decisions, work or family demands, and health or mental issues. In our fast-paced modern environment, chronic sleep deprivation is becoming more widespread [66]. An enormous section of the population suffers from chronic sleep deficits due to social transformation, such as increased TV viewing and internet usage [66]. Numerous chronic diseases are also directly linked to unhealthy lifestyles [67–70]. The main risk factors for the general population include poor stress management, self-actualisation, inactivity, and interpersonal relationships [8].

A healthy lifestyle is a multifaceted pattern of self-initiated views and behaviors that support and enhance one's health and well-being [8, 64]. These kinds of beliefs and behaviors can help to lessen illness occurrence, lower death rates, and improve the state of health. Bad lifestyle choices like smoking, drinking, eating poorly, and not exercising can lead to several chronic diseases and increase the risk of damage and illness [71]. According to the WHO, unhealthy behavior and lifestyle choices are among the top ten causes of death globally [15–19, 21, 72, 73].

## 5 Adolescent Period and SHS

The key adolescent years spanning from 10 to 24 years old are the time between childhood and adulthood [15–19]. Pubertal maturity, the transition to adult social roles, and the development of independence are characteristics of this time [74]. As a result, it is sometimes referred to as a time of "Stress and Storm" [75, 76]. Before a child becomes more focused on his or her peers, there is a small window of time when family health practices can be changed. Adolescents' physical activity is also influenced by their conception of the advantages of physical activity (beliefs), the social influences of family and friends on physical activity (social influences), and the growth of their self-efficacy (confidence in their own abilities to be physically active) [77]. During this period is more dangerous to be exposed to peer groups and engage in bad habits like drinking alcohol, smoking, eating poorly, etc. [74]. These effects have an impact on both present and future health status, yet, the adolescent stage offers plenty of opportunity for behavior to be positively influenced, leading to better long-term health outcomes [74].

According to epidemiological data, risky behaviors are the primary cause of adolescent illness and mortality worldwide [15–19]. Risk-taking is at its highest during adolescence, which shows that this is when people have a strong tendency or a natural desire to do so [21]. They frequently experience accidents or injuries due to their tendency to take high risks [78]. They are always at risk when engaging in this risk-taking activity during adolescence [76].

During adolescence, a person's body grows and changes their reproductive health, mental health, social life, and emotions. The most crucial time in one's life is when they are still young. Because of this, adulthood is a critical time for developing healthy or unhealthy behaviors, and those traits are linked to a higher chance of developing chronic diseases [79]. However, the increasing source of health hazards in old age may be determined by unhealthy practices and behavior and poor lifestyle choices made at a young age [64]. Adolescent harmful behavior can significantly impact the development of health issues later in life [80].

Risky behaviour among college and university students is also a big reason they get chronic diseases as they age [81]. The study showed that SHS was most common among high school students. Both physical and mental SHS were more often found in this age group [4]. Adolescence may be the best period to learn about health issues because of physical and psychological development. It would provide some proof of the degree of ill health. Health assessment data from a college or university may be more convincing if we want to explore how to avoid getting a chronic disease later in life [4].

It has been shown that SHS can be prevented if it is found and treated early. In predictive, preventive, and personalised medicine [5, 13, 14] (PPPM), a new therapeutic paradigm or mechanism has been made to give patients the power to treat diseases early [82].

In conclusion, SHS is a condition that comes from a person's physical, mental, and social stress between being healthy and being sick. Even though the body hasn't yet reached the disease stage, the general coordination of the body's systems gets out of whack and stops working. Physiological, psychological, and social functions are reduced as a result. SHS is linked to many long-term conditions, such as fatigue, headaches, dizziness, depression, anxiety, loss of appetite, trouble sleeping, and problems with functioning. Similar to this, several organ systems are linked to short- or long-term unfavourable health effects. SHS can affect people of any age, gender, job, or location and greatly affects the quality of life, leading to frequent visits and high treatment costs. Physical, mental, and social SHS strongly correlate with lifestyle variables. So, lifestyle factors are risk factors for SHS, and SHS is often linked to developing long-term illnesses. By screening the SHS in the community, figuring out how likely they are to get sick, and then making individualised interventions based on the PPPM model, there is a chance to avoid or delay many diseases. This significantly enhances the current medical model.

**Disclosure of Interests** There are no conflicts of interest, according to the authors.

**Ethical Approval** Each institution has granted ethical approval for the investigations covered in this book chapter. All procedures used in research involving human subjects complied with the 1964 Helsinki Statement and its later amendments, as well as the ethical guidelines established by institutional research committees.

**Declarations of Interest Statement** None.

## References

1. Wang W, Yan Y, Guo Z, Hou H, Garcia M, Tan X, Anto EO, Mahara G, Zheng Y, Li B, Kang T, Zhong Z, Wang Y, Guo X, Golubnitschaja O (2021) All around suboptimal health—a joint position paper of the Suboptimal Health Study Consortium and European Association for Predictive, Preventive and Personalised Medicine. EPMA J 12:403–433. https://doi.org/10.1007/s13167-021-00253-2
2. Wang Y, Ge S, Yan Y, Wang A, Zhao Z, Yu X, Qiu J, Alzain MA, Wang H, Fang H, Gao Q, Song M, Zhang J, Zhou Y, Wang W (2016) China suboptimal health cohort study: rationale, design and baseline characteristics. J Transl Med 14:291. https://doi.org/10.1186/s12967-016-1046-y
3. Yan Y-X, Liu Y-Q, Li M, Hu P-F, Guo A-M, Yang X-H, Qiu J-J, Yang S-S, Shen J, Zhang L-P, Wang W (2009) Development and evaluation of a questionnaire for measuring suboptimal health status in urban Chinese. J Epidemiol 19:333–341. https://doi.org/10.2188/jea.je20080086

4. Mahara G, Liang J, Zhang Z, Ge Q, Zhang J (2021a) Associated factors of suboptimal health status among adolescents in China: a cross-sectional study. J Multidiscip Healthc 14:1063–1071. https://doi.org/10.2147/JMDH.S302826
5. Wang W, Yan Y (2012) Suboptimal health: a new health dimension for translational medicine. Clin Transl Med 1:28. https://doi.org/10.1186/2001-1326-1-28
6. Xue Y, Huang Z, Liu G, Feng Y, Xu M, Jiang L, Xu J (2020a) Association analysis of suboptimal health status: a cross-sectional study in China. PeerJ 8:e10508–e10508. https://doi.org/10.7717/peerj.10508
7. Wang W (2012) Suboptimal health: a potential preventive instrument for non-communicable disease control and management. J Transl Med 10:A45–A45. https://doi.org/10.1186/1479-5876-10-S2-A45
8. Chen J, Xiang H, Jiang P, Yu L, Jing Y, Li F, Wu S, Fu X, Liu Y, Kwan H, Luo R, Zhao X, Sun X (2017) The role of healthy lifestyle in the implementation of regressing suboptimal health status among college students in China: a nested case-control study. Int J Environ Res Public Health 14:240. https://doi.org/10.3390/ijerph14030240
9. Reniers RLEP, Murphy L, Lin A, Bartolomé SP, Wood SJ (2016) Risk perception and risk-taking behaviour during adolescence: the influence of personality and gender. PLoS One 11:e0153842. https://doi.org/10.1371/journal.pone.0153842
10. Mahara G, Zhang J, Wang W (2021b) Is the sub-optimal health status shifting to chronic diseases pathway….? BMJ 331:3–4. https://doi.org/10.1136/bmj.331.7507.3
11. Dunstan RH, Sparkes DL, Roberts TK, Crompton MJ, Gottfries J, Dascombe BJ (2013) Development of a complex amino acid supplement, Fatigue Reviva™, for oral ingestion: initial evaluations of product concept and impact on symptoms of sub-health in a group of males. Nutr J 12:115. https://doi.org/10.1186/1475-2891-12-115
12. Levy M, Kolodziejczyk AA, Thaiss CA, Elinav E (2017) Dysbiosis and the immune system. Nat Rev Immunol 17:219–232. https://doi.org/10.1038/nri.2017.7
13. Bodrova TA, Kostyushev DS, Antonova EN, Slavin S, Gnatenko DA, Bocharova MO, Legg M, Pozzilli P, Paltsev MA, Suchkov SV (2012) Introduction into PPPM as a new paradigm of public health service: an integrative view. EPMA J 3:16–16. https://doi.org/10.1186/1878-5085-3-16
14. Lemke HU, Golubnitschaja O (2014) Towards personal health care with model-guided medicine: long-term PPPM-related strategies and realisation opportunities within "Horizon 2020". EPMA J 5:8–8. https://doi.org/10.1186/1878-5085-5-8
15. World Health Organization (2023) Non-communicable diseases. https://www.who.int/news-room/factsheets/detail/noncommunicable-diseases
16. World Health Organization (2023) Fact-sheet of noncommunicable diseasest. https://www.who.int/news-room/factsheets/detail/noncommunicable-diseases
17. World Health Organization (2023) Sustainable development goals. https://www.who.int/westernpacific/healthtopics/sustainable-development-goals
18. World Health Organization (2023) Adolescents' health-related behaviours. https://apps.who.int/adolescent/seconddecade/section4
19. World Health Organization (2023) Adolescent and young adult health. https://www.who.int/news-room/factsheets/detail/adolescents-health-risks-and-solutions
20. Chen J-Y, Yu K-Q, Sun X-M, Chen Z-W, Kuang L-Y, Ji Y-Z, Zhao X-S, Luo R (2017) Effect of health-promoting lifestyle on outcomes of suboptimal health status. J South Med Univer, 37(2):184–1910. https://doi.org/10.3969/j.issn.1673-4254.2017.02.07
21. Duell N, Steinberg L, Icenogle G, Chein J, Chaudhary N, Di Giunta L, Dodge KA, Fanti KA, Lansford JE, Oburu P, Pastorelli C, Skinner AT, Sorbring E, Tapanya S, Uribe Tirado LM, Alampay LP, Al-Hassan SM, Takash HMS, Bacchini D, Chang L (2018) Age patterns in risk taking across the world. J Youth Adolesc 47:1052–1072. https://doi.org/10.1007/s10964-017-0752-y
22. Lu J, Yu Z, Zhang X, Wu M, Lin S, Zhu Y, Xu Z, You L, Wei F, Tang M, Jin M, Wang J, Chen K (2020) Association between social health status and health-related quality of life among

community-dwelling elderly in Zhejiang. Health Qual Life Outcomes 18:110–110. https://doi.org/10.1186/s12955-020-01358-4
23. Chen J, Cheng J, Liu Y, Tang Y, Sun X, Wang T, Xiao Y, Li F, Xiang L, Jiang P, Wu S, Wu L, Luo R, Zhao X (2014) Associations between breakfast eating habits and health-promoting lifestyle, suboptimal health status in southern China: a population based, cross sectional study. J Transl Med 12:348–348. https://doi.org/10.1186/s12967-014-0348-1
24. Yan YX, Dong J, Liu YQ, Yang XH, Li M, Shia G, Wang W (2012) Association of suboptimal health status and cardiovascular risk factors in urban Chinese workers. J Urban Health 89:329–338. https://doi.org/10.1007/s11524-011-9636-8
25. GBD 2016 Disease and Injury Incidence and Prevalence Collaborators (2017) Global, regional, and national incidence, prevalence, and years lived with disability for 328 diseases and injuries for 195 countries, 1990–2016: a systematic analysis for the global burden of disease study 2016. Lancet 390:1211–1259. https://doi.org/10.1016/S0140-6736(17)32154-2
26. Sun Q, Xu X, Zhang J, Sun M, Tian Q, Li Q, Cao W, Zhang X, Wang H, Liu J, Zhang J, Meng X, Wu L, Song M, Liu H, Wang W, Wang Y (2020) Association of suboptimal health status with intestinal microbiota in Chinese youths. J Cell Mol Med 24:1837–1847. https://doi.org/10.1111/jcmm.14880
27. Opazo MC, Ortega-Rocha EM, Coronado-Arrázola I, Bonifaz LC, Boudin H, Neunlist M, Bueno SM, Kalergis AM, Riedel CA (2018) Intestinal microbiota influences non-intestinal related autoimmune diseases. Front Microbiol 9:432. https://doi.org/10.3389/fmicb.2018.00432
28. Mayer EA, Tillisch K, Gupta A (2015) Gut/brain axis and the microbiota. J Clin Invest 125:926–938. https://doi.org/10.1172/JCI76304
29. Betrapally NS, Gillevet PM, Bajaj JS (2016) Changes in the intestinal microbiome and alcoholic and nonalcoholic liver diseases: causes or effects? Gastroenterology 150:1745–1755.e3. https://doi.org/10.1053/j.gastro.2016.02.073
30. Jin M, Qian Z, Yin J, Xu W, Zhou X (2019) The role of intestinal microbiota in cardiovascular disease. J Cell Mol Med 23:2343–2350. https://doi.org/10.1111/jcmm.14195
31. Belizário JE, Napolitano M (2015) Human microbiomes and their roles in dysbiosis, common diseases, and novel therapeutic approaches. Front Microbiol 6:1050–1050. https://doi.org/10.3389/fmicb.2015.01050
32. Lanter BB, Sauer K, Davies DG (2014) Bacteria present in carotid arterial plaques are found as biofilm deposits which may contribute to enhanced risk of plaque rupture. mBio 5:e01206–e01214. https://doi.org/10.1128/mBio.01206-14
33. Li J, Zhao F, Wang Y, Chen J, Tao J, Tian G, Wu S, Liu W, Cui Q, Geng B, Zhang W, Weldon R, Auguste K, Yang L, Liu X, Chen L, Yang X, Zhu B, Cai J (2017) Gut microbiota dysbiosis contributes to the development of hypertension. Microbiome 5:14. https://doi.org/10.1186/s40168-016-0222-x
34. Tong X, Xu J, Lian F, Yu X, Zhao Y, Xu L, Zhang M, Zhao X, Shen J, Wu S, Pang X, Tian J, Zhang C, Zhou Q, Wang L, Pang B, Chen F, Peng Z, Wang J, Zhen Z, Fang C, Li M, Chen L, Zhao L (2018) Structural alteration of gut microbiota during the amelioration of human type 2 diabetes with hyperlipidemia by metformin and a traditional Chinese herbal formula: a multicenter, randomized, open label clinical trial. mBio 9:e02392–e02317. https://doi.org/10.1128/mBio.02392-17
35. Zhou Y, Ou Z, Tang X, Zhou Y, Xu H, Wang X, Li K, He J, Du Y, Wang H, Chen Y, Nie Y (2018) Alterations in the gut microbiota of patients with acquired immune deficiency syndrome. J Cell Mol Med 22:2263–2271. https://doi.org/10.1111/jcmm.13508
36. Zhu J, Ying W, Zhang L, Peng G, Chen W, Anto EO, Wang X, Lu N, Gao S, Wu G, Yan J, Ye J, Wu S, Yu C, Yue M, Huang X, Xu N, Ying P, Chen Y, Tan X, Wang W (2020) Psychological symptoms in Chinese nurses may be associated with predisposition to chronic disease: a cross-sectional study of suboptimal health status. EPMA J 11:551–563. https://doi.org/10.1007/s13167-020-00225-y
37. Dyrbye LN, Thomas MR, Shanafelt TD (2006) Systematic review of depression, anxiety, and other indicators of psychological distress among U.S. and Canadian medical students. Acad Med 81:354–373. https://doi.org/10.1097/00001888-200604000-00009

38. Ding G, Zhao X, Wang Y, Song D, Chen D, Deng Y, Xing W, Dong H, Zhou Y, Li D, Hou H (2020) Evaluation of the relationship between cognitive impairment and suboptimal health status in a northern Chinese population: a cross-sectional study. J Glob Health 10:010804. https://doi.org/10.7189/jogh.10.010804
39. Liang Y-Z, Chu X, Meng S-J, Zhang J, Wu L-J, Yan Y-X (2018) Relationship between stress-related psychosocial work factors and suboptimal health among Chinese medical staff: a cross-sectional study. BMJ Open 8:e018485. https://doi.org/10.1136/bmjopen-2017-018485
40. Grynderup MB, Mors O, Hansen ÅM, Andersen JH, Bonde JP, Kærgaard A, Kærlev L, Mikkelsen S, Rugulies R, Thomsen JF, Kolstad HA (2013) Work-unit measures of organisational justice and risk of depression—a 2-year cohort study. Occup Environ Med 70:380–385. https://doi.org/10.1136/oemed-2012-101000
41. Kapalla M, Kubáň J (2014) How to estimate health-related costs: economic aspect of healthy life style and its importance for PPPM. EPMA J 5:A103. https://doi.org/10.1186/1878-5085-5-S1-A103
42. Cheung T, Yip PSF (2015) Depression, anxiety and symptoms of stress among Hong Kong nurses: a cross-sectional study. Int J Environ Res Public Health 12:11072–11100. https://doi.org/10.3390/ijerph120911072
43. Gao Y-Q, Pan B-C, Sun W, Wu H, Wang J-N, Wang L (2012) Depressive symptoms among Chinese nurses: prevalence and the associated factors. J Adv Nurs 68:1166–1175. https://doi.org/10.1111/j.1365-2648.2011.05832.x
44. Fair DC, Rodriguez M, Knight AM, Rubinstein TB (2019) Depression and anxiety in patients with juvenile idiopathic arthritis: current insights and impact on quality of life, a systematic review. Open Access Rheumatol 11:237–252. https://doi.org/10.2147/OARRR.S174408
45. Hiriscau EI, Bodolea C (2019) The role of depression and anxiety in frail patients with heart failure. Diseases 7:45. https://doi.org/10.3390/diseases7020045
46. Wallace K, Zhao X, Misra R, Sambamoorthi U (2018) The humanistic and economic burden associated with anxiety and depression among adults with comorbid diabetes and hypertension. J Diabetes Res 2018:4842520. https://doi.org/10.1155/2018/4842520
47. Chaari L, Golubnitschaja O (2020) Covid-19 pandemic by the "real-time" monitoring: the Tunisian case and lessons for global epidemics in the context of 3PM strategies. EPMA Journal 11:133–138. https://doi.org/10.1007/s13167-020-00207-0
48. Golubnitschaja O (2010) Time for new guidelines in advanced diabetes care: paradigm change from delayed interventional approach to predictive, preventive & personalized medicine. EPMA J 1:3–12. https://doi.org/10.1007/s13167-010-0014-5
49. Golubnitschaja O, Baban B, Boniolo G, Wang W, Bubnov R, Kapalla M, Krapfenbauer K, Mozaffari MS, Costigliola V (2016) Medicine in the early twenty-first century: paradigm and anticipation - EPMA position paper 2016. EPMA J 7:23. https://doi.org/10.1186/s13167-016-0072-4
50. Golubnitschaja O, Watson ID, Topic E, Sandberg S, Ferrari M, Costigliola V (2013) Position paper of the EPMA and EFLM: a global vision of the consolidated promotion of an integrative medical approach to advance health care. EPMA J 4:12. https://doi.org/10.1186/1878-5085-4-12
51. Baban B, Liu JY, Payne S, Abebe W, Yu JC, Mozaffari MS (2016) Status of stem cells in diabetic nephropathy: predictive and preventive potentials. EPMA J 7:21. https://doi.org/10.1186/s13167-016-0070-6
52. Molacek J, Treska V, Zeithaml J, Hollan I, Topolcan O, Pecen L, Slouka D, Karlikova M, Kucera R (2019) Blood biomarker panel recommended for personalized prediction, prognosis, and prevention of complications associated with abdominal aortic aneurysm. EPMA J 10:125–135. https://doi.org/10.1007/s13167-019-00173-2
53. Wang Y, Liu X, Qiu J, Wang H, Liu D, Zhao Z, Song M, Song Q, Wang X, Zhou Y, Wang W (2017) Association between ideal cardiovascular health metrics and suboptimal health status in Chinese population. Sci Rep 7:14975. https://doi.org/10.1038/s41598-017-15101-5
54. Abebe W (2019) Review of herbal medications with the potential to cause bleeding: dental implications, and risk prediction and prevention avenues. EPMA J 10:51–64. https://doi.org/10.1007/s13167-018-0158-2

55. Adua E, Roberts P, Wang W (2017) Incorporation of suboptimal health status as a potential risk assessment for type II diabetes mellitus: a case-control study in a Ghanaian population. EPMA J 8:345–355. https://doi.org/10.1007/s13167-017-0119-1
56. Cheng T, Zhan X (2017) Pattern recognition for predictive, preventive, and personalized medicine in cancer. EPMA J 8:51–60. https://doi.org/10.1007/s13167-017-0083-9
57. Hsiao S-J, Tseng H-T (2020) The impact of the moderating effect of psychological health status on nurse healthcare management information system usage intention. Healthcare (Basel), 8(1):28. https://doi.org/10.3390/healthcare8010028
58. Wang W, Tan X (2019) Suboptimal health status and cardiovascular deficits. In: Golubnitschaja O (ed) Flammer syndrome: from phenotype to associated pathologies, prediction, prevention and personalisation, advances in predictive, preventive and personalised medicine. Springer International Publishing, Cham, pp 287–315. https://doi.org/10.1007/978-3-030-13550-8_17
59. Kastorini C-M, Milionis HJ, Esposito K, Giugliano D, Goudevenos JA, Panagiotakos DB (2011) The effect of Mediterranean diet on metabolic syndrome and its components: a meta-analysis of 50 studies and 534,906 individuals. J Am Coll Cardiol 57:1299–1313. https://doi.org/10.1016/j.jacc.2010.09.073
60. Lin Y-H, Tsai E-M, Chan T-F, Chou F-H, Lin Y-L (2009) Health promoting lifestyles and related factors in pregnant women. Chang Gung Med J 32:650–661
61. Mozaffarian D, Capewell S (2011) United Nations' dietary policies to prevent cardiovascular disease. BMJ 343:d5747. https://doi.org/10.1136/bmj.d5747
62. Mozaffarian D, Hao T, Rimm EB, Willett WC, Hu FB (2011) Changes in diet and lifestyle and long-term weight gain in women and men. N Engl J Med 364:2392–2404. https://doi.org/10.1056/nejmoa1014296
63. Xue Y, Liu G, Feng Y, Xu M, Jiang L, Lin Y, Xu J (2020) Mediating effect of health consciousness in the relationship of lifestyle and suboptimal health status: a cross-sectional study involving Chinese urban residents. BMJ Open 10:e039701–e039701. https://doi.org/10.1136/bmjopen-2020-039701
64. Lolokote S, Hidru TH, Li X (2017) Do socio-cultural factors influence college students' self-rated health status and health-promoting lifestyles? A cross-sectional multicenter study in Dalian, China. BMC Public Health 17:478. https://doi.org/10.1186/s12889-017-4411-8
65. Patel SR, Hu FB (2008) Short sleep duration and weight gain: a systematic review. Obesity (Silver Spring) 16:643–653. https://doi.org/10.1038/oby.2007.118
66. Van Cauter E, Spiegel K, Tasali E, Leproult R (2008) Metabolic consequences of sleep and sleep loss. Sleep Med 9(Suppl 1):S23–S28. https://doi.org/10.1016/S1389-9457(08)70013-3
67. Folsom AR, Yatsuya H, Nettleton JA, Lutsey PL, Cushman M, Rosamond WD, ARIC Study Investigators (2011) Community prevalence of ideal cardiovascular health, by the American Heart Association definition, and relationship with cardiovascular disease incidence. J Am Coll Cardiol 57:1690–1696. https://doi.org/10.1016/j.jacc.2010.11.041
68. Lin C-C, Li C-I, Liu C-S, Lin W-Y, Fuh MM-T, Yang S-Y, Lee C-C, Li T-C (2012) Impact of lifestyle-related factors on all-cause and cause-specific mortality in patients with type 2 diabetes: the Taichung diabetes study. Diabetes Care 35:105–112. https://doi.org/10.2337/dc11-0930
69. Okami Y, Kato T, Nin G, Harada K, Aoi W, Wada S, Higashi A, Okuyama Y, Takakuwa S, Ichikawa H, Kanazawa M, Fukudo S (2011) Lifestyle and psychological factors related to irritable bowel syndrome in nursing and medical school students. J Gastroenterol 46:1403–1410. https://doi.org/10.1007/s00535-011-0454-2
70. Sikorski C, Luppa M, Weyerer S, König H-H, Maier W, Schön G, Petersen JJ, Gensichen J, Fuchs A, Bickel H, Wiese B, Hansen H, van den Bussche H, Scherer M, Riedel-Heller SG (2014) Obesity and associated lifestyle in a large sample of multi-morbid German primary care attendees. PLoS One 9:e102587. https://doi.org/10.1371/journal.pone.0102587
71. Liebergall-Wischnitzer M, Buyum M, DeKeyser Ganz F (2016) Health promoting lifestyle among Israeli adult survivors of childhood cancer. J Pediatr Oncol Nurs 33:146–154. https://doi.org/10.1177/1043454215600177

72. Caring for Kids (2003) Age limits and adolescents. Paediatr Child Health 8(9):577. https://doi.org/10.1093/pch/8.9.577
73. Gokyildiz S, Alan S, Elmas E, Bostanci A, Kucuk E (2014) Health-promoting lifestyle behaviours in pregnant women in Turkey. Int J Nurs Pract 20:390–397. https://doi.org/10.1111/ijn.12187
74. Pringle J, Doi L, Jindal-Snape D, Jepson R, McAteer J (2018) Adolescents and health-related behaviour: using a framework to develop interventions to support positive behaviours. Pilot Feasibil Stud 4:69. https://doi.org/10.1186/s40814-018-0259-7
75. Casey BJ, Jones RM, Levita L, Libby V, Pattwell SS, Ruberry EJ, Soliman F, Somerville LH (2010) The storm and stress of adolescence: insights from human imaging and mouse genetics. Dev Psychobiol 52:225–235. https://doi.org/10.1002/dev.20447
76. Park E, McCoy TP, Erausquin JT, Bartlett R (2018) Trajectories of risk behaviors across adolescence and young adulthood: the role of race and ethnicity. Addict Behav 76:1–7. https://doi.org/10.1016/j.addbeh.2017.07.014
77. Gesell SB, Reynolds EB, Ip EH, Fenlason LC, Pont SJ, Poe EK, Barkin SL (2008) Social influences on self-reported physical activity in overweight Latino children. Clin Pediatr (Phila) 47:797–802. https://doi.org/10.1177/0009922808318340
78. Maslowsky J, Owotomo O, Huntley ED, Keating D (2019) Adolescent risk behavior: differentiating reasoned and reactive risk-taking. J Youth Adolesc 48:243–255. https://doi.org/10.1007/s10964-018-0978-3
79. Kazemi DM, Levine MJ, Dmochowski J, Roger Van Horn K, Qi L (2015) Health behaviors of mandated and voluntary students in a motivational intervention program. Prev Med Rep 2:423–428. https://doi.org/10.1016/j.pmedr.2015.05.004
80. Chan CQH, Lee KH, Low LL (2018) A systematic review of health status, health seeking behaviour and healthcare utilisation of low socioeconomic status populations in urban Singapore. Int J Equity Health 17(1):39. https://doi.org/10.1186/s12939-018-0751-y
81. Ay S, Yanikkerem E, Calim SI, Yazici M (2012) Health-promoting lifestyle behaviour for cancer prevention: a survey of Turkish university students. Asian Pac J Cancer Prev 13:2269–2277. https://doi.org/10.7314/APJCP.2012.13.5.2269
82. Wang H, Tian Q, Zhang J, Liu H, Zhang X, Cao W, Zhang J, Anto EO, Li X, Wang X, Liu D (2020) Population-based case-control study revealed metabolomic biomarkers of suboptimal health status in Chinese population-potential utility for innovative approach by predictive, preventive, and personalized medicine. EPMA J 11:147–160. https://doi.org/10.1007/s13167-020-00200-7

# Treatment Algorithm Tailored to Individuals with Non-communicable Diseases: The Innovative Utility of Suboptimal Health Concept from the Predictive, Preventive and Personalised Medical Care Perspective

**Enoch Odame Anto, Youxin Wang, and Wei Wang**

E. O. Anto (✉)
Department of Medical Diagnostics, Kwame Nkrumah University of Science and Technology, Kumasi, Ghana

School of Medical and Health Sciences, Edith Cowan University, Perth, Australia

Centre for Precision Health, Edith Cowan University, Perth, Australia

Suboptimal Health Study Consortium, Kumasi, Ghana

Suboptimal Health Study Consortium, Perth, Australia

Suboptimal Health Study Consortium, Beijing, China

Suboptimal Health Study Consortium, Bonn, Germany

European Association for Predictive, Preventive and Personalised Medicine, EPMA, Brussels, Belgium

Y. Wang
School of Medical and Health Sciences, Edith Cowan University, Perth, Australia

Suboptimal Health Study Consortium, Kumasi, Ghana

Suboptimal Health Study Consortium, Perth, Australia

Suboptimal Health Study Consortium, Beijing, China

Suboptimal Health Study Consortium, Bonn, Germany

European Association for Predictive, Preventive and Personalised Medicine, EPMA, Brussels, Belgium

Beijing Key Laboratory of Clinical Epidemiology, Capital Medical University, Beijing, China



W. Wang (ed.), *All Around Suboptimal Health*, Advances in Predictive, Preventive and Personalised Medicine 18,
https://doi.org/10.1007/978-3-031-46891-9_7

W. Wang
First Affiliated Hospital, Shantou University Medical College, Shantou, China

Beijing Key Laboratory of Clinical Epidemiology, Capital Medical University, Beijing, China

School of Public Health, Shandong First Medical University and Shandong Academy of Medical Sciences, Jinan, China

Centre for Precision Health, Edith Cowan University, Perth, Australia

Suboptimal Health Study Consortium, Kumasi, Ghana

Suboptimal Health Study Consortium, Perth, Australia

Suboptimal Health Study Consortium, Beijing, China

Suboptimal Health Study Consortium, Bonn, Germany

European Association for Predictive, Preventive and Personalised Medicine, EPMA, Brussels, Belgium
e-mail: wei.wang@ecu.edu.au

## Abbreviations

| | |
|---|---|
| CVH | Cardiovascular Health |
| EPMA | European Association for Predictive, Preventive and Personalised Medicine |
| FS | Flammer syndrome |
| HCC | Hepatocellular carcinoma |
| NCDs | Non-communicable chronic diseases |
| PCa | Prostate cancer |
| PE | Preeclampsia |
| PPPM/3PM | Predictive, preventive, and personalised medicine |
| SHS | Suboptimal health status |
| SHSQ-25 | Suboptimal Health Status Questionnaire-25 |
| T2DM | Type II diabetes mellitus |
| VD | Vaginal dryness |

## 1 Introduction

Worldwide, non-communicable disease (NCD) is one the leading cause of adverse health outcome and fatal rate. As such, several treatment strategies have evolved. Although most diseases are diagnosed before treatment, there are individuals who may experience poor health without a clear diagnosis but complain of general body weakness and vitality [1]. The latter group of individuals are termed to have suboptimal health, a physical stage between health and diseases. Nevertheless, these suboptimal health individuals can remain undiagnosed even for many decades of their life [1]. Individuals in pre-clinical phase of a health condition usually need to be treated with targeted drugs that help to avert or delay the development of a disease. However, suboptimal health individuals require no specific treatment and this increases their chances of poor health subsequent to a disease. Effective intervention tailored towards individuals with suboptimal health can only begin after the clinical manifestation of a disease. Thus, from the personalised medicine standpoint, this is a delayed intervention. Thus, identifying appropriate treatments tailored to individuals who suffer from NCDs is important in improving health and well-being.

## 2 The Healthcare System: PPPM as the Future Medicine?

Current healthcare systems practice more of a delayed treatment approach, which leads to several health complaints including drug resistance and reactions. The need to promote the paradigm change from the "wait-to-treat" approach to a more targeted predictive and personalisation of medical care is needed [2–5]. This concept has been coined as PPPM.

PPPM enables the early identification of individual's clinical signs prior to a clinical manifestation and thereby creates targeted preventive measures tailored to the affected individual. PPPM is more tailored to early prevention of childhood illness, general health screening, identification of high-risk population, categorisation of patients for the ideal regimen and reduction of adverse drug-to-disease or drug-to-drug interactions. PPPM concept utilises new technologies, including disease modelling, pathology-specific molecular patterns, pharmacogenetics, imaging techniques, and individual patient biochemical profiles to aid in disease prevention and treatment policies [5] making PPPM the precise future medicine [2, 3]. For decades, the concept of PPPM has contributed to health and policies on the treatment and management of diseases because of the all-inclusive approach it adopts in solving health problems [2, 5]. Global health organisations including the World Health Organisation and the European Union and the National Institutes of Health have recognised the concept of PPPM as a more cost-effective and economical in disease management [3, 4]. For several years, the European Association for Predictive, Preventive and Personalised Medicine (EPMA) has led the global effort to promote the concept of PPPM among patient organisations and in the communities, funding institutions, academic and research institutions, governmental institutions and healthcare stakeholders [3, 4].

# 3 Suboptimal Health Status Concept in the Perspective of Targeted Treatment Tailored to the Individual at Risk of NCDs

Over the past years, suboptimal health status (SHS) assessment has been considered as one of the public health concepts that explain the perspective of PPPM in that it recognises poor health in individual devoid of a diagnosable clinical condition and create the avenue for targeted personalisation of medical care [1, 6]. Even though the SHS evaluation using the SHS questionnaire-25 (SHSQ-25) is a cheap, reliable tool with a short turn-around processing time, and is readily available to both low- and high resource countries, it is a recognised measure that provides early phenotypic risk signs and predicts future NCD outcomes. Several researchers from across Africa, Asia, Australia and Europe who explored the SHSQ-25 as a screening tool found it to be suitable for patient's investigation, relative risk, prognosis, monitoring and targeted preventive therapeutic options that provide benefit to patients and the healthy population. Thus, the SHS concept is relevant and important for treatment algorithms tailored towards individuals at risk of developing a condition.

The ground-breaking evidence of PPPM via the use of SHS concept is the vital part of efforts in the healthcare treatment and management system aimed at preventing the occurrence of NCDs that include but are not limited to poor dental health, malignancies, hypertension, preeclampsia, mental disorders, cardiovascular diseases, diabetes mellitus and other familial pathologies.

## *3.1 Diabetes Mellitus and SHS Concept*

PPPM plays a key role in the management of diabetes conditions by providing support on prediction of effective treatment dose, adequate patient stratification and lifestyle modification [3, 7–9]. Taken together, this has improved the quality of life, promoted longevity and delayed the onset of complications leading to a better health outcome. Like other chronic diseases, screening and beginning treatment at the suboptimal or prediabetic phase is pivotal in PPPM, and it provides the support for starting prophylaxis, which prevents the manifestation of diabetes mellitus and its complications. The pre-diabetes mellitus represent a suboptimal stage of the diabetes condition; hence, can be explained as a stage between non-diabetes and diabetes patients. Recent studies have found that SHS is a predictor for type 2 diabetes mellitus (T2DM) co-existing with poor lifestyle modifications and imbalance in biochemical concentrations [10, 11]. For instance, in a cohort study in a Ghanaian population, primarily sedentary lifestyle (AOR = 2.97), high triglyceride concentrations (AOR = 2.39) and high systolic blood pressure (AOR = 1.86-fold) were independent predictors of SHS [11]. Among the Chinese population, the fourth (AOR = 1.70), third (AOR = 1.60) and second quartiles (AOR = 1.50) of SHS scores

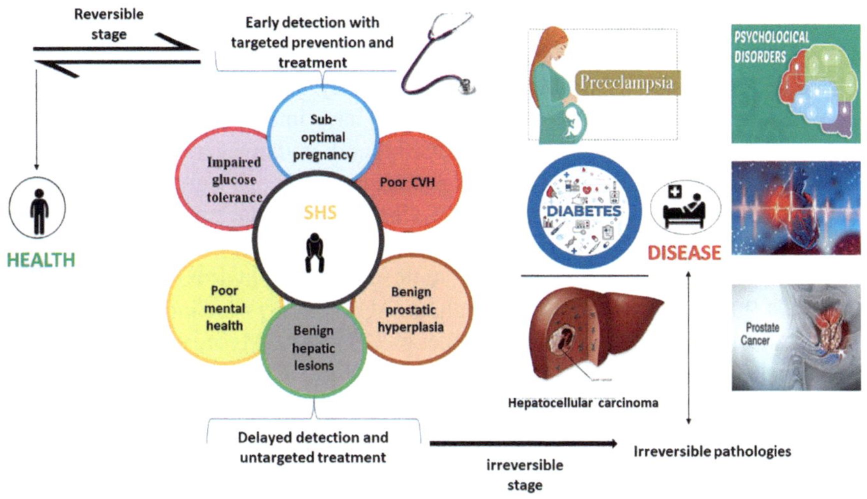


**Fig. 1** Treatment algorithm at the suboptimal health stage is instrumental for reversing chronic conditions

were identified as a predictor of T2DM [10]. In addition to the study in China, the SHS score yielded a discriminating power of 84.8% for predicting the onset of T2DM, indicating that SHS evaluation can identify more than 80% of individuals in the pre-diabetics phase. The management of T2DM is thus suboptimal, even though a higher number of individuals may remain undiagnosed, leading to adverse diabetes events and complications. Identifying early individuals with combined risk of prediabetes, poor lifestyle modifications and cardiometabolic syndrome in suboptimal health individuals would inform health professionals to initiate targeted preventive measures to prevent the onset of T2DM [12]. In the current health system, it is therefore important to move from a more reactive medical approach to PPPM (Fig. 1).

## *3.2 SHS Screening Is Highly Recommended in Preeclampsia Management*

The prediction of hypertensive disorder of pregnancy such as preeclampsia (PE) using SHS screening is highly recommended for maternal healthcare during pregnancy [13]. Particularly, a recent longitudinal cohort study in a Ghanaian population found that approximately 90% of suboptimal pregnant women who were between 10 and 20th weeks of gestation went on to develop preeclampsia [13]. In addition to this study, between 78.0% and 82.0% of the suboptimal pregnant women who developed were coexisting with dyslipidaemia, intrauterine growth restriction, stillbirth, HELLP (haemolysis elevated liver enzymes and low platelet count) syndrome and acute kidney injury in a prospective cohort study conducted in a Ghanaian population [13]. In our previous study, suboptimal health pregnant women who were normotensive were found to have imbalances in the concentrations of angiogenic growth mediators (AGMs) and oxidative stress (OS) biomarkers when measured at 10–20th weeks of gestation [14]. The first quartile for vascular endothelial growth factor-A (AOR = 5.35), and placental growth factor (AOR = 2.79), and the fourth quartile for soluble FMS-like tyrosine kinase receptor 1 (AOR = 1.84), soluble endoglins (AOR = 4.31), 8-hydroxydeoxyguanosine (AOR = 1.90) and 8-prostagliandinF2-alpha (AOR = 2.23) were independently predictors of suboptimal health [14] Even though OS and AGMs are significant factors in placental vascular development, an increased SHS score is an early sign of adverse pregnancy complication along with imbalance in OS and AGMs. SHS pregnancy is a call to start targeted treatment and monitoring tailored to prevent the clinical manifestation of preeclampsia (Fig. 1). From the prophylactic standpoint, targeted preventive approach and treatment options such as antioxidant and micronutrient supplementations tailored towards the suboptimal pregnant mothers are beneficial for alleviating new onset of preeclampsia [15]. The subjective measure, SHS along with objective biomarkers of OS and AGMs can be useful for the PPPM for pregnant women.

### *3.3 Suboptimal Health: The Link Between Vaginal Dryness and Flammer Syndrome*

Suboptimal health condition is known to contribute to the development of vaginal dryness (VD) among pre- and post-menopausal women. Even though hormonal disturbances, which occurs among women during their climacteric period is the main cause, most of the affected individual tends to be suboptimal [16]. Other causes of VD such as Flammer syndrome (FS) are obviously avoidable and, therefore, if well managed, tend to reduce the occurrence of VD. Thus, to manage VD, it is important to prevent modifiable risk factors linked to FS phenotype at the primary prevention and treatment level while screening individuals at the suboptimal level. Thus, future studies are recommended to use SHS criterion as a health screening tool for both pre- and post-menopausal women for VD.

### *3.4 SHS Criterion in the Management of Cardiovascular Diseases*

Maintaining optimal cardiovascular health (CVH) is a crucial component in the management of cardiovascular disease (CVD) [17]. The prevalence of SHS increased with increasing CVH metrics in a China suboptimal health cohort study

[17]. In the China study, SHS was associated with poor CVH metrics including dyslipidaemia, hypertension, hyperglycaemia and poor lifestyle characteristics (obesity, physical inactivity, cigarette smoking, and poor dietary habit). Early stratification of SHS individuals who have poor CVH metrics would create an avenue to initiate personalised medical care tailored to the affected individual [17]. Aside from poor CVH [11, 18], SHS has also been associated with behavioural factors [18, 19] and index of endothelial function, which the combined effect increases the individuals chances of cardiovascular disease [7]. From the personalised medical care perspective, it is imperative to monitor individuals at the suboptimal stage for poor CVH (Fig. 1).

### *3.5 SHS and Psychological Disorders*

Mental health, which is among the SHS domains, is a public health challenge affecting both the young and adult. Previous studies in a Chinese population have found an association of SHS with mental health-related factors such as reduced cognitive function [8], psychological symptoms [9] and increased incidence of self-reported suicidal ideation [20]. The prevalence of SHS was 21.0% among China University College students in a cross-sectional study by Hou et al. [9]. In the Study by Hou and colleagues, SHS was independently associated with interpersonal sensitivity (AOR = 1.88), obsessive-compulsive (AOR = 3.52), depression (AOR = 1.85) and somatisation (AOR = 3.18) [9]. Another study among Chinese individuals reported that SHS was three-fold increased odds of developing cognitive impairment [8] and that early indication of poor health in relation with poor behavioural, cognitive, and emotional well-being would inform healthcare providers to initiate preventive measures and treatment options for mental health disorders (Fig. 1). Effective management of mental health disorders may lead to neurological complications [21–23].

### *3.6 Targeted Treatment and Preventive Measure in Prostate Cancer*

Prostate cancer (PCa) is the one commonest cancer in men, globally. Although there are numerous causes of PCa, the need to improve the diagnosis and treatments is essential. The PCa management causes a remarkable divergence, i.e., permanently high prevalence of PCa cases on one hand and, stable or even slightly reducing fatal rates on the other hand [24]. In addition, there is always a delay in the time of prostate cancer diagnosis and therefore, to identify persons who may be at risk of developing prostate cancer, PPPM is the modern medical approach to use. Personalised treatment is beneficial for prostate cancer individuals since keeping urinary and sexual functions intact allows for a significantly higher quality of life for most PCa individuals without reducing the survival rates [24].

### 3.7 *Hepatocellular Carcinomas Management: From the PPPM Perspective*

Hepatocellular carcinoma (HCC) is the second leading cause of all cancer-related mortalities even though it is classified among the five top most common of all cancers [5]. This prevalence and mortality rate continues to increase due to inadequate facilities for effective screening programmes, tumour heterogeneity and late diagnosis. HCC is also multifactorial in origin and has erratic impacts of individual tumour growth and development. Thus the frequently untargeted treatment and its associated cancer resistance towards currently applied treatment approaches should be addressed [5]. The reactive medical approach is inappropriate in the management of hepatocellular carcinoma. A therapeutic system tailored towards HCC risk population would require an early evaluation of SHS. Early recognition of benign lesions at the suboptimal phase would create an opportunity for treatment options to reverse the growth of cancerous lesions (Fig. 1). Thus, there is an urgent need to change from reactive treatment toward predictive, preventive and personalised medicine.

## 4 Conclusion, Expert Recommendations and Future Perspective

Suboptimal health evaluation is recognised as an essential tool for PPPM. It is therefore important for healthcare to move from the reactive medical care to PPPM. Identifying persons at the suboptimal stage followed by an appropriate management strategy is essential for preventing the early onset of diseases and their adverse complications [13]. Implementing a targeted prophylactic therapeutic approach but not the 'wait' to 'treat' approach will create a window opportunity to prevent disease development and subsequent complications. The suboptimal stage, which is the flexible stage of chronic diseases, is the recommended stage to start a targeted treatment tailored to the individual. Evaluation of SHS using SHSQ-25 has become necessary and should be adapted as part of treatment strategies in monitoring and management of NCDs. As suggested in predictive, preventive and personalised medical care (PPPM), SHS-targeted treatment algorithms tailored towards persons are the future precision medicine for NCDs.

## References

1. Wang W, Russell A, Yan Y (2014) Traditional Chinese medicine and new concepts of predictive, preventive and personalized medicine in diagnosis and treatment of suboptimal health. EPMA J 5 4(1). https://doi.org/10.1186/1878-5085-5-4.
2. Lemke HU, Golubnitschaja O (2014) Towards personal health care with model-guided medicine: long-term PPPM-related strategies and realisation opportunities within 'horizon 2020'. EPMA Journal 5(1):8. https://doi.org/10.1186/1878-5085-5-8

3. Golubnitschaja O, Kinkorova J, Costigliola V (2014) Predictive, preventive and personalised medicine as the hardcore of 'horizon 2020': EPMA position paper. EPMA J 5(1):6. https://doi.org/10.1186/1878-5085-5-6
4. Golubnitschaja O (2012) Time for new guidelines in advanced healthcare: the mission of The EPMA Journal to promote an integrative view in predictive, preventive and personalized medicine. EPMA J 3(1):5. https://doi.org/10.1186/1878-5085-3-5.
5. Abraham JA, Golubnitschaja O (2016) Time for paradigm change in management of hepatocellular carcinoma: is a personalized approach on the horizon? Per Med 13(5):455–467. https://doi.org/10.2217/pme-2016-0013
6. Wang W, Yan Y, Guo Z, Hou H, Garcia M, Tan X, Anto EO, Mahara G, Zheng Y, Li B, Kang T, Zhong Z, Wang Y, Guo X, Golubnitschaja O (2021) Suboptimal health study consortium and European association for predictive, preventive and personalised medicine. All around suboptimal health - a joint position paper of the Suboptimal Health Study Consortium and European Association for Predictive, Preventive and Personalised Medicine. EPMA J 12(4):403–433. https://doi.org/10.1007/s13167-021-00253-2
7. Kupaev V, Borisov O, Marutina E, Yan YX, Wang W (2016) Integration of suboptimal health status and endothelial dysfunction as a new aspect for risk evaluation of cardiovascular disease. EPMA J 7(1):19. https://doi.org/10.1186/s13167-016-0068-0. Epub 2016/09/14. PubMed PMID: 27621756; PubMed Central PMCID: PMCPMC5018938
8. Ding G, Zhao X, Wang Y, Song D, Chen D, Deng Y, Xing W, Dong H, Zhou Y, Li D, Hou H (2020) Evaluation of the relationship between cognitive impairment and suboptimal health status in a northern Chinese population: a cross-sectional study. J Glob Health 10(1):010804. https://doi.org/10.7189/jogh.10.010804.
9. Hou H, Feng X, Li Y, Meng Z, Guo D, Wang F, Guo Z, Zheng Y, Peng Z, Zhang W, Li D, Ding G, Wang W (2018) Suboptimal health status and psychological symptoms among Chinese college students: a perspective of predictive, preventive and personalised health. EPMA J 9(4):367–377. https://doi.org/10.1007/s13167-018-0148-4.
10. Ge S, Xu X, Zhang J, Hou H, Wang H, Liu D, Zhang X, Song M, Li D, Zhou Y, Wang Y, Wang W (2019) Suboptimal health status as an independent risk factor for type 2 diabetes mellitus in a community-based cohort: the China suboptimal health cohort study. EPMA J 10(1):65–72. https://doi.org/10.1007/s13167-019-0159-9.
11. Adua E, Roberts P, Wang W (2017) Incorporation of suboptimal health status as a potential risk assessment for type II diabetes mellitus: a case-control study in a Ghanaian population. EPMA J 8(4):345–355. https://doi.org/10.1007/s13167-017-0119-1.
12. Duarte AA, Mohsin S, Golubnitschaja O (2018) Diabetes care in figures: current pitfalls and future scenario. EPMA J 9(2):125–131. https://doi.org/10.1007/s13167-018-0133-y. Epub 2018/06/14. PubMed PMID: 29896313; PubMed Central PMCID: PMCPMC5972141
13. Anto EO, Roberts P, Coall D, Turpin CA, Adua E, Wang Y, Wang W (2019) Integration of suboptimal health status evaluation as a criterion for prediction of preeclampsia is strongly recommended for healthcare management in pregnancy: a prospective cohort study in a Ghanaian population. EPMA J 10(3):211–226. https://doi.org/10.1007/s13167-019-00183-0. Epub 2019/08/30. PubMed PMID: 31462939; PubMed Central PMCID: PMCPMC6695466
14. Anto EO, Roberts P, Coall DA, Adua E, Turpin CA, Tawiah A,Wang Y, Wang W (2020) Suboptimal health pregnant women are associated with increased oxidative stress and unbalanced pro- and antiangiogenic growth mediators: a cross-sectional study in a Ghanaian population. Free Radic Res 54(1):27–42. https://doi.org/10.1080/10715762.2019.1685668
15. Anto EO, Coall DA, Addai-Mensah O, Wiafe YA, Owiredu W, Obirikorang C, Annani-Akollor ME, Adua E, Tawiah A, Acheampong E, Asamoah EA, Wang X, Opoku S, Boakye DK, Hou H, Wang Y, Wang W (2021) Suboptimal health study consortium (SHSC). Early gestational profiling of oxidative stress and angiogenic growth mediators as predictive, preventive and personalised (3P) medical approach to identify suboptimal health pregnant mothers likely to develop preeclampsia. EPMA J 12(4):517–534. https://doi.org/10.1007/s13167-021-00258-x. Epub 2021/12/28. PubMed PMID: 34956424; PubMed Central PMCID: PMCPMC8648887

16. Goncharenko V, Bubnov R, Polivka J Jr, Zubor P, Biringer K, Bielik T, Kuhn W, Golubnitschaja O (2019) Vaginal dryness: individualised patient profiles, risks and mitigating measures. EPMA J 10(1):73–79. https://doi.org/10.1007/s13167-019-00164-3.
17. Wang Y, Liu X, Qiu J, Wang H, Liu D, Zhao Z, Song M, Song Q, Wang X, Zhou Y, Wang W (2017) Association between Ideal Cardiovascular Health Metrics and Suboptimal Health Status in Chinese Population. Sci Rep 7(1):14975. https://doi.org/10.1038/s41598-017-15101-5. Epub 2017/11/05. PubMed PMID: 29101345; PubMed Central PMCID: PMCPMC5670124
18. Yan YX, Dong J, Liu YQ, Yang XH, Li M, Shia G, Wang W (2012) Association of suboptimal health status and cardiovascular risk factors in urban Chinese workers. J Urban Health 89(2):329–338. https://doi.org/10.1007/s11524-011-9636-8.
19. Chen J, Cheng J, Liu Y, Tang Y, Sun X, Wang T, Xiao Y, Li F, Xiang L, Jiang P, Wu S, Wu L, Luo R, Zhao X (2014) Associations between breakfast eating habits and health-promoting lifestyle, suboptimal health status in Southern China: a population based, cross sectional study. J Transl Med 12:348. https://doi.org/10.1186/s12967-014-0348-1.
20. Tu C, Huang Z, Fu L, Fang Y, Wang J, Guo T, Li M, Hao J, Tao F (2012) Predictors of suicidal ideation with sub-optimal health status and anxiety symptom among Chinese adolescents. J Trop Pediatr 58(4):314–319. https://doi.org/10.1093/tropej/fmr090
21. Chen AX, Conti TF, Hom GL, Greenlee TE, Raimondi R, Briskin IN, Rich CA, Kampani R, Engel R, Sharma S, Talcott KE, Singh RP (2021) Functional imaging of mitochondria in retinal diseases using flavoprotein fluorescence. Eye (London, England) 35(1):74–92. https://doi.org/10.1038/s41433-020-1110-y.
22. Polivka J Jr, Polivka J, Pesta M, Rohan V, Celedova L, Mahajani S, Topolcan O, Golubnitschaja O (2019) Risks associated with the stroke predisposition at young age: facts and hypotheses in light of individualized predictive and preventive approach. EPMA J 10(1):81–99. https://doi.org/10.1007/s13167-019-00162-5.
23. Koklesova L, Samec M, Liskova A, Zhai K, Büsselberg D, Giordano FA, Kubatka P, Golunitschaja O (2021) Mitochondrial impairments in aetiopathology of multifactorial diseases: common origin but individual outcomes in context of 3P medicine. EPMA J 12(1):1–14. https://doi.org/10.1007/s13167-021-00237-2.
24. Kucera R, Pecen L, Topolcan O, Dahal AR, Costigliola V, Giordano FA, Golubnitschaja O (2020) Prostate cancer management: long-term beliefs, epidemic developments in the early twenty-first century and 3PM dimensional solutions. EPMA J 11(3):399–418. https://doi.org/10.1007/s13167-020-00214-1.

# Approaches for Measuring Reversible Damage to the Health

**Yu-Xiang Yan and Wei Wang**

## Abbreviations

| | |
|---|---|
| M-M | Multi-trait-multi-method |
| MMSE | Mini-Mental State Examination |
| MPQ | McGill pain questionnaire |
| SHS | Suboptimal health status |
| SHSQ-25 | Suboptimal health status questionnaire-25 |

Y.-X. Yan (✉)
School of Public Health, Capital Medical University, Beijing, China
e-mail: yanyxepi@ccmu.edu.cn

W. Wang
First Affiliated Hospital, Shantou University Medical College, Shantou, China

Beijing Key Laboratory of Clinical Epidemiology, Capital Medical University, Beijing, China

School of Public Health, Shandong First Medical University and Shandong Academy of Medical Sciences, Jinan, China

Centre for Precision Health, Edith Cowan University, Perth, Australia

Suboptimal Health Study Consortium, Kumasi, Ghana

Suboptimal Health Study Consortium, Perth, Australia

Suboptimal Health Study Consortium, Beijing, China

Suboptimal Health Study Consortium, Bonn, Germany

European Association for Predictive, Preventive and Personalised Medicine, EPMA, Brussels, Belgium
e-mail: wei.wang@ecu.edu.au



W. Wang (ed.), *All Around Suboptimal Health*, Advances in Predictive, Preventive and Personalised Medicine 18,
https://doi.org/10.1007/978-3-031-46891-9_8

# 1 Introduction

Health questionnaires and scales have become the dominant instruments to measure various health, such as the existence of different symptoms or specific characteristics [1, 2]. Multiple items are constructed for comprehensive assessment of subjective health complaints prior to organic lesions. Nowadays, there are a variety of health scales and questionnaires have been constructed for the detection of reversible health damages that could not be measured directly [3], such as the "Suboptimal Health Status Questionnaire-25 (SHSQ-25)" [3], "Mini-Mental State Examination (BMI) [4]" and "McGill Pain Questionnaire (MPQ) [5]."

The SHSQ-25 was established to evaluate suboptimal health status (SHS), which includes various health complaints. The SHSQ-25 consists of 25 items concerning a series of symptoms on five dimensions. Based on previous qualitative and quantitative analysis, work stress has been proven to be an important influencing factor of SHS. Chronic activation of the stress response is associated with a number of diseases, such as cardiovascular disease, gastrointestinal disease, immunological diseases and mental illness [3]. According to the impacts of mental stress on health, the preliminary SHSQ-25 was established based on a literature review and focus group discussions. The validity and reliability of the SHSQ-25 were evaluated in a large-scale investigation.

# 2 Major Procedures of Establishing a Health Instrument

Before establishing a questionnaire, it is necessary to determine the purpose and theoretical hypothesis of the investigation. The main contents of the questionnaire should be outlined and relevant data and information should be collected for the item pool.

## *2.1 Selection of Items*

The individual questions of a new health instrument usually come from literature, existing questionnaires, expert opinions and focus group discussions [1, 2]. Exiting health questionnaires assessing a particular trait or disorder may be useful source of items. These instruments have been widely used and proved to be relevant, important and discriminating. So, some items of the newly developed questionnaire are derived from these widely used instruments.

It is a fact that potential subjects of a specific study are a good source of individual questions in establishing health instrument [1]. Focus group usually consisted of 5–10 individuals who have the disorder or health problem. The focus group discussion is led by a moderator, who adhered to a question guide with interesting theme. The discussions are conducted until no new items emerge. The opinions, experiences and perceived health were recorded, transcribed word for word, processed as text until no new themes appeared, and then analysed them by means of qualitative analysis [3]. Expert opinions are important to determine the most important characteristics of health complaints. The accumulated knowledge and experience of the experts, such as physicians, nurses and health managers, are necessary for the generation and choice of items [1].

### 2.2 *Construction of Health Questionnaire*

Once the individual questions have been selected, expert consults and focus groups will be performed again to evaluate whether these items are relevant, explicit, and whether they are written in a way that can be understood by interviewees. After that, a preliminary health instrument is developed according to the pool of questions. The researchers should consider the order of questions, logical structure of the questionnaire, convenience of the answers and potential psychological influence on the interviewees. For each question, we should pay attention to whether it is necessary and whether the answers are comprehensive and reasonable. Generally, a pilot survey will be conducted to evaluate whether the questions are feasible and relevant. According to the feedback of the interviewees, the instrument is then modified for formal investigation.

### 2.3 *Measurement and Rating of Responses*

To obtain effective answers, an appropriate scoring method to quantify the answers should be developed. A response of "yes/no" could not discriminate a person who has health problem from those who do not have. Rating scales are extensively utilised in the areas of health and social research for the measurement of characteristics that could not be evaluated directly [6–8]. Most of questionnaires have been constructed using thresholds of three or five classes with scores of "1, 2, 3" or "1, 2, 3, 4, 5," which correspond to the frequency or degree of health complaint suffered [6, 8]. For example, each item in the SHSQ-25 is evaluated using 5-point Likert-type scales anchored by 1 = "never or almost never," 2 = "now and then," 3 = "often," 4 = "very often," and 5 = "always" [3].

## 3 Assessment of Reliability

Reliability and validity are among the most important and fundamental characteristics in the assessment of any measuring methodology for data collection. They are important aspects in evaluating the accuracy and precision of an investigation.

Reliability refers to whether the same result can be attained consistently by applying the same methodology under similar conditions [9]. Reliability can be evaluated by the following methods:

### 3.1 Test–Retest Reliability

The test–retest reliability means whether the instrument produces stable scores over time. It is deemed an excellent test–retest reliability if the same instrument is repeated after a period of time and gives the same answers. The test–retest reliability is evaluated by correlation analysis between the first and second measurements by using the same instrument to the same subjects [10]. The environment should be as consistent as possible to minimise the external factors that may affect the measurements. The assumption of test–retest reliability is that the measured characteristic of the same subjects does not change over time.

### 3.2 Alternate Form Reliability

Alternate form reliability refers to equivalence between an alternate form of instrument and the original instrument. The alternate questionnaire has different items but equal means [11]. It is hypothesised that no significant differences should exist between the two forms of the instruments. Alternate form reliability is measured by the correlation coefficient between the scores of two parallel measurements administered in the same individuals or different group of individuals. Strong positive correlations between the two instruments indicate equivalent.

### 3.3 Split-Half Reliability

When alternate form of same measure is not available, split-half reliability can be used. The measurement is split into two half-tests that are as nearly parallel as possible, and the correlation between halves is calculated. The measurement can be split in ordered halves (first-half and second-half) or odd-even half. The correlation is likely to be an underestimate of the reliability coefficient for the full-length measurement instrument. To overcome this problem, the Spearman-Brown formula ($\mathrm{R} = 2r/(1 + r)$, $r$ indicates the correlation between halves, $R$ indicates the split-half reliability) is then used for correction [12, 13].

### 3.4 *Reliability of Internal Consistency*

Internal consistency refers to whether the items correlate with each other within the instrument. Cronbach's alpha is a measure that assesses internal consistency reliability [14]. It can be used with both polytomous and dichotomous data. It is the average of all possible split-half reliabilities assuming the halves are parallel to each other. It is also the lowest bound of estimate of reliability. A Cronbach's alpha coefficient greater than 0.70 is generally considered acceptable for group comparisons, and 0.90 for person-level comparisons [15]. Cronbach's alpha can be affected by the length of the scale, the correlation coefficient between items and the dimension of measurement. With the increase of item numbers and correlation between items, Cronbach's alpha will also increase. However, Cronbach's alpha will decrease with increase of dimension number.

## 4 Assessment of Validity

Validity is defined as how accurately a methodology measures a variable that it intends to measure [9]. Validity is difficult to assess but can be evaluated by comparing the results with other relevant conception or theory. Validity can be evaluated by the following methods:

### 4.1 *Content Validity*

Content validity refers to the relevance and representativeness of the contents of the instrument, that is, whether the relevant aspects of the idea being measured are included in an instrument. In most cases, content validity is evaluated by panels of professionals [9]. Unlike with other types of validation, there is no correlation coefficient or some other statistic that can be used to measure content validation. Usually, experts review all of the items for readability, clarity and comprehensiveness and decide which items should be included in the final questionnaire [16]. Content validity is also called logical validity, intrinsic validity or circular validity.

### 4.2 *Construct Validity*

Construct validity reflects the compliance of a measurement to the existing concept and theory. To establish construct validity, researcher has to make predictions based on the assumed construct. The predictions will further be proved to support the validity of the instrument [17]. Evidence based on the internal structure of an instrument is used to determine whether the items measure unidimensional construct or a multidimensional one. In addition, it is used to ascertain whether internal relationships between the variables are consistent with the definition of the construct to be measured and the intended structure of the instrument. Exploratory or confirmatory factor analyses are usually used methods for the evaluation of construct validity [18, 19].

## *4.3 Criterion Validity*

Criterion validity refers to the degree of association between the scores of a measurement instrument and a specific criterion, which can be measured by the correlation coefficient between the score of a measurement and a widely accepted measure of the same characteristics [20]. There are two types of criterion validity, including concurrent validity and predictive validity. Concurrent validity reflects the association between the new instrument and the current criterion. Predictive validity refers to the association between the new instrument and the future criterion (a criterion that is measured later), which reflects the accuracy of an instrument in predicting the individual's future performances. The more accurate an instrument predicts, the higher the predictive validity is.

## *4.4 Assessment of Discriminant and Convergent Validity*

Discriminant validity means that the measurements of an instrument should be significantly less correlated with those of conceptually unrelated instruments than other measurements of that instrument [21]. Convergent validity refers to the degree of similarity of the results obtained when using different instruments to measure the same characteristics or conception. There should be a high correlation between two or more instruments of the same characteristics.

The discriminant validity and convergent validity are usually evaluated by the multi-trait-multi-method (M-M) proposed by Campbell and Fiske [22]. The M-M method requires multiple (at least two) instruments to measure multiple (more than two) characteristics, respectively, so that the correlation coefficient between the scores of any two instruments of the same characteristics and the correlation coefficient between the scores of any two different characteristics of the same instrument can be calculated. However, M-M analysis is relatively complex, it is not widely used in practice.

## 5 Conclusions

Health questionnaires and scales are important instruments in evaluating reversible damage to the health, which could not be measured directly. They have become a routine instrument for assessing subjective health complaints. A well-established health questionnaire is important for predictive, preventive and personalised medicine. Reliability and validity are important and fundamental aspects of health questionnaires and scales.Declarations of InterestNone.

## References


1. Keszei AP, Novak M, Streiner DL (2010) Introduction to health measurement scales. J Psychosom Res 68(4):319–323. https://doi.org/10.1016/j.jpsychores.2010.01.006
2. McDowell I (2010) Measures of self-perceived well-being. J Psychosom Res 69(1):69–79. https://doi.org/10.1016/j.jpsychores.2009.07.002
3. Yan YX, Liu YQ, Li M, Hu PF, Guo AM, Yang XH, Qiu JJ, Yang SS, Shen J, Zhang LP, Wang W (2009) Development and evaluation of a questionnaire for measuring suboptimal health status in urban Chinese. J Epidemiol 19(6):333–341. https://doi.org/10.2188/jea.je20080086
4. Gagnon M, Letenneur L, Dartigues JF, Commenges D, Orgogozo JM, Barberger-Gateau P, Alpérovitch A, Décamps A, Salamon R (1990) Validity of the mini-mental state examination as a screening instrument for cognitive impairment and dementia in French elderly community residents. Neuroepidemiology 9(3):143–150. https://doi.org/10.1159/000110764
5. Melzack R (1975) The McGill pain questionnaire: major properties and scoring methods. Pain 1(3):277–299. https://doi.org/10.1016/0304-3959(75)90044-5
6. Panagiotakos D (2009) Health measurement scales: methodological issues. Open Cardiovasc Med J 3:160–165. https://doi.org/10.2174/1874192400903010160
7. Likert R (1932) A technique for the measurement of attitudes. Arch Psychol 140:5–55
8. Andrich D (2011) Rating scales and Rasch measurement. Expert Rev Pharmacoecon Outcomes Res 11(5):571–585. https://doi.org/10.1586/erp.11.59
9. Carmines E, Zeller R (1986) Reliability and validity assessment. Sage Publications, London
10. Lohr KN, Aaronson NK, Alonso J, Burnam MA, Patrick DL, Perrin EB, Roberts JS (1996) Evaluating quality-of-life and health status instruments: development of scientific review criteria. Clin Ther 18(5):979–992. https://doi.org/10.1016/s0149-2918(96)80054-3
11. Gage M, Noh S, Polatajko HJ, Kaspar V (1994) Measuring perceived self-efficacy in occupational therapy. Am J Occup Ther 48(9):783–790. https://doi.org/10.5014/ajot.48.9.783
12. Spearman C (1910) Correlation calculated from faulty data. Br J Psychol 3:271–295
13. Brown W (1910) Some experimental results in the correlation of mental abilities. Br J Psychol 3:296–322
14. Rosenthal R, Rosnow RL (1991) Essentials of behavioral research: methods and data analysis. McGraw-Hill, Boston, MA
15. Ware JE Jr, Gandek B (1998) Methods for testing data quality, scaling assumptions, and reliability: the IQOLA project approach. International quality of life assessment. J Clin Epidemiol 51(11):945–952. https://doi.org/10.1016/s0895-4356(98)00085-7

16. Polit DF, Beck CT, Owen SV (2007) Is the CVI an acceptable indicator of content validity? Appraisal and recommendations. Res Nurs Health 30(4):459–467. https://doi.org/10.1002/nur.20199
17. Cronbach LJ, Meehl PE (1955) Construct validity in psychological tests. Psychol Bull 52(4):281–302. https://doi.org/10.1037/h0040957
18. Comrey AL, Lee HB (1992) A first course in factor analysis, 2nd edn. Lawrence Erlbaum Associates, Hillsdale, NJ
19. Kline RB (1998) Principles and practice of structural equation modeling. Guilford Press, New York
20. Caracciolo B, Giaquinto S (2002) Criterion validity of the center for epidemiological studies depression (CES-D) scale in a sample of rehabilitation inpatients. J Rehabil Med 34(5):221–225. https://doi.org/10.1080/165019702760279215
21. Strauss ME, Smith GT (2009) Construct validity: advances in theory and methodology. Annu Rev Clin Psychol 5:1–25. https://doi.org/10.1146/annurev.clinpsy.032408.153639
22. Ferketich SL, Figueredo AJ, Knapp TR (1991) The multitrait-multimethod approach to construct validity. Res Nurs Health 14(4):315–320. https://doi.org/10.1002/nur.4770140410

# Leveraging Supervised Machine Learning for Determining the Link between Suboptimal Health Status and the Prognosis of Chronic Diseases

**Eric Adua, Ebenezer Afrifa-Yamoah, and Emmanuel Awuni Kolog**

## Abbreviations

| | |
|---|---|
| AI | Artificial intelligence |
| ANN | Artificial neural network |
| BMI | Body mass index |
| DT | Decision tree |
| HbA1c | Glycated haemoglobin |
| KNN | *k*-neural neighbour |
| ML | Machine learning |
| NB | Naïve Bayes |
| PCA | Principal component analysis |
| PPPM | Predictive, preventive and personalized medicine |
| RF | Random Forest |
| ROC | Receiver operating characteristic |
| SHS | Suboptimal Health Status |

E. Adua (✉)
School of Medical and Health Sciences, Edith Cowan University, Joondalup, WA, Australia

Rural Clinical Campus, School of Clinical Medicine, Medicine and Health, University of New South Wales, Sydney, NSW, Australia
e-mail: e.adua@unsw.edu.au

E. Afrifa-Yamoah
School of Science, Edith Cowan University, Joondalup, WA, Australia
e-mail: e.afrifayamoah@ecu.edu.au

E. A. Kolog
Department of OMIS, University of Ghana Business School, Accra, Ghana
e-mail: eakolog@ug.edu.gh



W. Wang (ed.), *All Around Suboptimal Health*, Advances in Predictive, Preventive and Personalised Medicine 18,
https://doi.org/10.1007/978-3-031-46891-9_9

| | |
|---|---|
| SHSQ-25 | Suboptimal Health Status Questionnaire-25 |
| SVM | Support vector machine |
| T2DM | Type II diabetes mellitus |
| TC | Total cholesterol |

## 1 Background

Advances in medical and health science research have informed a paradigm shift from reactive medicine to proactive approaches that personalise the prevention, stratification, diagnosis and treatment of a specific patient [1, 2]. This concept herein referred to as predictive, preventive and personalised medicine (PPPM) recognises individuals who are at risk of developing diseases by collecting and analysing large amounts of data including lifestyle, demographic, anthropometric and family history amongst others [3, 4]. With such information, tailored treatment can be administered to actualise optimal health outcomes for an individual. Moreover, PPPM is essential to allow the distinction between patients who are likely to respond to therapy, from those who would not and those likely to experience major side effects. Yet, the full potential of PPPM has not been realised as people have latent and varied subclinical presentations that are often missed. Suboptimal health status (SHS) is a concept that captures individuals with subclinical conditions and earmark them for treatment [2, 5]. Introduced in 2009, SHS identifies individuals who feel unwell, but their conditions cannot classify them as diseased. The concept is premised on the fact that the deterioration of health begins at least 30 years prior, with noticeable symptoms that range from general body weakness and vitality to loss of appetite, insomnia and recurring cold. Over time, these mild conditions progress into increased heart rate, weight gain, raised blood pressure and elevated plasma glucose until they worsen into cardiovascular diseases, metabolic syndrome [6], type II diabetes mellitus (T2DM) [6, 7], dyslipidaemia, amongst others. SHS is determined using validated subjective instrument, SHSQ-25 [4] that measures the health status of individuals from five domains including the immune system, cardiovascular, digestive, fatigue and mental system [5, 8, 9]. When combined with objective clinical makers, the link between SHS and diseases can be established (Fig. 1).

The implementation of PPPM requires massive research investment and innovations in biomedical, and social sciences, and health economics that inform the provision of equitable access to healthcare at the individual or population level. When implementing PPPM, it is important to consider the type of population and geographical location [10]. This is because, population subgroups have different genomic and environmental make-ups, which may affect their responses to therapy. For example, the implementation strategies for Africans, Caucasians and Asians are likely to differ because of the variations of climatic, demographic and socioeconomic status. There is a need to perform analysis and construct models that contextually suit specific populations. Moreover, implementation based on biomarkers poses a formidable challenge because biomarkers change in response to

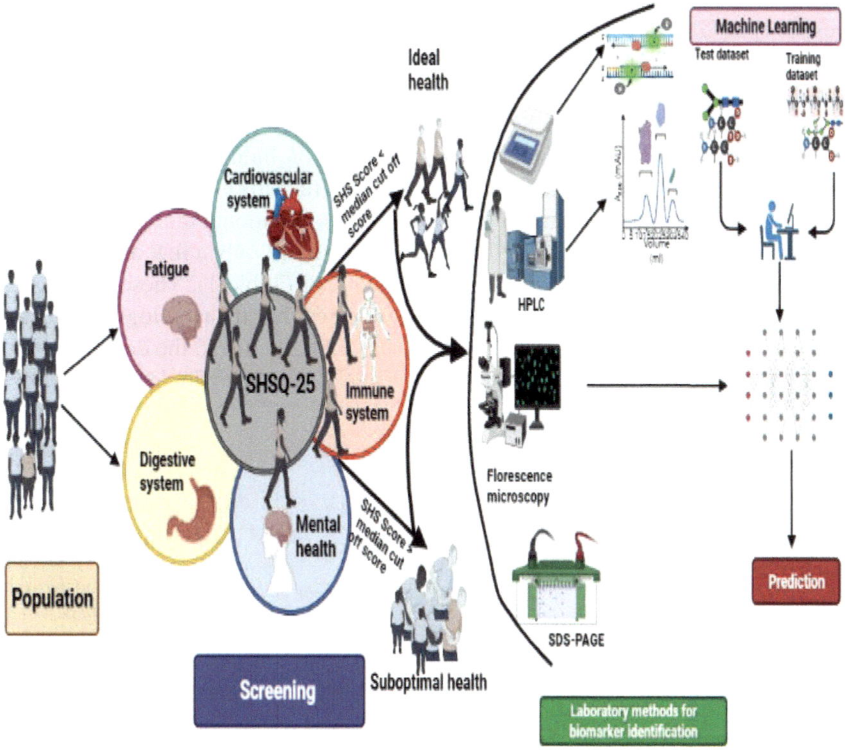


**Fig. 1** The recognition of persons with suboptimal health status begins with screening with SHSQ-25. Responses are rated and individuals who score above a median cut-off value are classified as suboptimal health whereas those with scores below the median cut-off value have ideal health. Both groups undergo further testing, using analytical/molecular biology techniques to establish diagnosis and identify biomarkers. ML can transform data into clinically useful information, while enabling better health planning, assessment, management, disease forecasting and characterisation of disease risk

genetic, epigenetic and environmental perturbations. Thus, there is no one-size-fits-all approach for implementing PPPM. Furthermore, implementation of the PPPM requires a simultaneous application of public policy, legal ethics, medicine and science [10].

The SHSQ-25 can be central to PPPM implementation, as its application is seen worldwide. Among Ghanaians, SHS was linked with T2DM [3]. Yan et al. [5] associated SHS with cardiovascular risk factors in 2012 in a Chinese population, which was also confirmed by Wang et al. [11]. Moreover, SHS was associated with psychological syndromes such as depression and anxiety among Chinese nurses [12]. Hou et al. [13] also confirmed that SHS was associated with psychological symptoms such as interpersonal sensitivity, depression, obsessive-compulsive, sleep and diet problems and somatisation.

Anto et al. [8] indicated that SHS could lead to pre-eclampsia and oxidative stress [14] in Ghanaian pregnant women. Kupaev et al. [9] established an association of SHS and endothelial dysfunction in a Russian population. Sun et al. [15] also revealed that altered intestinal microbiota was associated with SHS. The ability to detect association between SHS and disease states has been possible because of technologies that allow the precise quantification of biomarkers and statistical methods that transform generated data into meaningful information (Fig. 1).

Univariate analysis (such as ANOVA and *t*-tests), traditional multivariate analysis, logistic regression and cox-regression approaches are only a few of the statistical techniques that have already been published [16] (Table 1). These techniques have uncovered biomarkers associated with illnesses, but their biological interactions are not made immediately apparent. This is partially due to the daunting challenges posed by the 'big data' produced by analytical technologies, which have

**Table 1** Related studies on suboptimal health status

| Population | Analytical tool | Statistical method | Biomarker measured |
|---|---|---|---|
| Chinese [17] Sample size 3635 | Automatic clinical analyser | ANOVA, multivariable logistic regression, chi-square tests | BMI, BP, FPG TC, TG LDL-c, HDL-c |
| Ghanaians [3] Sample size 505 | Cobas Integra chemistry analyser | Kolmogov–Smirnov test, linear regression and multiple logistic regression, ANOVA, Chi-Square | BMI, BP, FPG TC, TG, LDL-c and HDL-c, non-HDL-c, HbA1c |
| Ghanaians [8] Sample size 262 | Cobas Integra chemistry analyser, haematology analyser | Kolmogov–Smirnov and multiple logistic regression, ANOVA, Chi-square | BMI, BP, FPG TC, TG, LDL-c and HDL-c, HbA1c, GGT, ALB, UA, Mg, Ca, Cl, K, LDH, ALP, Na, Urea, creatinine, AST, ALT |
| Russians [9] Sample size 459 | Brachial plethysmography | Student's *t*-test, multiple linear regression, cluster analysis | BMI, BP, FPG TC, TG LDL-c and HDL-c |
| Chinese [5] Sample size 4881 | Automatic clinical analyser radioimmunoassay | Univariate, multivariate analysis | BMI, BP, FPG TC, TG LDL-c and HDL-c, cortisol |
| Chinese Sample size 30 | Agilent 2100 Bioanalyzer | Student/Mann–Whitney *U* test, Shapiro–Wilk test, Benjamini–Hochberg method, multivariate binary logistic regression | GJA1, TWIST2, KRT1, TUBB3, AMHR2, BMP10, MT3, BMPER, NTM and TMEM98 |
| Chinese [18] Sample size 386 | Radioimmunoassay, qPCR, capillary gel electrophoresis | Pearson's correlation analysis, multiple linear regression analysis, general linear model | Cortisol, mRNA |

hampered the capacity of conventional statistical methodologies to thoroughly examine the data. These include, amongst others, over-fitting, curse of dimensionality, Simpson's paradox and multicollinearity [16, 19]. The limitations of the traditional statistical methods [20, 21] have ignited the need for more robust and advanced models from computational data analytical methods, such as machine learning (ML). The present study provides an overview of the ML process and algorithms and provides insights on their application in subclinical disease prediction based on SHSQ-25 data.

Machine learning (ML) has advanced the traditional approaches of artificial intelligence (AI) by capitalising on historical data to empower machines to make inform decisions. ML is defined as an application of algorithms that provides systems with the ability to automatically learn and improve from experience without being explicitly programmed [22]. The primary aim is to allow computers to learn automatically without or with minimal human intervention or assistance and adjust actions accordingly. The process of learning begins with observations or data, such as direct experience or instruction, to look for patterns in data and make better decisions in the future. The approach has widely been used to improve the landscape of data analysis and inference in many sectors, including health and medicine. Within the context of medicine,

ML can be used to transform medical data into clinically useful information, while enabling better health planning, assessment, management, disease forecasting and characterisation of disease risk. The application of ML in disease prediction has been mainly based on genotype data, which are generally expensive and time-consuming to collect and process. For instance, fasting plasma glucose, serum lipids, such as, total cholesterol, triglycerides, low-density lipoprotein cholesterols, resting pulse rate and high-density lipoprotein cholesterols have been identified as significant correlates for a range of cardiometabolic conditions. We hypothesise that suboptimal health status monitoring via SHSQ-25 could provide opportunity to gather worth of longitudinal data at a relatively cheaper cost, whose exploration could potentially confirm the SHSQ-25 as a 'pseudo' biomarker for cardiometabolic disease. However, the potential of ML methods to determine the trajectory from SHS to chronic diseases has not been previously investigated. Data-driven ML algorithms have improved disease prediction but there is limited evidence of their application in subclinical disease prediction. Recognition of SHS, prior to a cardiometabolic disease, is another area that ML can be leveraged. It can enable the identification of molecular intricacies that underpin the link between suboptimal health and metabolic disease.

ML can generally be classified into four: unsupervised, semi-supervised, supervised and reinforcement learning. For this study, we focused on supervised learning, as we presume that the ensuing SHSQ-25 datasets would be labelled, giving investigators some level of oversight in the implementation of the ML algorithms. Thus, the subsequent section delves deeper into the various supervised ML techniques for disease prediction (Fig. 2).

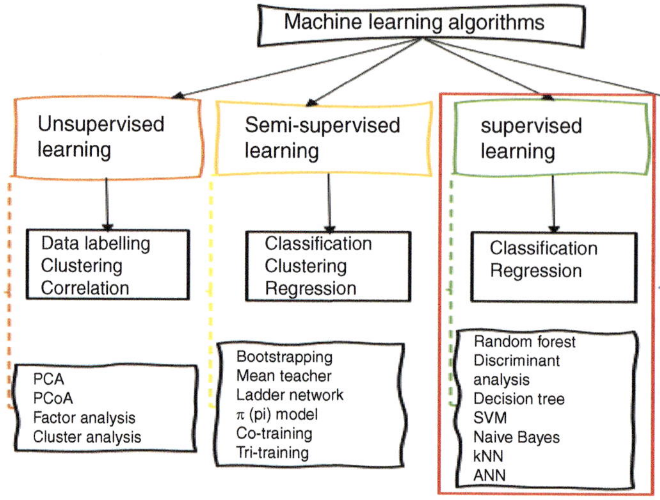


**Fig. 2** Machine learning algorithms in brief: Types of machine learning algorithm, application and various types of techniques that fall under each type. *PCA* principal component analysis, *PCoA* principal coordinate analysis, *SVM* support vector machine, *kNN* *k*-nearest neighbour, *ANN* artificial neural network

## 2 Machine Learning Process

In this section, we describe the various categories of ML-based techniques by providing a systematic evaluation of their applications in disease prediction. For example, while each of the ML approaches has its own process, data preparation is a characteristic associated with all of them.

### *2.1 Data Sources and Preparation*

Data from SHS and cardio-metabolic diseases are often generated in the health institutions and archive for possible exploration. In many cases, data can primarily be collected from the field depending on the intended purpose of the data. The type of data from SHS is numerical in nature. These data are usually managed structurally and archived in data warehouse. To pipeline data for classification and other ML techniques, it must be first pre-processed to improve the quality of the data. The accuracy of a predictive model largely depends on the quality of the data.

## 2.2 Feature Engineering

Feature engineering is the process of using domain knowledge to extract features from raw data. It forms one of the most important components of the ML pipeline. A robust predictive model does not only require clean and quality data but also the selection of features with high predictive strengths. The issues of curse of dimensionality and overfitting make this process very important in building models for prediction purposes. When there are several variables involved, it is necessary to target the most informative predictors. The technique can also be used to rank features based on their relevance. For example, Adua et al. [23] employed recursive feature elimination technique to rank predictive features of diabetes. In their study, glycated haemoglobin (HbA1c), total cholesterol (TC) and body mass index (BMI) were found as the most important features for predicting T2DM.

Feature selection methods are categorised according to filter methods, wrapper methods and embedded methods. The filter method applies a statistical measure to assign a score to each feature. Examples are the Chi-squared test, information gain and correlation coefficient. The wrapper feature selection methods consider the selection of a set of features as a search problem, where different combinations are prepared, evaluated and compared with other combinations. Examples are the use of feature elimination techniques and principal component analysis (PCA). Predominantly, PCA has been widely used to select features for ML. The embedded methods, on the other hand, learn which feature contributes to the best performance in the process of model building. Examples include elastic net, lasso and ridge regression.

SHS individuals generally suffer from a myriad of complaints including lethargy, physical exhaustion and mental fatigue. Association rules can be used to determine how the five health domains in the SHSQ-25 are connected. Subsequently, we can discover the relationships between SHS domains and clinical biomarkers of cardiometabolic health. For example, depending on how individuals rate their health status in each of the health domains, risk factors can be derived. In turn, the combination of variables or factors that lead to suboptimal health can be detected. We may detect that high SHS who frequently rate a question like "*How often were you bothered by heart palpitations?* (Subjective data) as 5 on the Likert scale also have raised blood pressure (objective data), and they can be said to be associated with each other. In addition, an improved version, called survival association rule mining that considers possible confounders and can be used to determine the interaction or interconnections between risk factors for high SHS and cardiometabolic disease. Undertaking these activities paves way for feature selection based on the SHSQ-25.

## 2.3 *Supervised Learning*

Supervised ML techniques have been widely used in the identification of clinical biomarkers for cardio-metabolic diseases. These techniques do lend themselves as suitable in studying the links between health status and cardio-metabolic diseases. Supervised learning aims at mapping input data to output data, thus, the input data ($x$) are tagged with the output ($y$) data, which yields a function $y = f(x)$. In supervised learning, a set of predictors is inputted and used to predict an outcome. For example, the ordinary least squares regression predicts an outcome based on the linear relationship between a continuous dependent variable and independent variables [24]. Broadly, supervised learning involves classification and regression processes. Hypothetically, clinical markers of patients could be used and mapped to their corresponding suboptimal health and cardio-metabolic health status. Such predictive models can be explored by training a supervised learning algorithm with labelled data.

### 2.3.1 Classification

Some supervised learning models, such as logistic regression are built for the classification purpose of predicting the response class based on some target attributes. Unlike traditional programming scenarios, both input and output (expected) variables/attributes are given to ML algorithms to learn. This implies that all instances of the input data (attributes) are given labels or come with its labels. Assume a diabetic dataset $D$, containing $m$ instances/observations, where $x < m$ is explanatory attributes and $y < m$ categorical target attribute (diabetes status), for building a model such that $x + y = m$. The $x$ attributes, also called predictive variables, may be numerical and/or categorical while the target attribute, $y$ has class labels. The goal of the classification is to maximise the predictive relations of the function $y = f(x)$. Figure 3 shows a typical ML classification pipeline. The dataset undergoes a data preparation stage by cleaning. The cleaned data is scaled to ensure standardisation of the data attributes, thereby avoiding any possible estimation bias. Important features from the data are extracted to increase the strength of prediction. Training an ML algorithm requires efficient techniques. Among existing techniques for training an ML algorithm, test/train and cross-validation techniques are the most widely used. The test/train technique requires dividing the dataset into two where one part of the data is used for training while the remaining data is used for testing or validating the algorithm (classifiers). Often, the test data ranges from 10% to 30% while the training data ranges from 70% to 90%.

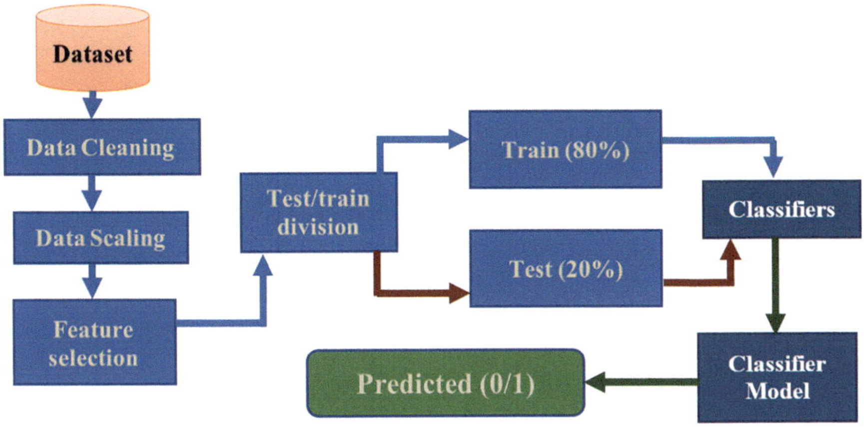


**Fig. 3** Workflow of data classification process. A classification model where 1 represents suboptimal health and 0 is ideal health. Cleaning, scaling, feature selection, test/train validation, classifier model development and evaluation are among the steps in the process model

ML algorithms can suffer from overfitting issues, where the analysis or patterns produced are based on a subset of the data rather than being representative of the general dataset. Hence, the predicted outcomes may not be reliable. To mitigate this risk, cross-validation, such as leave-one-out and *k*-fold, is performed. In cross-validation, a random fraction, or a control dataset algorithm with known outcome (disease or no disease) is trained ("training set"), and the trained algorithm is then tested on the "test set" (validation set). The overall performance is then determined using the test sample [24]. The procedure has a single parameter, *k* that refers to the number of groups that a given data sample is to be split into. As such, the procedure is often called *k*-fold cross-validation. The widely used approach is the ten-fold cross-validation. There are various algorithms used in classification. These algorithms are also referred to as classifiers. Notable and most widely used classification algorithms are described as follows:

### Random Forest

Random Forest (RF) comprises multiple regression trees with nodes at its base that resemble a forest and can be used for both classification and prediction purposes. A subset of the attributes is selected or evaluated at each split and trained separately on another dataset. The prediction is based on the mean of all trees under consideration. RF has been reported to be robust and computationally efficient because it selects complex and strong learners with low bias to reduce variance and error rates [25]. It ranks variables according to their importance. Random forest applies the Gini index that measures the frequency at which wrongly labelled element is chosen

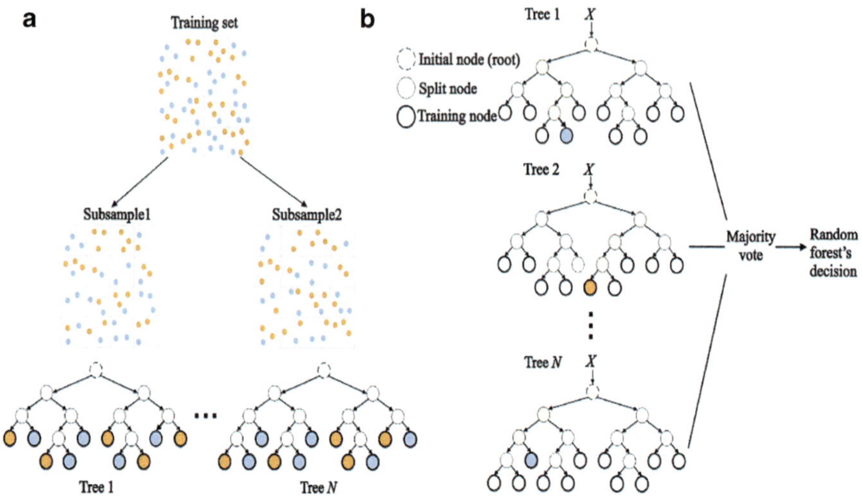


**Fig. 4** Illustration of random forest model for training and classification processes. (**a**) *Training process*: A random bootstrap is used to build each decision tree in the ensemble from the original data, which contains positive (orange labels) and negative (blue labels) outcomes. (**b**) *Classification process*: A majority voting procedure is used for the class prediction among all individual trees. For each new data point (i.e., X) in each tree, the algorithm starts at the root node of a decision tree and traverses down the tree testing the variables' values in each of the visited split nodes, to decide the next branch to follow. This process is repeated until a leaf node is reached, which assigns a class. At the end of the process, each tree casts a vote for the preferred class label, and the mode of the outputs is chosen as the final prediction [26]

by chance in dataset (Fig. 4). In calculating this index, the probability of each class is summed up and subtracted from 1. This way, predictive power is enhanced while potential biases from decision tree (DT) on a system are removed [27]. Moreover, RF is appropriate for non-linear models and ideal for small datasets. However, analysing with RF can be time-consuming and may be subject to overfitting [28].

### Decision Tree

Decision Tree (DT) is a tree-like structure comprising an internal node, root nodes and leaf nodes that form a hierarchy. The internal node stands for a test attribute, the test output is the branch, and the leaf node is a category [29, 30]. Decisions about an outcome variable are made in a hierarchical and sequential manner. Comparison of attributes is from the root to the leaves, and entropy assesses decisions at each internal node [27, 31]. Although the accuracy of prediction by DT may be affected by an overlap problem, its output is easy to visualise and interpret [28, 32].

### Naïve Bayes

Naïve Bayes (NB) uses Bayes rules, and it is based on conditional probability that assumes that all features are unrelated and independent of each other. For a given outcome variable, $Y$ and predictors, $X$, with realizations $y_i$ and $x_j$ respectively, the Bayes theorem is defined as:

$$(\forall i,j)P\left(Y=y_i \mid X=x_j\right)=\frac{P\left(X=x_j \mid Y=y_i\right)(P\left(Y=y_i\right)}{\Sigma_k P\left(X=x_j \mid Y=y_k\right)(P\left(Y=y_k\right)} \tag{1}$$

Naïve Bayes assumes conditional dependency between $X$ and $Y$, defined as:

$$P\left(X_1,\cdots,X_n \mid Y\right)=\prod_i P\left(X_i \mid Y\right) \tag{2}$$

Prediction on $Y$ is made based on the posterior distribution.

$$P\left(Y=y_k \mid X_1,\cdots,X_n\right)=\frac{P\left(Y=y_k\right)\Pi_i P\left(X_i \mid Y=y_k\right)}{\Sigma_j P\left(Y=y_j\right)\Pi_i P\left(X_i \mid Y=y_j\right)} \tag{3}$$

Decisions are made considering all possible information that reflects the way prognostic and diagnostic decisions are made by clinicians [33]. A posterior probability $P(Y = y_k| X_1, \cdots, X_n)$ of each class $y$ given an object $x$ is estimated from data after which further decisions are made based on the estimates. NB has been shown to be simple but computationally efficient, has low variance and is insensitive to noise and missing values in training data [34]. However, it is prone to skewed probabilities [28].

### Support-Vector Machine (SVM)

In this algorithm, datasets are represented as points with the number of features in a dimensional space and classes are separated by vectors. A hyperplane, which must be at the utmost of the margin, separates the datasets into various sorts. SVM achieves robustness when the hyperplane's margin is high and the distance between each class and the nearest data point is maximised. SVM has been applied in handwriting interpretation, text and facial recognition. It is ideal for detecting both linear and non-linear relationships in variables even for small datasets but not favourable for multi-class classification problems and large datasets [28]. The objective of SVM algorithm is to maximise the margin between the data points and the hyperplane (Fig. 5), using the hinge loss function [35]. For a given observed outcome and predictor variables, $y_i$ and $x_j$, respectively, a zero cost is observed when predicted

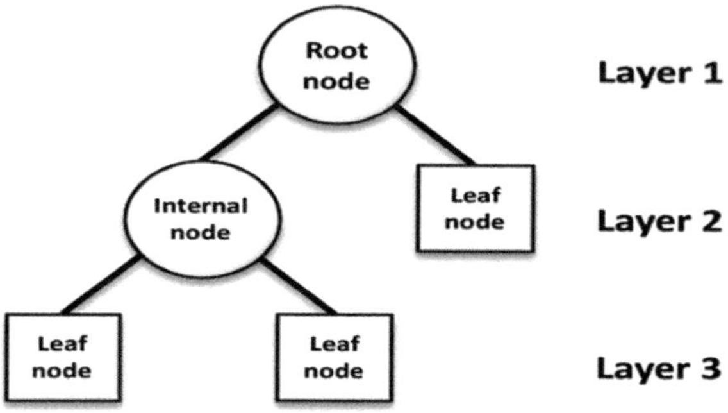


**Fig. 5** Illustration of the decision tree's basic structure with three distinct hierarchical layers

value and the actual value have the same sign, otherwise a loss value is calculated incorporating appropriate regularization parameter expressed as:

$$\min_{w} \lambda w^2 + \sum_{n}^{i=1} \left(1 - y_i x_i, w\right)_+ \tag{4}$$

where $w$ denotes the weights of the loss function. To find the gradient of the loss function, a partial derivative with respect to the weights is calculated, which can result in an iterative routine where the weights of our loss function can be updated as follows:

$$\frac{\delta}{\delta w_k} \lambda w^2 = 2\lambda w_k \tag{5}$$

$$\frac{\delta}{\delta w_k} \left(1 - y_i x_i, w\right)_+ = \left\{ \begin{array}{ll} 0, & \text{if } y_i x_i, w \geq 1 \\ -y_i x_{ik}, & \text{else} \end{array} \right. \tag{6}$$

If the model predicts the class of the data point correctly, the gradient is updated from the regularization parameter as follows:

$$w = w - \alpha \cdot (2\lambda w) \tag{7}$$

otherwise

$$w = w + \alpha \cdot (y_i \cdot x_i - 2\lambda w) \tag{8}$$

The illustration in Fig. 6 presents the pictorial representation of the optimization outcome of the SVM algorithm for data classification.

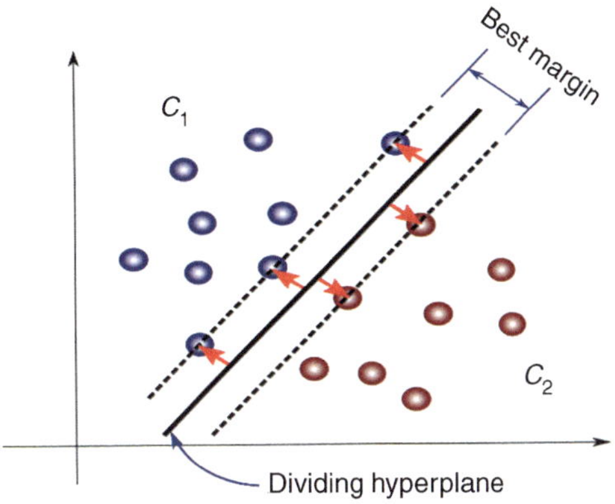


**Fig. 6** SVM classification on datapoints in high dimensional vector space

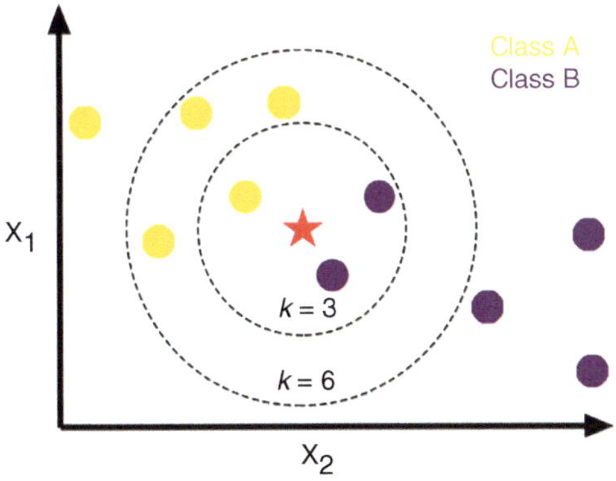


**Fig. 7** *K*-Nearest neighbour classification on datapoints

## *K*-Nearest Neighbour (KNN)

New objects are classified following data training and nearest neighbours to *K* forms the basis for classifying data. This is a memory-based classification that does not require a model [29]. Here, the minimum distance between the newly classified data and the *K*-nearest neighbours' Euclidean distance is calculated as follows:

$$d\left(x_i, x_j\right) = \sqrt{\left(x_{i1} - x_{j1}\right)^2 + \left(x_{i2} - x_{j2}\right)^2 + \ldots + \left(x_{ip} - x_{jp}\right)^2}. \tag{9}$$

The number of *k*-nearest neighbours obtained is used to predict the new data. In mathematical terms, $x_i$ represents the input sample with $p$ features ($x_{i1}$, $x_{i2}$, …, $x_{ip}$), $n$ = total number of input samples ($i = 1, 2, \ldots, n$) and $p$ the total number of features ($j = 1, 2, \ldots, p$). Euclidean distance and hamming distance are used for continuous and binary data, respectively [36]. KNN is useful for outlier detection, but interpretation of the results and the determination of the *k* can be challenging [28] (Fig. 7).

Artificial Neural Network (ANN)

ANN is a computational algorithm or classification method that mirrors the structure and function of neuronal cells in the human brain [37]. Here, nodes replace the neurons in the brain and are interconnected by weights that are automatically calculated during the training phase. It is made up of three entities. Information to be processed is received at the input unit; the results are displayed in the output unit and the hidden unit is sandwiched between the input and the output units. The input–output mapping can be determined after the network is trained on the dataset [38, 39]. This is followed by fixing the connections between the neurons and the classification of the new data is determined by the network. The output is the sum of the product of all the input layers and their associated weights through an activation function. The activation function in neurons of the hidden layer is often the same for those in the output layer [38]. The advantages of ANN include the ease of detection of relationship between variables, ease of visualisation and can be applied for non-linear modelling. However, it can be time-consuming and prone to overfitting [28].

Given a set of inputs ($x_1.x_2$, $x_3$), output ($Y$) and the corresponding synaptic weights ($w_1$, $w_2$, $w_3$) as shown in Fig. 8, the outputs in the network, either to the hidden layer or to the output layer, is defined by the activation function. An activation function controls the amplitude of the output. For example, an acceptable range of output is

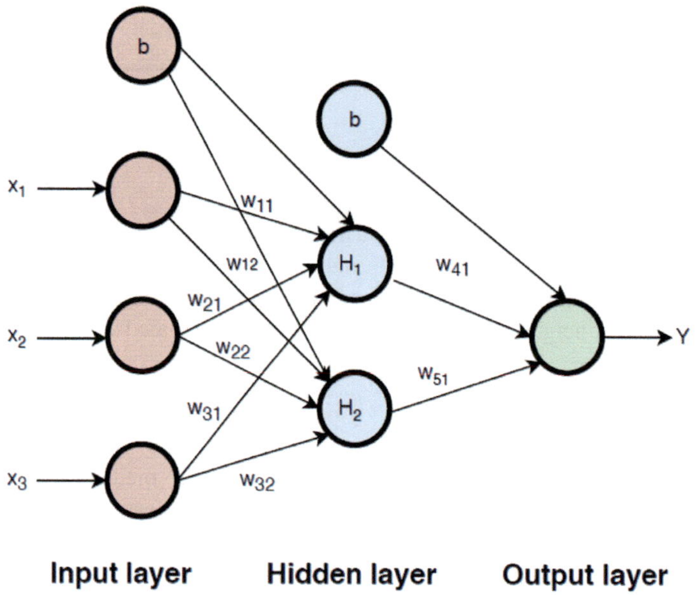


**Fig. 8** Structure of an ANN for classification of suboptimal health status. It shows a three-layered feed-forward ANN with the hidden layer connected to the output layer via a connection weight and the input layer connected to both by a connection weight

usually between 0 and 1, or it could be −1 and 1. To deduce the output, then mapping function of the input and output data is given in Eq. (10):

$$Y = f(x) \tag{10}$$

From Fig. 8, the output for the hidden functions, shown in Eq. (11), are simplified in Eqs. 12 and 13, where *b* is bias or error.

$$\text{Hidden layers}(H1, H2) = \begin{bmatrix} w_{11} & w_{21} & w_{31} \\ w_{12} & w_{22} & w_{32} \end{bmatrix} \times \begin{bmatrix} x_1 \\ x_2 \\ x_3 \end{bmatrix} \tag{11}$$

$$H_1 = x_1 \cdot w_{11} + x_2 \cdot w_{21} + x_3 \cdot w_{31} + b \tag{12}$$

$$H_2 = x_1 \cdot w_{12} + x_2 \cdot w_{22} + x_3 \cdot w_{32} + b \tag{13}$$

Sigmoid function (*S*) given in Eq. 14, where *x* is an input variable and *e* is a mathematical exponent:

$$S(x) = \frac{1}{1 + e^{-x}} \tag{14}$$

Applying sigmoid function to the hidden layers in Eqs. 12 and 13:

$$H_1 = S(x_1 \cdot w_{11} + x_2 \cdot w_{21} + \cdot w_{31} + b) \tag{15}$$

$$H_2 = S(x_1 \cdot w_{12} + x_2 \cdot w_{22} + x_3 \cdot w_{32} + b) \tag{16}$$

From the hidden to the output nodes, with feed-forward algorithm, the final output by using sigmoid function is given in Eq. 17:

$$Y(\text{output}) = S(H_1 \cdot w_{41} + H_2 \cdot w_{51} + b) \tag{17}$$

## 2.4 Evaluation of Supervised Learning Models

Building a reliable model with a supervised learning technique requires a robust ML algorithm. ML models are expected to predict unseen data with a high level of performance. Thus, there is the need for ML models to be evaluated thereby ascertaining their efficacy in predicting unseen data such as data from optimal health status and cardio-metabolic diseases. ML models with high predictive relevance and accuracy levels are suitable for predicting unseen data, especially when it is concerned with predicting disease. Researchers often build models with competing ML algorithms and use various performance measures to select the best model. In the subsequent subsections, we discuss some existing ML performance measures. To improve the performance of the model, ensemble techniques have been developed to boost the accuracy of the training dataset. The most widely used ensemble for ML are Boosting, Bagging and Majority voting. The commonly used matrices for evaluating machine learning algorithms include classification accuracy (including Recall, Precision, F-Measure and Confusion Matrix), area under ROC curve, logarithmic loss, confusion matrix and root mean square error.

### 2.4.1 Recall, Precision, F-Measure and Confusion Matrix

Recall, Precision and F-Measure are widely used for evaluating the performance of ML algorithms. Precision estimates the number of positive class predictions that belong to the positive class. In Eq. (18), TP is true positive, and FP is false positive.

$$\text{Recall} = \frac{\text{TP}}{\text{TP} + \text{FP}} \tag{18}$$

Recall quantifies the number of positive class predictions made from all positive examples in the dataset. It can also be described as the proportion of the data that an ML algorithm identifies. The Recall is represented in Eq. (19). In Eq. 19, TP is true positive, FN is false negative:

$$\text{Precision} = \frac{\text{TP}}{\text{TP} + \text{FN}} \tag{19}$$

*F*-Measure is the harmonic mean of the recall and F-measure. It is a representation of both the recall and Precision. Researchers often report and discuss the *F*-measure towards efficacy of machine learning algorithms because it offers the balance between the Precision and Recall.

$$F - \text{measure} = 2 \times \frac{\text{Precision} \times \text{Recall}}{\text{Precision} + \text{Recall}} \tag{20}$$

Confusion Matrix is a matrix that summarizes the prediction results of classification by taken. The results show the extent to which a classification model is confused. It gives insight not only into the errors being made by the classifier but more importantly the types of errors that are being made. Tables 2 and 3 are confusion matrices.

### 2.4.2 Receiver Operating Characteristics Curve (ROC)

Area under the curve-Receiver operating characteristics (AUC-ROC) is a graphical plot that illustrates the diagnostic ability of a binary classifier system as its discrimination threshold is varied. The curve serves as a performance indicator for

**Table 2** Confusion matrix showing a recall

| | | Predicted | |
|---|---|---|---|
| | | Negative | Positive |
| Actual | Negative | True Negative | False Positive |
| | Positive | False Negative | True Positive |

True Positive + False Positive = Total Predicted Positive

**Table 3** Confusion matrix showing precision

| | | Predicted | |
|---|---|---|---|
| | | Negative | Positive |
| Actual | Negative | True Negative | False Positive |
| | Positive | False Negative | True Positive |

True Positive + False Negative = Actual Positive

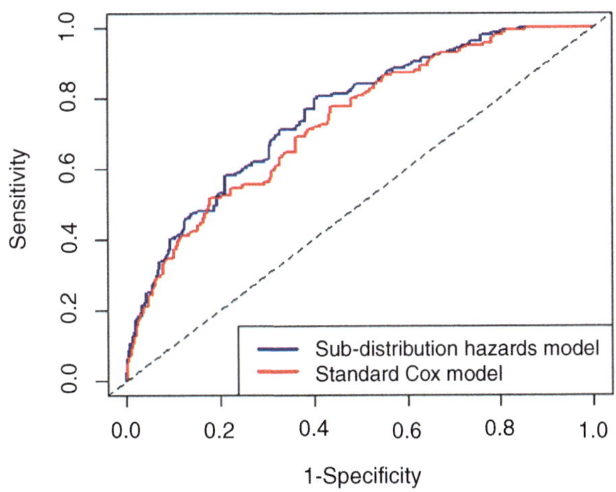


**Fig. 9** ROC curves for diabetes risk prediction model showing sub-distribution hazards model and Standard Cox model. A study conducted on competing risk-based score for predicting twenty-year risk of incident diabetes in Beijing based on a Longitudinal Study of Ageing study [40]

categorisation issues at different threshold levels. AUC highlights the degree or measurement of separability, and ROC is a probability curve. It indicates the degree of class distinction the model is capable of. The model's accuracy in classifying 0 as 0 and 1 as 1 increases with the AUC score. Accordingly, the higher the AUC, the better the model's ability to differentiate between diseased and healthy people. In AUC-ROC, true positive rate (sensitivity) is plotted against the false positive rate (specificity). Figure 9 is an example of AUC-ROC showing sub-distribution hazards model and Standard Cox model. As indicated on the graph, the sensitivity is plotted at the *y*-axis against the specificity at the *x*-axis.

## 3 Unravelling the Link Between Suboptimal Health and Chronic Diseases Using Machine Learning

SHSQ-25 questionnaire is a diagnostic algorithm, which comprises 25 items that multidimensionally capture health constructs of individuals from five health domains: immune system (3 items), mental health (7 items), fatigue (9 items), digestive system (3 items) and cardiovascular system (3 items) (Fig. 1). Participants rate how they feel in the previous 3 months by providing the following responses on a Likert type scale: (1) never or almost never, (2) occasionally, 3) often, (4) very often and (5) always. The discriminatory ability of the SHSQ-25 for diseased and non-diseased individuals has been reported for multiple chronic conditions [3, 4, 6, 8, 9, 14]. This screening is not only non-invasive, but it also provides a cheaper means of building a large database for an individual.

A lack of lifestyle modification of SHS may manifest as a life-threatening clinical condition in the future, with multiple studies already associating it with cardiometabolic diseases [3, 6], endothelial dysfunction [9], psychological stress [18] and digestive disorders [15]. Unfortunately, these studies have been cross-sectional, providing limited evidence to support the cause–effect relationships. Longitudinal studies will provide the opportunity for researchers to access big data that are scalable, and analysable to obtain more robust cause–effect outcomes that would inform effective and efficient practices. Thus far, the only study that has attempted to investigate the progression from SHS to a chronic disease was by Ge et al. [17]. In this study, authors analysed multiple clinical biomarkers and showed that SHS individuals developed T2DM in 3.1 years. Although the connection between SHS and T2DM was established, the period of investigation was short to concretise this link.

Serial SHS screening, conducted over an extended period will enable a comprehensive exploration of human health, while highlighting the interaction between multiple factors in disease progression. Indeed, each subscale of the SHSQ-25 represents an aspect of a person's health status, which could be explored in the disease continuum. For example, symptoms of fatigue may progress into myalgic encephalomyelitis/chronic fatigue syndrome, cardiovascular system domain may be indicative of heart diseases (e.g., cardiomyopathy, pericarditis, arrhythmia etc.), mental health complaints may indicate depression, schizophrenia, psychosis, complains in the digestion system can precede digestive disorders (gastroesophageal, reflux disease, ulcerative colitis amongst others) while immune system decline may result in coeliac disease, lupus, type 1 diabetes and rheumatoid arthritis. Each of these diseases are diagnosed based on the elevation or aberration of objective biomarkers (Fig. 10). When these biomarkers are matched with the responses on SHSQ-25, the path to and the pattern to developing chronic diseases can be revealed. This is where ML becomes valuable, as it can train models on database to understand patterns and relationships through a hierarchical learning process [22].

In ML applications, the SHS data observed longitudinally will enable the accurate generalisation of patterns for future unseen data. The diverse range of methods

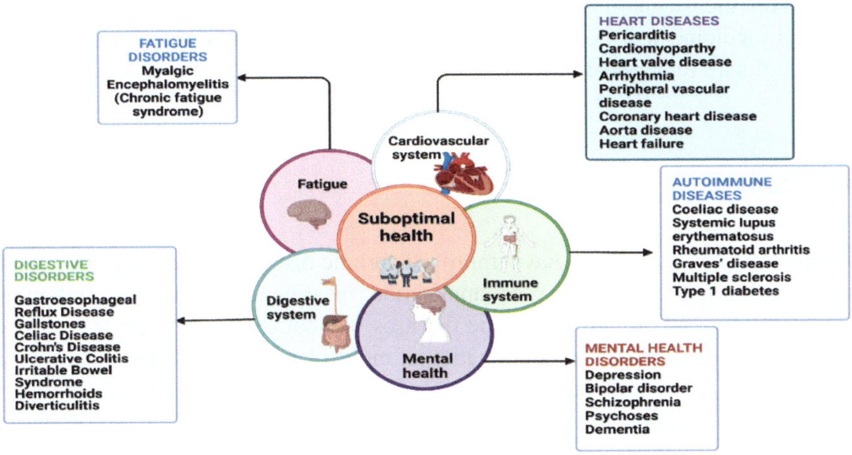


**Fig. 10** The association between SHSQ-25 domains and chronic disease development. Longitudinal and repeated screening with the SHSQ-25 can reveal how each subscale correlates with chronic diseases. Poor ratings in each of the domains can be indicative of future cardiovascular, immune system, digestive, fatigue and mental disorders

in ML underpins its broad applications in classification, clustering, regression, features, and neural networks, depending on the type of the data system. For example, for a given data obtained from the administration of the SHS questionnaire over time, ANN can be applied to stimulate the working function of the five thematic connections of the scale, to achieve a massive parallel distributed process [41] that predicts likely chronic conditions. The process of chronic disease development and progression can be explained by the activations flowing through networks that link together nodes. In this process, new events will lead to changes in the strength of connections among relevant units in the database, by altering the connection weights for the nodes. Consequently, units in the database developing different chronic conditions are likely to respond based on their experiences. Most ML algorithms have adaptive-learning and fault-tolerance capabilities, making them highly suitable for pattern recognition applications, which is fundamental in the diagnosis of chronic conditions.

The integration of ML in suboptimal health studies is vital in the pursuit of PPPM, as confirmed chronic diseases among population in the database over time can be traced to the responses provided for the domains of SHSQ-25. This will offer opportunities to establish robust thresholds for the domains and their alignment to known chronic conditions. The thresholds will become standardized benchmarks for highlighting predisposed domains of SHSQ-25, to inform targeted lifestyle changes and healthcare to prevent and/or effectively manage chronic diseases. Targeted personalised lifestyle changes, such as diet and exercise [40], stimulate varying molecular pathways that can greatly influence the functioning of the human body in building resistance against chronic diseases. For example, diet and regular exercise have been identified as key regulating risk factors for T2DM, and interventions targeting these behaviours can help to prevent or postpone this disease [42,

43]. With the standardized benchmarks for the domains of SHSQ-25, patient-centred medicine will be promoted, ultimately complementing, and reducing the burden of care in our healthcare systems and institutions.

## 4 Outlook

Data-driven ML algorithms have improved chronic disease prediction [44, 45], but there is limited evidence of its application in subclinical disease prediction. Recognition of SHS, before chronic diseases, is another area in that ML can be leveraged. It can enable the identification of molecular intricacies that underpin the link between suboptimal health and metabolic disease. ML develops models from a dataset, cross-validate, test, and evaluate the models and detect the best correlative or associative features. Thus, ML can optimise the accuracy of predictive models for suboptimal health. The application of ML approaches on longitudinal data will be more valuable in the prediction of chronic diseases compared to approaches that rely on conventional risk factors and cross-sectional data [46]. Over time, confirmed chronic diseases among population in the database can be linked to the responses to the domains of SHSQ-25. This will provide opportunities to establish robust thresholds for the domains and their alignment to known chronic conditions.

ML learning encompasses supervised learning, semi-supervised learning, unsupervised learning, and reinforcement learning. These areas have attracted diverse interest depending on the type of knowledge and data within the health ecosystem. While we aim to explore all these areas in the health ecosystem in the future, this study only focused on the application of supervised learning in disease detection. We envision that this study will provide the needed foundation for practitioners who aim to establish the association between SHS and cardio-metabolic diseases.

## 5 Conclusion

One could argue that modern society takes medical knowledge and technological progress for granted. In this chapter, several ML algorithms including random forest, Naïve Bayes, *k*-neural network, and support vector machine have been discussed. ML can make it easier to analyse data of individuals and discover disease patterns that would support early detection of chronic diseases. In the context of PPPM, ML can pinpoint the intricate molecular processes that underlie the connection between poor health and cardiometabolic diseases, enabling accurate precision to be brought to medicine.

**Author Contributions** EA[1,2], EA-Y[3] and EA[4] conceived the study and wrote the manuscript. All authors edited the ideas and concepts presented. All authors read and approved the final manuscript.

**Competing Interests** Authors have no competing interest to declare.

## References

1. Russell A, Adua E, Ugrina I, Laws S, Wang W (2018) Unravelling immunoglobulin G Fc N-glycosylation: a dynamic marker potentiating predictive, preventive and personalised medicine. Int J Mol Sci 19(2):390
2. Wang W, Yan Y (2012) Suboptimal health: a new health dimension for translational medicine. Clin Transl Med 1(1):e28
3. Adua E, Roberts P, Wang W (2017) Incorporation of suboptimal health status as a potential risk assessment for type II diabetes mellitus: a case-control study in a Ghanaian population. EPMA J 8(4):345–355
4. Adua E, Afrifa-Yamoah E, Frimpong K, Adama E, Karthigesu SP, Anto EO, Aboagye E, Yan Y, Wang Y, Tan X, Wang W (2021) Construct validity of the suboptimal health status questionnaire-25 in a Ghanaian population. Health Qual Life Outcomes 19, 180
5. Yan YX, Dong J, Liu YQ, Yang XH, Li M, Shia G, Wang W (2012) Association of suboptimal health status and cardiovascular risk factors in urban Chinese workers. J Urban Health 89(2):329–338
6. Adua E, Memarian E, Russell A, Trbojević-Akmačić I, Gudelj I, Jurić J, Roberts P, Lauc G, Wang W (2019) Utilization of Nglycosylation profiles as risk stratification biomarkers for suboptimal health status and metabolic syndrome in a Ghanaian population. Biomark Med 13(15):1273–1287
7. Adua E, Roberts P, Sakyi SA, Yeboah FA, Dompreh A, Frimpong K, Anto EO, Wang W (2017) Profiling of cardio-metabolic risk factors and medication utilisation among type II diabetes patients in Ghana: a prospective cohort study. Clin Transl Med 6(1):32
8. Anto EO, Roberts P, Coall D, Turpin CA, Adua E, Wang Y, Wang W (2019) Integration of suboptimal health status evaluation as a criterion for prediction of preeclampsia is strongly recommended for healthcare management in pregnancy: a prospective cohort study in a Ghanaian population. EPMA J 10(3):211–226
9. Kupaev V, Borisov O, Marutina E, Yan YX, Wang W (2016) Integration of suboptimal health status and endothelial dysfunction as a new aspect for risk evaluation of cardiovascular disease. EPMA J 7(1):1–7
10. Mogaka JJ, James SE, Chimbari MJ (2020) Leveraging implementation science to improve implementation outcomes in precision medicine. Am J Transl Res 12(9):4853–4872
11. Wang Y, Liu X, Qiu J, Wang H, Liu D, Zhao Z, Song M, Song Q, Wang X, Zhou Y, Wang W (2017) Association between ideal cardiovascular health metrics and suboptimal health status in Chinese population. Sci Rep 7(1):14975
12. Zhu J, Ying W, Zhang L, Peng G, Chen W, Anto EO, Wang X, Lu N, Gao S, Wu G, Yan J, Ye J, Wu S, Yu C, Yue M, Huang X, Xu N, Ying P, Chen Y, Tan X, Wang W (2020) Psychological symptoms in Chinese nurses may be associated with predisposition to chronic disease: a cross-sectional study of suboptimal health status. EPMA J 11(4):551–563
13. Hou H, Feng X, Li Y, Meng Z, Guo D, Wang F, Guo Z, Zheng Y, Peng Z, Zhang W, Li D, Ding G, Wang W (2018) Suboptimal 1,2 3 4 health status and psychological symptoms among Chinese college students: a perspective of predictive, preventive and personalised health. EPMA J 9(4):367–377
14. Anto EO, Roberts P, Coall DA, Adua E, Turpin CA, Tawiah A, Wang Y, Wang W (2020) Suboptimal health pregnant women are associated with increased oxidative stress and unbalanced pro-and antiangiogenic growth mediators: a cross-sectional study in a Ghanaian population. Free Radic Res 54(1):27–42
15. Sun Q, Xu X, Zhang J, Sun M, Tian Q, Li Q, Cao W, Zhang X, Wang H, Liu J, Zhang J, Meng X, Wu L, Song M, Liu H, Wang W, Wang Y (2020) Association of suboptimal health status with intestinal microbiota in Chinese youths. J Cell Mol Med 24(2):1837–1847
16. Libbrecht MW, Noble WS (2015) Machine learning applications in genetics and genomics. Nat Rev Genet 16(6):321–332

17. Ge S, Xu X, Zhang J, Hou H, Wang H, Liu D, Zhang X, Song M, Li D, Zhou Y, Wang Y, Wang W (2019) Suboptimal health status as an independent risk factor for type 2 diabetes mellitus in a community-based cohort: the China suboptimal health cohort study. EPMA J 10(1):65–72
18. Yan Y-X, Dong J, Liu YQ, Zhang J, Song MS, He Y, Wang W (2015) Association of suboptimal health status with psychosocial stress, plasma cortisol and mRNA expression of glucocorticoid receptor α/β in lymphocyte. Stress 18(1):29–34
19. Leclercq M, Vittrant B, Martin-Magniette ML, Scott Boyer MP, Perin O, Bergeron A, Fradet Y and Droit A (2019) Large-scale automatic feature selection for biomarker discovery in high-dimensional OMICs data. Front Genet 10:452
20. Wang Y, Adua E, Russell AC, Roberts P, Ge S, Zeng Q, Wang W (2016) Glycomics and its application potential in precision medicine. American Association for the Advancement of Science
21. Adua E, Memarian E, Russell A, Trbojević-Akmačić I, Gudelj I, Jurić J, Roberts P, Lauc G, Wang W (2019) High throughput profiling of whole plasma N-glycans in type II diabetes mellitus patients and healthy individuals: a perspective from a Ghanaian population. Arch Biochem Biophys 661:10–21
22. Najafabadi MM, Villanustre F, Khoshgoftaar TM, Seliya N, Wald R, Muharemagic E (2015) Deep learning applications and challenges in big data analytics. J Big Data 2(1):1–21
23. Adua E, Kolog EA, Afrifa-Yamoah E, Amankwah B, Obirikorang C, Anto EO, Acheampong E, Wang W, Tetteh AY (2021) Predictive model and feature importance for early detection of type II diabetes mellitus. Transl Med Commun 6(1):17
24. Buskirk TD, Kirchner A, Eck A, Signorino CS (2018) An introduction to machine learning methods for survey researchers. Surv Pract 11(1):1–10
25. Kuhn M, Johnson K (2013) Applied predictive modeling in RR. Springer, New York
26. Machado G, Mendoza MR, Corbellini LG (2015) What variables are important in predicting bovine viral diarrhea virus? A random forest approach. Vet Res 46(1):1–15
27. Yu C-S, Lin YJ, Lin CH, Wang ST, Lin SY, Lin SH, Wu JL, Chang SS (2020) Predicting metabolic syndrome with machine learning models using a decision tree algorithm: retrospective cohort study. JMIR Med Inform 8(3):e17110
28. Krittanawong C, Virk HUH, Bangalore S, Wang Z, Johnson KW, Pinotti R, Zhang H, Kaplin S, Narasimhan B, Kitai T, Baber U, Halperin JL, Tang WHW (2020) Machine learning prediction in cardiovascular diseases: a meta-analysis. Sci Rep 10(1):1–11
29. Zhang L, Wang Y, Niu M, Wang C, Wang Z (2020) Machine learning for characterizing risk of type 2 diabetes mellitus in a rural Chinese population: the Henan rural cohort study. Sci Rep 10(1):1–10
30. Kolog EA, Montero CS, Toivonen T (2018) Using machine learning for sentiment and social influence analysis in text. In International Conference on Information Technology & Systems. Springer
31. Chiu M-H, Yu Y-R, Liaw HL, Chun-Hao L (2016) The use of facial micro-expression state and Tree-Forest Model for predicting conceptual-conflict based conceptual change. In Jari Lavonen, Kalle Juuti, Jarkko Lampiselkä, Anna Uitto & Kaisa Hahl (Eds.). Science Education Research: Engaging learners for a sustainable future (ESERA eproceeding, ISBN 978-951-51-1541-6)
32. Tang Z, Bo L, Liu X, Wei D (2021) An autoencoder with adaptive transfer learning for intelligent fault diagnosis of rotating machinery. Meas Sci Technol 32(5):055110
33. Choe EK, Rhee H, Lee S, Shin E, Oh SW, Lee JE, Choi SH (2018) Metabolic syndrome prediction using machine learning models with genetic and clinical information from a nonobese healthy population. Genomics Inform 16(4):e31
34. Webb GI, Keogh E, Miikkulainen R (2010) Naïve Bayes. Encyclopedia Mach Learn 15:713–714
35. Bishop CM (2006) Pattern recognition. Mach Learn 128:9
36. Altman NS (1992) An introduction to kernel and nearest-neighbor nonparametric regression. Am Stat 46(3):175–185
37. Kavakiotis I, Tsave O, Salifoglou A, Maglaveras N, Vlahavas I, Chouvarda I (2017) Machine learning and data mining methods in diabetes research. Comput Struct Biotechnol J 15:104–116

38. Zhang Z, Beck MW, Winkler DA, Huang B, Sibanda W, Goyal H; written on behalf of AME Big-Data (2018) Opening the black box of neural networks: methods for interpreting neural network models in clinical applications. Ann Transl Med 6(11):216
39. Mehdy MM, Ng PY, Shair EF, Saleh NIM, Gomes C (2017) Artificial neural networks in image processing for early detection of breast cancer. Comput Math Methods Med 2017:1–15
40. Du Vaure CB, Dechartres A, Battin C, Ravaud P, Boutron I (2016) Exclusion of patients with concomitant chronic conditions in ongoing randomized controlled trials targeting 10 common chronic conditions and registered at ClinicalTrials.gov: a systematic review of registration details. BMJ Open 6(9):e012265
41. Afrifa-Yamoah E, Adua E, Anto EO, Peprah-Yamoah E, Opoku-Yamoah V, Aboagye E, Hashmi R. (2023) Conceptualised psychomedical footprint for health status outcomes and the potential impacts for early detection and prevention of chronic diseases in the context of 3P medicine. EPMA J. 10.1007/s13167-023-00344-2
42. Roumen C, Corpeleijn E, Feskens EJ, Mensink M, Saris WH, Blaak EE et al (2008) Impact of 3-year lifestyle intervention on postprandial glucose metabolism: the SLIM study. Diabet Med 25(5):597–605
43. Vlaar EM, Nierkens V, Nicolaou M, Middelkoop BJC, Busschers WB, Stronks K, van Valkengoed IGM (2017) Effectiveness of a targeted lifestyle intervention in primary care on diet and physical activity among south Asians at risk for diabetes: 2-year results of a randomised controlled trial in The Netherlands. BMJ Open 7(6):e012221
44. Sarker IH (2021) Machine learning: algorithms, real-world applications and research directions. SN Comput Sci 2(3):1–21
45. Weng SF, Reps J, Kai J, Garibaldi JM, Qureshi N (2017) Can machine-learning improve cardiovascular risk prediction using routine clinical data? PLoS One 12(4):e0174944
46. Zhao J, Feng Q, Wu P, Lupu RA, Wilke RA, Wells QS, Denny JC, Wei WQ (2019) Learning from longitudinal data in electronic health record and genetic data to improve cardiovascular event prediction. Sci Rep 9(1):717

# Integrative Approach to Investigate Suboptimal Health Status and Endothelial Dysfunction

**Vitalii Kupaev, Madina Zhalbinova, and Wei Zhang**

## Abbreviations

| | |
|---|---|
| BMI | Body mass index |
| DBP | Diastolic blood pressure |
| ET-1 | Enddothelin-1 |
| GLU | Plasma glucose |
| IEF | Index of the endothelial function |
| IR | Index of reflection at the baseline |
| IR2 | Index of reflection of the second measure |
| IS | Stiffness index at the baseline |
| IS2 | Stiffness index of the second measure |
| NO | Nitric oxide |
| PPPM/3 PM | Predictive, preventive, and personalised medicine |
| SBP | Systolic blood pressure |
| SHS | Suboptimal health status |
| SHSQ-25 | Suboptimal health status-25 questionnaire |
| TCH | Total cholesterol |

V. Kupaev
Samara State Medical University, Russian Federation, Samara, Russia
e-mail: vk1964sam@rambler.ru

M. Zhalbinova
National Laboratory Astana, Nazarbayev University, Astana, Kazakhstan
e-mail: madina.zhalbinova@nu.edu.kz

W. Zhang (✉)
Department of Neurology, Beijing Tiantan Hospital, Centre for Cognitive Neurology, Capital Medical University, Beijing, China



W. Wang (ed.), *All Around Suboptimal Health*, Advances in Predictive, Preventive and Personalised Medicine 18,
https://doi.org/10.1007/978-3-031-46891-9_10

# 1 Introduction

There have been many significant changes occurred in Russia in the past decades. The rapid economic growth and socio-demographic changes caused the increased risk for people to suffer from chronic diseases with increased morbidity and mortality [1]. The early detection of cardiovascular diseases at their preclinical status is one of the important parts in the promotion of the essential medical services at the primary healthcare setting. There has been a demand in screening the risks of the development of the chronic diseases, which should be cost-effective and time-efficient. For instance, the SHSQ-25 is a tool designed for screening the early stages of chronic diseases [2]. Initially, this method was developed and validated in a Chinese population [2]. SHSQ-25 gives a new opportunity for primary health workers to identify the risk factors that are associated with cardiovascular diseases [3].

SHS is characterised by the feelings of health complaints, chronic fatigue and complex of physical symptoms and lack of strength, a preclinical illness stage [3]. The previous studies showed that SHS has a significant contribution to the identification of the progression or development of the chronic disease among the people who have continued exposure to the risk factors [4]. The linear relationship between SHS and cardiovascular risk factors, as well as a decrease of cholesterol shows clear association of SHS with cardiovascular health [3].

The intervention of the pathological processes in patients with cardiovascular diseases is related to the assessment of their endothelium function. Endothelial dysfunction and vascular stiffness are the integral indicators, reflecting the structural function of vascular wall and blood pressure [5–7].

## *1.1 Endothelial Dysfunction*

### 1.1.1 Current View of the Endothelial Dysfunction

The vascular endothelium carries on many important functions as it is an active receptor-effector organ with a dynamic structure. It releases substances during exposure to a chemical or physical stimulus. In normal case, vascular endothelium maintains vascular-tissue homeostasis and vasomotor balance [8–10].

Endothelial dysfunction could be considered as an imbalance between the production of the prothrombotic, vasoconstrictive and proliferative endothelial factors. The loss of homeostasis of angioprotective, antiproliferative and vasodilating factors occurs during endothelial dysfunction [11]. Progression of the vascular lesions is caused by the imbalance between vasoconstrictors and vasodilators, which forms vasospasm [12]. Thus, the endothelium is a selective barrier for the various substances that penetrate from the bloodstream into tissues. This is a central link in the regulation of vasomotor tone [13].

The most damaging element in the endothelium is the endothelial factor known as nitric oxide (NO). The basal release of NO from the vascular endothelium reduces the tone of the muscular arteries and the resistant vasculature [14]. NO is responsible for the vasodilative effect of the relaxing factor, which is secreted by the endothelium. A number of aminopeptidases and endothelins are produced when the vascular endothelium is damaged. Investigations show that the vasodilative effect of NO counteracts the vasoconstrictor effect of endothelins [15, 16].

Endothelins are a family of the biologically active peptides with a wide spectrum of the effects. They are one of the most important regulators of the functional conditions of the endothelium. Violations in systemic and regional hemodynamics are observed as a result of their vasoconstrictor action. Endothelin-1 is currently considered as a biomarker for assessing the severity of the coronary heart disease. The normal concentration of endothelin-1 in the healthy human blood plasma is 0.1–1 fmol/mL or undetectable at all. The half-life of the endothelin-1 is not more than 4–7 min. There are about 80–90% of the endothelin-1 inactivated during their passage through the lungs' blood vessels. It revealed that the level of endothelin-1 in the blood plasma is significantly higher in individuals at the initial stage of hypertension compared to healthy individuals [17]. Based on this, it is evident that endothelins play a role in the pathogenesis of cardiovascular disease during the early stages. Endothelial dysfunction is considered the primary triggering mechanism in the development of cardiovascular pathology [18, 19].

### 1.1.2 New Methods of Determination of Endothelial Dysfunction

Currently, mechanical properties of the arteries are being actively studied due to their high clinical and prognostic significance. Extensibility, compliance and rigidity are important determinants of the elastic properties of the vascular wall. Elongation is determined by the ratio of the compliance to the initial volume of the artery. Arterial stiffness is the value reciprocal to the tensile.

Non-invasive methods are widely recommended, for example, ultrasound examination of the vascular wall, magnetic resonance imaging, the method of volumetric sphygmography with the determination of PWV in the area from the brachial artery to the ankle, rheovasography of the forearm and laser Doppler flowmetry.

One of the most accessible methods for the determination of vascular stiffness is the method of computer photoplethysmography that estimates the shape of the peripheral pulse wave [20]. Registration of the peripheral pulse wave is based on the passage of the infrared radiation through the finger vessels. The amount of the light is directly proportional to the volume of the blood pulsing in the finger. The pulse curve is recorded by photoplethysmography, which consists of two components: a direct wave that goes to the periphery and a vessel wave. Reflection index and stiffness index are determined. A clear parameter that measures vascular tone and allows assessing vascular endothelial function, calculated as the ratio of the amplitude of the diastolic and systolic peaks, is the reflection index (RI). Investigations revealed a correlation between the RI and vascular tone (diameter of the large vessels) [21].

In addition, the stiffness index (IS) is a measurement that associates with the pulse wave speed (in seconds). Furthermore, the index of the endothelial function (IEF) is the index value that reflects changes during reactive hyperemia at the third minute of the post-occlusive blood flow (RI-3 min) in comparison to the pre-test baseline measure. It is defined as the ratio of growth to the pulse wave's spread time from the lower part of the body to the finger. The advantage of the computed photoplethysmography is the availability of the method as the pulse wave of the finger could be obtained very easily. This fact makes possible the usage of this method in real-world population-based epidemiological health surveys.

The results were compared with the flow on the other arm. Furthermore, the following parameters of the photoplethysmogram were analysed: reflection index, stiffness index (IS) and the index of the endothelial function (IEF).

# 2 Comparison of the Correlation Between Vascular Endothelial Function Parameters with Indicators of Suboptimal Health Status and the Factors of Cardiovascular Risk

## *2.1 Investigation of Suboptimal Health Status in a Russian Population*

The cross-sectional study was performed on 459 patients. Most of them were Russian residents aged 18–40 years (34.01 ± 14.; male 41.4%). Participants had no diseases and any prescribed treatments within the last 2 weeks. The study was conducted in the health centers at the medical clinics in Samara city with a population of more than one million. We used SHSQ-25 to assess SHS, along with family history, sedentary lifestyle, smoking, alcohol consumption and unhealthy diet. Specially trained doctors examined participants to ensure quality control of results. The study was approved by the scientific and ethical committees of Samara State Medical University and the medical institution of Samara region of the Russian Federation.

The arterial blood pressure was measured three times using standard methods. The average of the second and third measurements was used to estimate the systolic blood pressure (SBP) and diastolic blood pressure (DBP). Venous blood samples were obtained from the overnight fasting for the measurement of the plasma glucose and serum lipids. Plasma glucose, high-density lipoprotein, cholesterol, low-density lipoprotein (LDL) cholesterol, and triglycerides were measured using the enzyme-linked immunosorbent assay (ELISA), a commonly employed analytical biochemistry technique ("Biomedica," Austria). During the interview, our specialists measured the body weight and height of the participants two times.

Indicators of the arterial stiffness and endothelial dysfunction were determined using the standard method of the shoulder plethysmography technique "Eldar" [22].

The index of endothelial function (IEF) was determined in two stages, before and after the reactive hyperemia test. By occlusion of the brachial artery, reactive hyperemia was created. For occlusion, a cuff was used to measure blood pressure, which was applied at the level of the upper third of the shoulder, where pressure was gained above the systolic pressure by 30 mm Hg. This pressure was maintained for 5 min and then quickly vented. Then, a photoplethysmogram was recorded and analysed at the third minute of post-occlusive blood flow.

We used the SHSQ-25 for measurement of the SHS [2]. The SHS score was calculated for each participant by summarising the 25-item scores. The high score represented a high level of SHS (poor health). The total score of more than 35 points indicates a suboptimal condition that requires more examination according to five scales [23, 24].

## 2.2 *Statistical Analysis*

Continues variables were reported as mean ± standard deviation. Categorical variables were presented as frequency. Participants were divided into two groups: Group 1—healthy ($n = 295$), and Group 2—participants with risk factors of cardiovascular diseases ($n = 164$). Participants of Group 2 were with higher levels of blood pressure (>140/90 mmHg), glucose (>6.1 mmol/L), lipids (TCP > 5 mmol/L) and BMI (>24.5 kg/m$^2$). The difference of the SHSQ-25 scores between the two groups was performed by Student's $t$-test. According to the Pearson's correlation analysis and linear regression analysis, the relationship between SHS and endothelial dysfunction was identified by using the score of the SHSQ as dependent and endothelial dysfunction as independent. Cluster analysis was carried out to identify systemic patterns resulting from exposure to various risk factors. Subjects were identified as separate local subsets (clusters), according to the grouping attributes with k-means clustering. The statistical analysis was performed in SPSS program version 10.0.

## 2.3 *Results*

All participants completed a questionnaire, along with laboratory and instrumental measurements. Their mean age was 34.01 ± 14.10 years (males = 41.4%). The cardiovascular risk group was dominated by men (51.2%), older age (74.4% against) and labour workers (51.83%) (Table 1).

Although there was no statistically significant difference in the incidences of individuals with suboptimal health status between the healthy and cardiovascular risk groups (7.8% vs. 8.8%, $p > 0.05$), the SHSQ-25 scores showed differences between the two groups on three SHS subscales: (1) fatigue, (2) cardiovascular and 3) immune ($p < 0.05$). The largest discrepancy was concentrated in the cardiovascular and fatigue subscales. The average score of the cardiovascular system according

**Table 1** Characteristics of the studied groups

| Variables | Group 1 $n = 295$ | Group 2 $n = 164$ | $\chi^2$ | $P$ |
|---|---|---|---|---|
| Gender | | | | |
| Male | 106 (35.9%) | 84 (51.2%) | 10.15 | <0.01 |
| Female | 189 (64.1%) | 80 (48.8%) | | |
| Age | | | | |
| 18–40 years | 256 (86.8%) | 42 (25.6%) | 173.19 | <0.01 |
| 41–60 years | 39 (13.2%) | 122 (74.4%) | | |
| Occupation | | | | |
| Labour workers | 28 (8.5%) | 86 (51.83%) | | |
| Office workers | 267 (90.5%) | 79 (48.17%) | 103.16 | <0.01 |
| Suboptimal health status | 23 (7.8%) | 14 (8.8%) | 0.029 | >0.05 |

Note: *Group 1* healthy group, *Group 2* cardiovascular risk group

**Table 2** Comparison of the cardiovascular risk factors between the healthy and cardiovascular risk groups

| Variables | Group 1 | Group 2 | $t$ | $P$ |
|---|---|---|---|---|
| BMI (kg/m$^2$) | 22.1 ± 4.2 | 28.55 ± 5.0 | 14.12 | <0.001 |
| Index smoker | 1.66 ± 10.2 | 7.9 ± 15.5 | 4.801 | <0.001 |
| SBP (mmHg) | 111.73 ± 12.7 | 129.5 ± 11.9 | 13.611 | <0.001 |
| DBP (mmHg) | 73.86 ± 8.2 | 80.86 ± 8.3 | 8.803 | <0.001 |
| GLU (mmol/L) | 4.03 ± 0.86 | 4.67 ± 0.96 | 6.403 | <0.001 |
| TCH (mmol/L) | 4.28 ± 0.8 | 5.6 ± 0.96 | 6.441 | <0.001 |
| TG (mmol/L) | 1.11 ± 0.57 | 1.56 ± 0.87 | 2.801 | 0.010 |
| LDL (mmol/L) | 2.85 ± 0.17 | 3.01 ± 0.37 | 2.562 | 0.006 |
| Endothelin-1, (fmol/L) | 2.3 ± 2.2 | 6.1 ± 5.42 | 3.3 | <0.01 |

Note: Continuous variables are presented as mean ± SD; The statistical significance: $p < 0.05$
Abbreviations: *Group 1* healthy group, *Group 2* cardiovascular risk group, *BMI* body mass index, *SBP* systolic blood pressure, *DBP* diastolic blood pressure, *GLU* plasma glucose, *TCH* total cholesterol, *TG* triglyceride, *LDLC* low-density lipoprotein cholesterol

to the scale was 1.95 ± 1.81 in patients with cardiovascular risk, which is significantly higher than that in the control group ($p < 0.001$).

The group with risk factors for cardiovascular disease is presented in Table 2. Group 2 with cardiovascular risk had significantly higher levels of BMI, smoker index, SBP, DBP, GLU, TCH, TG, LDL and endothelin-1 ($p < 0.01$).

The method of computer photoplethysmography was used for assessment of the endothelial function. The higher the index of endothelial function (IEF), the less the exhibition of endothelial dysfunction. The endothelial function parameters are presented in Table 3.

Some important differences were revealed according to the index of the endothelial function by age: for people 41–50 years old, the index of endothelial function –(IEF) value was 9.4 ± 9.3%; for over 50 years old, IEF value was 6.4 ± 9.0% which were significantly lower than in people aged 18–40 years who had

**Table 3** Index of endothelial function

| Characteristics | IEF (%) | *t* | *P* |
|---|---|---|---|
| 18–40 years | 16.5 ± 8.4 | 4.97 | 0.0001 |
| 41–60 years | 9.4 ± 9.3 | | |
| Males | 14.3 ± 9.7 | 0.15 | 0.88 |
| Females | 14.5 ± 9.2 | | |
| Smokers | 6.4 ± 8.1 | −6.4 | <0.0001 |
| Non-smokers | 15.1 ± 9.9 | | |
| Office workers | 16.4 ± 9.5 | −2.17 | 0.03 |
| Labour workers | 12.0 ± 9.0 | | |
| BMI < 25 | 16.6 ± 8.6 | 8.19 | <0.0001 |
| BMI ≥ 25 | 7.8 ± 9.6 | | |

Note: Continuous variables are presented as mean ± SD; Significant *p* value: <0.05
Abbreviations: *BMI* body mass index

**Table 4** Index of endothelial function in comparison groups

| Groups | IEF (%) | IR (%) | IR-2 2 (%) | IS (m/s) | IS-2 m/s |
|---|---|---|---|---|---|
| Group 1- SHS < 14, *n* = 181 | 16.4 ± 8.6 | 68.1 ± 12.2 | 59.1 ± 11.3 | 11.3 ± 4.3 | 8.2 ± 4.1 |
| Group 2- SHS ≥ 14, *n* = 146 | 6.6 ± 10.5 | 71.8 ± 12.4 | 63.3 ± 10.7 | 12.3 ± 8 | 9.3 ± 3.3 |
| *P* | <0.0001 | 0.01 | 0.001 | 0.22 | 0.01 |

Notes: *IEF* index of endothelial function, *IR* index of reflection at the baseline, *IR2* index of reflection of the second measure, *IS* stiffness index at the baseline, *IS2* stiffness index of the second measure

IEF value at 16.5 ± 8.4%, $p = 0.0001$. IEF value was significantly higher in the office workers than that in the labour workers (16.4 ± 9.5% vs. 12.0 ± 9.0%, $p = 0.03$); while IEF value was significantly lower in the individuals with overweight than that in the individuals with normal body weight who had higher IEF value (7.8 ± 9.6% vs. 16.6 ± 8.6%, $p < 0.0001$).

In our investigation, we also identified a significant difference of IEF value ($r = -0.43$, $p < 0.05$), between smokers and non-smokers. IEF value was significantly higher in the non-smoker individuals than that in the smokers (15.1 ± 9.9% vs. 6.4 ± 8.1%, $p < 0.0001$). An inverse relationship was also found with the level of blood pressure ($r = -0.44$, $p < 0.05$) and total cholesterol ($r = -0.23$, $p < 0.05$).

The comparison groups that were divided according to the average score of SHS had significant differences of characteristics such as: IEF (Group 1, 16.4 ± 8.6%; Group 2, 6.6 ± 10.5%, $p < 0.0001$), index reflections outgoing (IR) (Group 1, 68.1 ± 12.2%, Group 2, 71.7 ± 12.4%; $p < 0.01$), IR after the test (IR2) (Group 1, 59.1 ± 11.3%; Group 2, 63.3 ± 10.7%, $p < 0.001$) and stiffness index after the test (SI 2) (Group 1, 8.2 ± 4.1 m/s; Group 2, 9.3 ± 3.3 m/s, $p = 0.01$) (Table 4). This indicated higher vascular tone and stiffness in individuals with suboptimal health status.

Furthermore, we studied the indicators of endothelial function in participants as we divided them for comparison into two groups according to their average score of

SHS. There were significant differences in the group of participants with SHS score > 14 on IEF, reflection of index outgoing before the sample (IR 1) and after the sample (IR 2), and index of stiffness after the sample (S 2) (Table 4). This indicates higher vascular tone and stiffness in participants with higher suboptimal health status score.

## 2.4 Discussion

Our research confirmed about the importance of the measurement of the wall stiffness by using photoplethysmography assessment. Thus, our investigation revealed a significant correlation between the index of endothelial function and general indicators of the suboptimal health status (SHS) (Table 5).

Changes in the lipid level affect the state of the vascular wall of the endothelium. We assessed vascular wall health using photoplethysmography to measure the IEF. Among the variables, SHS score and IEF value ($p = 0.0001$) and also age ($p = 0.013$) showed a significant association, respectively, by linear regression analysis respectively (Table 5).

The endothelin-1 index had a significant connection with index of endothelial function ($r = -0.72$, $p < 0.05$), SHS-total ($r = 0.62$, $p < 0.05$), with an indicator of sub-optimal status by scale "cardiovascular system" ($r = 0.79$, $p < 0.05$). Association of suboptimal health status with endothelin-1 index ($r = 0.62$, $p < 0.05$) once again provided a potential sensitivity method for assessing suboptimal health status tests for predicting the risk of cardiovascular diseases.

We further examined the integral relationship between endothelial dysfunction scores and CVD risk factors according to the correlation analysis between endothelial dysfunction and SHSQ-25 scores. A multivariate statistical analysis of the following parameters was used: " the total score of SHSQ-25, the respective subscale scores of the SHSQ-25 (fatigue, mental state, cardiovascular system, digestive system, immune system"), smoker index, BMI, SBP, DBP and endothelial function

**Table 5** The results of the regression analysis (dependent variable SHSQ-25 total score)

| | Unstandardised coefficients | | Standardised coefficients | | |
|---|---|---|---|---|---|
| Variables | Beta | Std. error | Beta | *t* | *P* |
| Age | −0.132 | 0.053 | −0.209 | −2.491 | 0.013 |
| BMI | 0.139 | 0.145 | 0.079 | 0.958 | 0.339 |
| Index smoker | 0.034 | 0.085 | 0.026 | 0.398 | 0.691 |
| SBP | 0.069 | 0.054 | 0.102 | 1.288 | 0.199 |
| DBP | −0.040 | 0.049 | 0.052 | −0.815 | 0.416 |
| IEF | −0.248 | 0.068 | −0.284 | −3.679 | 0.0001 |

Note: The significant $p$ value is <0.05

Abbreviations: *BMI* body mass index, *SBP* systolic blood pressure, *DBP* diastolic blood pressure, *IEF* index of endothelial function indices, vascular stiffness index, pulse wave reflectance index, blood glucose and total cholesterol (Fig. 1).

According to the cluster analysis of cardiovascular risk factors and indicators of SHS, all participants were divided into five clusters (Fig. 1) [25]. The first cluster included $n = 99$ young people with lower total index of SHSQ-25, normal body weight, normal blood pressure, absence of the endothelial dysfunction and lower level of glucose and cholesterol. These individuals were rated with optimal health. The second cluster contained 121 cases. This cluster was characterised by the young age of the participants with average value of the total SHSQ-25 index, abnormalities in the mental status and immune system, normal weight, blood pressure, absence of the endothelial dysfunction, and reduced level of the glucose and cholesterol. This cluster was described with low risk of SHS cluster. The third cluster ($n = 91$ cases) differs from the other two with high values of the cumulative index of SHSQ-25, especially on the scale of the mental status, digestive system and immune system. This cluster was described as an SHS cluster with a high risk of a non-cardiac pathology profile. The fourth cluster included $n = 94$ participants with a higher age of 35 years, with average values of the total SHSQ-25 index, but with at least 1–2 risk factors for cardiovascular diseases. This cluster primarily consisted of overweight participants with a long history of smoking. We designated this cluster as a low-risk cardiovascular syndrome phenotype. The fifth cluster ($n = 54$ cases) was characterised with significant variations in the total SHSQ-25 score, the cardiovascular disease scale, the presence of the risk factors for cardiovascular diseases and endothelial dysfunction. These participants were assigned to our SHS cardiovascular phenotype with a high risk of suffering from cardiovascular disease.

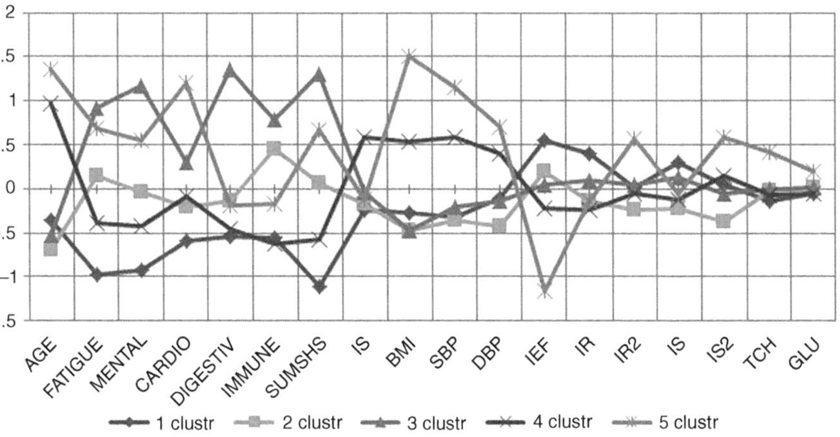


**Fig. 1** Cluster analysis of integration of the suboptimal health status, cardiovascular risk and endothelial dysfunction. *SUMSHS* the total amount of SHS:25, *IS* index smoker, *BMI* body mass index, *SBP* systolic blood pressure, *DBP* diastolic blood pressure, *IEF* index of endothelial function, *IR* index of reflection before the sample, *IR2* index of reflection after the sample, *IS* stiffness index before the sample, *IS2* stiffness index after the sample, *TCH* total cholesterol, *GLU* glucose. Figure source: Kupaev et al. The EPMA Journal (2016)

We saw a strong association between SHS scores and cardiovascular risk factors by using cluster analysis. We noted the largest distance and significant dependence between the clusters, which indicates the presence of the relationship between health conditions and vascular wall rigidity. Cluster analysis showed the association between SHS scores, risk factors of cardiovascular disease and endothelial dysfunction scores ($p < 0.001$). Among the risk factors for cardiovascular diseases, the largest distance was mentioned between clusters 1, 2, 3, and between 4 and 5 clusters. The most significant dependencies were found in age, body mass index, and blood pressure, indicating the presence of a relationship between vascular wall rigidity and several traditional determinants of cardiovascular pathology at a suboptimal stage of health.

In the present study, the assessment of SHS was combined with analysis of the endothelial dysfunction condition, which allowed to identify the risks of the development of the cardiovascular diseases and to interfere early in the framework of predictive, preventive and personalised medicine (PPPM) [26, 27].

However, the present study had limitations: information on the physical activity habits, dietary profile, frequency of the meal intake and sleeping habits that were not able to be collected for assessment [28]. All these parameters are also important for the measurement of the suboptimal health status [29–31].

## 3 Conclusions and Recommendations

1. Suboptimal health status has a significant relationship with risk factors for cardiovascular disease. SHSQ-25 could be used as a useful predictor for the cardiovascular diseases for community-based population surveys at a primary care setting.
2. This study identified the association of endothelial dysfunction with age, blood glucose levels and systolic blood pressure and also relationships with SHS index and metabolic factors such as body mass index and total cholesterol levels.
3. SHSQ-25 can be used as a tool for health measures following the context of PPPM concept.

The assessment of the SHS index, combined with the analysis of the state of the endothelial dysfunction, allows to identify the risk of the developing cardiovascular diseases at the early stage and gives an example of early intervention from the perspective of PPPM in a Russian population.

## References

1. Boytsov SA, Deev AD, Shalnova SA (2017) Mortality and risk factors for non-communicable diseases in Russia: specific features, trends, and prognosis. Ter Arkh 89(1):5–13. https://doi.org/10.17116/terarkh20178915-13

2. Yan YX, Liu YQ, Li M, Hu PF, Guo AM, Yang XH, Qiu JJ, Yang SS, Shen J, Zhang LP, Wang W (2009) Development and evaluation of a questionnaire for measuring suboptimal health status in urban Chinese. J Epidemiol 19(6):333–341. https://doi.org/10.2188/jea.je20080086
3. Yan YX, Dong J, Liu YQ, Yang XH, Li M, Shia G, Wang W (2012) Association of suboptimal health status and cardiovascular risk factors in urban Chinese workers. J Urban Health 89(2):329–338. https://doi.org/10.1007/s11524-011-9636-8
4. Yan YX, Dong J, Liu YQ, Zhang J, Song MS, He Y, Wang W (2015) Association of suboptimal health status with psychosocial stress, plasma cortisol and mRNA expression of glucocorticoid receptor α/β in lymphocyte. Stress 18(1):29–34. https://doi.org/10.3109/10253890.2014.999233. Epub 2015 Jan 23
5. Kaess BM, Rong J, Larson MG, Hamburg NM, Vita JA, Levy D, Benjamin EJ, Vasan RS, Mitchell GF (2012) Aortic stiffness, blood pressure progression, and incident hypertension. JAMA 308(9):875–881. https://doi.org/10.1001/2012.jama.10503
6. Li Z, Yang X, Wang A, Qiu J, Wang W, Song Q, Wang X (2015) Association between ideal cardiovascular health metrics and depression in Chinese population: a cross-sectional study. Sci Rep 5:11564. https://doi.org/10.1038/srep11564
7. Qiu J, Zhou Y, Yang X, Zhang Y, Li Z, Yan N, Wang Y, Ge S, Wu S, Zhao X, Wang W (2016) The association between ankle-brachial index and asymptomatic cranial-carotid stenosis: a population-based, cross-sectional study of 5440 Han Chinese. Eur J Neurol 23(4):757–762. https://doi.org/10.1111/ene.12935
8. Forstermann U, Munzel T (2006) Endothelial nitric oxide synthase in vascular disease: from marvel to menace. Circulation 113(13):1708–1714. https://doi.org/10.1161/CIRCULATIONAHA.105.602532
9. Forstermann U, Li Huege (2011) Therapeutic effect of enhancing endothelial nitric oxide synthase (eNOS) expression and preventing eNOS uncoupling. Br J Pharmacol 164(2):213–223. https://doi.org/10.1111/j.1476-5381.2010.01196.x
10. Trovato GM (2016) Clinical research and methodology: the paradigm of fatty liver and atherosclerosis behind the chicken or the egg dilemma. Atherosclerosis 249:228–229. https://doi.org/10.1016/j.atherosclerosis.2016.02.031
11. Wilson SH, Simari RD, Lerman A (2001) The effect of endothelin-1 on nuclear factor kappa B in macrophages. Biochem Biophys Res Commun 286(5):968–972. https://doi.org/10.1006/bbrc.2001.5485
12. Wilkinson IB, MacCallum H, Cockcroft JR, Webb DJ (2002) Inhibition of basal nitric oxide synthesis increases aortic augmentation index and pulse wave velocity in vivo. Br J Clin Pharmacol 53(2):189–192. https://doi.org/10.1046/j.1365-2125.2002.1528adoc.x
13. Endemann DH, Schiffrin EL (2004) Endothelial dysfunction. J Am Soc Nephrol 15(8):1983–1992. https://doi.org/10.1097/01.ASN.0000132474.50966.DA
14. O'Gallagher K, Shabeeh H, Shahzad M, Roomi A, Jiang B, Guilcher A, Brett S, Chowienczyk P (2020) Effects of inhibition of nitric oxide synthase on muscular arteries during exercise: nitric oxide does not contribute to vasodilation during exercise or in recovery. J Am Heart Assoc 9(16):e013849. https://doi.org/10.1161/JAHA.119.013849
15. Fitch RM, Vergona R, Sullivan ME, Wang YX (2001) Nitric oxide synthase inhibition increasers aortic stiffness measured by pulse wave velocity in rats. Cardiovasc Res 51(2):351–358. https://doi.org/10.1016/s0008-6363(01)00299-1
16. Cockcroft JR (2005) Exploring vascular benefits of endothelium-derived nitric oxide. Am J Hypertens 18(12 Pt2):177–183. https://doi.org/10.1016/j.amjhyper.2005.09.001
17. Boffa GM, Zaninotto M, Bacchiega E, Nalli C, Forni M, Tiso E, Cacciavillani L, Razzolini R, Plebani M (2005) Correlations between clinical presentation, brain natriuretic peptide, big endothelin-1, tumor necrosis factor-alpha and cardiac troponins in heart failure patients. Ital Heart J 6(2):125–132
18. Cecelja M, Chowienczyk P (2009) Dissociation of aortic pulse wave velocity with risk factors for cardiovascular disease other than hypertension. A systematic review. Hypertension 54(6):1328–1336. https://doi.org/10.1161/HYPERTENSIONAHA.109.137653.

19. Katz SD, Hryniewiez K, Hriljac I, Balidemaj K, Dimayuga C, Hudaihed A, Yasskiy A (2005) Vascular endothelial dysfunction and mortality risk in patients with chronic heart failure. Circulation 111(3):310–314. https://doi.org/10.1161/01.CIR.0000153349.77489.CF
20. Widlansky ME, Gokce N, Keaney JF, Vita JA (2003) The clinical implications of endothelial dysfunction. J Am Coll Cardiol 42(7):1149–1160. https://doi.org/10.1016/s0735-1097(03)00994-x
21. Wilkinson IB, Qasem A, McEniery CM, Webb DJ, Avolio AP, Cockcroft JR (2002) Nitric oxide regulates local arterial distensibility in vivo. Circulation 105(2):213–217. https://doi.org/10.1161/hc0202.101970
22. Wierzbicki AS, Chowienczyk PJ, Cockcroft JR, Brett SE, Watts GF, Jenkins BS, Ritter JM (2004) Cardiovascular risk factors and endothelial dysfunction. Clin Sci (Lond) 107(6):609–615. https://doi.org/10.1042/CS20040078
23. Yan YX, Dong J, Li M, Yang SS, Wang W (2011) Establish the cut off point for suboptimal health status using SHSQ-25. Chinese J Health Stat 28(3):256–258. (in Chinese)
24. Wang W, Russell A, Yan Y, On behalf of Global Health Epidemiology Reference Group (GHERG) (2014) Traditional Chinese medicine and new concepts of predictive, preventive and personalized medicine in diagnosis and treatment of suboptimal health. EPMA J 5(1):12. https://doi.org/10.1186/1878-5085-5-4
25. Kupaev V, Borisov O, Marutina E, Yan Y, Wei W (2016) Integration of suboptimal health status and endothelial dysfunction as a new aspect for risk evaluation of cardiovascular disease. EPMA J 7:19. https://doi.org/10.1186/s13167-016-0068-0
26. Trovato GM (2012) Behavior, nutrition and lifestyle in a comprehensive health and disease paradigm: skills and knowledge for a predictive, preventive and personalized medicine. EPMA J 3(1):8. https://doi.org/10.1007/s13167-012-0141-2
27. Golubnitschaja O, Costigliola V (2012) General report and recommendations in predictive, preventive and personalised medicine 2012: white paper of the European Association for Predictive, Preventive and Personalised Medicine. EPMA J 3(1):14. https://doi.org/10.1186/1878-5085-3-14
28. Slobodjanjuk AL, Krylova IA, Kupaev VI (2019) Primary care: how to increase physical activity in your patient. Russian Arch Intern Med 9(4):269–279. [In Russian]. https://doi.org/10.20514/2226-6704-2019-9-4-269-279
29. Trovat FM, Martines GF, Brischetto D, Catalano D, Musumeci G, Trovato GM (2016) Fatty liver disease and lifestyle in youngsters: diet, food intake frequency, exercise, sleep shortage and fashion. Liver Int 36(3):427–433. https://doi.org/10.1111/liv.12957
30. Kupaev VI, Krylova IA, Slobodyanuk AL (2019) The role of questionnaires for the assessment of physical activity and suboptimal health status for primary screening of cardiovascular diseases. Cardiovasc Therapy Prevent 18(4):47–52. https://doi.org/10.15829/1728-8800-2019-4-47-52
31. Krylova IA, Kupaev VI, Ljamin AV (2021) Microbiological characteristics of intestinal biocenosis of ambulator patients having behavioral risk factors for chronic noncommunicable diseases. Russian Archiv Intern Med 11(3):217–224. https://doi.org/10.20514/2226-6704-2021-11-3-217-224

# Individualised Preventive Measurements of Suboptimal Health

Zheng Guo, Yulu Zheng, and Manshu Song

## Abbreviations

| | |
|---|---|
| ADCC | Antibody-dependent cellular cytotoxicity |
| BMI | Body mass index |
| CH2 | Constant heavy 2 |
| E2 | Estradiol |
| Fc | Fragment crystallisable |
| FcγRIIB | Fc gamma receptor type IIB |
| FSH | Follicle-stimulating hormone |
| GlcNAc | N-acetylglucosamine |
| IgG | Immunoglobulin G |
| LH | Luteinising hormone |
| MBL | Mannose-binding lectin |
| NCDs | Non-communicable chronic diseases |
| PPPM/3PM | Predictive, preventive, and personalised medicine |
| PTM | Post-translational modification |
| RCT | Randomised controlled trial |
| SHS | Suboptimal health status |
| SHSQ-25 | Suboptimal Health Status Questionnaire-25 |
| TNF-α | Tumour necrosis factor alpha |
| WHO | World Health Organization |

Z. Guo · Y. Zheng
Centre for Precision Health, Edith Cowan University, Perth, WA, Australia
e-mail: zguo0@our.ecu.edu.au; yuluz@our.ecu.edu.au

M. Song (✉)
School of Medical and Health Sciences, Edith Cowan University, Perth, WA, Australia
e-mail: m.song@ecu.edu.au


W. Wang (ed.), *All Around Suboptimal Health*, Advances in Predictive, Preventive and Personalised Medicine 18,
https://doi.org/10.1007/978-3-031-46891-9_11

# 1 Disease Prevention

Phases of the disease's natural history include the underlying, susceptible, subclinical, clinical, and recovery/disability/death stages [1]. According to the guidelines from the World Health Organization, health prevention is classified into primary, secondary, and tertiary prevention [2]. Comprehensive preventive strategies can prevent diseases by reducing the risk of morbidity and the subsequent complications of overt disease [1].

**Primary prevention** also called aetiology prevention is the fundamental action to prevent, control, and eliminate diseases. From both individual and population levels, it focuses on actions that endeavour to control the effects of risk factors [3]; thus, the target population of primary prevention is those whose diseases have not yet occurred [1, 4]. Primary prevention consists of two components: health promotion and health protection. Health promotion aims to reduce an individual's exposure to the causes (risk factors) of diseases by creating a health-promoting environment. In such case, the susceptibility can be altered, and the individual can be protected from disease, thus the morbidity rate can be reduced [2]. Health protection is a measure taken for diseases with clear causes (risk factors) or specific ways of prevention, for example, the vaccination against *hepatitis B* to prevent *hepatitis B* [5]. The two-pronged strategy is often employed for primary prevention, combining universal prevention for the whole population and focused prevention for high-risk population. Both components complement each other to improve efficiency [3].

**Secondary prevention** also known as preclinical prevention aiming to control the development and deterioration of the disease and prevent the disease from recurring or turning into chronic status [2]. The core of secondary prevention is early diagnosis, with its premise being early detection and early diagnosis, which can contribute to early treatment and thus improve the prognosis [1]. An ideal secondary prevention requires the dissemination of disease prevention knowledge to the public, the improvement of clinicians' diagnosis, and the establishment of a reliable and an accurate disease surveillance system [6]. Due to the long period of the occurrence and the development of chronic diseases, it is feasible to achieve early detection and early treatment of those diseases, such as cervical cancer, coronary heart disease, and hypertension. Activities for early detection include census, screening, regular medical examinations, and establishment of specialist clinics [3, 4].

**Tertiary prevention** also termed as clinical prevention refers to taking timely and effective treatment for those who have already suffered from the disease [2]. It aims to prevent deterioration, complications, and disability for those who have already diagnosed with diseases. It mainly promotes functional recovery, psychological rehabilitation, and home care guidance [7–9]. In that case, patients can restore their living and working abilities as far as possible and can participate in social activities and prolong their life. Symptomatic treatment, which can relieve pain, reduces the adverse effects of the disease, and prevents complications and disability, and rehabilitation, which mainly involves functional, psychological, social and vocational rehabilitation, are the primary tertiary preventive strategies [9].

**Individualised prevention** also refers to personalised prevention, [10, 11]. It cannot be separated from the development of precision medicine, which is an innovation and development based on traditional medicine. Related fields including medical informatics, molecular medicine, health economics, and medical sociology [11, 12]. The individualised medicine is relied on the development of molecular diagnostics and molecular pharmacodynamics [2]. Progresses in genomics and proteomics have greatly contributed to the development of molecular medicine [11]. The application of high-throughput gene microarrays and protein microarrays has made molecular typing of various diseases possible [11]. The molecular spectrum of specific patients has gradually become a very important basis and evidence in clinical diagnosis and treatment [12]. From the concept of predictive, preventive, and personalised medicine (PPPM), the present assessment applications for human health status involved both subjective and objective measurements. With regard to subjective measurements, they are typically referred to self-reported questionnaires, contingent on subjects' feelings, opinions, and general impressions. In preventive medicine, the subjective tool Suboptimal Health Status Questionnaire-25 (SHSQ-25), which has been coined and validated as a reliable and robust health measurement, is employed to evaluate Suboptimal Health Status (SHS) in five domains: cardiovascular system, digestive system, fatigue immune system, and mental status [13]. SHS is defined as an intermediate physical state between health and disease [13]. Additionally, it is reversible and helps predicted or prevented non-communicable diseases (NCDs) before the onset of diseases [14–16]. While objective measurements are more impartial compared with subjective measurements. One of the most prevalent methods to objectively quantifying outcome of interest is the application of biomarkers, such as classical inflammatory biomarkers, such as tumour necrosis factor alpha [TNF-α], and multi-omics molecular biomarkers, such as analyses in genome, transcriptome, epigenome, proteome, metabolome, and glycome. Of note, glycosylation is the most common and diverse form of post-translational modification (PTM) of protein. N-glycosylation, the binding of a glycan to an asparagine residue of a protein, is the most common and best understood. A variety of biological processing (such as protein folding, cell adhesion, and receptor activation) can be affected by glycosylation. Immunoglobulin G (IgG) is the most abundant antibody in human blood circulation, accounting for about 80% of the antibodies. The alterations in IgG N-glycans have been associated with SHS (PMID: 35719133). Moreover, IgG N-glycosylation have linked to SHS-related diseases or disorders, such as cardiovascular diseases [17] and type 2 diabetes mellitus [18]. This connection may offer insights and strategies for reversing SHS.

On one hand, the objective of individualised prevention is to supplant current traditional, community- or population-based public health efforts. On the other hand, individualised prevention also strives to ensure that individuals have access to the appropriate preventative measures at the right dose and timing in order to maximise the effectiveness and safety of all interventions and optimise the benefit-risk ratio [19]. Thus, the cost-effective, time-efficient, and tailored prevention programmes for reversing SHS can be provided from the precise application of primary and secondary prevention [12, 19].

## 2 Prevention of SHS Defined by Subjective Measurements

The timely screening for SHS has the potential for early prediction and prevention of non-communicable diseases (NCDs), and effective SHS prevention may be an effective and economical way to prevent NCDs [16]. To assess the SHS efficiently and economically, our team developed and validated the innovative and robust health assessment tool, SHSQ-25. This is in line with the conceptualisation of PPPM/3PM [20].

Disease prevention, especially for chronic NCDs, requires an emphasis on SHS according to PPPM/3PM strategies to prevent the development of diseases in advance (Fig. 1). Ideally, interventions should be delivered when a person presents with symptoms that suggest a non-healthy state but does not yet meet existing diagnostic criteria for the disease. When it comes to SHS prevention, it is important to pay attention to identifying physical health conditions, as well as mental and emotional states. In summary, it is essential to implement people-oriented interventions based on the comprehensive concept of PPPM/3PM and to provide rapid, economical, and targeted preventive measures. In this chapter, we demonstrated the effectiveness of preventive measurements of SHS through cases studies.

**Case Study 1: Examine the Effect of Baduanjin Exercise on SHS Individuals**
There is increasing proof exercise or physical activity can help to improve one's physical and mental condition [21]. Additionally, traditional Chinese exercises, such as Baduanjin exercise, have proven to be successful workout regimens for promoting both physical and mental health, as well as improving body composition [22–24]. There are eight separate, delicate, and smooth exercise movements in

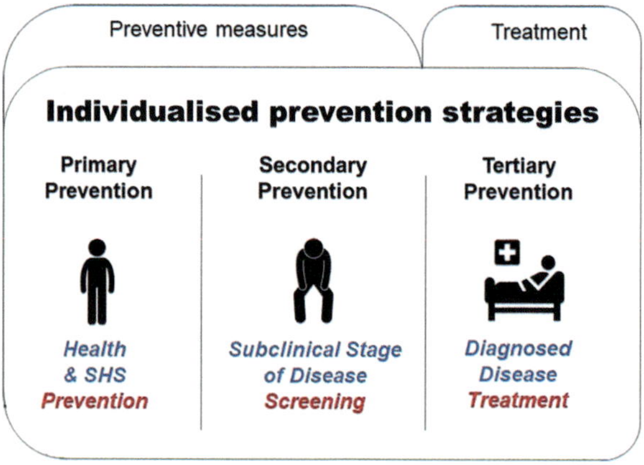


**Fig. 1** Strategies in accordance with the individualised prevention. Primary prevention focuses on actions that endeavour to control the effects of risk factors of disease at both individual and population levels. Secondary prevention refers to early detection of diseases. Tertiary prevention represents taking timely and effective treatment for those who have already suffered from the disease

*Baduanjin* exercise (1 raise hands to hold up the sky; 2 draw two bows to shoot vultures; 3 raise one arm to control the stomach and spleen; 4 turn head to eliminate fatigue; 5 lean forwards and backwards to release heart fire; 6 pull your toes together with both hands to support your waist and kidneys; 7 clench the fists and glare fiercely; 8 tiptoe up and down), and each movement helps certain body parts or organs by improving their capacity for function [25].

A clinical trial was carried out to examine the impact of Baduanjin exercise on the symptom of fatigue in SHS participants [26].

To determine the long-lasting impact of Baduanjin exercise on SHS, participants were monitored for a period of 12 weeks after the intervention. Statistical comparisons of the SHS score were carried out at several time points, including preintervention, the fourth and sixth week following the intervention, and the 12th and 18th week during the post-intervention follow-ups. The findings revealed the Baduanjin exercise group had substantially decreased SHS scores ($P < 0.05$). The study suggests that Baduanjin exercise has an effect on relieving fatigue in people with SHS [26].

**Case Study 2: Effectiveness of Mild Moxibustion for SHS in Pre- and Post-menopausal Women**

Women, who are at the peri-menopausal stage of life, would frequently experience SHS, which is characterised by uncomfortable symptoms such as difficulty concentrating, fatigue, headache, hot flashes, insomnia, irritability, and mental confusion [27]. Chinese and other Asian people have been reported to use moxibustion, which is a kind of heat treatment in dried "moxa" burned on acupoints, as a way of clinical therapy and for self-healthcare [28]. A randomised controlled study (RCT) with 60 participants randomised to the intervention (moxibustion) and control groups was carried out to examine the safety and effectiveness of moxibustion for improving SHS in peri-menopausal women. Mild moxibustion was administered to the moxibustion group, and vitamin E soft capsules were given to the control group as a placebo [29]. According to the results in the study, the intervention in the (moxibustion) group dramatically improved SHS when compared to the control group. Pre-menopausal women had more pronounced improvements in SHS compared to post-menopausal women. Additionally, after treatment, the moxibustion group had substantially higher estradiol (E2) levels than the control group, and pre-menopausal women in the moxibustion group had higher E2 levels than post-menopausal women. Pre-menopausal women had considerably greater levels of E2, prolactin (PBL), and progesterone, while post-menopausal women had significantly higher levels of luteinising hormone (LH) and follicle-stimulating hormone (FSH).

**Case Study 3: Effects of Pulsatile Cupping on Body Pain and Quality of Life in People with SHS**

A traditional medical practice known as cupping therapy uses heated cups to apply pressure to the skin in order to clear blockages and promote "Qi" flow [30]. Cupping has been widely employed in China and other Asian populations because of its non-invasive nature, straightforward procedure, and quick results [31]. Cupping was identified as a primary clinical treating way to relieve SHS and improve patients' overall well-being in clinical practice [32].

The effects of pneumatic pulsatile cupping on pain and life quality in SHS patients were examined in a four-arm randomised clinical experiment [33]. In this study, 96 SHS patients were recruited and assigned to receive low-frequency (LF) or high-frequency (HF) pulsating cupping, traditional cupping (TC), or wait-list (WL) therapy.

Compared to the TC group, pain symptoms dramatically declined in both LF and HF groups, whereas the life quality was significantly improved in both the LF and HF groups. Additionally, compared to the WL group, the quality of life was significantly improved in both LF and HF groups and pain symptoms were significantly reduced. However, there was no statistically significant difference between the LF and HF groups.

## 3 Prevention of SHS Defined by Objective Measurements

While no statement meets the clinical diagnostic criteria for health declines (i.e. in SHS), the molecular processes are already measurably perturbed.

Glycans are thought of as one of the ideal objective measures for detecting SHS as glycosylation plays a crucial role in the inflammatory processing at the molecular level (42). Immunoglobulin G (IgG) is one of the most thoroughly studied glycoproteins overall, connecting the innate and adaptive immune system branches [34]. Conserved N-glycans linked to the constant heavy 2 (CH2) region of the IgG fragment crystallisable (Fc) domain mediate downstream immunological responses in addition to directly influencing the conformation of the fragment crystallisable (Fc) region (Fig. 2) [35, 36]. In addition, alternations of the IgG N-glycosylation can elicit inflammageing, which is a generalised term describing the process of ageing at the molecular level through inflammation [37]. IgG N-glycans can serve as a

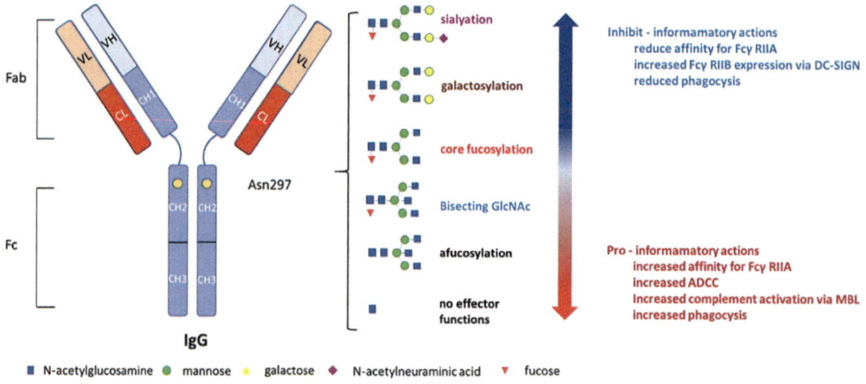


**Fig. 2** Fc-bound N-glycans modulate IgG effector functions, adapted from [35, 36]. *ADCC* antibody-dependent cellular cytotoxicity; *FcγRIIB* Fc gamma receptor type IIB; *GlcNAc* N-acetylglucosamine; *MBL* mannose-binding lectin

molecular parameter for individualised monitoring and prevention of SHS, as they are important dynamic biomarkers for identifying SHS and offer a window opportunity for its management.

SHS is on the rise, posing a new threat to both societal and individual health due to the epidemics of poor lifestyle such as physical inactivity. The cost of managing non-communicable diseases is increasing, placing growing pressure on healthcare budgets. Shifting the emphasis on SHS prevention can effectively address this issue. It is feasible to track the impact of the outcomes of helpful interventions because IgG N-glycome can be utilised as a biomarker for SHS and interventions can influence IgG N-glycome compositions.

**Case Study 1: Intense Physical Exercise Induces an Anti-inflammatory Change in IgG N-glycosylation Profile**

A longitudinal intervention research involving 29 males was carried out to demonstrate the impact of high intensity physical exercise programme on the IgG N-glycosylation profile [38]. IgG N-glycosylation profiling was assessed from blood samples at three time points: (1) baseline, (2) post-intervention (EXC), and (3) recovery period (REC). The outcomes from the baseline, EXC, and REC time periods were compared after the IgG N-glycosylation study. Analysis was conducted on the following derived glycan characteristics: agalactosylation (G0), monogalactosylation (G1), digalactosylation (G2), monosialylation (S1), disialylation (S2), bisection (B), and core fucosylation (CF). IgG N-glycome compositions at the REC time point were significantly different from the baseline due to the effects of exercise (Table 1).

**Case Study 2: Effects of Estradiol on Biological Age Measured Using the Glycan Age Index**

A randomised controlled trial (RCT) was carried out to estimate the effects of estradiol supplementation on glycan age [39]. This research involved 36 healthy young women in total and underwent 5 months treatment of gonadotropin-releasing hormone agonist (GnRHAG) to suppress ovarian gonadal hormones. Participants were

**Table 1** Effects of intense physical exercise on levels of IgG N-glycosylation [38]

| Structural feature | Estimate EXC | *P*-value EXC | Adj. *P*-value EXC | Estimate REC | *P*-value REC | Adj. *P*-value REC |
|---|---|---|---|---|---|---|
| Agalactosylation (G0) | −0.2009 | 0.5394 | 0.6152 | −0.8080 | 0.0190 | **0.0473** |
| Monogalactosylation (G1) | −0.1040 | 0.5388 | 0.6152 | −0.1710 | 0.3149 | 0.4409 |
| Digalactosylation (G2) | 0.3049 | 0.4554 | 0.6152 | 0.9950 | 0.0203 | **0.0473** |
| Monosialylation (S1) | 0.2688 | 0.1283 | 0.6152 | 0.5270 | 0.0048 | **0.0339** |
| Disialylation (S2) | 0.1430 | 0.2206 | 0.6152 | 0.2465 | 0.0399 | 0.0698 |
| Bisection (B) | 0.0901 | 0.5807 | 0.6152 | 0.1095 | 0.5030 | 0.5868 |
| Core fucosylation (CF) | −0.0373 | 0.6152 | 0.6152 | −0.0339 | 0.6479 | 0.6479 |

then randomly assigned to estradiol (E2) intervention (GnRHAG + E2, $n = 15$) and placebo control group (GnRHAG + PL, $n = 21$) [40].

IgG N-glycosylation profiling was assessed from blood samples at three time points: (1) baseline, (2) post-intervention, and (3) recovery period (Fig. 3). Estradiol supplementation significantly reduced glycan age (−0.23 years), which was significantly increased by 9.1 years when gonadal hormones were suppressed. Glycan age in both groups returned to baseline levels following the recovery period.

**Case Study 3: Extensive Weight Loss Reduces Glycan Age by Altering IgG N-glycosylation**

Bariatric surgery is considered as one of the most effective methods to treat severe obesity [41]. To explore if weight loss can improve glycan age, 37 obese patients were recruited in an exploratory cohort from Oxford University Hospitals and 2146 participants were included in a replication cohort from the Twins UK cohort. Participants recruited from the exploratory cohort underwent bariatric surgery after low-calorie diet for 3 weeks.

The IgG N-glycome compositions were assessed at three time points: (1) baseline, (2) the day of the bariatric surgery, and (3) the day of 20% of weight loss. Subsequently, the replication cohort longitudinally monitored IgG N-glycome of 3742 participants with information on body mass index (BMI) [42]. The results indicated that low-calorie diet causes a decrease in bisecting GlcNAc that reflected a decreased pro-inflammatory trend (Fig. 4). During the one year follow-up after the bariatric surgery, an increase in digalactosylation and sialylation was observed, while agalactosylation and core fucosylation was decreased.

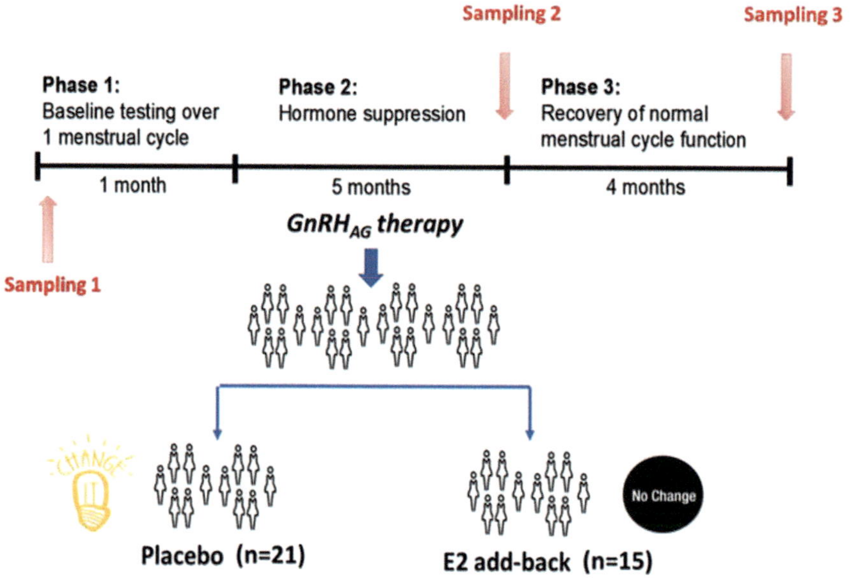


**Fig. 3** Flowchart of the study design

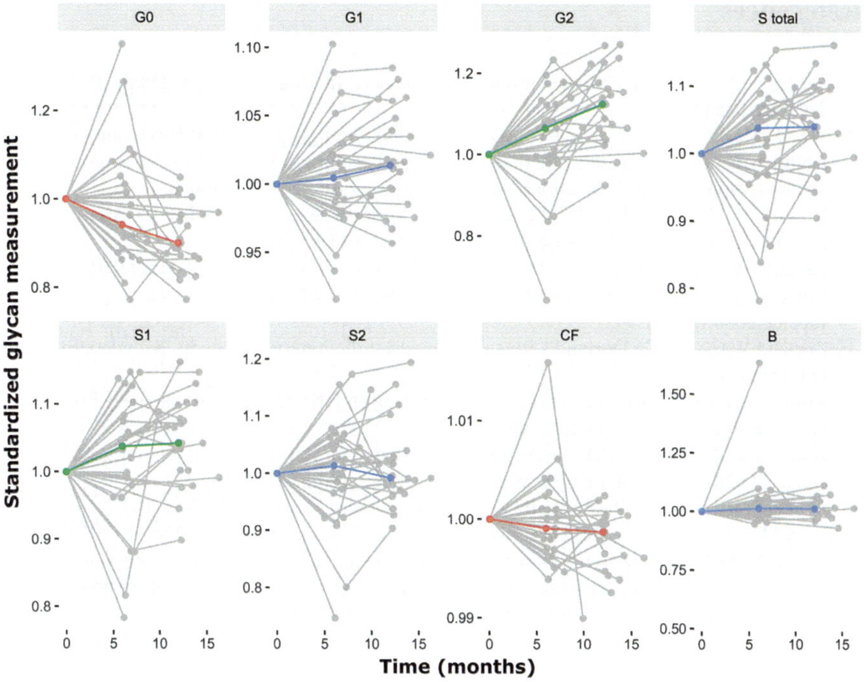


**Fig. 4** Effect of Bariatric surgery on IgG N-glycosylation [41]. *G0* agalactosylation; *G1* monogalactosylation; *G2* digalactosylation; *S total* total sialylation; *S1* monosialylation; *S2* disialylation; *CF* core fucosylation; *B* bisecting N-acetylglucosamine

# 4 Conclusion, Expert Recommendations, and Future Perspective

In conclusion, personalised SHS measurements provide a reliable and robust platform for effective prevention measures. The established SHS assessments, such as SHSQ-25 and IgG N-glycosylation profile, should thus serve as the foundation for individualised preventative strategies for SHS. The examples of targeted interventions for prevention aforementioned showed how the combination of subjective and objective SHS assessments has a positive impact on health improvement. From the perspectives of PPPM, it provided a thorough strategy for the individualised prevention of SHS from progressing into the disease phase.

**Declaration of Interest Statement** Declarations of interest: none.

## References


1. Kisling LA, Das JM (2021) Prevention strategies. In: StatPearls. StatPearls Publishing, Treasure Island, FL
2. WHO. Health promotion and disease prevention through population-based interventions, including action to address social determinants and health inequity. http://www.emro.who.int/about-who/public-health-functions/health-promotion-disease-prevention.html
3. Kirch W (2008) Encyclopedia of public health. Springer Science & Business Media
4. Health AIo, Welfare (2014) Australia's health 2014. AIHW, Canberra
5. Zanetti AR, Van Damme P, Shouval D (2008) The global impact of vaccination against hepatitis B: a historical overview. Vaccine 26(49):6266–6273. https://doi.org/10.1016/j.vaccine.2008.09.056
6. Dorland WAN (2012) Dorland's illustrated medical dictionary, 32nd edn. Saunders/Elsevier, Philadelphia, PA
7. Nolte E (2008) Disease prevention. In: Heggenhougen HK (ed) International encyclopedia of public health. Academic, Oxford, pp 222–234
8. Greenfield SF (2010) Tertiary prevention. The corsini encyclopedia of psychology, pp 1–2
9. Quah SR (2016) International encyclopedia of public health. Academic
10. Boccia S, Ricciardi W, Pastorino R, Adany R, Barnhoorn F, Boffetta P, Cornel MC, De Vito C, Gray M, Jani A, Lang M, Roldan J, Rosso A, Sánchez JM, Van Dujin CM, Van El CG, Villari P, Zawati MH (2019) How to integrate personalized medicine into prevention? recommendations from the personalized prevention of chronic diseases (PRECeDI) consortium. Public Health Genomics 22(5-6):208-214. https://doi.org/10.1159/000504652
11. Pastorino R, Loreti C, Giovannini S, Ricciardi W, Padua L, Boccia S (2021) Challenges of prevention for a sustainable personalized medicine. J Pers Med 11(4):311. https://doi.org/10.3390/jpm11040311
12. Davies S (2017) Annual report of the chief medical officer 2016, generation genome
13. Guo Z, Meng R, Zheng Y, Li X, Zhou Z, Yu L, Tang Q, Zhao Y, Garcia M, Yan Y, Song M, Balmer L, Wen J, Hou H, Tan X, Wang W (2022) Suboptimal health study consortium (SHSC) and the global health epidemiology research group (GHERG). Translation and cross-cultural validation of a precision health tool, the suboptimal health status questionnaire-25, in Korean. J Glob Health 1(12):04077. https://doi.org/10.7189/jogh.12.04077
14. Wang Y, Ge S, Yan Y, Wang A, Zhao Z, Yu X, Qiu J, Alzain MA, Wang H, Fang H, Gao Q, Song M, Zhang J, Zhou Y, Wang W (2016) China suboptimal health cohort study: rationale, design and baseline characteristics. J Transl Med 14(1):291. https://doi.org/10.1186/s12967-016-1046-y
15. Wang W (2020) Cardiovascular health in China: low level vs high diversity. Lancet Reg Health West Pac 3. https://doi.org/10.1016/j.lanwpc.2020.100038
16. Wang H, Tian Q, Zhang J, Liu H, Zhang X, Cao W, Zhang J, Anto EO, Li X, Wang X, Liu D, Zheng Y, Guo Z, Wu L, Song M, Wang Y, Wang W (2020) Population-based case-control study revealed metabolomic biomarkers of suboptimal health status in Chinese population-potential utility for innovative approach by predictive, preventive, and personalized medicine. EPMA J 11(2):147–160. https://doi.org/10.1007/s13167-020-00200-7
17. Kupaev V, Borisov O, Marutina E, Yan YX, Wang W (2016) Integration of suboptimal health status and endothelial dysfunction as a new aspect for risk evaluation of cardiovascular disease. EPMA J 7(1):19. https://doi.org/10.1186/s13167-016-0068-0
18. Ge S, Wang Y, Song M, Li X, Yu X, Wang H, Wang J, Zeng Q, Wang W (2018) Type 2 diabetes mellitus: integrative analysis of multiomics data for biomarker discovery. OMICS 22(7):514–523. https://doi.org/10.1089/omi.2018.0053

19. Boccia S, Ricciardi W (2020) Personalized prevention and population health impact: how can public health professionals be more engaged? Eur J Pub Health 30(3):391–392. https://doi.org/10.1093/eurpub/ckaa018
20. Yan YX, Liu YQ, Li M, Hu PF, Guo AM, Yang XH, Qiu JJ, Yang SS, Shen J, Zhang LP, Wang W (2009) Development and evaluation of a questionnaire for measuring suboptimal health status in urban Chinese. J Epidemiol 19(6):333–341. https://doi.org/10.2188/jea.je20080086
21. Penedo FJ, Dahn JR (2005) Exercise and well-being: a review of mental and physical health benefits associated with physical activity. Curr Opin Psychiatry 18(2):189–193. https://doi.org/10.1097/00001504-200503000-00013
22. Jones BM (2001) Changes in cytokine production in healthy subjects practicing Guolin qigong: a pilot study. BMC Complement Altern Med 1:8. https://doi.org/10.1186/1472-6882-1-8
23. McCaffrey R, Fowler NL (2003) Qigong practice: a pathway to health and healing. Holist Nurs Pract 17(2):110–116. https://doi.org/10.1097/00004650-200303000-00006
24. Sancier KM (1999) Therapeutic benefits of qigong exercises in combination with drugs. J Altern Complementary Med (New York, NY) 5(4):383–389. https://doi.org/10.1089/acm.1999.5.383
25. Liu XY, Gao J, Yin BX, Yang XY, Bai DX (2016) Efficacy of Ba Duan Jin in improving balance: a study in Chinese community-dwelling older adults. J Gerontol Nurs 42(5):38–46. https://doi.org/10.3928/00989134-20160201-03
26. Liao Y, Lin Y, Zhang C, Xue XL, Mao QX, Zhang Y, Dai JG, Wang TF (2015) Intervention effect of baduanjin exercise on the fatigue state in people with fatigue-predominant sub-health: a cohort study. J Altern Complement Med 21(9):554-562 https://www.liebertpub.com/doi/10.1089/acm.2014.0395
27. Dalal PK, Agarwal M (2015) Postmenopausal syndrome. Indian J Psychiatry 57(Suppl 2):S222–SS32. https://doi.org/10.4103/0019-5545.161483
28. Zheng L, Jing Y (2011) Clinical analysis on combined acupuncture and ginger-partitioned moxibustion for perimenopause syndrome. Shanghai J Acu-mox 30(10):673–674
29. Shen J, Ai B, Shen M (2018) Effectiveness of mild moxibustion for sub-health conditions in pre- and post-menopausal women: a randomized controlled clinical trial. Med Sci Monit 24:2907–2911. https://doi.org/10.12659/msm.909721
30. Lauche R, Spitzer J, Schwahn B, Ostermann T, Bernardy K, Cramer H, Dobos G, Langhorst J (2016) Efficacy of cupping therapy in patients with the fibromyalgia syndrome-a randomised placebo controlled trial. Sci Rep 6:37316. https://doi.org/10.1038/srep37316
31. Huber R, Emerich M, Braeunig M (2011) Cupping—is it reproducible? Experiments about factors determining the vacuum. Complement Ther Med 19(2):78–83. https://doi.org/10.1016/j.ctim.2010.12.006
32. Chi LM, Lin LM, Chen CL, Wang SF, Lai HL, Peng TC (2016) The effectiveness of cupping therapy on relieving chronic neck and shoulder pain: a randomized controlled trial. Evid Based Complement Alternat Med 2016:7358918. https://doi.org/10.1155/2016/7358918
33. Yang Y, Ma LX, Niu TL, Niu X, Yang XZ, Wang JX, Lu Y, Gao LJ, Chen TY, Zhang YJ, Wu YJ, Song Y (2018) Effects of pulsatile cupping on body pain and quality of life in people with suboptimal health: a randomized controlled exploratory trial. Med Acupuncture 30(6):326–335. https://doi.org/10.1089/acu.2018.1313
34. Martinić Kavur M, Lauc G, Pezer M (2021) Systems glycobiology: immunoglobulin G Glycans as biomarkers and functional effectors in aging and diseases. Comprehensive Glycoscience (Second Edition), Elsevier 1:439-478. https://doi.org/10.1016/B978-0-12-819475-1.00086-9
35. Russell A, Adua E, Ugrina I, Laws S, Wang W (2018) Unravelling immunoglobulin G fc N-glycosylation: a dynamic marker potentiating predictive, preventive and personalised medicine. Int J Mol Sci 19(2):390. https://doi.org/10.3390/ijms19020390
36. Štambuk T, Klasić M, Zoldoš V, Lauc G (2020) N-glycans as functional effectors of genetic and epigenetic disease risk. Mol Asp Med 79:100891. https://doi.org/10.1016/j.mam.2020.100891

37. Franceschi C, Garagnani P, Parini P, Giuliani C, Santoro A (2018) Inflammaging: a new immune-metabolic viewpoint for age-related diseases. Nat Rev Endocrinol 14(10):576–590. https://doi.org/10.1038/s41574-018-0059-4
38. Tijardović M, Marijančević D, Bok D, Kifer D, Lauc G, Gornik O, Keser T (2019) Intense physical exercise induces an antiinflammatory change in IgG N-glycosylation profile. Front Physiol 10:1522. https://doi.org/10.3389/fphys.2019.01522
39. Jurić J, Kohrt WM, Kifer D, Gavin KM, Pezer M, Nigrovic PA, Lauc G (2020) Effects of estradiol on biological age measured using the glycan age index. Aging 12(19):19756–19765. https://doi.org/10.18632/aging.104060
40. Shea KL, Gavin KM, Melanson EL, Gibbons E, Stavros A, Wolfe P, Kittelson JM, Vondracek SF, Schwartz RS, Wierman ME, Kohrt WM (2015) Body composition and bone mineral density after ovarian hormone suppression with or without estradiol treatment. Menopause (New York, NY) 22(10):1045–1052. https://doi.org/10.1097/gme.0000000000000430
41. Nguyen NT, Kim E, Vu S, Phelan M (2018) Ten-year outcomes of a prospective randomized trial of laparoscopic gastric bypass versus laparoscopic gastric banding. Ann Surg 268(1):106–113. https://doi.org/10.1097/sla.0000000000002348
42. Greto VL, Cvetko A, Štambuk T, Dempster NJ, Kifer D, Deriš H, Cindrić A, Vučković F, Falchi M, Gillies RS, Tomlinson JW, Gornik O, Sgromo B, Spector TD, Menni C, Geremia A, Arancibia-Cárcamo CV, Lauc G (2021) Extensive weight loss reduces glycan age by altering IgG N-glycosylation. Int J Obes (Lond) 45(7):1521–1531. https://doi.org/10.1038/s41366-021-00816-3

# Early Vascular Aging in Young Adults Is Instrumental as the Screening Tool to Combat CVD Epidemics in the Population

**M. E. Evsevieva, O. V. Sergeeva, M. V. Eremin, E. V. Simches, M. V. Rostovceva, V. D. Kudriavceva, M. J. Martynov, I. V. Koshel, and O. Golubnitschaja**

## Abbreviations

| | |
|---|---|
| ABI | Ankle-brachial index |
| AC | Atherogenic coefficient |
| AGEs | Advanced glycation end products |
| AH | Arterial hypertension |
| BH | Burdened heredity |
| BM | Body mass |
| BMI | Body mass index |
| BP | Blood pressure |
| CAVI | Cardio-ankle vascular index |
| CR | Calorie restriction |
| CV | Cardiovascular |
| CVD | Cardiovascular diseases |
| CVRF | Cardiovascular risk factors |
| DASH | Dietary Approaches to Stop Hypertension |
| DBP | Diastolic blood pressure |
| DSR | Dietary sodium restriction |

M. E. Evsevieva · O. V. Sergeeva · M. V. Eremin · E. V. Simches · M. V. Rostovceva · V. D. Kudriavceva · I. V. Koshel
Stavropol State Medical University, Stavropol, Russia

M. J. Martynov
Pirogov Russian National Research Medical University, Moscow, Russia

O. Golubnitschaja (✉)
Predictive, Preventive and Personalized (3P) Medicine, Department of Radiation Oncology, University Hospital Bonn, Rheinische Friedrich-Wilhelms-Universität Bonn, Bonn, Germany
e-mail: olga.golubnitschaja@ukbonn.de



W. Wang (ed.), *All Around Suboptimal Health*, Advances in Predictive, Preventive and Personalised Medicine 18,
https://doi.org/10.1007/978-3-031-46891-9_12

| | |
|---|---|
| EDD | Endothelium-dependent dilation |
| eNOS | Endothelial nitric oxide-synthase |
| ET-1 | Endothelin-1 |
| EVA | Early vascular aging |
| HDL | High-density lipoproteins |
| HR | Heart rate |
| LDL | Low-density lipoproteins |
| MitoQ | Mitochondria-targeted antioxidant |
| MMPs | Matrix metalloproteinases |
| MnSOD | Manganese superoxide dismutase |
| mTOR | Mammalian target of rapamycin |
| NAD | Nicotinamide adenine dinucleotide |
| NMN | Nicotinamide mononucleotide |
| NO | Nitric oxide |
| NR | Nicotinamide riboside |
| PH | Prehypertension |
| PWV | Pulse wave velocity |
| RF | Risk factors |
| ROS | Reactive oxygen species |
| SBP | Systolic blood pressure |
| SIRT-1 | Sirtuin 1 |
| TC | Total cholesterol |
| TG | Triglycerides |
| VA | Vascular age |
| VS | Vascular stiffness |
| YP | Young people |

## 1 Preamble

Although modern cardiology is characterized by a high level of implementation of innovative therapeutic and diagnostic technologies, cardiovascular diseases (CVD) still remain the leading causes of death worldwide [1]. The problem is aggravated by the fact that the process of rejuvenation of morbidity and mortality from these diseases is widely reported [2]. Contextually, more attention should be paid to studying early preclinical stages of CVD pathogenetic continuum, in particular at young age [3–5], in order to cost-effectively protect populations against health-to-disease transition and vascular aging at the stage of suboptimal health [6, 7]. To this end, specifically stroke of unclear etiology affects a big portion of altogether over 101.5 million individuals diagnosed with stroke worldwide including patients at teenager age. The World Stroke Organization prognosed 1 in 4 adults over the age of 25 getting a stroke in their lifetime with associated global costs estimated at 721 billion US dollars annually. The overall number of affected individuals is assumed to be about 14-times greater than clinically recorded, due to undiagnosed "silent" brain infarction related to early and unpredictable vascular aging [8].

The key point is to change the paradigm from reactive medical services (applied to patients affected by downstream pathologies such as clinically manifested myocardial infarction and ischemic stroke, among others) to a predictive approach applied to individuals in suboptimal health conditions, in order to protect them against the health-to-disease transition based on a multi-parametric health risk assessment and application of artificial intelligence in medicine [8].

## 2 Vascular Stiffness as an Early Stratification Indicator for 3PM Approach

A number of authors believe that preventive CV technologies should be based on the concept of vascular aging, the main determinant of which is arterial stiffness [9, 10]. Increased vascular stiffness (VS), meaning the loss of elastic properties of the medial layer of the wall of large-caliber arteries, is a highly significant predictor of total and CV mortality [11, 12], as is a decrease in the ankle-brachial index (ABI), which reflects abnormalities mainly in the inner layer of the arterial wall [13]. In the case of increased stiffness of the vascular wall, large arteries lose their ability to damping, due to which the impact of the energy of shock blood ejection on internal organs is reduced. For this reason, conditions are created for realization of the damaging effect of excessive pulse wave on target organs, and also the load on myocardium increases, its blood supply is disturbed and the risk of development of major CVD increases [14].

The assessment of vascular stiffness indices allows differentiating young people from their elastic potential of the arterial wall into certain phenotypes. However, until now, young people as carriers of preclinical athero- and arteriosclerosis have not been studied, and these phenotypes have not been investigated in terms of their relationship with major risk factors, including AH, which in turn is considered a leading cardiovascular risk factor (CVRF). Some experts believe that VS and AH are in a continuous bidirectional mutual influence with each other [15].

We are about to develop an approach aimed at identifying carriers of premature vascular aging or EVA (Early Vascular Aging) syndrome among young people in order to include them in the CV risk group as soon as possible and to initiate individualized and targeted preventive programs under control of not only BP and other traditional RF but also VS indices [16]. The goal of such preventive interventions, according to leading experts, should be the restoration of healthy vascular aging and its maintenance on the basis of differentiated preventive interventions under dynamic control of arterial stiffness parameters—in the form of pulse wave velocity (PWV) or cardio-ankle vascular index CAVI (cardio-ankle vascular index). The prognostic significance of VS has been confirmed both in relation to the development of CV complications in mature and elderly individuals [11, 17], and in the aspect of the occurrence of CVD in 35–45 years old individuals, in whom EVA syndrome was detected in childhood and adolescence according to the results of angiological instrumental screening [18].

Interval division of samples homogeneous by sex and age by this index allowed P. Nilsson and his colleagues to substantiate the doctrine of vascular aging phenotypes [10]. In accordance with this approach, three main variants of vascular aging are distinguished: premature (or EVA syndrome), normal, and favorable. This approach creates a prospect for improving the existing dispensary models, as well as for creating a system of effective monitoring of arterial biological age parameters and real management of it in each person starting from the early stages of its pathogenetic CV continuum [19]. Young people are of particular importance in the discussed aspect since it has already been shown that the main behavioral stereotypes, which then act as the main RF, are finally formed exactly at this age [15]. However, the youth features of vascular aging are still poorly studied.

## 3 Complexity of Mechanisms of Premature Vascular Aging

In the process of vascular aging, mechanisms of functional and structural damaging synergistically form arteriosclerosis as a pathology of predominantly (1) middle sheath of arteries and (2) media [15]. Risk factors of the first include increased blood plasma levels of endothelin-1, insufficient NO bioavailability, impaired balance of sympatho-adrenal, immune, renin-angiotensin-aldosterone systems resulting in non-compensated oxidative stress by excessive formation of ROS.

Structural damage to the media side includes the shifted ratio of proteins of the medial membrane such as collagen and elastin, due to the altered activity of metalloproteinases and formation of glycation end products (AGEs). The latter create conditions for "piercing" of proteins promoting arterial stiffness. The functional component of arterial stiffness depends on vasoconstrictor tone, which, in turn, increases the tone of smooth muscle of blood vessels [20]. Age-related neurohumoral dysfunction resulting from a decrease in the baroreflex combined with an increased sympathetic activation also contributes to inadequately enhanced arterial stiffness [21]. Systemic inflammation, which increases with age, may predispose to increased arterial stiffness through immune activation pathways and the development of hypertension. Age-related endothelial dysfunction also interacts closely with arterial stiffness, as it is favored by dissociation of endothelial NO synthase (eNOS) resulting in significantly decreased NO bioavailability, which may be further exacerbated by non-compensated oxidative stress. Age-related structural remodeling of the extracellular matrix of the middle layer is accompanied by pathological changes in the composition and ratio of elastin and collagen in the wall of large elastic arteries. Extended fragmentation and degradation of elastin, which are largely mediated by the activation of matrix metalloproteinases (MMPs) followed by collagen deposition replacing the loss of elastin molecules have been observed [22]. Accelerated formation of glycation end products (AGEs) strongly contributing to the "cross-linking" of protein structures further exacerbate increased arterial stiffness. Oxidative stress and inflammation synergistically lead to proliferation of smooth muscle cells, their transformation, collagen deposition, and remodeling associated with AH. Angiotensin II may also modulate the structural contribution to arterial stiffness by stimulating the formation of collagen, reducing elastin synthesis, and promoting remodeling of the vascular matrix.

Regarding the functional interrelationship between AH and VS, there is still an uncertainty on what is primary and what is secondary in the development of vascular aging, namely an increase BP or vascular stiffness. However, accumulated data indicate that not only AH predisposes to increased vascular stiffness, but also a systematic increase in arterial stiffness may significantly contribute to BP increase with the systolic hypertension as a consequence [23, 24].

Arterial hypertension may contribute to aortic stiffness, and increased stiffness of large elastic arteries may precede and contribute to SBP increase. Rigidity of large elastic arteries is an independent predictor of arterial hypertension in many longitudinal cohorts [25]. Experimental data are consistent with such clinical findings—in rodents fed a diet high in fat and sucrose, an increase in aortic pulse wave velocity was found before an increase in systolic AH [26].

As large elastic arteries become stiffer with age, systolic BP increases while diastolic BP decreases due to decreased elastic recoil of the aorta; as a result, pulse pressure increases with age [8]. Isolated systolic hypertension is the most common form of arterial hypertension in individuals aged 50 years and older. Increased stiffness of large elastic arteries is the main cause of AH changes with age, ultimately contributing to the development of systolic hypertension [27]. Age-related endothelial dysfunction, characterized by decreased nitric oxide (NO) bioavailability and increased endothelin-1 production, also contributes to both increased SBP levels and impaired regulation of vascular tone [21]. These phenomena are partially mediated by increased oxidative stress associated with excessive superoxide production. There may also be an interaction between the immune system and hypertension, as immune activation and inflammation induced by oxidative stress are involved in the development of hypertension [28]. As already indicated, the activity of the sympathetic nervous system increases with age and the association between it and BP levels becomes stronger, especially in women [29]. In addition, chronic activation of the renin-angiotensin system contributes to damage to target organs, including the kidneys and heart, because angiotensin II promotes both BP and the production of reactive oxygen species [15, 30].

## 4 Vascular Stiffness as an Early Indicator of the EVA Syndrome in Youth

According to the recommendations of international experts, in order to determine whether a particular person belongs to one or another variant or phenotype of vascular aging, a sample homogeneous by sex and age should be subjected to interval analysis within its various variants [10, 31]. This approach makes it possible to determine the quantitative criteria of each phenotype by one or another VS indicator—PWV, CAVI, and others.

We examined 346 students (young adults) of the Stavropol State Medical University (131 males and 215 females) to evaluate such VS index as cardio-ankle vascular index or CAVI (cardio-ankle vascular index) on the VaSera device (model VS-1500N, Fukuda Denshi, Japan). Unlike the used PWV, the CAVI index does not depend on the level of current BP stretching the arterial wall at the moment of its measurement [32]. Elevated VS in young adults has already demonstrated its potential to detect an increased risk of CV events later in life [33, 34].

All young adults were divided into tertile groups according to a sex-specific measure of vascular stiffness, the CAVI index. Consideration of biological sex is considered necessary because it has already been established that CAVI index values are on average 0.2 higher in men than in women in all age groups [32]. It was found that male sex is an independent factor determining a higher CAVI level.

With the proposed approach we succeeded with phenotyping of premature aging—see Figs. 1 and 2. To this end, CAVI-R levels correlated well with BP values on the right hand, as well as CAVI-L levels correlated well with BP on the left hand. The system works well for screening and phenotyping of affected individuals and allows for individualized diagnostics and follow-up recommendations. For the EVA syndrome carriers, CAVI-R values ≥6.10 and ≥5.87 are characteristic for young males and females, respectively; CAVI-L values ≥6.16 and ≥6.08 are characteristic for them (see Figs. 1 and 2).

Particular accents should be put to the upper tertile (the group at highest risk) for the targeted disease prevention and treatments tailored to the individualized patient profile [14]. This is the key point for changing the paradigm from reactive medical

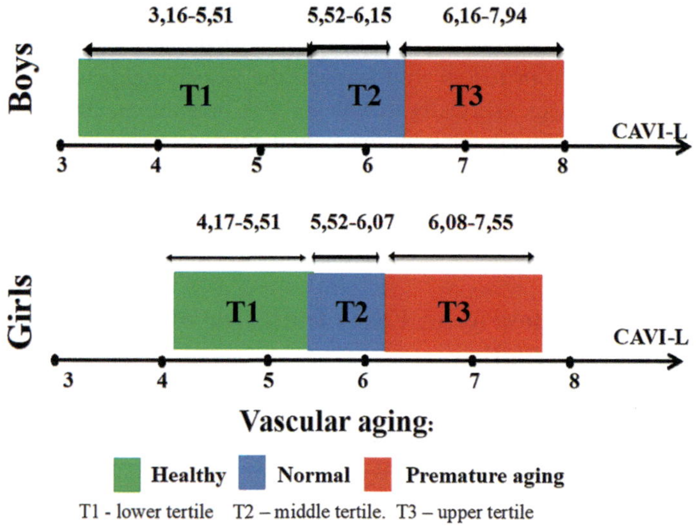


**Fig. 1** Tertile distribution of young people taking into account CAVI-L ($n = 346$)

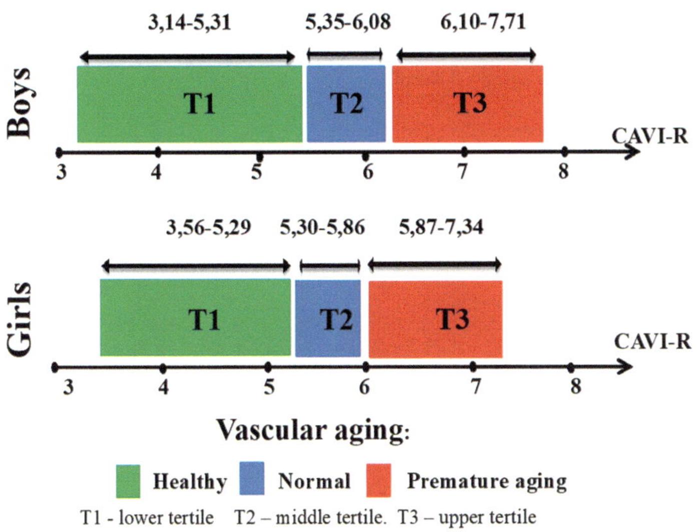


**Fig. 2** Tertile distribution of young adults under consideration stratified by CAVI-R ($n = 346$)

services (applied to patients affected by downstream pathologies such as sudden heart attack, clinically manifested myocardial infarction and ischemic stroke, among others) to healthy individuals in suboptimal conditions to protect them against the transition from health-to-disease based on a multi-parametric analysis (including VS and BP) and application of artificial intelligence in medicine [8].

## 5 Phenotyping of Vascular Aging in Youth Correlated with Blood Pressure

Because of the continuing uncertainty as to whether EVA or arterial hypertension is primary or secondary in the development of the pathogenetic CV continuum, it was important to study BP levels in young adults with different variants of vascular aging.

Table 1 shows that among young males and females from the first to the third group SBP did not increase as expected, but, on the contrary, even slightly decreased. Moreover, the differences in this indicator between the extreme groups in both groups reached a reliable level ($P_{1-3} = 0.048$; $P_{1-3} = 0.037$). No particularly clear trends were found in DBP in either young males or females between the groups. HR was higher in males with favorable phenotype of vascular aging compared with carriers of phenotypes of normal and especially early vascular aging, but the differences between the groups were not significant. In young females, there were no particular differences in HR between groups.

**Table 1** Hemodynamic parameters of young people by phenotyping of vascular aging

| Parameters | First group Healthy aging | Second group Normal aging | Third group Early aging | p | ANOVA |
|---|---|---|---|---|---|
| Young males, *n* = 131 | | | | | |
| *n* | 42 | 44 | 45 | | |
| SBP, mmHg | 134.6 ± 1.8 | 135.1 ± 2.2 | 129.8 ± 1.6 | $P_{1-2} = 0.872$<br>$P_{2-3} = 0.051$<br>$P_{1-3} = 0.048$ | 0.084 |
| DBP, mmHg | 77.4 ± 1.2 | 79.3 ± 1.5 | 77.7 ± 0.9 | $P_{1-2} = 0.861$<br>$P_{2-3} = 0.364$<br>$P_{1-3} = 0.330$ | 0.504 |
| HR, beats/min | 79.2 ± 2.2 | 74.3 ± 2.1 | 72.9 ± 2.3 | $P_{1-2} = 0.109$<br>$P_{2-3} = 0.636$<br>$P_{1-3} = 0.050$ | 0.110 |
| Young females, *n* = 215 | | | | | |
| *n* | 73 | 71 | 71 | | |
| SBP, mmHg | 119.8 ± 1.2 | 116.9 ± 1.3 | 116.3 ± 1.1 | $P_{1-2} = 0.109$<br>$P_{2-3} = 0.735$<br>$P_{1-3} = 0.037$ | 0.097 |
| DBP, mmHg | 71.9 ± 0.9 | 72.3 ± 0.9 | 71.8 ± 0.7 | $P_{1-2} = 0.819$<br>$P_{2-3} = 0.677$<br>$P_{1-3} = 0.865$ | 0.921 |
| HR, beats/min | 73.9 ± 1.2 | 74.6 ± 1.3 | 71.6 ± 1.2 | $P_{1-2} = 0.705$<br>$P_{2-3} = 0.104$<br>$P_{1-3} = 0.192$ | 0.225 |

*SBP* systolic blood pressure; *DBP* diastolic blood pressure; *HR* heart rate

Having received the presented data on the absence of association of AN/PH with CAVI-phenotypes reflecting the level of arterial wall remodeling relative to the middle muscular sheath in young people, we decided to study the peculiarities of occurrence of various hemodynamic variants in the aspect of isolated EVA syndrome, isolated BP increase and their combination. It is equally important to determine among young people the representation of carriers of a favorable combination, including the presence of normotonia with good vascular elasticity. This approach to the analysis of the obtained data allows us to understand how the process of development of the main cardiovascular pathology starts long before its clinical manifestation, as young people correspond to the very beginning of the pathogenetic CV continuum.

The data of another analysis (Fig. 3) show that a certain part of the examined young people are carriers of isolated VS increase, i.e., they have increased VS combined with office normotension and even with hypotension. This phenomenon is somewhat more frequent among young females, but the differences with young men in terms of VS do not reach a significant level. There is also an isolated presence of office BP increase in conditions of preserved elastic potential of the vascular wall. This variant of hemodynamic status is observed three times more often among young men compared to their female counterparts ($p = 0.000$). The combined variant of increased VS together with increased BP was also registered 2.6 times more often ($p = 0.024$) in the representatives of the stronger sex. More than a half of

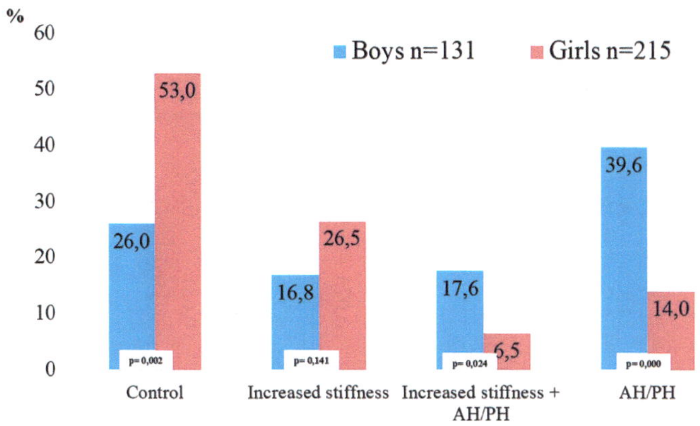


**Fig. 3** Hemodynamic variants in young people according to the CAVI-L index ($n$ = 346)

young females and only a quarter of young males ($p = 0.02$) were carriers of favorable hemodynamic status, which in the discussed aspect means a combined presence of non-elevated BP and sufficiently preserved elastic status of arteries within the framework of untimely vascular aging, which corresponds to the first and third CAVI-tertiles.

In other words, the obtained data clearly show that both EVA syndrome and increased BP can act as the primary event at the early preclinical stage of the development of major CVD in young people. At the same time, there are clear sex differences in young people with respect to the presence of the hemodynamic variants we have identified, associated with two important CV parameters such as BP and arterial stiffness. Such subdivision of the youth population according to the presented variants of hemodynamic status based on the results of preventive angio-screening may provide very effective tools for preclinical diagnosis of the features of vascular remodeling at the very beginning of the pathogenetic cardiovascular continuum.

Follow-up studies are required to elucidate both the causes of the identified differences and the peculiarities of further clinical course of these hemodynamic variants. Their identification also dictates the need to study the possibilities of differentiated approaches to preventive interventions aimed at restoration and maintenance of healthy vascular aging in EVA syndrome depending on the level of background BP.

## 6 Phenotyping of Vascular Aging Correlated with BMI: The Youth Obesity Paradox

The study of vascular stiffness (VS) in young people from the point of view of the peculiarities of the correlation of its index such as CAVI with the main RF (Table 2) allowed us to find out that the most significant correlation of this index was with body weight and BMI. The correlation between these parameters in young men and

**Table 2** Correlation of the indicator CAVI with the main risk factors in investigated groups of young males and females

| Parameters | Statistical significance | Age | Height | Weight | BMI | TC | HDL | TG | LDL | AC | Glucose |
|---|---|---|---|---|---|---|---|---|---|---|---|
| **Young males, $n = 93$** | | | | | | | | | | | |
| CAVI-R | Pearson correlation coefficient | 0.193 | −0.145 | −0.428[b] | −0.417[b] | −0.054 | 0.091 | −0.017 | −0.084 | −0.013 | −0.058 |
| | *p* | 0.064 | 0.165 | 0.000 | 0.000 | 0.666 | 0.466 | 0.895 | 0.505 | 0.920 | 0.647 |
| CAVI-L | Pearson correlation coefficient | 0.210[a] | −0.124 | −0.453[b] | −0.456[b] | −0.048 | 0.131 | −0.006 | −0.091 | −0.022 | −0.043 |
| | *p* | 0.044 | 0.237 | 0.000 | 0.000 | 0.699 | 0.294 | 0.960 | 0.465 | 0.867 | 0.739 |
| **Young females, $n = 171$** | | | | | | | | | | | |
| CAVI-R | Pearson correlation coefficient | 0.152[a] | −0.058 | −0.108 | −0.109 | 0.002 | 0.020 | −0.128 | 0.025 | −0.086 | −0.067 |
| | *p* | 0.047 | 0.454 | 0.160 | 0.157 | 0.982 | 0.830 | 0.178 | 0.796 | 0.380 | 0.487 |
| CAVI-L | Pearson correlation coefficient | 0.135 | −0.046 | −0.112 | −0.122 | 0.017 | 0.030 | −0.153 | 0.039 | −0.105 | −0.036 |
| | *p* | 0.079 | 0.548 | 0.143 | 0.111 | 0.860 | 0.750 | 0.105 | 0.681 | 0.281 | 0.707 |

*CAVI-R* cardio-ankle vascular index right; *CAVI-L* cardio-ankle vascular index left; *BMI* body mass index; *TC* total cholesterol; *HDL* high-density lipoproteins; *TG* triglycerides; *LDL* low-density lipoproteins; *AC* atherogenicity coefficient

[a] The significance of the connection at the level of 0.05 (*p*)

[b] The significance of the connection at the level of 0.01 (*p*)

young females is negative and moderate, and in the former it was also highly significant.

We also studied the features of VS association with weight, BMI, and waist from the standpoint of the above-described phenotypes of vascular aging, which we determined by CAVI-tertile groups presented above (Table 2). It turned out that body weight, BMI, and waist volume in both—young males and females from the first to the third group, i.e., as the arterial aging phenotype worsened, the differences between the groups of comparison for the first two parameters reached a significant level among young males. Table 3 summarizes selected cardio-metabolic RF in groups of comparison stratified by phenotypes of corresponding vascular aging.

The results of analyzing the parameters of vascular status and basic RF in three groups formed according to BMI level (Table 4) demonstrated that as BMI increases, the CAVI index in both young males and females steadily decreases. We called the phenomenon we have identified "the youth obesity paradox." An analysis of the current literature has shown the absence of such a phenomenon in older individuals [35]. At the same time, similar results have been recorded in children [36].

The "youth obesity paradox" described by us demonstrates clear sex differences. The described trend is particularly clear among young men—the difference in mean CAVI values between the extreme groups on both sides is 1.4, while in young

**Table 3** Selected cardio-metabolic RF in groups of comparison stratified by phenotypes of corresponding vascular aging

| Parameters | 1 g Healthy aging | 2 g Normal aging | 3 g Early aging | *p* | ANOVA |
|---|---|---|---|---|---|
| Young males, *n* = 131 | | | | | |
| *n* | 42 | 44 | 45 | | |
| Body weight, kg | 81.8 ± 1.8 | 75.4 ± 2.2 | 71.4 ± 2.1 | $P_{1-2} = 0.026$<br>$P_{2-3} = 0.205$<br>$P_{1-3} = 0.000$ | 0.002 |
| BMI, kg/m$^2$ | 25.2 ± 0.5 | 23.6 ± 0.6 | 22.1 ± 0.6 | $P_{1-2} = 0.052$<br>$P_{2-3} = 0.087$<br>$P_{1-3} = 0.000$ | 0.001 |
| Waist, cm | 86.3 ± 1.7 | 82.3 ± 1.8 | 81.3 ± 2.0 | $P_{1-2} = 0.110$<br>$P_{2-3} = 0.710$<br>$P_{1-3} = 0.062$ | 0.139 |
| Young females, *n* = 215 | | | | | |
| *n* | 73 | 71 | 71 | | |
| Body weight, kg | 62.1 ± 1.2 | 59.3 ± 1.2 | 57.8 ± 1.1 | $P_{1-2} = 0.111$<br>$P_{2-3} = 0.376$<br>$P_{1-3} = 0.011$ | 0.038 |
| BMI, kg/m$^2$ | 22.5 ± 0.5 | 21.3 ± 0.4 | 20.9 ± 0.4 | $P_{1-2} = 0.043$<br>$P_{2-3} = 0.569$<br>$P_{1-3} = 0.010$ | 0.019 |
| Waist, cm | 70.9 ± 0.9 | 70.0 ± 1.3 | 69.0 ± 0.9 | $P_{1-2} = 0.594$<br>$P_{2-3} = 0.529$<br>$P_{1-3} = 0.174$ | 0.460 |

*BMI* body mass index

**Table 4** CAVI values and the main risk factors in groups of comparison stratified by BMI

| Parameters | Young males, $n = 93$ | | | $p_{1-2}$ $p_{2-3}$ $p_{1-3}$ | Young females, $n = 171$ | | | $p_{1-2}$ $p_{2-3}$ $p_{1-3}$ |
|---|---|---|---|---|---|---|---|---|
| | Group 1 Insufficient BW $n = 12$ | Group 2 Normal BW $n = 56$ | Group 3 Excess BW $n = 25$ | | Group 1 Insufficient BW $n = 32$ | Group 2 Normal BW $n = 119$ | Group 3 Excess BW $n = 20$ | |
| CAVI-R | 6.7 ± 0.2 | 5.7 ± 0.1 | 5.3 ± 0.1 | $P_{1-2 = 0.000}$ $P_{2-3 = 0.008}$ $P_{1-3 = 0.000}$ | 5.8 ± 0.14 | 5.6 ± 0.06 | 5.5 ± 0.13 | $P_{1-2 = 0.141}$ $P_{2-3 = 0.286}$ $P_{1-3 = 0.091}$ |
| CAVI-L | 6.8 ± 0.2 | 5.9 ± 0.1 | 5.4 ± 0.1 | $P_{1-2 = 0.000}$ $P_{2-3 = 0.002}$ $P_{1-3 = 0.000}$ | 6.1 ± 0.11 | 5.9 ± 0.05 | 5.7 ± 0.13 | $P_{1-2 = 0.298}$ $P_{2-3 = 0.134}$ $P_{1-3 = 0.053}$ |
| SBP, mmHg | 127.8 ± 3.2 | 131.9 ± 1.3 | 136.04 ± 3.5 | $P_{1-2 = 0.211}$ $P_{2-3 = 0.183}$ $P_{1-3 = 0.145}$ | 114 ± 1.2 | 117 ± 0.86 | 125.15 ± 2.0 | $P_{1-2 = 0.091}$ $P_{2-3 = 0.000}$ $P_{1-3 = 0.000}$ |
| DBP, mmHg | 74.6 ± 1.5 | 77.8 ± 1.02 | 77.72 ± 1.9 | $P_{1-2 = 0.174}$ $P_{2-3 = 0.983}$ $P_{1-3 = 0.314}$ | 70.8 ± 1.01 | 70.9 ± 0.6 | 74.65 ± 1.5 | $P_{1-2 = 0.925}$ $P_{2-3 = 0.030}$ $P_{1-3 = 0.031}$ |
| HR, beats/min | 81.9 ± 6.3 | 74.3 ± 1.5 | 73.96 ± 2.7 | $P_{1-2 = 0.087}$ $P_{2-3 = 0.907}$ $P_{1-3 = 0.177}$ | 76.5 ± 1.6 | 72.1 ± 1.1 | 74.6 ± 2.5 | $P_{1-2 = 0.056}$ $P_{2-3 = 0.369}$ $P_{1-3 = 0.514}$ |
| TC, mmol/L | 3.5 ± 0.2 | 3.5 ± 0.1 | 4 ± 0.2 | $P_{1-2 = 0.904}$ $P_{2-3 = 0.038}$ $P_{1-3 = 0.097}$ | 4.02 ± 0.2 | 3.94 ± 0.08 | 4.6 ± 0.16 | $P_{1-2 = 0.652}$ $P_{2-3 = 0.003}$ $P_{1-3 = 0.033}$ |
| HDL, mmol/L | 1.02 ± 0.08 | 0.99 ± 0.04 | 0.95 ± 0.06 | $P_{1-2 = 0.776}$ $P_{2-3 = 0.538}$ $P_{1-3 = 0.502}$ | 1.5 ± 0.08 | 1.35 ± 0.03 | 1.13 ± 0.13 | $P_{1-2 = 0.028}$ $P_{2-3 = 0.014}$ $P_{1-3 = 0.013}$ |

| | | | | | | | | |
|---|---|---|---|---|---|---|---|---|
| TG, mmol/L | 1.1 ± 0.3 | 1.04 ± 0.1 | 1.6 ± 0.2 | $P_{1-2 = 0.821}$<br>$P_{2-3 = 0.020}$<br>$P_{1-3 = 0.218}$ | 0.7 ± 0.04 | 0.82 ± 0.04 | 1.35 ± 0.2 | $P_{1-2 = 0.417}$<br>$P_{2-3 = 0.000}$<br>$P_{1-3 = 0.006}$ |
| LDL, mmol/L | 1.9 ± 0.3 | 2.1 ± 0.1 | 2.32 ± 0.14 | $P_{1-2 = 0.688}$<br>$P_{2-3 = 0.188}$<br>$P_{1-3 = 0.198}$ | 2.1 ± 0.2 | 2.21 ± 0.08 | 2.8 ± 0.2 | $P_{1-2 = 0.620}$<br>$P_{2-3 = 0.006}$<br>$P_{1-3 = 0.011}$ |
| AC | 3.5 ± 0.2 | 3.7 ± 0.2 | 4.23 ± 0.3 | $P_{1-2 = 0.731}$<br>$P_{2-3 = 0.131}$<br>$P_{1-3 = 0.094}$ | 2.75 ± 0.2 | 2.9 ± 0.09 | 4.38 ± 0.37 | $P_{1-2 = 0.422}$<br>$P_{2-3 = 0.000}$<br>$P_{1-3 = 0.000}$ |
| Glucose, mmol/L | 4.9 ± 0.05 | 4.99 ± 0.1 | 5.02 ± 0.15 | $P_{1-2 = 0.830}$<br>$P_{2-3 = 0.877}$<br>$P_{1-3 = 0.671}$ | 4.75 ± 0.1 | 5.1 ± 0.07 | 4.89 ± 0.2 | $P_{1-2 = 0.065}$<br>$P_{2-3 = 0.373}$<br>$P_{1-3 = 0.499}$ |

*AH* arterial hypertension; *BW* body weight; *TC* total cholesterol; *HDL* high-density lipoproteins; *TG* triglycerides; *LDL* low-density lipoproteins; *AC* atherogenicity coefficient, *SBP* systolic blood pressure; *DBP* diastolic blood pressure; *HR* heart rate, *CAVI-L* cardio-ankle vascular index left; *CAVI-R* cardio-ankle vascular index right females it is only 0.3 for CAVI-R and 0.4 for CAVI-L. At the same time, thin young males have markedly higher values than thin young females, and in contrast, obese young males have lower values than obese young females. At the same time, the differences between the groups reach significant differences. It is noteworthy that this trend on the part of VS indicator is observed despite the increase in both SBP and DBP from group 1 to group 3. An unfavorable tendency was also revealed in the above groups on the side of lipidogram parameters, and it was especially strong in young females.

The data presented in the tables in their totality characterize the age specificity of vascular aging at the young stage of the life cycle. It is shown that there is no special influence of the main RF on VS and its, in fact, paradoxical reaction to the increase in BM. Moreover, this seemingly positive rearrangement of the arterial wall occurs in young individuals despite the obvious deterioration of hemodynamics and lipid status associated with overweight and/or obesity.

According to the current literature [37, 38], the correlation between VS and overweight and/or obesity in older age groups is quite different—in adulthood the correlation between these parameters is close to zero, and in old age it becomes positive. At the same time, our data coincide with the results of pediatric studies indicating a lower level of VS in obese children compared to their normal-weight peers [39, 40]. The authors explain this phenomenon in children by the inclusion of a peculiar adaptation mechanism as a consequence of the training effect of excessive BM on the activity of their CV system by analogy with physical exercise. This adaptation moment is limited in time and therefore some researchers call it a "honeymoon period" [41].

Summarizing these data with our results on young people, we can conclude that the directionality of the effect of the above RF on the arterial wall in terms of its stiffness has clear age-specific features that should be taken into account when planning preventive interventions for individuals of different ages. We believe that despite the youthful "obesity paradox" described by us, the correction of metabolic and hemodynamic disorders should be started in youth, even in the presence of seemingly different rejuvenating effect of obesity on the vascular wall, which we described above. Only from such long-term positions in the planning and implementation of preventive interventions can we expect to slow down vascular aging in mature and elderly people in full compliance with the principles of 3P-medicine.

## 7 Arterial Hypertension in Young Adults: Particularities of Metabolic and Hemodynamic Status

Since elevated BP of all RF makes the most significant contribution to CV mortality of the adult population, we believe that the study of AH features at the beginning of the pathogenetic continuum, to which young people correspond, deserve special attention.

The data in Table 5 show that in young males the index of vascular stiffness CAVI on both sides of its registration slightly decreases with increasing BP although the differences between the groups do not reach a significant level ($p = 0.099$ on the left and $p = 0.105$ on the right). It should be reminded that this index characterizes the state of the middle shell of the arterial wall and its increase indicates an increase in arterial stiffness due to the development of arteriosclerosis and loss of its elastic potential. Therefore, the data obtained in young males with AH on the decrease of CAVI index indicate the improvement of elastic properties of arteries, which we can explain by the higher BMI in this group and for this reason associated with the previously described youth obesity paradox. At the same time, the ankle-brachial index (ABI), which reflects, with its decrease, the impairment of mainly the internal arterial sheath due to atherosclerosis, also slightly decreases and for this parameter the differences between the groups reach significant values for both sides of the registration ($p = 0.000$ on the left and $p = 0.004$ on the right). BMI and waist score show an increase in the presence of AN/PH, but it is not significant ($p = 0.074$) and ($p = 0.103$), respectively. Most of the atherogenic lipid status parameters tend to be increased, anti-atherogenic HDL tend to be decreased, but the differences between normo- and hypertensive young males are not significant. Fasting blood glucose is unchanged. The incidence of aggravated heredity (BH) for the development of early

**Table 5** Selected hemodynamic, metabolic, and other parameters at AH/PH in young males ($n = 131$)

| Parameters | Normotension $n = 58$ | AH/PH $n = 73$ | $p$ |
|---|---|---|---|
| Young males | | | |
| HR, beats/min | 74.7 ± 15.2 | 75.9 ± 13.9 | 0.630 |
| CAVI-R | 5.83 ± 0.8 | 5.60 ± 0.74 | 0.105 |
| CAVI-L | 5.98 ± 0.8 | 5.76 ± 0.73 | 0.099 |
| ABI on the right | 1.07 ± 0.1 | 1.02 ± 0.08 | 0.004 |
| ABI on the left | 1.08 ± 0.08 | 1.02 ± 0.08 | 0.000 |
| BMI, kg/m$^2$ | 22.89 ± 4.4 | 24.2 ± 3.7 | 0.074 |
| Waist, cm | 81.4 ± 8.9 | 84.8 ± 11.5 | 0.103 |
| TC, mmol/L | 3.58 ± 0.76 | 3.70 ± 0.86 | 0.552 |
| HDL, mmol/L | 1.03 ± 0.21 | 1.01 ± 0.29 | 0.805 |
| TG, mmol/L | 1.13 ± 0.64 | 1.25 ± 0.91 | 0.532 |
| LDL, mmol/L | 2.06 ± 0.7 | 2.16 ± 0.68 | 0.559 |
| AC | 3.56 ± 0.88 | 3.77 ± 1.30 | 0.464 |
| Glucose, mmol/L | 5.03 ± 0.68 | 5.03 ± 0.73 | 0.992 |
| Smoking, *n* (%) | 6 (10.3) | 9 (12.3) | 0.674 |
| BH, *n* (%) | 17 (29.3) | 30 (41.1) | 0.160 |

Note: *AH* arterial hypertension; *PH* prehypertension; *HR* heart rate; *CAVI-R* cardio-ankle vascular index right; *CAVI-L* cardio-ankle vascular index left; *ABI* ankle-shoulder index; *BMI* body mass index; *TC* total cholesterol; *TG* triglycerides; *HDL* high-density lipoproteins; *LDL* low lipoproteins; *AC* atherogenicity coefficient; *BH* burdened heredity

CVD in families among young hypertensive males reached 41% versus almost 30% in normotensive males, but the difference is not significant ($p = 0.160$). The number of smokers in the compared groups is almost the same, but it is slightly higher in the group with AN/PH. Table 6 summarizes selected hemodynamic, metabolic, and other parameters at AH/PH in investigated young females.

Among the examined young females (Table 6), the changes in the vascular stiffness index CAVI on the left and right sides show a similar tendency to its decrease with increasing BP. Moreover, on one side the differences between the groups reach quite a significant level ($p = 0.012$ on the left and $p = 0.133$ on the right). The ABI in young females also showed a similar trend to that of young males, with a significant decrease in ABI in AN/PH carriers compared to normotensive peers ($p = 0.003$ on the left and $p = 0.007$ on the right). In young females, BMI and waist also showed an increase in the presence of AH/PH, with the former parameter showing significant differences between groups ($p = 0.000$). As in young males, most atherogenic lipid status indicators in the weaker sex tend to increase, anti-atherogenic HDL—to decrease, but the differences between normo- and hypertensive young females are not significant. Fasting blood glucose in young females does not show a significant increase with increasing BP ($p = 0.174$), and its mean values do not exceed the acceptable norm. BH on early CVD among hypertensive young females was

**Table 6** Selected hemodynamic, metabolic, and other parameters at AH/PH in investigated young females ($n = 215$)

| Parameters | Normotension $n = 168$ | AH/PH $n = 47$ | $p$ |
|---|---|---|---|
| Young females | | | |
| HR, beats/min | 72.0 ± 10.1 | 78.3 ± 11.8 | 0.002 |
| CAVI-R | 5.62 ± 0.7 | 5.46 ± 0.6 | 0.133 |
| CAVI-L | 5.87 ± 0.64 | 5.63 ± 0.5 | 0.012 |
| ABI on the right | 1.08 ± 0.08 | 1.04 ± 0.08 | 0.007 |
| ABI on the left | 1.07 ± 0.07 | 1.03 ± 0.07 | 0.003 |
| BMI, kg/m$^2$ | 20.99 ± 2.7 | 23.82 ± 4.6 | 0.000 |
| Waist, cm | 69.5 ± 7.4 | 72.11 ± 8.5 | 0.132 |
| TC, mmol/L | 4.00 ± 0.8 | 3.99 ± 0.8 | 0.920 |
| HDL, mmol/L | 1.39 ± 0.3 | 1.25 ± 0.35 | 0.129 |
| TG, mmol/L | 0.85 ± 0.5 | 0.89 ± 0.49 | 0.702 |
| LDL, mmol/L | 2.27 ± 0.7 | 2.28 ± 0.78 | 0.944 |
| AC | 3.02 ± 0.8 | 3.33 ± 1.26 | 0.298 |
| Glucose, mmol/L | 4.91 ± 0.5 | 5.22 ± 0.96 | 0.174 |
| Smoking, *n* (%) | 2 (1.2) | 1 (2.1) | 0.620 |
| BH, *n* (%) | 55 (32.7) | 21 (44.7) | 0.173 |

*AH* arterial hypertension; *PH* prehypertension; *HR* heart rate; *CAVI-R* cardio-ankle vascular index right; *CAVI-L* cardio-ankle vascular index left; *ABI* ankle-shoulder index; *BMI* body mass index; *TC* total cholesterol; *TG* triglycerides; *HDL* high-density lipoproteins; *LDL* low lipoproteins; *AC* atherogenicity coefficient; *BH* burdened heredity detected in almost every second, while in the normotensive group only in every third. The number of young females who smoked did not exceed 1.5% of all those examined in the two groups.

In general, the materials presented in this subchapter once again show the presence of specific associations between arterial stiffness and BP at young age, which predetermine the possibility of AH development in young people at overweight despite the presence of a favorable vascular status in the form of a reduced VS indicating a good elastic status of the arteries. Usually in the literature, when describing the relationship between AH and VS in the traditional mature population, it is stated that there is a direct relationship between these parameters of hemodynamic status [42]. The favorable variant of AH presented by us was practically not described. Meanwhile, based on our own results, carriers of this form of elevated BP among young males are almost 40%, and among young females—14%. Taken together, our data indicate the need to use in the practice of dispensary measures among young people the method of angiological screening to assess the VS index and identify vascular phenotypes with mandatory and timely consideration of BP level in each young person.

## 8 3PM-Related Concepts to Maintain Vascular Health in the Population

Vascular aging phenotypes can be determined at both clinical and preclinical stages of the CV continuum. In patients with overt CV pathology, assessment of vascular age (VA) can be used to improve compliance with treatment and to assess the effect of therapy on VS as one important indicator of its efficacy. These are technologies within the framework of reactive or disease-oriented medicine. In the case of young students, we should talk about preclinical diagnostics, which in essence corresponds to health-oriented medicine and aims to inhibit or even stop the process of initial development of CV pathology, which, in turn, is the most effective way to reduce CVD and mortality. This approach is fully consistent with the principles of 3P-medicine. The main stake in this contingent is made not on traditional pharmaceutical therapy, but on preventive interventions aimed not only at correction of traditional RF, but at restoration of favorable vascular aging or its maintenance. For this reason, we advocate the introduction of instrumental assessment of VS, which is the main determinant of vascular age, and its further correction as the main technologies of the youth dispensary system.

What are the main principles of corrective measures after determination of VA phenotype in young people? Of course, first and foremost, these should be strategies based on a rational lifestyle.

In this section, we focus on the mechanisms by which lifestyle-based strategies can modulate arterial stiffness without much effect on BP [43]. The authors suggest that lifestyle-based strategies designed to maintain or restore healthy vascular aging appear more likely to influence the functional components of arterial stiffness. After all, it is difficult to identify any structural changes that might occur during the time period that is usually assessed in traditional prospective studies [21].

## 8.1 *Physical Activity*

The results of studies aimed at investigating the cellular and molecular mechanisms of the positive effects of aerobic exercise on cardiovascular function in aging have shown the important role of inhibition of oxidative stress and inflammation during such exercise [44]. In an experiment on mice, it has been shown that aerobic exercise can improve the status of vascular mitochondria in elderly animals [45], and lifelong exercise can prevent age-related decline in the functional status of mitochondria in the vascular wall [46]. Older adults who engage in aerobic exercise have also been found to have lower markers of endothelial cell senescence compared to their sedentary peers [47]. These markers include, for example, less blood flow-mediated dilatation of the brachial artery. The authors conclude that the described effect of aerobic exercise on vascular function is to inhibit various signs of aging in arterial wall structures through suppression of oxidative stress and inflammation or both simultaneously. To this end, starting with early age, for example, in subpopulations of school children, personalized couching of body exercises is essential to meet individual needs and effectively promote health conditions [48].

## 8.2 *Impacts by Healthy Dietary Patterns*

### 8.2.1 Calorie Restriction (CR)

Reducing total caloric intake (by approximately 30–40%) while maintaining adequate micronutrient intake is one of the most well-studied and documented methods of beneficial effects on the CV system [49]. In an experiment, it has been shown that lifelong CR in mice can prevent endothelial dysfunction, arterial stiffness and increased SBP by partially preventing excess oxidative stress, as well as preserving NO bioavailability and the balance of arterial wall structural proteins (collagen and elastin). It was still found that lifelong CR could preserve the abundance and/or activity of SIRT-1 and mTOR (with no differences compared to young control groups), which allowed the authors to suggest that CR contributes to the preservation of vascular function throughout life, partially affecting a hallmark of aging such as "unregulated nutrient uptake" [50]. CR may also improve CV system health during aging by enhancing autophagy, suggesting that CR may also affect another hallmark of aging, "impaired proteostasis" [51].

Diet-induced weight loss (consumption of a diet designed to reduce body weight by 10%) in young and elderly people with overweight and/or obesity has also been shown to improve vascular endothelial function and arterial stiffness [52]. Moreover, the improvement in endothelial function was associated with a reduction in oxidative stress as assessed by circulating oxidized low-density lipoprotein cholesterol. It has also been demonstrated that diet-induced weight loss in overweight and obese adults can reduce arterial stiffness and SBP by 7–8 mmHg [53, 54]. Taken together, these results suggest that CR-mediated weight loss may be an effective dietary approach to improve cardiovascular health at different ages.

### 8.2.2 Limiting Dietary Sodium Intake

Given the clear association between excessive dietary sodium intake and cardiovascular dysfunction [55], reducing sodium intake is recommended as a lifestyle/nutritional strategy for individuals at increased risk of CVD (e.g., adults with overweight and/or obesity). Historically, dietary sodium restriction (DSR) has been promoted as a therapeutic strategy to reduce BP—for example, the DASH diet is an important component of the dietary approach to the treatment of hypertension [56]; however, excessive dietary sodium intake has adverse effects independent of BP. It has been found that DSR can improve endothelial function in arteries by increasing NO bioavailability secondary to a reduction in excess suppression of endothelial function associated with oxidative stress [57]. DSR has also been found to be associated with reduced aortic stiffness in adults with overweight and/or obesity [58, 59]. Some investigators suggest that DSR may improve endothelial function by altering arteriolar deoxyribonucleic acid methylation patterns (i.e., through epigenetics) [60]. In other words, DSR may be a safe and effective dietary strategy to improve CV health in adults with overweight and/or obesity.

### 8.2.3 Relevant Dietary Models

As mentioned earlier, the DASH diet was specifically designed to reduce BP, and its efficacy for reducing BP in adults with overweight and/or obesity has already been established. Data from a large cohort longitudinal study also suggest that the DASH diet independently inhibits the increase in arterial stiffness between the ages of 36 and 64 years [61]. However, the effect of the DASH diet on endothelial function is equivocal [62, 63].

The Mediterranean diet is defined as a diet rich in whole grains, vegetables, legumes, fruits, seeds, herbs, spices, olive oil and, in moderation, seafood, dairy products and poultry. It has demonstrated clear efficacy to improve arterial stiffness, endothelial function, normalize SBP [64, 65] and prevent CVD [66]. In the elderly, effects on arterial stiffness and SBP levels have been found [67]. The cardiovascular function-promoting effects of both the DASH and Mediterranean diets are thought to be due in part to the high intake of soluble fiber that accompanies these diets. Numerous epidemiological and intervention studies involving large cohorts have shown that high-fiber diets reduce CVD-related morbidity and mortality [68–71].

Unfortunately, a low percentage of individuals with overweight and/or obesity follow the recommended daily intake of total dietary fiber (25–30 g/day) [71]. The DASH diet and Mediterranean diet as a dietary style may represent effective approaches to increase fiber intake in adults with overweight and/or obesity. Recently, a group of researchers from Colorado conducted a controlled nutrition study in children and adolescents under 18 years of age to determine the effects of dietary fiber on arterial function, in which one part of the study included a short-term (7-day) high-fiber diet. The results of this study showed that increasing dietary fiber in this population was a safe and effective strategy to improve endothelial function and SBP (4 mmHg reduction in 7 days), and that these improvements may be due to a reduction in vascular oxidative stress [72]. However, more work is required to determine whether high-fiber diets directly affect vascular function in aging and to explore the potential mechanisms underlying these effects.

The European Association of Preventive Cardiology (EAPC) in the latest version of its recommendations for the prevention of major CVD [73] presents for practical use the following positions of the formation of a rational diet, which in general coincide with the principles of the above-described diets.

Characteristics of a healthy diet (EARS, 2021):

1. The basis of the diet is predominantly plant foods rather than animal foods.
2. Saturated fatty acids account for <10% of daily calories and are replaced by polyunsaturated fatty acids, monounsaturated fatty acids, and whole-grain carbohydrates
3. Trans-unsaturated fatty acids should be minimized where possible, eliminating their intake from processed foods.
4. <5 g of table salt per day.
5. 30–45 g dietary fiber per day, preferably from whole-grain products.
6. ≥200 g of fruit per day (≥2–3 servings).
7. ≥200 g of vegetables per day (≥2–3 servings).
8. Limiting red meat intake to 350–500 g/week, especially processed meat should be minimized.
9. Consumption of fish one to two times per week, especially oily fish is recommended.
10. 30 g of unsalted nuts per day.
11. Limit alcohol consumption to 100 g/week.
12. Avoid sugary drinks such as soft drinks and fruit juices.

## 8.3 *Dietary Supplements*

Regular aerobic exercise, a healthy diet, reducing caloric intake (if necessary) and restricting certain nutrients (e.g., DSRs) are likely to be the most effective approaches to promote healthy aging of the CV system. From a public health perspective, these interventions should be considered first-line strategies [74, 75]. A complementary approach could be the use of "natural" therapies such as nutraceuticals, defined as dietary supplements that may benefit human health in the aspect of inhibition of premature aging [76, 77] or certain synthetic pharmacological agents based on consideration of physiological functions and with favorable safety profiles. In this aspect, it is worth highlighting the long-term research data of the already mentioned group from Colorado [15, 21], as such an approach to influence the primary mechanisms of age-related vascular dysfunction is particularly relevant for the young population in accordance with the principles of 3P medicine. Their research concerns compounds that target: (1) nitric oxide (NO) bioavailability; (2) mitochondrial health and mitophagy involvement; (3) inflammation; (4) energy perception and NAD+ homeostasis; (5) cellular senescence.

## 8.4 *Bioavailability of Nitric Oxide (NO)*

NO bioavailability decreases with age and can be increased with certain lifestyle modifications [78]. Therefore, NO represents a therapeutic target for the correction and/or prevention of CV aging [79]. Supplementation of inorganic nitrite to old and young mice in their diet has been shown to completely reverse age-related endothelial dysfunction by increasing NO bioavailability secondary to a reduction in oxidative stress, as well as reducing arterial stiffness [80]. Similar changes have been described in adult subjects by sodium nitrite administration [78, 81]. The mechanism of such anti-aging effects has been deciphered. It has been shown that sodium nitrite supplementation leads to a decrease in free oxygen radical (ROS) levels in the mitochondria of the vascular wall and thereby contributes to mitochondrial stress resistance [81]. Research is now ongoing with inorganic nitrate supplementation using nitrate-rich beetroot juice to increase NO bioavailability to improve vascular function and normalize BP in patients with chronic kidney disease. If beetroot juice is shown to be safe and effective, it could be a very useful nutraceutical to improve vascular function and reduce the risk of CVD in chronic kidney disease, as these diseases are the leading cause of death in these patients [82].

## 8.5 *Mitochondrial Health as the Target for Anti-aging Strategies*

Mitochondria are frequently the major source of excessive oxidative stress in aging. Therefore, targeting the mitochondrial health becomes an effective therapeutic approach for preventing and treating age-related vascular dysfunction [83]. It was found that the addition of the mitochondria-targeted antioxidant MitoQ to the diet of aged mice completely restores (returns to youthful levels) endothelial function by increasing NO bioavailability, reducing ROS in mitochondria and, in part, by increasing mitochondrial resistance to stress [84]. The same effect was obtained in adults with overweight and/or obesity [85].

It has been shown that the disaccharide and natural autophagy enhancer trehalose can reverse age-related endothelial dysfunction by increasing NO bioavailability and reducing ROS-related EDD over-suppression and may also reduce age-related arterial stiffness. These changes have been associated with reduced inflammation and increased activation of mitochondrial quality control and autophagy pathways in the vascular network [86, 87]. In addition, trehalose reduced vascular mitochondrial oxidative stress, suggesting an improvement in mitochondrial status [87]. In adults with overweight and/or obesity, it was found that trehalose supplementation could improve arterial resistance to EDD by increasing NO bioavailability and reducing excess oxidative stress; however, trehalose had no effect on arterial stiffness in this cohort [88]. As trehalose is a disaccharide (carbohydrate), long-term administration requires body weight control [88]. The natural polyamine spermidine has also been studied in terms of its effect on autophagy, and it was found that spermidine is generally safe and can restore age-related impairment of NO-mediated endothelial function and reverse aortic stiffness in mice [89]. The improvement in arterial function was mediated by a reduction in vascular oxidative stress and was associated with increased activation of autophagic pathways [89]. Clinical studies showed that dietary spermidine intake is inversely associated with BP and cardiovascular disease risk [90]. More information about the mitochondrial health—associated medical conditions is provided in the chapter "*Mitochondrion: The Subordinated Partner Who Agreed to Come Short but Insists in Healthy Life*" by Golubnitschaja O.

## 8.6 Adverse Effects by Inflammation

Inflammation is a well-known mechanism of CV system aging [91, 92]. A study of the anti-inflammatory nutraceutical curcumin (the main polyphenol contained in turmeric) in an experiment showed that its administration could restore NO-mediated endothelial function and normalize arterial stiffness in old mice by reducing excess oxidative stress [93]. In humans, curcumin supplementation was able to improve NO-mediated resistance and arterial endothelial function by reducing excess oxidative stress, but had no effect on arterial stiffness [94]. Curcumin may be a promising nutraceutical for the treatment of vascular dysfunction in different groups of patients with accelerated vascular aging, but further studies are required.

## 8.7 Bioavailability of NAD+

Decreased NAD+ bioavailability is thought to be an important mechanism for age-related decline in physiological functions, in part because of NAD+'s role as a substrate for SIRT-1 and its association with unregulated nutrient uptake. NAD+ is also an important coenzyme for various cellular reactions that regulate DNA repair, inflammation, metabolism, and other processes [95]. Consequently, the addition of a precursor for NAD+ biosynthesis has become one of the most popular ways to increase NAD+ levels and promote healthy aging. Increasing NAD+ bioavailability is a compelling therapeutic approach to treat and/or prevent vascular dysfunction in aging, given that increasing the amount/activity of SIRT-1 is an effective strategy to improve vascular function in aging [96]. The administration of the NAD+ precursor, nicotinamide mononucleotide (NMN) in the diet of aged experimental animals can restore NO-mediated endothelial function by reducing excessive ROS bioactivity and reverse arterial stiffness, favorably modulating the intrinsic mechanical stiffness of the aortic wall and structural protein levels (more elastin and less collagen) [97]. The use of another NAD+ precursor, nicotinamide-riboside (NR) increases NAD+ bioavailability, that is evidenced by an increase in NAD+ metabolites in peripheral blood mononuclear cells. It was also found that NR could reduce SBP by 4 mmHg and reduce arterial stiffness with particular efficacy (SBP reduction by 9 mmHg) in patients with baseline SBP above normal (i.e., CAD ≥120 mmHg) [98].

## *8.8 Cellular Senescence*

Different effects on cellular senescence to improve various age-related conditions are now being intensively studied [99]. Given that cellular senescence is among the fundamental mechanisms underlying vascular aging, targeting cellular senescence to treat CV aging is very promising [100–102]. Currently, the most widely accepted approach to reduce the burden of senescent cells is treatment with compounds that selectively clear/kill senescent cells and are therefore called senolytics. Typically, senolytic compounds are administered intermittently, with the aim of removing excess senescent cells in a single step, while maintaining basal cellular senescence levels and not interfering with processes such as wound healing [103] and cancer suppression [104]. Currently, synthetic pharmacological senolytics (e.g., dasatinib + quercetin) are undergoing clinical trials in various pathological conditions [105, 106] for their side effects, making it very difficult to introduce this senolytic strategy to adults without clinical disease. Accordingly, there is great interest in studying natural senolytics to improve age-related vascular dysfunction, as experts believe that these compounds have the greatest potential to restore and maintain a healthy aging CV system. A candidate natural senolytic is the flavonoid fisetin, which has been shown to exert senolytic effects in vivo and increase longevity and health markers in mouse models of both chronological and accelerated aging [107]. Experiments in aged mice show that administration of fisetin markedly increases NO-mediated endothelial function and reduces arterial stiffness, and that these improvements result from suppression of excess cellular senescence in the vascular wall [108]. However, further studies in adults with overweight and/or obesity are needed.

## 9 Conclusions and Expert Recommendations in the Framework of 3PM

Above presented data motivate follow-up research on EVA syndrome and application of innovative screening programs to the needs of young populations following the paradigm change from reactive medical services (clinically manifested disorders) to 3PM approach based on predictive diagnostics, targeted prevention, and treatments tailored to individualized patient profiles [8]. To maximize cost-efficacy, 3PM approach should be applied as early as possible in life. School children and students at Universities are certainly the target groups to reach the aims of 3PM in populations [18, 109–111].

In the context of the chapter, it is strongly recommended to implement below listed 3PM-related tools and relevant parameters to combat CVD epidemics in the population.

**Suboptimal health status screening** is instrumental to protect individuals against the transition from health to disease [6].

**Endothelin-1 axes** are involved in the regulation of vascular status and a myriad of processes highly relevant for physical and mental well-being. ET-1 blood plasma patterns are instrumental as a sensor of lifestyle quality and transition from suboptimal health conditions to diseases and as a predictor of aging and related pathologies [112].

**Homocysteine metabolism** presents the key pathways in post-genomic and epigenetic regulation mechanisms crucial for regulating methionine availability, protein homeostasis, and DNA-methylation. In particular, mild hyperhomocysteinemia remains frequently underdiagnosed although it is a strong indicator of an induced oxidative stress, systemic inflammation, impaired healing, compromised mitochondrial health, and increased risks of systemic disorders including coronary artery diseases, atherosclerosis, myocardial infarction, and ischemic stroke, among others [113].

**Mitochondrial health risk assessment** is instrumental for systemic effects including but not restricted to individualized cardiovascular health status. Mitophagy and mitochondrial "burnout" signals trigger SOS signals of developing downstream diseases such as chronic fatigue, accelerated aging, and associated pathologies. Contextually, a holistic predictive diagnostic test based on the mitochondrial health quality control is a powerful tool for advanced 3PM approach in primary and secondary care [114, 115].

**Multi-parametric analysis and individualized phenotyping by artificial intelligence** is instrumental for individualized health risk assessment in primary and secondary care for predictive approach and targeted prevention of potential risks [8].

## References

1. Tsao CW, Aday AW, Almarzooq ZI, Anderson CAM, Arora P, Avery CL, Baker-Smith CM, Beaton AZ, Boehme AK, Buxton AE, Commodore-Mensah Y, Elkind MSV, Evenson KR, Eze-Nliam C, Fugar S, Generoso G, Heard DG, Hiremath S, Ho JE, Kalani R, Kazi DS, Ko D, Levine DA, Liu J, Ma J, Magnani JW, Michos ED, Mussolino ME, Navaneethan

SD, Parikh NI, Poudel R, Rezk-Hanna M, Roth GA, Shah NS, St-Onge MP, Thacker EL, Virani SS, Voeks JH, Wang NY, Wong ND, Wong SS, Yaffe K, Martin SS (2023) American Heart Association Council on Epidemiology and Prevention Statistics Committee and Stroke Statistics Subcommittee. Heart disease and stroke statistics-2023 update: a report from the American Heart Association. Circulation 147(8):e93–e621. https://doi.org/10.1161/CIR.0000000000001123

2. Sagris M, Antonopoulos AS, Theofilis P, Oikonomou E, Siasos G, Tsalamandris S, Antoniades C, Brilakis ES, Kaski JC, Tousoulis D (2022) Risk factors profile of young and older patients with myocardial infarction. Cardiovasc Res 118(10):2281–2292. https://doi.org/10.1093/cvr/cvab264
3. Gooding HC, Gidding SS, Moran AE, Redmond N, Allen NB, Bacha F, Burns TL, Catov JM, Grandner MA, Harris KM, Johnson HM, Kiernan M, Lewis TT, Matthews KA, Monaghan M, Robinson JG, Tate D, Bibbins-Domingo K, Spring B (2020) Challenges and opportunities for the prevention and treatment of cardiovascular disease among young adults: report from a National Heart, Lung, and Blood Institute working group. J Am Heart Assoc 9(19):e016115. https://doi.org/10.1161/JAHA.120.016115
4. Aatola H, Koivistoinen T, Tuominen H, Juonala M, Lehtimäki T, Viikari JSA, Raitakari OT, Kähönen M, Hutri-Kähönen N (2017) Influence of child and adult elevated blood pressure on adult arterial stiffness: the cardiovascular risk in young Finns study. Hypertension 70(3):531–536. https://doi.org/10.1161/HYPERTENSIONAHA.117.09444. Epub 2017 Jul 3
5. Evsevyeva MY, Eremin MV, Rostovtseva MV, Sergeeva OV, Rusidi AV, Kudryavtseva VD, Shchetinin EV (2022) Preventive screening of young people from the perspective of vascular aging phenotypes: the role of body weight. Ration Pharmacother Cardiol 18(1):42–48. https://doi.org/10.20996/1819-6446-2022-02-14
6. Wang W, Yan Y, Guo Z, Hou H, Garcia M, Tan X, Anto EO, Mahara G, Zheng Y, Li B, Wang Y, Guo X, Golubnitschaja O (2021) ALL AROUND SUBOPTIMAL HEALTH. A joint position paper of the suboptimal health study consortium and European Association for Predictive, Preventive and Personalised Medicine. EPMA J 12(4):1–31. https://doi.org/10.1007/s13167-021-00253-2
7. Evsevieva M, Sergeeva O, Mazurakova A, Koklesova L, Prokhorenko-Kolomoytseva I, Shchetinin E, Birkenbihl C, Costigliola V, Kubatka P, Golubnitschaja O (2022) Pre-pregnancy check-up of maternal vascular status and associated phenotype is crucial for the health of mother and offspring. EPMA J 13(3):351–366. https://doi.org/10.1007/s13167-022-00294-1
8. Golubnitschaja O, Potuznik P, Polivka J Jr, Pesta M, Kaverina O, Pieper CC, Kropp M, Thumann G, Erb C, Karabatsiakis A, Stetkarova I, Polivka J, Costigliola V (2022) Ischemic stroke of unclear aetiology: a case-by-case analysis and call for a multi-professional predictive, preventive and personalised approach. EPMA J 13(4):535–545. https://doi.org/10.1007/s13167-022-00307-z
9. Nilsson PM (2015) Early vascular aging (EVA): new directions in cardiovascular protection. Academic, pp 129–136. ISBN 97801280138782015. https://doi.org/10.1016/B978-0-12-801387-8.00013-2
10. Laurent S, Boutouyrie P, Cunha P, Lacolley P, Nilsson P (2019) Concept of extremes in vascular aging from early vascular aging to supernormal vascular aging. Hypertension 74:218–228. https://doi.org/10.1161/HYPERTENSIONAHA.119.12655
11. Ben-Shlomo Y, Spears M, Boustred C, May M, Anderson SG, Benjamin EJ, Boutouyrie P, Cameron J, Chen CH, Cruickshank JK, Hwang SJ, Lakatta EG, Laurent S, Maldonado J, Mitchell GF, Najjar SS, Newman AB, Ohishi M, Pannier B, Pereira T, Vasan RS, Shokawa T, Sutton-Tyrell K, Verbeke F, Wang KL, Webb DJ, Willum Hansen T, Zoungas S, McEniery CM, Cockcroft JR, Wilkinson IB (2014) Aortic pulse wave velocity improves cardiovascular event prediction: an individual participant metaanalysis of prospective observational data from 17,635 subjects. J Am Coll Cardiol 63(7):636–646. https://doi.org/10.1016/j.jacc.2013.09.063
12. Mitchell GF, Hwang SJ, Vasan RS, Larson MG, Pencina MJ, Hamburg NM, Vita JA, Levy D, Benjamin EJ (2010) Arterial stiffness and cardiovascular events: the Framingham heart study. Circulation 121(4):505–511. https://doi.org/10.1161/CIRCULATIONAHA.109.886655

13. Visseren FLJ, Mach F, Smulders YM, Carballo D, Koskinas KC, Bäck M, Benetos A, Biffi A, Boavida JM, Capodanno D, Cosyns B, Crawford C, Davos CH, Desormais I, Di Angelantonio E, Franco OH, Halvorsen S, Hobbs FDR, Hollander M, Jankowska EA, Michal M, Sacco S, Sattar N, Tokgozoglu L, Tonstad S, Tsioufis KP, van Dis I, van Gelder IC, Wanner C, Williams B, National Cardiac Societies ESC, ESC Scientific Document Group (2021) 2021 ESC guidelines on cardiovascular disease prevention in clinical practice. Eur Heart J 42(34):3227–3337. https://doi.org/10.1093/eurheartj/ehab484. Erratum in: Eur Heart J. 2022 Nov 7;43(42):4468
14. Teemu JN, Bindu K, Gary FM, Ramachandran SV (2019) Relative contributions of pulse pressure and arterial stiffness to cardiovascular disease. The Framingham Heart Study Hypertension 73(3):712–717. https://doi.org/10.1161/HYPERTENSIONAHA.118.12289
15. Nowak KL, Rossman MJ, Chonchol M, Seals DR (2018) Strategies for achieving healthy vascular aging. Hypertension 71(3):389–402. https://doi.org/10.1161/HYPERTENSIONAHA.117.10439
16. LaRocca TJ, Martens CR, Seals DR (2017) Nutrition and other lifestyle influences on arterial aging. Ageing Res Rev 39:106–119. https://doi.org/10.1016/j.arr.2016.09.002
17. Vlachopoulos C, Aznaouridis K, Stefanadis C (2010) Prediction of cardiovascular events and all-cause mortality with arterial stiffness: a systematic review and meta-analysis. J Am Coll Cardiol 55:1318–1327. https://doi.org/10.1016/j.jacc.2009.10.061
18. Aatola H, Hutri-Kähönen N, Juonala M, Laitinen TT, Pahkala K, Mikkilä V, Telama R, Koivistoinen T, Lehtimäki T, Viikari JS, Raitakari OT, Kähönen M (2014) Prospective relationship of change in ideal cardiovascular health status and arterial stiffness: the cardiovascular risk in young Finns study. J Am Heart Assoc 3(2):e000532. https://doi.org/10.1161/JAHA.113.000532
19. Wu F, Ahola-Olli A, Pahkala K, Hakala JO, Juonala M, Salo P, Lehtimäki T, Hutri-Kähönen N, Kähönen M, Laitinen T, Tossavainen P, Taittonen L, Jokinen E, Viikari JSA, Magnussen CG, Raitakari OT, Rovio SP (2022) Risk factor profile in youth, genetic risk, and adulthood cognitive function: the cardiovascular risk in young Finns study. Neuroepidemiology 56(3):201–211. https://doi.org/10.1159/000524986
20. Ungvari Z, Tarantini S, Donato AJ, Galvan V, Csiszar A (2018) Mechanisms of vascular aging. Circ Res 123:849–867. https://doi.org/10.1161/CIRCRESAHA.118.311378
21. Clayton ZS, Craighead DH, Darvish S, Coppock M, Ludwig KR, Brunt VE, Seals DR, Rossman MJ (2022) Promoting healthy cardiovascular aging: emerging topics. J Cardiovasc Aging 2:43. https://doi.org/10.20517/jca.2022.27
22. Kirkman DL, Robinson AT, Rossman MJ, Seals DR, Edwards DG (2021) Mitochondrial contributions to vascular endothelial dysfunction, arterial stiffness, and cardiovascular diseases. Am J Physiol Heart Circ Physiol 320(5):H2080–H2100. https://doi.org/10.1152/ajpheart.00917.2020
23. Pucci G, Martina MR, Bianchini E, D'abbondanza M, Curcio R, Battista F, Anastasio F, Crapa ME, Sanesi L, Gemignani V, Vaudo G (2023) Relationship between measures of adiposity, blood pressure and arterial stiffness in adolescents. The MACISTE study. J Hypertens 41(7):1100–1107. https://doi.org/10.1097/HJH.0000000000003433. Epub 2023 May 19
24. Agbaje AO (2022) Arterial stiffness precedes hypertension and metabolic risks in youth: a review. J Hypertens 40(10):1887–1896. https://doi.org/10.1097/HJH.0000000000003239
25. Nilsson PM (2020) Early vascular aging in hypertension. Front Cardiovasc Med 7:6. https://doi.org/10.3389/fcvm.2020.00006
26. Weisbrod RM, Shiang T, Al Sayah L, Fry JL, Bajpai S, Reinhart-King CA, Lob HE, Santhanam L, Mitchell G, Cohen RA, Seta F (2013) Arterial stiffening precedes systolic hypertension in diet-induced obesity. Hypertension 62:1105–1110. https://doi.org/10.1161/HYPERTENSIONAHA.113.01744
27. Mitchell GF (2021) Arterial stiffness in aging: does it have a place in clinical practice?: recent advances in hypertension. Hypertension 77(3):768–780. https://doi.org/10.1161/HYPERTENSIONAHA.120.14515
28. Wu J, Saleh MA, Kirabo A, Itani HA, Montaniel KR, Xiao L, Chen W, Mernaugh RL, Cai H, Bernstein KE, Goronzy JJ, Weyand CM, Curci JA, Barbaro NR, Moreno H, Davies SS, Rob-

erts LJ 2nd, Madhur MS, Harrison DG (2016) Immune activation caused by vascular oxidation promotes fibrosis and hypertension. J Clin Invest 126(1):50–67. https://doi.org/10.1172/JCI80761
29. Narkiewicz K, Phillips BG, Kato M, Hering D, Bieniaszewski L, Somers VK (2005) Gender-selective interaction between aging, blood pressure, and sympathetic nerve activity. Hypertension 45:522–525. https://doi.org/10.1161/01.HYP.0000160318.46725.46
30. Valisno JAC, May J, Singh K, Helm EY, Venegas L, Budbazar E, Goodman JB, Nicholson CJ, Avram D, Cohen RA, Mitchell GF, Morgan KG, Seta F (2021) BCL11B regulates arterial stiffness and related target organ damage. Circ Res 128(6):755–768. https://doi.org/10.1161/CIRCRESAHA.120.316666
31. Wadström BN, Engström G, Nilsson P (2021) Exploring and comparing definitions of healthy vascular ageing in the population: characteristics and prospective cardiovascular risk. J Hum Hypertens 35(5):428–436. https://doi.org/10.1038/s41371-020-0353-1
32. Miyoshi T, Ito H (2021) Arterial stiffness in health and disease: the role of cardio–ankle vascular index review. J Cardiol 78(6):493–501. https://doi.org/10.1016/j.jjcc.2021.07.011
33. Kjøllesdal MKR, Carslake D, Smith GD, Shaikh F, Næss Ø (2022) The role of family factors in the association between early adulthood BMI and risk of cardiovascular disease. An intergenerational study of BMI in early adulthood and cardiovascular mortality in parents, aunts and uncles. Int J Obes 46(1):228–234. https://doi.org/10.1038/s41366-021-00987-z
34. Catov JM, McNeil RB, Marsh DJ, Mercer BM, Bairey Merz CN, Parker CB, Pemberton VL, Saade GR, Chen YI, Chung JH, Ehrenthal DB, Grobman WA, Haas DM, Parry S, Polito L, Reddy UM, Silver RM, Simhan HN, Wapner RJ, Kominiarek M, Kreutz R, Levine LD, Greenland P (2021) NHLBI nuMoM2b Heart Health Study. Early pregnancy Atherogenic profile in a first pregnancy and hypertension risk 2 to 7 years after delivery. J Am Heart Assoc 10(5):e017216. https://doi.org/10.1161/JAHA.120.017216
35. Nilsson PM, Laurent S, Cunha PG, Olsen MH, Rietzschel E, Franco OH, Ryliškytė L, Strazhesko I, Vlachopoulos C, Chen CH, Boutouyrie P, Cucca F, Lakatta EG, Scuteri A (2018) Metabolic syndrome, Arteries REsearch (MARE) Consortium. Characteristics of healthy vascular ageing in pooled population-based cohort studies: the global metabolic syndrome and artery REsearch consortium. J Hypertens 36(12):2340–2349. https://doi.org/10.1097/HJH.0000000000001824
36. Dangardt F, Osika W, Volkmann R, Gan LM, Friberg P (2008) Obese children show increased intimal wall thickness and decreased pulse wave velocity. Clin Physiol Funct Imaging 28:287–293. https://doi.org/10.1111/j.1475-097X.2008.00806.x
37. Corden B, Keenan NG, de Marvao AS, Dawes TJ, Decesare A, Diamond T, Durighel G, Hughes AD, Cook SA, O'Regan DP (2013) Body fat is associated with reduced aortic stiffness until middle age. Hypertension 61(6):1322–1327. https://doi.org/10.1161/HYPERTENSIONAHA.113.01177
38. Li P, Wang L, Liu C (2017) Overweightness, obesity and arterial stiffness in healthy subjects: a systematic review and metaanalysis of literature studies. J Postgrad Med 129(2):224–230. https://doi.org/10.1080/00325481.2017.1268903
39. Charakida M, Deanfield JE (2018) BMI trajectories from childhood: the slippery slope to adult obesity and cardiovascular disease. Eur Heart J 39(24):2271–2273. https://doi.org/10.1093/eurheartj/ehy218
40. Lurbe E, Torro I, Garcia-Vicent C, Alvarez J, Fernandez-Fornoso JA, Redon J (2012) Blood pressure and obesity exert independent influences on pulse wave velocity in youth. Hypertension 60(2):550–555. https://doi.org/10.1161/HYPERTENSIONAHA.112.194746
41. Charakida M, Jones A, Falaschetti E, Khan T, Finer N, Sattar N, Hingorani A, Lawlor DA, Smith GD, Deanfield JE (2012) Childhood obesity and vascular phenotypes: a population study. J Am Coll Cardiol 60:2643–2650. https://doi.org/10.1016/j.jacc.2012.08.1017
42. Onuh JO, Qiu H (2020) New progress on the study of aortic stiffness in age-related hypertension. J Hypertens 38(10):1871–1877. https://doi.org/10.1097/HJH.0000000000002452
43. Brook RD, Appel LJ, Rubenfire M, Ogedegbe G, Bisognano JD, Elliott WJ, Fuchs FD, Hughes JW, Lackland DT, Staffileno BA, Townsend RR, Rajagopalan S (2013) Beyond medications and diet: alternative approaches to lowering blood pressure: a scientific statement

from the American Heart Association. Hypertension 61:1360–1383. https://doi.org/10.1161/HYP.0b013e318293645f
44. Seals DR, Edward F (1985) Adolph distinguished lecture: the remarkable anti-aging effects of aerobic exercise on systemic arteries. J Appl Physiol 2014(117):425–439. https://doi.org/10.1152/japplphysiol.00362.2014
45. Gioscia-Ryan RA, Battson ML, Cuevas LM, Zigler MC, Sindler AL, Seals DR (2016) Voluntary aerobic exercise increases arterial resilience and mitochondrial health with aging in mice. Aging (Albany NY) 8:2897–2914. https://doi.org/10.18632/aging.101099
46. Gioscia-Ryan RA, Clayton ZS, Zigler MC, Richey JJ, Cuevas LM, Rossman MJ, Battson ML, Ziemba BP, Hutton DA, VanDongen NS, Seals DR (2021) Lifelong voluntary aerobic exercise prevents age- and Western diet-induced vascular dysfunction, mitochondrial oxidative stress and inflammation in mice. J Physiol 599(3):911–925. https://doi.org/10.1113/JP280607
47. Rossman MJ, Kaplon RE, Hill SD, McNamara MN, Santos-Parker JR, Pierce GL, Seals DR, Donato AJ (2017) Endothelial cell senescence with aging in healthy humans: prevention by habitual exercise and relation to vascular endothelial function. Am J Physiol Heart Circ Physiol 313(5):H890–H895. https://doi.org/10.1152/ajpheart.00416.2017
48. Dębiec-Bąk A, Skrzek A, Podbielska H, Golubnitschaja O, Stefańska M (2021) Superficial temperature distribution patterns before and after physical activity in school children are indicative for personalized exercise coaching and disease prevention. EPMA J 12(4):435–447. https://doi.org/10.1007/s13167-021-00262-1
49. Weiss EP, Fontana L (2011) Caloric restriction: powerful protection for the aging heart and vasculature. Am J Physiol Heart Circ Physiol 301(4):H1205–H1219. https://doi.org/10.1152/ajpheart.00685.2011
50. Donato AJ, Walker AE, Magerko KA, Bramwell RC, Black AD, Henson GD, Lawson BR, Lesniewski LA, Seals DR (2013) Life-long caloric restriction reduces oxidative stress and preserves nitric oxide bioavailability and function in arteries of old mice. Aging Cell 12(5):772–783. https://doi.org/10.1111/acel.12103
51. Wohlgemuth SE, Julian D, Akin DE, Fried J, Toscano K, Leeuwenburgh C, Dunn WA Jr (2007) Autophagy in the heart and liver during normal aging and calorie restriction. Rejuvenation Res 10(3):281–292. https://doi.org/10.1089/rej.2006.0535
52. Pierce GL, Beske SD, Lawson BR, Southall KL, Benay FJ, Donato AJ, Seals DR (2008) Weight loss alone improves conduit and resistance artery endothelial function in young and older overweight/obese adults. Hypertension 52(1):72–79. https://doi.org/10.1161/HYPERTENSIONAHA.108.111427
53. Dengo AL, Dennis EA, Orr JS, Marinik EL, Ehrlich E, Davy BM, Davy KP (2010) Arterial destiffening with weight loss in overweight and obese middle-aged and older adults. Hypertension 55(4):855–861. https://doi.org/10.1161/HYPERTENSIONAHA.109.147850
54. Brinkley TE, Leng I, Bailey MJ, Houston DK, Hugenschmidt CE, Nicklas BJ, Hundley WG (2021) Effects of exercise and weight loss on proximal aortic stiffness in older adults with obesity. Circulation 144(9):684–693. https://doi.org/10.1161/CIRCULATIONAHA.120.051943
55. O'Donnell M, Mente A, Yusuf S (2015) Sodium intake and cardiovascular health. Circ Res 116:1046–1057. https://doi.org/10.1161/CIRCRESAHA.116.303771
56. Svetkey LP, Simons-Morton DG, Proschan MA, Sacks FM, Conlin PR, Harsha D, Moore TJ (2001) Effects on blood pressure of reduced dietary sodium and the dietary approaches to stop. Hypertension (DASH) diet. DASH-Sodium Collaborative Research Group. N Engl J Med 344:3–10. https://doi.org/10.1056/NEJM200101043440101
57. Jablonski KL, Racine ML, Geolfos CJ, Gates PE, Chonchol M, McQueen MB, Seals DR (2013) Dietary sodium restriction reverses vascular endothelial dysfunction in middle-aged/older adults with moderately elevated systolic blood pressure. J Am Coll Cardiol 61:335–343. https://doi.org/10.1016/j.jacc.2012.09.010
58. Ablonski KL, Fedorova OV, Racine ML, Geolfos CJ, Gates PE, Chonchol M, Fleenor BS, Lakatta EG, Bagrov AY, Seals DR (2013) Dietary sodium restriction and association with urinary marinobufagenin, blood pressure, and aortic stiffness. Clin J Am Soc Nephrol 8:1952–1959. https://doi.org/10.2215/CJN.00900113

59. Gates PE, Tanaka H, Hiatt WR, Seals DR (2004) Dietary sodium restriction rapidly improves large elastic artery compliance in older adults with systolic hypertension. Hypertension 44:35–41. https://doi.org/10.1161/01.HYP.0000132767.74476.64
60. Kidambi S, Pan X, Yang C, Liu P, Roberts ML, Li Y, Wang T, Laud PW, Liu Y, Rubens M, Thomas R, Widlansky ME, Beyer AM, Liu Y, Cowley AW Jr, Kotchen TA, Munyura Y, Moosreiner A, Mattson DL, Liang M (2021) Dietary sodium restriction results in tissue-specific changes in DNA methylation in humans. Hypertension 78:434–446. https://doi.org/10.1161/HYPERTENSIONAHA.120.17351
61. Maddock J, Ziauddeen N, Ambrosini GL, Wong A, Hardy R, Ray S (2018) Adherence to a dietary approaches to stop hypertension (DASH)-type diet over the life course and associated vascular function: a study based on the MRC 1946 British birth cohort. Br J Nutr 119:581–589. https://doi.org/10.1017/S0007114517003877
62. Hodson L, Harnden KE, Roberts R, Dennis AL, Frayn KN (2010) Does the DASH diet lower blood pressure by altering peripheral vascular function? J Hum Hypertens 24:312–319. https://doi.org/10.1038/jhh.2009.65
63. Couch SC, Saelens BE, Khoury PR, Dart KB, Hinn K, Mitsnefes MM, Daniels SR, Urbina EM (2021) Dietary approaches to stop hypertension dietary intervention improves blood pressure and vascular health in youth with elevated blood pressure. Hypertension 77:241–251. https://doi.org/10.1161/HYPERTENSIONAHA.120.16156
64. Torres-Peña JD, Rangel-Zuñiga OA, Alcala-Diaz JF, Lopez-Miranda J, Delgado-Lista J (2020) Mediterranean diet and endothelial function: a review of its effects at different vascular bed levels. Nutrients 12:2212. https://doi.org/10.3390/nu12082212
65. Estruch R, Ros E, Salas-Salvadó J, Covas MI, Corella D, Arós F, Gómez-Gracia E, Ruiz-Gutiérrez V, Fiol M, Lapetra J, Lamuela-Raventos RM, Serra-Majem L, Pintó X, Basora J, Muñoz MA, Sorlí JV, Martínez JA, Martínez-González MA (2013) PREDIMED Study Investigators Primary prevention of cardiovascular disease with a Mediterranean diet. N Engl J Med 368:1279–1290. https://doi.org/10.1056/NEJMoa1200303
66. Jennings A, Berendsen AM, de Groot LCPGM, Feskens EJM, Brzozowska A, Sicinska E, Pietruszka B, Meunier N, Caumon E, Malpuech-Brugère C, Santoro A, Ostan R, Franceschi C, Gillings R, O' Neill CM, Fairweather-Tait SJ, Minihane AM, Cassidy A (2019) Mediterranean-style diet improves systolic blood pressure and arterial stiffness in older adults. Hypertension 73:578–586. https://doi.org/10.1161/HYPERTENSIONAHA.118.12259
67. Park Y, Subar AF, Hollenbeck A, Schatzkin A (2011) Dietary fiber intake and mortality in the NIH-AARP diet and health study. Arch Intern Med 171:1061–1068. https://doi.org/10.1001/archinternmed.2011.18
68. Todd S, Woodward M, Tunstall-Pedoe H, Bolton-Smith C (1999) Dietary antioxidant vitamins and fiber in the etiology of cardiovascular disease and all-causes mortality: results from the Scottish heart health study. Am J Epidemiol 150:1073–1080. https://doi.org/10.1093/oxfordjournals.aje.a009931
69. Streppel MT, Ocké MC, Boshuizen HC, Kok FJ, Kromhout D (2008) Dietary fiber intake in relation to coronary heart disease and all-cause mortality over 40 y: the Zutphen study. Am J Clin Nutr 88:1119–1125. https://doi.org/10.1093/ajcn/88.4.1119
70. Lubin F, Lusky A, Chetrit A, Dankner R (2003) Lifestyle and ethnicity play a role in all-cause mortality. J Nutr 133:1180–1185. https://doi.org/10.1093/jn/133.4.1180
71. Grooms KN, Ommerborn MJ, Pham DQ, Djoussé L, Clark CR (2013) Dietary fiber intake and cardiometabolic risks among US adults, NHANES 1999-2010. Am J Med 126:1059–67.e1. https://doi.org/10.1016/j.amjmed.2013.07.023
72. Casso AG, Burnsed-Torres ML, Lubieniecki KL, Rossman MJ, Adam EC, Lally HM, Chonchol M, Davy KP, Seals DR, Brunt VE (2022) Consumption of a high-fiber diet improves systolic blood pressure and vascular endothelial function and may reduce oxidative stress in middle-aged to older adults. FASEB J 36. https://doi.org/10.1096/fasebj.2022.36.S1.R4104
73. Visseren FLJ, Mach F, Smulders YM, Carballo D, Koskinas KC, Bäck M, Benetos A, Biffi A, Boavida JM, Capodanno D, Cosyns B, Crawford C, Davos CH, Desormais I, Di Angelantonio E, Franco OH, Halvorsen S, Hobbs FDR, Hollander M, Jankowska EA, Michal M, Sacco S, Sattar N, Tokgozoglu L, Tonstad S, Tsioufis KP, van Dis I, van Gelder IC, Wanner

C, Williams B (2021) ESC Scientific Document Group. 2021 ESC guidelines on cardiovascular disease prevention in clinical practice. Eur Heart J 42(34):3227–3337. https://doi.org/10.1093/eurheartj/ehab484
74. Seals DR, Justice JN, LaRocca TJ (2016) Physiological geroscience: targeting function to increase healthspan and achieve optimal longevity. J Physiol 594:2001–2024. https://doi.org/10.1113/jphysiol.2014.282665
75. Mozaffarian D, Appel LJ, Van Horn L (2011) Components of a cardioprotective diet: new insights. Circulation 123:2870–2891. https://doi.org/10.1161/CIRCULATIONAHA.110.968735
76. Seals DR, Kaplon RE, Gioscia-Ryan RA, LaRocca TJ (2014) You're only as old as your arteries: translational strategies for preserving vascular endothelial function with aging. Physiology (Bethesda) 29:250–264. https://doi.org/10.1152/physiol.00059.2013
77. Zuchi C, Ambrosio G, Lüscher TF, Landmesser U (2010) Nutraceuticals in cardiovascular prevention: lessons from studies on endothelial function. Cardiovasc Ther 28:187–201. https://doi.org/10.1111/j.1755-5922.2010.00165.x
78. Rossman MJ, LaRocca TJ, Martens CR, Seals DR (1985) Healthy lifestyle-based approaches for successful vascular aging. J Appl Physiol 2018(125):1888–1900. https://doi.org/10.1152/japplphysiol.00521.2018
79. Gates PE, Boucher ML, Silver AE, Monahan KD, Seals DR (1985) Impaired flow-mediated dilation with age is not explained by L-arginine bioavailability or endothelial asymmetric dimethylarginine protein expression. J Appl Physiol 2007(102):63–71. https://doi.org/10.1152/japplphysiol.00660.2006
80. Sindler AL, Fleenor BS, Calvert JW, Marshall KD, Zigler ML, Lefer DJ, Seals DR (2011) Nitrite supplementation reverses vascular endothelial dysfunction and large elastic artery stiffness with aging. Aging Cell 10:429–437. https://doi.org/10.1111/j.1474-9726.2011.00679.x
81. Rossman MJ, Gioscia-Ryan RA, Santos-Parker JR, Ziemba BP, Lubieniecki KL, Johnson LC, Poliektov NE, Bispham NZ, Woodward KA, Nagy EE, Bryan NS, Reisz JA, D'Alessandro A, Chonchol M, Sindler AL, Seals DR (2021) Inorganic nitrite supplementation improves endothelial function with aging: translational evidence for suppression of mitochondria-derived oxidative stress. Hypertension 77:1212–1222. https://doi.org/10.1161/HYPERTENSIONAHA.120.16175
82. Jankowski J, Floege J, Fliser D, Böhm M, Marx N (2021) Cardiovascular disease in chronic kidney disease: pathophysiological insights and therapeutic options. Circulation 143:1157–1172. https://doi.org/10.1161/CIRCULATIONAHA.120.050686
83. Rossman MJ, Gioscia-Ryan RA, Clayton ZS, Murphy MP, Seals DR (2020) Targeting mitochondrial fitness as a strategy for healthy vascular aging. Clin Sci (Lond) 134:1491–1519. https://doi.org/10.1042/CS20190559
84. Gioscia-Ryan RA, LaRocca TJ, Sindler AL, Zigler MC, Murphy MP, Seals DR (2014) Mitochondria-targeted antioxidant (MitoQ) ameliorates age-related arterial endothelial dysfunction in mice. J Physiol 592:2549–2561. https://doi.org/10.1113/jphysiol.2013.268680
85. Rossman MJ, Santos-Parker JR, Steward CAC, Bispham NZ, Cuevas LM, Rosenberg HL, Woodward KA, Chonchol M, Gioscia-Ryan RA, Murphy MP, Seals DR (2018) Chronic supplementation with a mitochondrial antioxidant (MitoQ) improves vascular function in healthy older adults. Hypertension 71:1056–1063. https://doi.org/10.1161/HYPERTENSIONAHA.117.10787
86. LaRocca TJ, Hearon CM Jr, Henson GD, Seals DR (2014) Mitochondrial quality control and age-associated arterial stiffening. Exp Gerontol 58:78–82. https://doi.org/10.1016/j.exger.2014.07.008
87. LaRocca TJ, Henson GD, Thorburn A, Sindler AL, Pierce GL, Seals DR (2012) Translational evidence that impaired autophagy contributes to arterial ageing. J Physiol 590:3305–3316. https://doi.org/10.1113/jphysiol.2012.229690
88. Kaplon RE, Hill SD, Bispham NZ, Santos-Parker JR, Nowlan MJ, Snyder LL, Chonchol M, LaRocca TJ, McQueen MB, Seals DR (2016) Oral trehalose supplementation improves resistance artery endothelial function in healthy middle-aged and older adults. Aging (Albany NY) 8:1167–1183. https://doi.org/10.18632/aging.100962

89. LaRocca TJ, Gioscia-Ryan RA, Hearon CM Jr, Seals DR (2013) The autophagy enhancer spermidine reverses arterial aging. Mech Ageing Dev 134:314–320. https://doi.org/10.1016/j.mad.2013.04.004
90. Eisenberg T, Abdellatif M, Schroeder S, Primessnig U, Stekovic S, Pendl T, Harger A, Schipke J, Zimmermann A, Schmidt A, Tong M, Ruckenstuhl C, Dammbrueck C, Gross AS, Herbst V, Magnes C, Trausinger G, Narath S, Meinitzer A, Hu Z, Kirsch A, Eller K, Carmona-Gutierrez D, Büttner S, Pietrocola F, Knittelfelder O, Schrepfer E, Rockenfeller P, Simonini C, Rahn A, Horsch M, Moreth K, Beckers J, Fuchs H, Gailus-Durner V, Neff F, Janik D, Rathkolb B, Rozman J, de Angelis MH, Moustafa T, Haemmerle G, Mayr M, Willeit P, von Frieling-Salewsky M, Pieske B, Scorrano L, Pieber T, Pechlaner R, Willeit J, Sigrist SJ, Linke WA, Mühlfeld C, Sadoshima J, Dengjel J, Kiechl S, Kroemer G, Sedej S, Madeo F (2016) Cardioprotection and lifespan extension by the natural polyamine spermidine. Nat Med 22:1428–1438. https://doi.org/10.1038/nm.4222
91. Seals DR, Jablonski KL, Donato AJ (2011) Aging and vascular endothelial function in humans. Clin Sci (Lond) 120:357–375. https://doi.org/10.1042/CS20100476
92. Lakatta EG (2003) Arterial and cardiac aging: major shareholders in cardiovascular disease enterprises: part III: cellular and molecular clues to heart and arterial aging. Circulation 107:490–497. https://doi.org/10.1161/01.cir.0000048894.99865.02
93. Fleenor BS, Sindler AL, Marvi NK, Howell KL, Zigler ML, Yoshizawa M, Seals DR (2013) Curcumin ameliorates arterial dysfunction and oxidative stress with aging. Exp Gerontol 48:269–276. https://doi.org/10.1016/j.exger.2012.10.008
94. Santos-Parker JR, Strahler TR, Bassett CJ, Bispham NZ, Chonchol MB, Seals DR (2017) Curcumin supplementation improves vascular endothelial function in healthy middle-aged and older adults by increasing nitric oxide bioavailability and reducing oxidative stress. Aging (Albany NY) 9:187–208. https://doi.org/10.18632/aging.101149
95. Zapata-Pérez R, Wanders RJA, van Karnebeek CDM, Houtkooper RH (2021) NAD+ homeostasis in human health and disease. EMBO Mol Med 13:e1394. https://doi.org/10.15252/emmm.202113943
96. Donato AJ, Magerko KA, Lawson BR, Durrant JR, Lesniewski LA, Seals DR (2011) SIRT-1 and vascular endothelial dysfunction with ageing in mice and humans. J Physiol 589:4545–4554. https://doi.org/10.1113/jphysiol.2011.211219
97. de Picciotto NE, Gano LB, Johnson LC, Martens CR, Sindler AL, Mills KF, Imai S, Seals DR (2016) Nicotinamide mononucleotide supplementation reverses vascular dysfunction and oxidative stress with aging in mice. Aging Cell 15:522–530. https://doi.org/10.1111/acel.12461
98. Martens CR, Denman BA, Mazzo MR, Armstrong ML, Reisdorph N, McQueen MB, Chonchol M, Seals DR (2018) Chronic nicotinamide riboside supplementation is well-tolerated and elevates NAD+ in healthy middle-aged and older adults. Nat Commun 9:1286. https://doi.org/10.1038/s41467-018-03421-7
99. Childs BG, Durik M, Baker DJ, van Deursen JM (2015) Cellular senescence in aging and age-related disease: from mechanisms to therapy. Nat Med 21:1424–1435. https://doi.org/10.1038/nm.4000
100. Mahoney S, Hutton D, Rossman M, Brunt, V (2021) Late-life treatment with the senolytic ABT-263 reverses aortic stiffening and improves endothelial function with aging. FASEB J 35. https://doi.org/10.1096/fasebj.2021.35.S1.02642
101. Venkatasubramanian R, Mahoney SA, Rossman MJ, Hutton DA, Brunt VE, VanDongen NS, Casso, AG, Greenberg, NT, Quiros YB, Melov S, Campisi J, Seals DR, Clayton ZS (2022) Cellular senescence and the associated secretome contribute to age-related vascular dysfunction. FASEB J 36. https://doi.org/10.1096/fasebj.2022.36.S1.R2053
102. Roos CM, Zhang B, Palmer AK, Ogrodnik MB, Pirtskhalava T, Thalji NM, Hagler M, Jurk D, Smith LA, Casaclang-Verzosa G, Zhu Y, Schafer MJ, Tchkonia T, Kirkland JL, Miller JD (2016) Chronic senolytic treatment alleviates established vasomotor dysfunction in aged or atherosclerotic mice. Aging Cell 15:973–977. https://doi.org/10.1111/acel.12458
103. Demaria M, Ohtani N, Youssef SA, Rodier F, Toussaint W, Mitchell JR, Laberge RM, Vijg J, Van Steeg H, Dollé ME, Hoeijmakers JH, de Bruin A, Hara E, Campisi J (2014) An essential

role for senescent cells in optimal wound healing through secretion of PDGF-AA. Dev Cell 31:722–733. https://doi.org/10.1016/j.devcel.2014.11.012
104. Demaria M, O'Leary MN, Chang J, Shao L, Liu S, Alimirah F, Koenig K, Le C, Mitin N, Deal AM, Alston S, Academia EC, Kilmarx S, Valdovinos A, Wang B, de Bruin A, Kennedy BK, Melov S, Zhou D, Sharpless NE, Muss H, Campisi J (2017) Cellular senescence promotes adverse effects of chemotherapy and cancer relapse. Cancer Discov 7:165–176. https://doi.org/10.1158/2159-8290.CD-16-0241
105. Hickson LJ, Langhi Prata LGP, Bobart SA, Evans TK, Giorgadze N, Hashmi SK, Herrmann SM, Jensen MD, Jia Q, Jordan KL, Kellogg TA, Khosla S, Koerber DM, Lagnado AB, Lawson DK, LeBrasseur NK, Lerman LO, McDonald KM, McKenzie TJ, Passos JF, Pignolo RJ, Pirtskhalava T, Saadiq IM, Schaefer KK, Textor SC, Victorelli SG, Volkman TL, Xue A, Wentworth MA, Wissler Gerdes EO, Zhu Y, Tchkonia T, Kirkland JL (2019) Senolytics decrease senescent cells in humans: preliminary report from a clinical trial of Dasatinib plus quercetin in individuals with diabetic kidney disease. EBioMedicine 47:446–456. https://doi.org/10.1016/j.ebiom.2019.08.069
106. Justice JN, Nambiar AM, Tchkonia T, LeBrasseur NK, Pascual R, Hashmi SK, Prata L, Masternak MM, Kritchevsky SB, Musi N, Kirkland JL (2019) Senolytics in idiopathic pulmonary fibrosis: results from a first-in-human, open-label, pilot study. EBioMedicine 40:554–563. https://doi.org/10.1016/j.ebiom.2018.12.052
107. Yousefzadeh MJ, Zhu Y, McGowan SJ, Angelini L, Fuhrmann-Stroissnigg H, Xu M, Ling YY, Melos KI, Pirtskhalava T, Inman CL, McGuckian C, Wade EA, Kato JI, Grassi D, Wentworth M, Burd CE, Arriaga EA, Ladiges WL, Tchkonia T, Kirkland JL, Robbins PD, Niedernhofer LJ (2018) Fisetin is a senotherapeutic that extends health and lifespan. EBioMedicine 36:18–28. https://doi.org/10.1016/j.ebiom.2018.09.015
108. Mahoney SA, Venkatasubramanian R, Rossman M, VanDongen, N (2022) Fisetin supplementation improves age-related vascular endothelial function by suppressing cellular senescence and mitochondrial oxidative stress. FASEB J 36. https://doi.org/10.1096/fasebj.2022.36.S1.R1931
109. Evsevyeva ME, Eremin MV, Rostovtseva MV, Fursova EN, Rusydi AV, Gal'kova IY, Kudryavtseva VD (2021) Vascular aging phenotypes based on VaSera-screening results in young people with hypertension. Place of hereditary disorders of connective tissue. The arterial. Hypertension 27(2):188–205. https://doi.org/10.18705/1607-419X-2021-27-2-188-205
110. Evsevyeva ME, Koshel VI, Eremin MV, Galkova IY, Rusidi AV, Chudnovsky EV, Korobova E, Frantseva, V (2015) Students' health resources screening and formation of intrauniversity preventive environment: clinical, educational, instructional and pedogogical aspects. Med News North Caucasus 10(1):64–69. https://doi.org/10.14300/mnnc.2015.10009
111. Evsevyeva ME, Eremin MV, Sergeeva OV, Simkhes EV, Barabash IV, Kudryavtseva VD, Kryuchkov MS (2023) Prospective analysis of the main risk factors and vascular status of students during their studies at a medical university. Russ J Cardiol 28(2):5143. https://doi.org/10.15829/1560-4071-2023-5143
112. Torres Crigna A, Link B, Samec M, Giordano FA, Kubatka P, Golubnitschaja O (2021) Endothelin-1 axes in the framework of predictive, preventive and personalised (3P) medicine. EPMA J 12(3):1–41. https://doi.org/10.1007/s13167-021-00248-z
113. Koklesova L, Mazurakova A, Samec M, Biringer K, Samson Mathews Samuel SM, Büsselberg D, Kubatka P, Golubnitschaja O (2021) Homocysteine metabolism as the target for predictive medical approach, disease prevention, prognosis, and treatments tailored to the person. EPMA J 12(4):1–29. https://doi.org/10.1007/s13167-021-00263-0
114. Koklesova L, Mazurakova A, Samec M, Kudela E, Biringer K, Kubatka P, Golubnitschaja O (2022) Mitochondrial health quality control: measurements and interpretation in the framework of predictive, preventive, and personalized medicine. EPMA J 13:177–193. https://doi.org/10.1007/s13167-022-00281-6
115. Golubnitschaja O (2023) What is the routine mitochondrial health check-up good for? A holistic approach in the framework of 3P medicine. In: Podbielska H, Kapalla M (eds) Predictive, preventive and personalised medicine: from bench to bedside. Advances in predictive, preventive and personalised medicine, vol 17. Springer, Cham. https://doi.org/10.1007/978-3-031-34884-6_3

# Personalized Management of Physiologic/Ophthalmologic Particularities for Predictive Approach and Targeted Prevention of Primary Angle Closure Glaucoma Applied to Persons at Risk

**Natalia I. Kurysheva, Oxana Y. Rodionova, Alexey L. Pomerantsev, and Galina A. Sharova**

## Abbreviations

| | |
|---|---|
| ACA | Anterior chamber angle |
| ACD | Anterior chamber depth |
| ACV | Anterior chamber volume |
| AS-OCT | Anterior segment optical coherence tomography |
| AL | Axial length |
| AOD | Angle opening distance |
| AODA | Angle opening distance area |
| ARA | Angle recess area |
| I-Area | Iris area |
| ICurv | Iris curvature |
| IOL | Intraocular lens |
| IOP | Intraocular pressure |
| IT | Iris thickness |
| ITC | Iridotrabecular contact |
| IVol | Iris volume |

N. I. Kurysheva (✉)
Medical Biological University of Innovations and Continuing Education, Burnazyan Federal Biophysical Center, Federal Medical and Biological Agency, Moscow, Russia

Ophthalmological Center, Burnazyan Federal Biophysical Center, Federal Medical and Biological Agency, Moscow, Russia

O. Y. Rodionova · A. L. Pomerantsev
Federal Research Center for Chemical Physics RAS, Moscow, Russia
e-mail: oksana@chph.ras.ru; forecast@chph.ras.ru

G. A. Sharova
Ophthalmology Clinic of Dr. Belikova, Moscow, Russia


W. Wang (ed.), *All Around Suboptimal Health*, Advances in Predictive, Preventive and Personalised Medicine 18,
https://doi.org/10.1007/978-3-031-46891-9_13

| | |
|---|---|
| LE | Lens extraction |
| LPI | Laser peripheral iridotomy |
| LT | Lens thickness |
| LV | Lens vault |
| ML | Machine learning |
| GON | Glaucomatous optic neuropathy |
| PAC | Primary angle closure |
| PACD | Primary angle closure disease |
| PACG | Primary angle closure glaucoma |
| PACs | Primary angle closure suspect |
| PAS | Peripheral anterior goniosynechia |
| POAG | Primary open angle glaucoma |
| PD | Pupil diameter |
| SE | Spherical equivalent |
| SFCT | Subfoveal choroidal thickness |
| SLT | Selective laser trabeculoplasty |
| TIA | Trabecular iris angle |
| TISA | Trabecular-iris space area |
| TICV | Trabecular-iris circumference volume |

# 1 Introduction

One of the features of modern medicine is the improvement of treatment from traditional (reactive) and to personalized one, based on individual predictors. This approach forms the new paradigm of treatment called the predictive, preventive, and personalized medicine (3PM/PPPM). The modern diagnostic technologies in ophthalmology provide a huge variety of clinical and anatomical parameters, which are sometimes difficult to assess in their totality. To this end, the search for individual biomarkers is of great relevance, which not only provide a personalized approach to the choice of treatment, but also make it as cost-effective as possible. At the same time, the development of quantitative predictors is recognized as the leading approach in modern paradigm of personalized medicine since they are the basis for the strategy of identifying different categories of the patients for whom standard treatment will not be successful. It is worth noting that the criteria for a personalized approach were initially of empirical nature, while the foundations of personalized medicine involve the use of evidence-based predictors of individualization. This review shows how the modern technologies with the use of machine learning methods allow using a differentiated approach to the treatment of primary anterior chamber angle closure.

Primary angle closure glaucoma (PACG) is still one of the leading causes of irreversible blindness. It is predicted that the number of glaucoma patients will have increased to 32 million by 2040 [1]. The risk of developing bilateral blindness is three times higher in PACG than in primary open angle glaucoma (POAG) [2].

Among many urgent problems associated with primary angle closure disease (PACD), the most important one is to determine the plan to treat primary angle closure suspect (PACs) and primary angle closure (PAC) to avoid the disease progression. Moreover, with the advancement of technologies for visualization of the anterior segment on optical coherence tomography (AS-OCT) and machine learning (ML) methods, the identification of both principle anatomical and topographic parameters, the determination of their threshold values [3, 4], as well as the development of classifications of ML-based AS-OCT images [5, 6], which allow to differentiate between the norm and pathology (PACs, PAC, PACG), are of great practical importance.

In early PACD, the choice of treatment tactics varies from complete refusal of treatment [7] to laser [8] and surgical interventions [9, 10]. Laser peripheral iridotomy (LPI) is a traditional method [11].

The ZAP study particularly clearly demonstrated the need for an individual approach to the choice of treatment for patients with early stage of PACD. In this study patients with bilateral PACs were observed, while one eye was randomly chosen for LPI, and the paired eye remained intact and served as a control [7]. After 6 years of follow-up, progression in the eyes with LPI was detected in 2% of cases (19 eyes out of 889), and in paired eyes in 4% of cases (36 eyes out of 889). Taking into account the data obtained, the authors recommended to abandon the widespread use of LPI for PACs. At the same time, the question of management of PACS remains open until now since its solution lies in the field of personalized medicine.

Some recent studies have reported on the higher efficiency of treatment of PACD with lens extraction (LE), including the removal of a transparent lens [12–14]. The EAGLE study (Effectiveness in Angle-closure Glaucoma of Lens Extraction Study Group) showed that LE has some advantages over LPI in PAC/PACG [12]. LE is associated with the higher risk of complications and the loss of physiological accommodation in relatively young patients, while LPI is a non-invasive, more accessible, and less expensive procedure. Therefore, the question rises how to choose LPI or LE should be the treatment of choice for PAC [15]. Obviously, the answer to this question lies in the field of personalized medicine. To solve this problem, it is necessary to search for the predictors of LPI and LE efficiency in each specific case [16].

It should be noted that the literature data on the predictors of LPI and LE efficiency in the treatment of PAC are ambiguous [17–21]. This fact is associated with the large number of estimated predictors correlating with each other, which makes it impossible to compare them in one study. It is possible to analyze clinical and anatomical parameters only with the use of machine learning methods, namely, the projection methods of multivariate statistical analysis that simultaneously take into account all available variables to assess treatment prognosis [22–27]. Moreover, the identification of predictors of treatment efficiency opens up the prospects for a personalized approach.

In cases of insufficient post-LPI IOP reduction and in the presence of contraindications to LE early PACD may be treated with the use of selective laser trabeculoplasty (SLT) [28–30].

Thus, the current studies are aimed at a personalized approach to the treatment of patients with early PACD, based on the predictive medicine data.

## 2 Differential Diagnosis of Early Stages of Primary Angle Closure Disease

According to the P. J. Foster classification, PACD includes PACs, PACs, and PACGs [31]. PACs are characterized by iridotrabecular contact (ITC) extending over two quadrants, normal intraocular pressure (IOP), the absence of increased IOP, peripheral anterior goniosynechia (PAS) and glaucomatous optic neuropathy (GON). PAC is diagnosed if there are more than two quadrants of ITC in combination with increased IOP and/or PAS, but without GON. In the presence of GON, PACG is diagnosed.

The assessment of the anterior chamber angle (ACA) by gonioscopy is essential to differentiate between appositional and goniosynechial closure of the ACA. Nevertheless, subjectivity, insufficient reproducibility of the method, unintentional compression during the examination can reduce the accuracy of the method [32]. Automatic gonioscopy is rather effective [33]; however, AS-OCT is currently an important method in detecting the early stages of PACD [34]. An example of ACA visualization of PAC on AS-OCT CASIA2, Tomey, Japan is shown in Fig. 1.

PACD differs from the norm in the values of the following anatomical parameters of an eye: axial length (AL), spherical equivalent (SE), anterior chamber depth (ACD), ACA, lens, iris, and choroid parameters.

### *2.1 Axial Length, Spherical Equivalent, Anterior Chamber Depth*

According to the literature, short AL and shallow ACD are associated with occlusion angles [35]. The study by Y. Zhang demonstrated that PACs eyes significantly differ from the norm in short AL, shallow ACD, and high SE [6]. Moreover, S. Zhou et al. (2023) showed that the risk of PACD progression increases significantly in hypermetropia and minor ACD [36]. In addition, short AL in paired eyes with an acute PAC attack is associated with reduced angle opening distance (AOD750) [37].

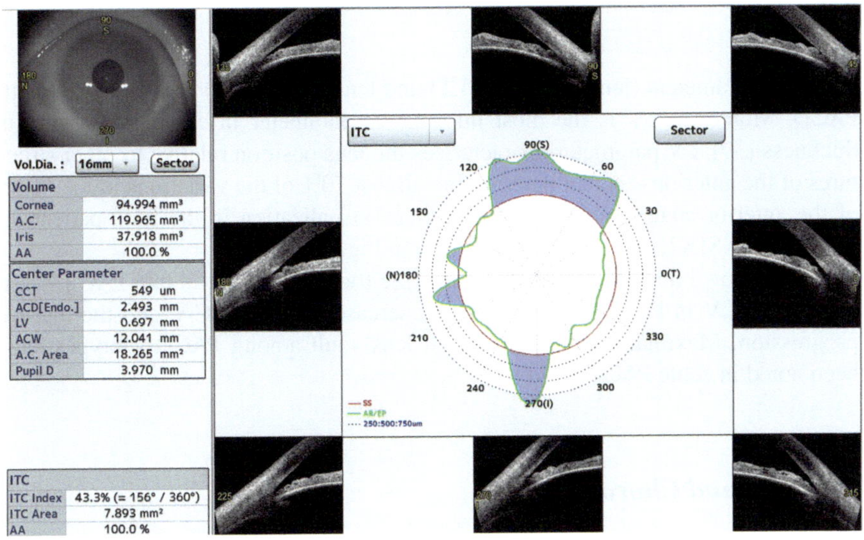


**Fig. 1** Clinical example of anterior chamber angle imaging of a patient with primary angle closure on AS-OCT CASIA2, Tomey, Japan. Note: areas of goniosynechia, determined automatically during scanning, are highlighted in blue

## 2.2 *Parameters of Anterior Chamber Angle*

PACD is characterized by smaller ACA [4, 6, 38]. Thus, E. K. Melese et al. studied ACA parameters to determine the threshold values of occlusion angles in comparison with open angles, analyzing the data of the patients with POAG and PACG/PAC/PACs in a comparative aspect [4]. AOD750 in the lower sector, as well as trabecular-iris circumference volume (TICV) demonstrated high diagnostic value.

N.I. Kurysheva et al. revealed the threshold ACA values that allow distinguishing not only between the early PACD and the norm, but also between PACs and PAC [3]. TISA500 in the lower sector showed the highest accuracy in determining the early transition of PACs to PAC.

Y. Zhang et al. used three prediction algorithms for the detection of PACs (backward logistic regression, naïve Bayes' classification, and neural network) [6]. According to the study results, the ACA parameters in PACs were significantly less than normal (AOD500, trabecular-iris space area (TISA500), angle recess area, ARA750). It is worth noting that none of the algorithms met the requirements of population screening for PACD. The authors explained this fact by different mechanisms of ACA closure.

Nevertheless, in 2023 Y. Eslami et al. classified AS-OCT images into normal, PACs and PAC/PACG using deep learning [5].

## 2.3 *Lens*

The lens parameters (lens thickness (LT) and lens vault, (LV)) are associated with PACD. Moreover, LV is the most informative parameter in comparison with its thickness [39]. LV parameter characterizes the lens position relative to other structures of the anterior segment determining almost 70% of the variations in the width of the anterior chamber. An example of lens visualization in the PAC patient on AS-OCT CASIA2, Tomey, Japan is shown in Fig. 2.

It was shown that LV values determine the transition of PACs into PAC [3]. An increase in LV in PACD [38] leads to a decrease in ACD, ACA, and the disease progression. Maximal lens thickness and lens vault among PACD subtypes have been noted in acute PAC [40, 41].

## 2.4 *Iris and Choroid*

The parameters of the iris and foveal choroid are of particular interest to researchers as the markers of PACD.

It has been shown that an increase in iris curvature (ICurv), iris area (I-Area), iris thickness (IT750) on AS-OCT is associated with narrow angles even with the account of age, sex, ACD, AL, and pupil diameter [42]. Interestingly, W. Huang et al. reported on an IT750 increase in PACs/PAC, but not in PACG [43]. The authors explained this fact with a higher IOP in the PACG group leading to a decrease of the initially increased iris thickness.

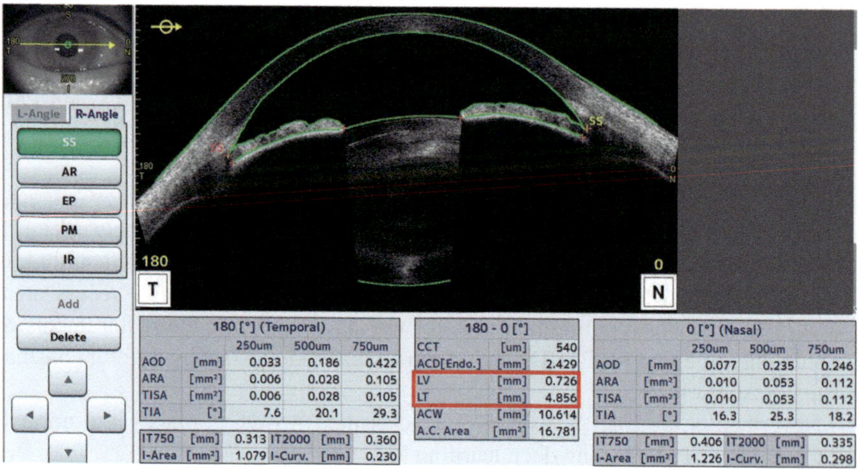


**Fig. 2** Clinical example of visualization of the lens of a patient with primary angle closure on AS-OCT CASIA2, Tomey, Japan. Note: lens thickness (LV) and lens vault (LV) are highlighted in red

According to the literature, increased subfoveal choroidal thickness (SFCT) may be a predictor of early PACD [3, 44, 45]. Nevertheless, some authors described the choroidal thinning with prolonged AL in response to an IOP increase during dark room prone provocative testing in eyes with PAC [46]. W. Song suggested that if during the onset of an attack the choroidal thickness increases with an IOP increase, then it can become thinner again due to significant hypertension [47].

The correlation between the parameters of iris and choroid is of a particular interest. W. Huang et al. revealed an inverse correlation between the thickness of the iris and the foveal choroid in PACs/PAC/PACG, but not in the control group [43]. The authors explained this fact with the presence of a single blood supply system from the ophthalmic artery. With an increase in resistance to blood flow in the long posterior ciliary artery, blood flow increases in the short posterior ciliary artery, followed by the choroidal expansion. Subsequently, this mechanism was confirmed in another study on a group of patients with PACs and PAC [3].

Moreover, PAC treatment has been found to result in a change in the foveolar choroid thickness [14]. Thus, the post-LPI choroidal thickness significantly increased in all sectors, except for the upper and temporal ones, 3 mm from the center of the foveola, as well as in the foveola itself. The post-LE choroidal thickness increased in all sectors, except for the nasal one, 3 mm from the center of the foveola. There was no significant difference in SFCT between the groups after the treatment.

Therefore, the collected data demonstrate an increase in the choroidal thickness almost in all sectors after LPI, which is consistent with the results of other authors. It has been noticed that a 1 mmHg IOP decrease is associated with 3.4 μm SFCT increase [48]. Other studies comparing choroidal thickness before and after trabeculectomy [49, 50] have also demonstrated the involvement of the choroid in the PACD pathogenesis.

Thus, the biometric parameters of the patients with early PACD differ from the norm. AS-OCT image analysis is a key area in the development of predictive medicine in the field of PACD. Further research and the development of machine learning methods (neural network) are required to identify the threshold values of parameters in PACs and PAC for early detection of the disease.

## 3 Predictors of Treatment Efficiency in Early Stages of Primary Angle Closure Disease

### *3.1 Predictors of Laser Peripheral Iridotomy Efficiency*

The current literature on the search for predictors of laser peripheral iridotomy success in PACD is rather ambiguous. This fact is explained by the choice of various postoperative clinical and topographic parameters taken by researchers for the success of treatment: hypotensive effect (ΔIOP), change in ACA, including according to AS-OCT, AOD500, AOD750, TISA500, TISA750, ARA500, ARA750, TICV500,

TICV750, trabecular iris angle (TIA500), angle opening distance area (AODA750), ICurv, and ACD [8, 11, 17, 18, 22, 51–59]. The authors differently interpret the choice of one or another parameter as a criterion for assessing the success of treatment. It is known that AOD is a predictor of ACA closure, significantly correlated with gonioscopy data [60]; therefore, Δpost-LPI AOD750 is a criterion for the effectiveness of PACD treatment [17, 51–54]. The choice of a change in the trabecular-iris space area after LPI as a criterion for the treatment success is due to the fact that it is less affected by the variability of the iris relief in contrast to the AOD linear parameter [55]. Other researchers choose a change in post-LPI ΔAODA750 to avoid the influence of local changes in the iris relief [18].

The following predictors of LPI success in PACD were identified according to the literature:

- old age [22, 57, 59] and young age [54]
- high preoperative IOP [22, 51]
- increased lens thickness and lens vault [8, 18, 22, 51, 53, 54, 58] and the presence of cataracts [22]
- уменьшенная anterior chamber depth [22] и увеличенные ACD [17, 53] and anterior chamber volume (ACV) [59]
- smaller anterior chamber angle parameters (AOD750) [17, 52, 53] and Shaffer angle opening degree in superior sector [22]
- reduced axial length [53]
- increased iris curvature [11, 17, 22, 53, 57]
- smaller iris area [17, 57] and iris volume [18]
- increased iris thickness [51] and decreased IT [22, 55]
- reduced spherical equivalent [18]
- superior LPI location [17]
- reduced pupil diameter (PD) [17]

The discrepancy in age values as predictors of LPI success in PACD is associated with a different composition of patients in terms of age, ethnicity, and stage of PACD. The study by B. C. Ang et al., where young age was one of the predictors of treatment success, included the Japanese with PACs, PAC, and PACG with a mean age of 75 years [54], and the studies, where old age was a predictor, included the patients from India with PACs of 55 years old [59], mixed ethnicity group with PACs of 65 years old [57], and the Caucasians with PACs of 63 years old [22]. The inclusion of glaucoma patients in the study indicates a worse outcome in the elderly patients, possibly due to the trabecular meshwork pathological changes damaging the outflow of intraocular fluid [61]. Early intervention, at the stage of PACs and PAC, on the contrary, leads to a favorable result in elderly patients. The treatment outcome may also be influenced by ethnicity, suggesting different mechanisms of ACA closure [62].

A high initial IOP determining the success of LPI [22, 51] has been reported by all authors [56]. However, the lack of correlation between the LPI success and preoperative hypertension occurs due to a decrease in the number of topical hypotensive drugs [56].

The best result of LPI is associated with increased LV and LT [8, 18, 22, 51, 53, 54, 58] since lens enlargement with age [63] leads to narrowing and displacement of the iris-lens diaphragm, ACA narrowing, and pupillary block. S. Han et al. showed that the PACD patients with high LV and shallow ACD (Cluster 1 is a marker of pupillary block mechanism) had more pronounced post-LPI angle opening than the patients with relatively deeper ACD and lower LV (Cluster 2 is a marker of plateau iris configuration) [64]. Thus, the authors recommended personalizing the treatment of PACD depending on the pathogenetic mechanism of the anterior chamber angle closure.

The discrepancy in the values of ACD parameters as predictors of LPI success [17, 22, 53, 59] can be explained by the different composition of the participants. Therefore increased ACD was a predictor of success in the PACs groups, and shallow ACD—the PAC groups.

The researchers agree that initially low AOD750 values predetermine post-treatment ACA opening [17, 52, 53]. It is an interesting fact that the decreased ACA parameters measured by AS-OCT (TISA500) and by gonioscopy are predictors of PAC progression after LPI [65]. An example of visualization of the residual ACA closure of a PAC patient after LPI on AS-OCT CASIA2, Tomey, Japan is presented in Fig. 3.

The correlation between reduced axial length and a treatment success is discussed. Some authors have not revealed this correlation [18, 51, 52, 58], while others consider reduced AL to be a predictor of ACA expansion [53]. These discrepancies may be associated with different age composition of the groups and different stages of PACD in the patients included in the study, as well as the use of different devices for measuring the anterior segment parameters.

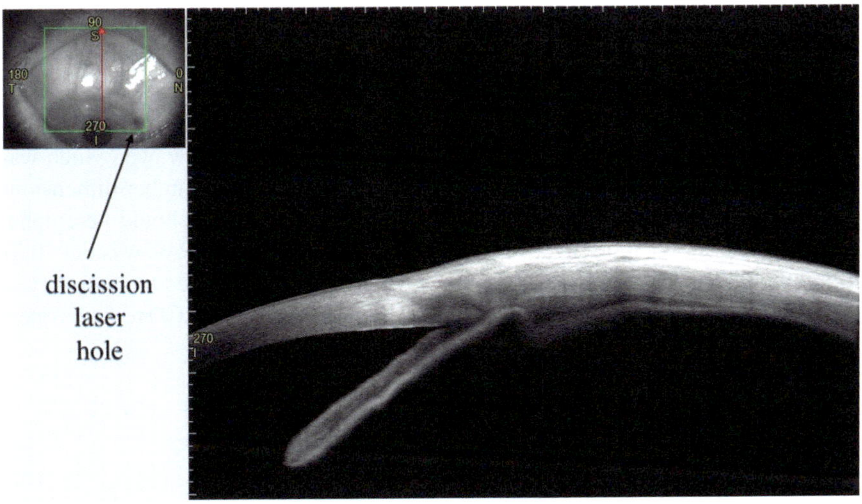


**Fig. 3** Clinical example of residual closure of the anterior chamber angle of a patient with primary angle closure after laser peripheral iridotomy on AS-OCT CASIA2, Tomey, Japan

It is known that a steep iris is a marker of pupillary block [66]. Laser treatment results in iris flattening and ACA opening. So, increased iris curvature serves as a predictor of LPI success [11, 17, 22, 53, 57].

The issue concerning iris thickness as a predictor of LPI success in PACD is currently unresolved. It has been demonstrated that an ACA increase and a decrease in the iris curvature, regarded as the predictors of LPI success in PACs, are associated with thin irises [55]. Similar data were obtained by G. Huang et al., who showed that post-LPI AOD500 increase correlated with an initially smaller iris area [57]. It is known that the hypotensive effect of LPI is also determined by a thin iris [22]. T.A. Tun et al. reported that the LPI success was predetermined by a smaller initial iris volume [18]. R.Y. Lee et al. [55] explained the correlation between thin irises and wider ACA opening after LPI with the studies demonstrating the relationship between high elasticity of thin irises and low content of type I collagen in the iris stroma [67]. An increase in the iris stiffness may provoke a change in its mechanical properties, which negatively affects the results of LPI [68].

In contrast to the abovementioned studies, the study by A.C. How et al. associated an increase in AOD750 after LPI in PACs with initially thick irises (IT2000), which surprised the authors [51]. Therefore, they refer to the discrepancy between their obtained result and the mathematical model of J.S. Tiedeman describing the mechanism of pupillary block [69].

Superior LPI location, which provides the best topographic LPI result in PACs [17], is associated with the fact that the upper angle is the narrowest one [20] with the highest probability of goniosynechia [32]. According to the foregoing, it is clear that the predictors of LPI success are manifold.

It is worth noting that 11–25% of PACS eyes remain persistently closed after LPI [70]. According to other data, this figure is 19.4% [71]. Moreover, iridotrabecular contact ≥1 quadrant is detected in 59% of eyes [72]. Therefore, the maximum personalized approach to the choice of a PACD treatment method seems to be extremely relevant, taking into account the identification of the mechanisms of ACA closure [64] and the parameters determining the post-LPI risk of disease progression. In the 14-year longitudinal study of LPI efficiency in PACS patients, the risk of PACS-to-PAC conversion was reduced by 2/3 compared to a control fellow eye, which was not treated with LPI. Higher baseline IOP and lower anterior chamber dimensions were associated with the transition from PACS to PAC [73]. It should be emphasized that this study reported that the risk ratio for progression to PAC was only 0.31 (95% confidence interval, 0.21–0.46) in LPI-treated eyes compared to control eyes. Thus, the question of the feasibility of LPI in the early stages of PACD remains open.

## 3.2 Predictors of Lens Extraction Efficiency

Currently, lens extraction is used more often in the early stages of PACD [12–14, 20, 21], including PACs [9, 10], proving its effectiveness. There are relatively few studies aimed at the search for the predictors of LE efficacy in PACD [19–22,

74–76]. In most of the existing studies, the hypotensive effect of LE was considered as a criterion for assessing the treatment success [19, 21, 22, 74, 75]. The following parameters have been identified to determine the success of LE:

- elderly age [20, 22]
- male [20, 22, 76]
- high preoperative IOP [21, 22, 74–76]
- increased amount of preoperative glaucoma medications [75]
- increased lens thickness and lens vault [19, 22] and the presence of cataracts [22]
- smaller anterior chamber depth [22, 74] and higher ACD [19, 21, 76]
- reduced anterior chamber angle parameters [22, 75] and higher ACA values [76]
- low degrees of irido-trabecular contact [20]
- reduced axial length [22]
- increased iris curvature [22]
- reduced iris thickness [22]
- increased spherical equivalent [22]
- weak intraocular lens (IOL) power [20]
- lower preoperative visual acuity [22, 76]

In the study by T. Dada et al. based on multivariate analysis, baseline IOP in PAC was the most significant factor of the hypotensive effect of LE ($p < 0.0001$) [21]. At the same time, not all researchers report on this effect in the case of PAC treatment. According to C.E. Traverso et al. the hypotensive effect of LE is associated with high preoperative IOP only in the case of PACG treatment, but not the PAC treatment [19]. A possible cause may be pathological processes in the trabecular meshwork in PACG [61]. In addition, it may be associated with different study designs. In the mentioned study of C.E. Traverso et al. lensectomy in PAC was preceded by LPI in 47% of cases and by iridoplasty in 12%, and in PACG—38% LPI was performed without iridoplasty [19]. C.J. Liu et al. associated the hypotensive effect with high baseline IOP also only in the PACG group but not in the PAC group. The design of this study involved a joint group of PAC with PACs, and the eyes with pre-LPI were also analyzed [74].

The association of the LE success in PAC/PACs with male gender was found in the studies conducted by E. Melese et al. [20] and N.I. Kurysheva et al. [22]. Women are known to be at a higher risk of developing PACG, probably due to an anatomical predisposition [77]. According to H.A. Quigley et al., the prevalence of PACG is associated with female sex, while in POAG this relation has not been confirmed [78]. IOP increase has been shown to be associated with the onset of menopause [79]. In addition, a decreased level of female sex hormones negatively affects ocular hemodynamics [80]. Probably, hormonal factors also influence the post-LE ocular hemodynamics.

According to the literature, a small ACD [22, 74] and a narrow ACA profile [20, 22, 75] were the anatomical and topographic predictors of the hypotensive success of LE. LE-based ACA reconstruction eliminates several mechanisms of pupillary block (both lens and pupillary) by iris flattening after IOL implantation, occupying a smaller volume of the anterior chamber. It is known that the anterior-posterior size of IOL (1 mm) compared to the natural lens (4–5 mm) creates the conditions for an increased ACA profile due to the deepening of the anterior chamber with a subsequent decrease in ophthalmotonus. An example of the anterior chamber visualization of a PAC patient after LE at AS-OCT CASIA2, Tomey, Japan is shown in Fig. 4.

Figure 5 shows how a post-LE decreased lens volume leads to an increase in ACD, the size of ACA and the irido-trabecular space.

The correlation between the post-LE IOP decrease and the initially high lens vault and a steep iris is explained by more pronounced normalization of the ACA topography. Increased LV and a steep iris have been shown to be associated with pupillary block [64, 66].

The relation of thin irises with a pronounced hypotensive effect [22] is explained by the mathematical model of Tiedeman J.S [69]. Thick irises can exacerbate the treatment outcome by affecting ACA reconstruction due to the involvement of both pupillary and extrapupillary blocks simultaneously or sequentially [81]. Peripheral thick irises prevent the outflow of intraocular fluid through the trabecular meshwork.

The inverse correlation between the LE success and the IOL optical power is explained by Melese et al. with a small sample (28 eyes), including eyes with the same biometric parameters (AL, ACD, PD, and corneal curvature) taken into account when calculating IOL, although no significant correlations were obtained with any of the listed parameters [20].

Thus, the predictors of LE success in early PACD are currently ambiguous and further research is required. However, the positioning of LE in the early stages of PACD, including PACs, is becoming more common, proving its effectiveness over 10 years of follow-up [82].

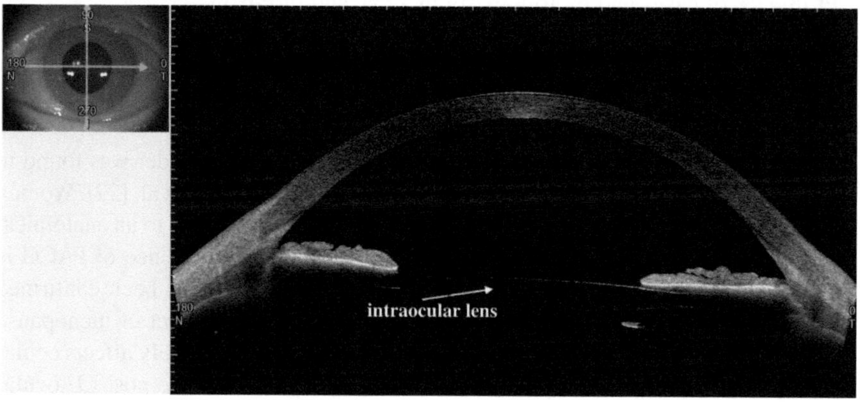


**Fig. 4** Clinical example of visualization of the anterior chamber of the eye of a patient with primary angle closure after lens extraction on AS-OCT. CASIA2, Tomey, Japan

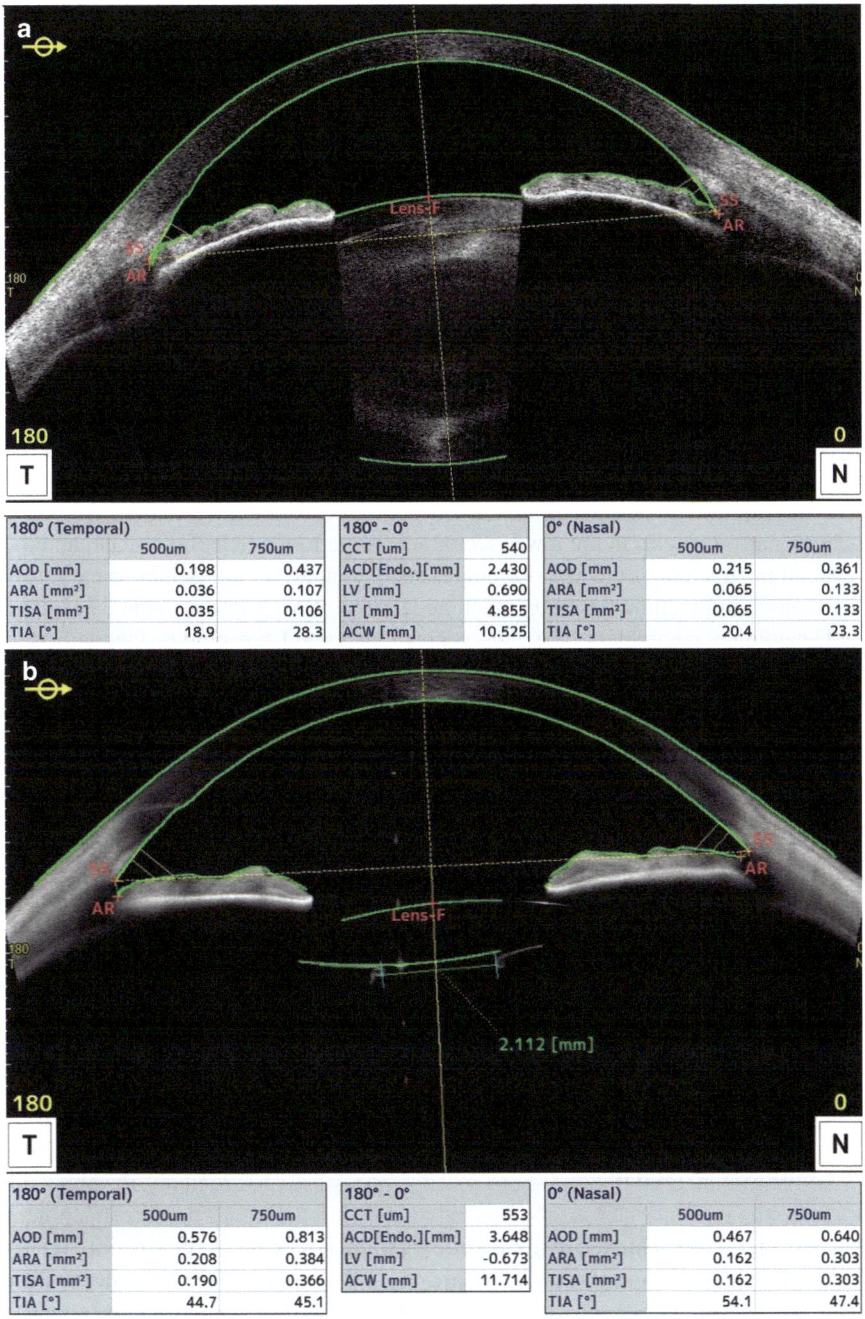


(a)

| 180° (Temporal) | 500um | 750um |
|---|---|---|
| AOD [mm] | 0.198 | 0.437 |
| ARA [mm²] | 0.036 | 0.107 |
| TISA [mm²] | 0.035 | 0.106 |
| TIA [°] | 18.9 | 28.3 |

| 180° - 0° | |
|---|---|
| CCT [um] | 540 |
| ACD[Endo.][mm] | 2.430 |
| LV [mm] | 0.690 |
| LT [mm] | 4.855 |
| ACW [mm] | 10.525 |

| 0° (Nasal) | 500um | 750um |
|---|---|---|
| AOD [mm] | 0.215 | 0.361 |
| ARA [mm²] | 0.065 | 0.133 |
| TISA [mm²] | 0.065 | 0.133 |
| TIA [°] | 20.4 | 23.3 |

(b)

| 180° (Temporal) | 500um | 750um |
|---|---|---|
| AOD [mm] | 0.576 | 0.813 |
| ARA [mm²] | 0.208 | 0.384 |
| TISA [mm²] | 0.190 | 0.366 |
| TIA [°] | 44.7 | 45.1 |

| 180° - 0° | |
|---|---|
| CCT [um] | 553 |
| ACD[Endo.][mm] | 3.648 |
| LV [mm] | -0.673 |
| ACW [mm] | 11.714 |

| 0° (Nasal) | 500um | 750um |
|---|---|---|
| AOD [mm] | 0.467 | 0.640 |
| ARA [mm²] | 0.162 | 0.303 |
| TISA [mm²] | 0.162 | 0.303 |
| TIA [°] | 54.1 | 47.4 |

**Fig. 5** Anterior chamber of a patient with PAC before (**a**) and after (**b**) LE on AS-OCT Casia2, Tomey, Japan. (**a**) Anterior chamber of a patient with primary angle closure before phacoemulsification. (**b**) Increase of the anterior chamber angle of the same patient after phacoemulsification and the implantation of the intraocular lens

## 4 Personalized Choice Between Laser Peripheral Iridotomy and Lens Extraction to Treat Early Primary Angle Closure Disease

Most of the studies aimed at the search for the predictors of treatment efficiency in the early stages of PACD are devoted to only one treatment method: either LPI [8, 11, 17, 18, 51–56], or LE, including eyes with prior LPI [21, 74, 75] and/or iridoplasty [19]. Only two studies compare the success predictors of both treatment methods [20, 22]. E. Melese et al. identified the factors that predict the effectiveness only of LE (elderly age, male gender, weak IOL power, low degree of the irido-trabecular contact, the Caucasians versus the African Americans) [20]. The common predictors of success for both treatment methods have been identified: elderly age, the presence of initial cataract, low corrected visual acuity, high preoperative IOP, narrow angles in the upper sector according to the Schaffer's scale, high LV, shallow ACD, steep and thin iris [22]. At the same time, the LE-specific parameters determining the hypotensive effect of the treatment were: high SE, short AL, male gender, narrow angles in the lower sector according to the Schaffer's scale, and the reduced parameters of the anterior angle. Such an analysis was achieved by applying a modeling method based on machine learning, taking into account 37 clinical and anatomical parameters. The authors concluded that LE should be the method of choice in short AL, a high spherical equivalent and a narrow ACA profile.

Using the machine learning methods [25–27], it is possible to predict the hypotensive effect of LE and LPI in each patient using regression models built for both treatment methods based on 37 clinical and anatomical parameters [83]. The authors assessed the result of the predictive calculation of the hypotensive effect of LPI or LE and suggested choosing a more effective method of treatment. By applying the significant variables selection method [26], a total of 4 parameters can be used, taking into account the availability of measurement in routine clinical practice (gender, IOP, AL, and ACD) to determine the treatment method (LE or LPI) [83].

Thus, one of the ways to solve the problem of choosing a treatment method for the initial stages of PACD is to use the machine learning methods that have proven their effectiveness in personalized medicine [23].

## 5 Selective Laser Trabeculoplasty to Treat Primary Angle Closure Disease

Selective laser trabeculoplasty is the most common treatment for POAG [84]. At the same time, SLT is known as an alternative treatment method of PACD in the eyes with previously performed LPI, provided that the trabecular meshwork is sufficiently visualized [29, 30, 85, 86], which is dictated by the risk of damage to the corneal endothelium [29]. The choice of SLT to treat PACD is associated with the forced use of topical hypotensive therapy after LPI with the risk of low compliance in the long term, including due to the economic component [87]. Furthermore, the role of SLT is undeniable in the case of allergies and systemic side effects to antiglaucoma drugs, as well as during pregnancy. In 2012, R. Sihota et al. used scanning electron biomicroscopy to study ACA structures in PACG and POAG [61]. They revealed similar histological changes in the trabecular meshwork of both groups, which made it possible to apply SLT in PACG as well.

It is known that the hypotensive effect of SLT is comparable with the use of prostaglandin analogues [85].

In PAC/PACG, a 20% IOP decrease from baseline without topical hypotensive drugs is observed in almost half of the cases 6 months after LPI [86]. L. Ali Aljasim et al. demonstrated that the LPI success at 1 year was 84.7% in the PAC/PACG group [88]. The long-term effect (6 years) of SLT in PACG is better than the effect of POAG and allows stabilizing glaucomatous optic neuropathy in the early stages of glaucoma [89].

S. Raj et al. reported that at 1 year after SLT 46.4% PAC/PACG patients achieved an IOP decrease of greater than 6 mmHg without the use of topical hypotensive drugs [28]. The mean IOP in both the PAC and PACG groups was comparable at all follow-up visits, except for the first week after SLT. IOP in PACG was significantly higher than in PAC ($p = 0.035$). The maximum hypotensive effect was noted on the first day, and the minimum—a week after laser intervention. High preoperative IOP was the only factor correlating with the hypotensive effect of SLT. The authors concluded that SLT is an effective post-LPI procedure.

In contrast to the abovementioned studies, N.I. Kurysheva et al. analyzed for the first time the effectiveness of SLT in PAC after LPI in the long-term period [30]. Already at the first year after the procedure, a significant difference in the IOP decrease in PAC in relation to PACG was revealed. This difference persisted throughout the entire follow-up period. Moreover, at 2 years after the treatment the need for topical hypotensive therapy was less in PAC than in PACG. The need for less use of antiglaucoma drugs is most likely associated with the deeper anterior chamber, the smaller lens thickness, fewer goniosynechia, and therefore the wider area of exposure in SLT.

Since the pathogenesis of primary angle closure disease is determined by the relative topographic features of the anterior segment, the treatment strategy is aimed at reconstructing ACA and reducing IOP, therefore, isolated SLT is not acceptable and SLT should be performed only after laser iridotomy. SLT is justified in the cases when LE is impossible, including due to the presence of contraindications, long surgery waiting period, refusal of intervention, and in some cases due to the refusal of lensectomy by the patients with high visual functions who are not always ready to replace the transparent lens. SLT after LPI as an alternative to LE may be considered as a replacement for continuous topical hypotensive therapy under dynamic follow-up.

Thus, SLT is an effective method for reducing IOP not only in PACG, but also in PAC, in cases of insufficient reduction in IOP after LPI. It can be assumed that in such eyes SLT is an alternative method in relation to LE, preventing the development of glaucomatous optic neuropathy.

## 6 Conclusions in the Framework of 3P Medicine

The present review follows the principles of 3P medicine in the research field of glaucoma. Recent international studies demonstrated great benefits of the paradigm change from reactive medical services to multi-level predictive diagnostics approach, phenotyping and patient stratification, targeted prevention and treatment algorithms tailored to individualized patient profiles which are pillars of predictive, preventive, and personalized medicine (3PM/PPPM) [90–98].

It is devoted to the problem of anterior chamber angle closure and highlights how the early detection of this condition, determination of its prognosis, and the formation of a personalized treatment algorithm allow preventing the development of one of the most severe forms of ophthalmopathology—primary angle closure glaucoma. Modern visualization technologies of the structures of the anterior and posterior segments, as well as the analysis of the data obtained on their basis by using machine learning methods provide the high level of **predictive** diagnostics. This makes it possible to select those patients who need an early start of treatment just in the early stage of PACD that corresponds to the concept of the **targeted prevention** of progression to the PACG development. The choice of a specific treatment method (in the context of PAC it is a peripheral laser iridotomy or lens extraction) is also based on an individual approach. This review shows how the determination of only four clinical parameters developed on the basis of machine learning methods contributes to making this choice and providing a **personalized** treatment of early stages of PACD.

## References


1. Tham YC, Li X, Wong TY, Quigley HA, Aung T, Cheng CY (2014) Global prevalence of glaucoma and projections of glaucoma burden through 2040: a systematic review and meta-analysis. Ophthalmology 121(11):2081–2090. https://doi.org/10.1016/j.ophtha.2014.05.013
2. Friedman DS, Foster PJ, Aung T, He M (2012) Angle closure and angle-closure glaucoma: what we are doing now and what we will be doing in the future. Clin Exp Ophthalmol 40(4):381–387. https://doi.org/10.1111/j.1442-9071.2012.02774.x
3. Kurysheva NI, Sharova GA (2023) Anatomical and topographical characteristics of the eye in the early stages of primary angle closure disease. Nat J Glaucoma 22(1):42–53. (In Russ.). https://doi.org/10.53432/2078-4104-2023-22-1-42-53
4. Melese EK, Chan JD, Blieden LS, Chuang AZ, Baker LA, Bell NP, Feldman RM (2016) Determination and validation of thresholds of anterior chamber parameters by dedicated anterior segment optical coherence tomography. Am J Ophthalmol 169:208–217. https://doi.org/10.1016/j.ajo.2016.06.032
5. Eslami Y, Mousavi Kouzahkanan Z, Farzinvash Z et al (2023) A deep learning approach for classification of the primary angle-closure disease Spectrum based on anterior segment optical coherence tomography. J Glaucoma 32(6):540–547. https://doi.org/10.1097/IJG.0000000000002194
6. Zhang Y, Zhang Q, Li L, Thomas R, Li SZ, He MG, Wang NL (2020) Establishment and comparison of algorithms for detection of primary angle closure suspect based on static and

dynamic anterior segment parameters. Transl Vis Sci Technol 9(5):16. https://doi.org/10.1167/tvst.9.5.16
7. He M, Jiang Y, Huang S, Chang DS, Munoz B, Aung T, Foster PJ, Friedman DS (2019) Laser peripheral iridotomy for the prevention of angle closure: a single-Centre, randomised controlled trial. Lancet 393(10181):1609–1618. https://doi.org/10.1016/S0140-6736(18)32607-2
8. Chen X, Wang X, Tang Y, Sun X, Chen Y (2022) Optical coherence tomography analysis of anterior segment parameters before and after laser peripheral iridotomy in primary angle-closure suspects by using CASIA2. BMC Ophthalmol 22(1):144. https://doi.org/10.1186/s12886-022-02366-2
9. Yan C, Han Y, Yu Y, Wang W, Lyu D, Tang Y, Yao K (2019) Effects of lens extraction versus laser peripheral iridotomy on anterior segment morphology in primary angle closure suspect. Graefes Arch Clin Exp Ophthalmol 257(7):1473–1480. https://doi.org/10.1007/s00417-019-04353-8
10. Yan C, Yu Y, Wang W, Han Y, Yao K (2023) Long-term effects of mild cataract extraction versus laser peripheral iridotomy on anterior chamber morphology in primary angle-closure suspect eyes. Br J Ophthalmol. https://doi.org/10.1136/bjo-2022-322698
11. Koh V, Keshtkaran MR, Hernstadt D, Aquino MCD, Chew PT, Sng C (2019) Predicting the outcome of laser peripheral iridotomy for primary angle closure suspect eyes using anterior segment optical coherence tomography. Acta Ophthalmol 97(1):e57–e63. https://doi.org/10.1111/aos.13822
12. Azuara-Blanco A, Burr J, Ramsay C, Cooper D, Foster PJ, Friedman DS, Scotland G, Javanbakht M, Cochrane C, Norrie J; EAGLE study group (2016) Effectiveness of early lens extraction for the treatment of primary angle-closure glaucoma (EAGLE): a randomised controlled trial. Lancet 388(10052):1389–1397. https://doi.org/10.1016/S0140-6736(16)30956-4
13. Mitchell WG, Azuara-Blanco A, Foster PJ, Halawa O, Burr J, Ramsay CR, Cooper D, Cochran C, Norrie J, Friedman D, Chang D (2023) Predictors of long-term intraocular pressure control after lens extraction in primary angle closure glaucoma: results from the EAGLE trial. Br J Ophthalmol 107(8):1072–1078. https://doi.org/10.1136/bjophthalmol-2021-319765
14. Kurysheva NI, Pomerantsev AL, Rodionova OY, Sharova GA (2023) Comparison of lens extraction versus laser Iridotomy on anterior segment, choroid, and intraocular pressure in primary angle closure using machine learning. J Glaucoma 32(6):e43–e55. https://doi.org/10.1097/IJG.0000000000002145
15. Bo J, Changulani T, Cheng ML, Tatham AJ (2018) Outcome following laser peripheral Iridotomy and predictors of future lens extraction. J Glaucoma 27(3):275–280. https://doi.org/10.1097/IJG.0000000000000863
16. Kwon J, Sung KR, Han S (2018) Long-term changes in anterior segment characteristics of eyes with different primary angle-closure mechanisms. Am J Ophthalmol 191:54–63. https://doi.org/10.1016/j.ajo.2018.04.005
17. Xu BY, Friedman DS, Foster PJ, Jiang Y, Pardeshi AA, Jiang Y, Munoz B, Aung T, He M (2021) Anatomic changes and predictors of angle widening after laser peripheral Iridotomy: the Zhongshan angle closure prevention trial. Ophthalmology 128(8):1161–1168. https://doi.org/10.1016/j.ophtha.2021.01.021
18. Tun TA, Sawicki A, Wilkos-Kuc A, Aung T, Zarnowski T (2021) Circumferential assessment of changes in anterior segment characteristics and baseline predictors of angle widening after laser Iridotomy in Caucasian eyes. J Glaucoma 30(9):839–845. https://doi.org/10.1097/IJG.0000000000001866
19. Traverso CE, Cutolo CA (2017) The effects of phacoemulsification and intraocular lens implantation on anatomical and functional parameters in patients with primary angle closure: a prospective study. (an American ophthalmological society thesis). Trans Am Ophthalmol Soc 115:T7
20. Melese E, Peterson JR, Feldman RM, Baker LA, Bell NP, Chuang AZ, Blieden LS (2016) Comparing laser peripheral Iridotomy to cataract extraction in narrow angle eyes using anterior segment optical coherence tomography. PLoS One 11(9):e0162283. https://doi.org/10.1371/journal.pone.0162283

21. Dada T, Rathi A, Angmo D, Agarwal T, Vanathi M, Khokhar SK, Vajpayee RB (2015) Clinical outcomes of clear lens extraction in eyes with primary angle closure. J Cataract Refract Surg 41(7):1470–1477. https://doi.org/10.1016/j.jcrs.2014.10.029
22. Kurysheva NI, Rodionova OY, Pomerantsev AL, Sharova GA (2023) Comparative study of predictors of hypotensive efficacy of laser peripheral iridotomy and lensectomy in patients with primary anterior chamber angle closure based on machine learning methods, 104884. Biomed Signal Process Control 85. https://doi.org/10.1016/j.bspc.2023.104884
23. Rodionova OY, Kurysheva NI, Sharova GA, Pomerantsev AL (2023) Expanding the DD-SIMCA concept: a case study of precision medicine, 340958. Anal Chim Acta 1250. https://doi.org/10.1016/j.aca.2023.340958
24. Kurysheva NI, Pomerantsev AL, Rodionova OY, Sharova GA (2022) Machine learning methods in the comparative evaluation of various approaches to the surgical treatment of primary angle closure. Ophthalmol Russia 19(3):549–556. (In Russ.). https://doi.org/10.18008/1816-5095-2022-3-549-556
25. Pomerantsev AL, Rodionova OY (2021) New trends in qualitative analysis: performance, optimization, and validation of multi-class and soft models. Trends Anal Chem 143:116372. https://doi.org/10.1016/j.trac.2021.116372
26. Kucheryavskiy S (2020) Mdatools—R package for chemometrics. Chemom Intell Lab Syst 198:103937. https://doi.org/10.1016/j.chemolab.2020.103937
27. Rodionova OY, Pomerantsev AL (2020) Detection of outliers in projection-based modeling. Anal Chem 92:2656–2664. https://doi.org/10.1021/acs.analchem.9b04611
28. Raj S, Tigari B, Faisal TT, Gautam N, Kaushik S, Ichhpujani P, Pandav SS, Ram J (2018) Efficacy of selective laser trabeculoplasty in primary angle closure disease [published correction appears in Eye (Lond). 2021 Mar;35(3):1028]. Eye (Lond) 32(11):1710–1716. https://doi.org/10.1038/s41433-018-0165-5
29. Kurysheva NI, Lepeshkina LV, Kapkova SG (2021) Factors affecting the corneal endothelium after selective laser trabeculoplasty in primary open angle and angle closure glaucoma. BMJ Open Ophthalmol 6(1):e000638. https://doi.org/10.1136/bmjophth-2020-000638
30. Kurysheva NI, Sharova GA (2022) Role of selective laser Trabeculoplasty in the treatment of primary angle closure of the anterior chamber. Eff Pharmacother 18(11):22–28. (In Russ.). https://doi.org/10.33978/2307-3586-2022-18-11-22-28
31. Foster PJ, Buhrmann R, Quigley HA, Johnson GJ (2002) The definition and classification of glaucoma in prevalence surveys. Br J Ophthalmol 86(2):238–242. https://doi.org/10.1136/bjo.86.2.238
32. Sakata LM, Lavanya R, Friedman DS, Aung HT, Gao H, Kumar RS, Foster PJ, Aung T (2008) Comparison of gonioscopy and anterior segment ocular coherence tomography in detecting angle closure in different quadrants of the anterior chamber angle. Ophthalmology 115(5):769–774. https://doi.org/10.1016/j.ophtha.2007.06.030
33. Correia Barão R, Cutolo C, Tanito M, Hommer A, Faschinger C, Abegão Pinto L, Traverso C (2021) Agreement analysis on angle characteristics with automated gonioscopy. J Glaucoma 30(12):1039–1046. https://doi.org/10.1097/IJG.0000000000001940
34. Chansangpetch S, Rojanapongpun P, Lin SC (2018) Anterior segment imaging for angle closure. Am J Ophthalmol 188:xvi–xxix. https://doi.org/10.1016/j.ajo.2018.01.006
35. George R, Paul PG, Baskaran M, Ramesh SV, Raju P, Arvind H, McCarty C, Vijaya L (2003) Ocular biometry in occludable angles and angle closure glaucoma: a population based survey. Br J Ophthalmol 87(4):399–402. https://doi.org/10.1136/bjo.87.4.399
36. Zhou S, Pardeshi AA, Burkemper B, Apolo G, Cho A, Jiang X, Torres M, McKean-Cowdin R, Varma R, Xu BY (2023) Refractive error and anterior chamber depth as risk factors in primary angle closure disease: the Chinese American eye study. J Glaucoma 32(4):257–264. https://doi.org/10.1097/IJG.0000000000002154
37. Atalay E, Nongpiur ME, Baskaran M, Sharma S, Perera SA, Aung T (2016) Biometric factors associated with acute primary angle closure: comparison of the affected and fellow eye. Invest Ophthalmol Vis Sci 57(13):5320–5325. https://doi.org/10.1167/iovs.16-20006

38. Huang W, Li X, Gao X, Zhang X (2020) Anterior and posterior segment structural features of acute primary angle-closure eyes: date based on AS-OCT and SS-OCT. Ann Eye Sci 5:35. https://doi.org/10.21037/aes-20-87
39. Foo LL, Nongpiur ME, Allen JC, Perera SA, Friedman DS, He M, Cheng CY, Wong TY, Aung T (2012) Determinants of angle width in Chinese Singaporeans. Ophthalmology 119(2):278–282. https://doi.org/10.1016/j.ophtha.2011.07.049
40. Guzman CP, Gong T, Nongpiur ME, Perera SA, How AC, Lee HK, Cheng L, He M, Baskaran M, Aung T (2013) Anterior segment optical coherence tomography parameters in subtypes of primary angle closure. Invest Ophthalmol Vis Sci 54(8):5281–5286. https://doi.org/10.1167/iovs.13-12285
41. Moghimi S, Vahedian Z, Fakhraie G, Ghaffari R, Eslami Y, Jabarvand M, Zarei R, Mohammadi M, Lin S (2013) Ocular biometry in the subtypes of angle closure: an anterior segment optical coherence tomography study. Am J Ophthalmol 155:664–673. https://doi.org/10.1016/j.ajo.2012.10.014
42. Wang B, Sakata LM, Friedman DS, Chan YH, He M, Lavanya R, Wong TY, Aung T (2010) Quantitative iris parameters and association with narrow angles. Ophthalmology 117(1):11–17. https://doi.org/10.1016/j.ophtha.2009.06.017
43. Huang W, Li X, Gao X, Zhang X (2021) The anterior and posterior biometric characteristics in primary angle-closure disease: data based on anterior segment optical coherence tomography and swept-source optical coherence tomography. Indian J Ophthalmol 69(4):865–870. https://doi.org/10.4103/ijo.IJO_936_20
44. Huang W, Wang W, Gao X, Li X, Li Z, Zhou M, Chen S, Zhang X (2013) Choroidal thickness in the subtypes of angle closure: an EDI-OCT study. Invest Ophthalmol Vis Sci 54:7849–7853. https://doi.org/10.1167/iovs.13-13158
45. Nguyen DT, Giocanti-Aurégan A, Benhatchi N, Greliche N, Beaussier H, Sustronck P, Hammoud S, Jeanteur MN, Kretz G, Abitbol O, Lachkar Y (2020) Increased choroidal thickness in primary angle closure measured by swept-source optical coherence tomography in Caucasian population. Int Ophthalmol 40(1):195–203. https://doi.org/10.1007/s10792-019-01171-z
46. Hata M, Hirose F, Oishi A, Hirami Y, Kurimoto Y (2012) Changes in choroidal thickness and optical axial length accompanying intraocular pressure increase. Jpn J Ophthalmol 56(6):564–568. https://doi.org/10.1007/s10384-012-0173-0
47. Song W, Huang P, Dong X, Li X, Zhang C (2016) Choroidal thickness decreased in acute primary angle closure attacks with elevated intraocular pressure. Curr Eye Res 41(4):526–531. https://doi.org/10.3109/02713683.2015.1037002
48. Saeedi O, Pillar A, Jefferys J, Arora K, Friedman D, Quigley H (2014) Change in choroidal thickness and axial length with change in intraocular pressure after trabeculectomy. Br J Ophthalmol 98(7):976–979. https://doi.org/10.1136/bjophthalmol-2013-304433
49. Usui S, Ikuno Y, Uematsu S, Morimoto Y, Yasuno Y, Otori Y (2013) Changes in axial length and choroidal thickness after intraocular pressure reduction resulting from trabeculectomy. Clin Ophthalmol 7:1155–1161. https://doi.org/10.2147/OPTH.S44884
50. Kara N, Baz O, Altan C, Satana B, Kurt T, Demirok A (2013) Changes in choroidal thickness, axial length, and ocular perfusion pressure accompanying successful glaucoma filtration surgery. Eye (Lond) 27(8):940–945. https://doi.org/10.1038/eye.2013.116
51. How AC, Baskaran M, Kumar RS, He M, Foster PJ, Lavanya R, Wong HT, Chew PT, Friedman DS, Aung T (2012) Changes in anterior segment morphology after laser peripheral iridotomy: an anterior segment optical coherence tomography study. Ophthalmology 119(7):1383–1387. https://doi.org/10.1016/j.ophtha.2012.01.019
52. Moghimi S, Chen R, Johari M, Bijani F, Mohammadi M, Khodabandeh A, He MG, Lin SC (2016) Changes in anterior segment morphology after laser peripheral iridotomy in acute primary angle closure. Am J Ophthalmol 166:133–140. https://doi.org/10.1016/j.ajo.2016.03.032
53. Zebardast N, Kavitha S, Krishnamurthy P, Friedman DS, Nongpiur ME, Aung T, Quigley HA, Ramulu PY, Venkatesh R (2016) Changes in anterior segment morphology and predictors of angle widening after laser Iridotomy in south Indian eyes. Ophthalmology 123(12):2519–2526. https://doi.org/10.1016/j.ophtha.2016.08.020

54. Ang BC, Nongpiur ME, Aung T, Mizoguchi T, Ozaki M (2016) Changes in Japanese eyes after laser peripheral iridotomy: an anterior segment optical coherence tomography study. Clin Exp Ophthalmol 44(3):159–165. https://doi.org/10.1111/ceo.12673
55. Lee RY, Kasuga T, Cui QN, Porco TC, Huang G, He M, Lin SC (2014) Association between baseline iris thickness and prophylactic laser peripheral iridotomy outcomes in primary angle-closure suspects. Ophthalmology 121(6):1194–1202. https://doi.org/10.1016/j.ophtha.2013.12.027
56. Kansara S, Blieden LS, Chuang AZ, Baker LA, Bell NP, Mankiewicz KA, Feldman RM (2016) Effect of laser peripheral iridotomy on anterior chamber angle anatomy in primary angle closure spectrum eyes. J Glaucoma 25(5):e469–e474. https://doi.org/10.1097/IJG.0000000000000293
57. Huang G, Gonzalez E, Lee R, Osmonavic S, Leeungurasatien T, He M, Lin SC (2012) Anatomic predictors for anterior chamber angle opening after laser peripheral iridotomy in narrow angle eyes. Curr Eye Res 37(7):575–582. https://doi.org/10.3109/02713683.2012.655396
58. Liu YM, Hu D, Zhou LF, Lan J, Feng CC, Wang XY, Pan XJ (2021) Associations of lens thickness and axial length with outcomes of laser peripheral iridotomy. Int J Ophthalmol 14(5):714–718. https://doi.org/10.18240/ijo.2021.05.11
59. Mansoori T, Balakrishna N (2018) Anterior segment morphology after laser iridotomy in primary angle closure suspects. Clin Exp Optom 101(3):333–338. https://doi.org/10.1111/cxo.12631
60. Narayanaswamy A, Sakata LM, He MG, Friedman DS, Chan YH, Lavanya R, Baskaran M, Foster PJ, Aung T (2010) Diagnostic performance of anterior chamber angle measurements for detecting eyes with narrow angles: an anterior segment OCT study. Arch Ophthalmol 128(10):1321–1327. https://doi.org/10.1001/archophthalmol.2010.231
61. Sihota R, Goyal A, Kaur J, Gupta V, Nag TC (2012) Scanning electron microscopy of the trabecular meshwork: understanding the pathogenesis of primary angle closure glaucoma. Indian J Ophthalmol 60(3):183–188. https://doi.org/10.4103/0301-4738.95868
62. Wang YE, Li Y, Wang D, He M, Lin S (2013) Comparison of factors associated with occludable angle between American Caucasians and ethnic Chinese. Invest Ophthalmol Vis Sci 54(12):7717–7723. https://doi.org/10.1167/iovs.13-12850
63. Sun JH, Sung KR, Yun SC, Cheon MH, Tchah HW, Kim MJ, Kim JY (2012) Factors associated with anterior chamber narrowing with age: an optical coherence tomography study. Invest Ophthalmol Vis Sci 53(6):2607–2610. https://doi.org/10.1167/iovs.11-9359
64. Han S, Sung KR, Lee KS, Hong JW (2014) Outcomes of laser peripheral iridotomy in angle closure subgroups according to anterior segment optical coherence tomography parameters. Invest Ophthalmol Vis Sci 55(10):6795–6801. https://doi.org/10.1167/iovs.14-14714
65. Bao YK, Xu BY, Friedman DS, Cho A, Foster PJ, Jiang Y, Porporato N, Pardeshi AA, Jiang Y, Munoz B, Aung T, He M (2023) Biometric risk factors for angle closure progression after laser peripheral Iridotomy. JAMA Ophthalmol 141:e230937. https://doi.org/10.1001/jamaophthalmol.2023.0937
66. Nonaka A, Iwawaki T, Kikuchi M, Fujihara M, Nishida A, Kurimoto Y (2007) Quantitative evaluation of iris convexity in primary angle closure. Am J Ophthalmol 143(4):695–697. https://doi.org/10.1016/j.ajo.2006.11.018
67. Konstas AG, Marshall GE, Lee WR (1990) Immunocytochemical localisation of collagens (I-V) in the human iris. Graefes Arch Clin Exp Ophthalmol 228(2):180–186. https://doi.org/10.1007/BF00935730
68. He M, Lu Y, Liu X, Ye T, Foster PJ (2008) Histologic changes of the iris in the development of angle closure in Chinese eyes. J Glaucoma 17(5):386–392. https://doi.org/10.1097/IJG.0b013e31815c5f69
69. Tiedeman JS (1991) A physical analysis of the factors that determine the contour of the iris. Am J Ophthalmol 111(3):338–343. https://doi.org/10.1016/s0002-9394(14)72319-0
70. Radhakrishnan S, Chen PP, Junk AK, Nouri-Mahdavi K, Chen TC (2018) Laser peripheral iridotomy in primary angle closure: a report by the American Academy of Ophthalmology. Ophthalmology 125(7):1110–1120. https://doi.org/10.1016/j.ophtha.2018.01.015

71. He M, Friedman DS, Ge J, Huang W, Jin C, Lee PS, Khaw PT, Foster PJ (2007) Laser peripheral iridotomy in primary angleclosure suspects: biometric and gonioscopic outcomes: the Liwan eye study. Ophthalmology 114(3):494–500. https://doi.org/10.1016/j.ophtha.2006.06.053
72. Kong X, Foster PJ, Huang Q, Zheng Y, Huang W, Cai X, He M (2011) Appositional closure identified by ultrasound biomicroscopy in population-based primary angle-closure glaucoma suspects: the Liwan eye study. Invest Ophthalmol Vis Sci 52(7):3970–3975. https://doi.org/10.1167/iovs.10-6412
73. Yuan Y, Wang W, Xiong R, Zhang J, Li C, Yang S, Friedman DS, Foster PJ, He M (2023) 14-year outcome of angle-closure prevention with laser Iridotomy in the Zhongshan angle closure prevention study: extended follow-up of a randomized controlled trial. Ophthalmology S0161-6420(23):00201–00204. https://doi.org/10.1016/j.ophtha.2023.03.024
74. Liu CJ, Cheng CY, Wu CW, Lau LI, Chou JC, Hsu WM (2006) Factors predicting intraocular pressure control after phacoemulsification in angle-closure glaucoma. Arch Ophthalmol 124(10):1390–1394. https://doi.org/10.1001/archopht.124.10.1390
75. Shams PN, Foster PJ (2012) Clinical outcomes after lens extraction for visually significant cataract in eyes with primary angle closure. J Glaucoma 21(8):545–550. https://doi.org/10.1097/IJG.0b013e31821db1db1
76. Ün Y, Cömerter D (2022) Phacoemulsification results of eyes with primary angle closure and primary angle closure glaucoma using the Pentacam system. Acta Med Austriaca 53:333–341. https://doi.org/10.32552/2022
77. Lee CS, Lee ML, Yanagihara RT, Lee AY (2021) Predictors of narrow angle detection rate-a longitudinal study of Massachusetts residents over 1.7 million person years. Eye (Lond) 35(3):952–958. https://doi.org/10.1038/s41433-020-1003-0
78. Quigley HA, Broman AT (2006) The number of people with glaucoma worldwide in 2010 and 2020. Br J Ophthalmol 90(3):262–267. https://doi.org/10.1136/bjo.2005.081224
79. Altintaş O, Caglar Y, Yüksel N, Demirci A, Karabaş L (2004) The effects of menopause and hormone replacement therapy on quality and quantity of tear, intraocular pressure and ocular blood flow. Ophthalmologica 218(2):120–129. https://doi.org/10.1159/000076148
80. Toker E, Yenice O, Akpinar I, Aribal E, Kazokoglu H (2003) The influence of sex hormones on ocular blood flow in women. Acta Ophthalmol Scand 81(6):617–624. https://doi.org/10.1111/j.1395-3907.2003.00160.x
81. Wang N, Ouyang J, Zhou W, Lai M, Ye T, Zeng M, Chen J. [Multiple patterns of angle closure mechanisms in primary angle closure glaucoma in Chinese]. Zhonghua Yan Ke Za Zhi. 2000;36(1):46–6. Chinese.
82. Sakai D, Yamamoto S, Yoshimizu S, Hirose F, Fujihara M, Nakamura M, Kurimoto Y (2023) Ten-year outcomes of cataract surgery for glaucoma management in patients with primary angle-closure disease. Jpn J Ophthalmol 67(2):129–137. https://doi.org/10.1007/s10384-022-00971-8
83. Kurysheva NI, Rodionova OY, Pomerantsev AL, Sharova GA (2023) Personalized choice of treatment for patients with primary anterior chamber angle closure. Poster, World Glaucoma Congress, Rome
84. Katz LJ, Steinmann WC, Kabir A, Molineaux J, Wizov SS, Marcellino G; SLT/Med Study Group (2012) Selective laser trabeculoplasty versus medical therapy as initial treatment of glaucoma: a prospective, randomized trial. J Glaucoma 21(7):460–468. https://doi.org/10.1097/IJG.0b013e318218287f
85. Narayanaswamy A, Leung CK, Istiantoro DV, Perera SA, Ho CL, Nongpiur ME, Baskaran M, Htoon HM, Wong TT, Goh D, Su DH, Belkin M, Aung T (2015) Efficacy of selective laser trabeculoplasty in primary angle-closure glaucoma: a randomized clinical trial. JAMA Ophthalmol. 133(2):206–212. https://doi.org/10.1001/jamaophthalmol.2014.4893
86. Ho CL, Lai JS, Aquino MV, Rojanapongpun P, Wong HT, Aquino MC, Gerber Y, Belkin M, Barkana Y (2009) Selective laser trabeculoplasty for primary angle closure with persistently elevated intraocular pressure after iridotomy. J Glaucoma 18(7):563–566. https://doi.org/10.1097/IJG.0b013e318193c2d1

87. Peng PH, Nguyen H, Lin HS, Nguyen N, Lin S (2011) Long-term outcomes of laser iridotomy in Vietnamese patients with primary angle closure. Br J Ophthalmol 95(9):1207–1211. https://doi.org/10.1136/bjo.2010.181016
88. Ali Aljasim L, Owaidhah O, Edward DP (2016) Selective laser trabeculoplasty in primary angle-closure glaucoma after laser peripheral Iridotomy: a case-control study. J Glaucoma 25(3):e253–e258. https://doi.org/10.1097/IJG.0000000000000282
89. Kurysheva NI, Lepeshkina LV, Shatalova EO (2018) Predictors of outcome in selective laser trabeculoplasty: a long-term observation study in primary angle-closure glaucoma after laser peripheral Iridotomy compared with primary open-angle glaucoma. J Glaucoma 27(10):880–886. https://doi.org/10.1097/IJG.0000000000001048
90. Golubnitschaja O, Baban B, Boniolo G, Wang W, Bubnov R, Kapalla M, Krapfenbauer K, Mozaffari MS, Costigliola V (2016) Medicine in the early twenty-first century: paradigm and anticipation—EPMA position paper 2016. EPMA J 7(1):23. https://doi.org/10.1186/s13167-016-0072-4
91. Zhang Q, Wang N, Rui Y, Xia Y, Xiong S, Xia X (2023) New insight of metabolomics in ocular diseases in the context of 3P medicine. EPMA J 14(1):53–71. https://doi.org/10.1007/s13167-023-00313-9
92. Zhou W, Sabel BA (2023) Vascular dysregulation in glaucoma: retinal vasoconstriction and normal neurovascular coupling in altitudinal visual field defects. EPMA J 14(1):87–99. https://doi.org/10.1007/s13167-023-00316-6
93. Evsevieva M, Sergeeva O, Mazurakova A, Koklesova L, Prokhorenko-Kolomoytseva I, Shchetinin E, Birkenbihl C, Costigliola V, Kubatka P, Golubnitschaja O (2022) Pre-pregnancy check-up of maternal vascular status and associated phenotype is crucial for the health of mother and offspring. EPMA J 13(3):351–366. https://doi.org/10.1007/s13167-022-00294-1
94. Golubnitschaja O, Potuznik P, Polivka J Jr, Pesta M, Kaverina O, Pieper CC, Kropp M, Thumann G, Erb C, Karabatsiakis A, Stetkarova I, Polivka J, Costigliola V (2022) Ischemic stroke of unclear aetiology: a case-by-case analysis and call for a multiprofessional predictive, preventive and personalised approach. EPMA J 13(4):535–545. https://doi.org/10.1007/s13167-022-00307-z
95. Zhan X, Li J, Guo Y, Golubnitschaja O (2021) Mass spectrometry analysis of human tear fluid biomarkers specific for ocular and systemic diseases in the context of 3P medicine. EPMA J 12(4):449–475. https://doi.org/10.1007/s13167-021-00265-y
96. Li S, Qiu Y, Yu J, Shao M, Li Y, Cao W, Sun X (2021) Association of systemic inflammation indices with visual field loss progression in patients with primary angle-closure glaucoma: potential biomarkers for 3P medical approaches. EPMA J 12(4):659–675. https://doi.org/10.1007/s13167-021-00260-3
97. Koklesova L, Samec M, Liskova A, Zhai K, Büsselberg D, Giordano FA, Kubatka P, Golunitschaja O (2021) Mitochondrial impairments in aetiopathology of multifactorial diseases: common origin but individual outcomes in context of 3P medicine. EPMA J 12(1):27–40. https://doi.org/10.1007/s13167-021-00237-2
98. Sabel BA, Wang J, Fähse S, Cárdenas-Morales L, Antal A (2020) Personality and stress influence vision restoration and recovery in glaucoma and optic neuropathy following alternating current stimulation: implications for personalized neuromodulation and rehabilitation. EPMA J 11(2):177–196. https://doi.org/10.1007/s13167-020-00204-3

# Multi-faceted Medical Care to Meet Individual Needs of Subjects with Excessive BMI: Professional Oral Hygiene and Periodontal Health Are in Focus of 3PM

**E. S. Loboda, L. Y. Orekhova, R. A. Rozov, V. V. Tachalov, T. V. Kudryavtseva, E. V. Grinenko, and O. Golubnitschaja**

## Abbreviations

| | |
|---|---|
| API | Plaque index of proximal surfaces |
| BMI | Body mass index |
| BOP | Bleeding index of gingival papillae |
| KPU | Caries intensity index |
| PMA | Papillary-marginal-alveolar index |
| PPPM/3PM | Predictive, preventive, and personalized medicine |
| PSAF-ADA | Psycho-sensorial-anatomical-functional autodeadaptation |

E. S. Loboda · L. Y. Orekhova · E. V. Grinenko
Therapeutic Dentistry and Periodontology Department, Pavlov First Saint Petersburg State Medical University, St. Petersburg, Russia

City Periodontology Centre, "PAKS", St. Petersburg, Russia

R. A. Rozov · V. V. Tachalov · T. V. Kudryavtseva
Therapeutic Dentistry and Periodontology Department, Pavlov First Saint Petersburg State Medical University, St. Petersburg, Russia

O. Golubnitschaja (✉)
3P Medicine Research Unit, University Hospital, Rheinische Friedrich-Wilhelms Universität Bonn, Bonn, Germany
e-mail: olga.golubnitschaja@ukbonn.de


W. Wang (ed.), *All Around Suboptimal Health*, Advances in Predictive, Preventive and Personalised Medicine 18,
https://doi.org/10.1007/978-3-031-46891-9_14

## 1 Overall Management of Periodontal Health in Patients with Comorbidities Remains Challenging

It is customary to call comorbid states the coexistence of two and/or more diseases in one patient, pathogenetically and genetically interconnected, while the negative impact on the body does not add up arithmetically but multiplies geometrically. Today, there is no doubt that somatic pathology can provoke the appearance of many dental diseases or aggravate their course [1–3]. According to epidemiological studies, the prevalence of periodontal diseases tends to 100% and in the structure of dental morbidity is it second to the most prevalent caries. The modern etiopathogenetic concept of the development of periodontal diseases includes three mandatory components: the presence of periodontopathogenic microflora as part of a biofilm on the tooth surface, the necessary local conditions in periodontal tissues for the formation of a dysbiotic shift in the oral microbiota and the accumulation of inflammatory mediators, as well as general factors that regulate the metabolism of oral tissues, which determine the response to pathological effects and the rate of recovery of periodontal tissues damaged during inflammation [4–6]. In connection with the emergence of new data on the development of periodontal diseases, the emphasis on biofilm as the primary etiological factor was shifted towards the compensatory capabilities of the body associated with common factors. Microbial invasion, in turn, triggers processes that destroy periodontal tissues, the result of which depends on the state of the body's defense reactions that can both limit and provoke destructive processes in the periodontium [6].

## 2 Health Risk Assessment and Predictive Approach Are Crucial for Maintaining Periodontal Health

Health risk assessment is crucial for both—diagnosing and treatment algorithms of periodontal diseases and predicting the results. Obviously, in patients with concomitant systemic diseases, such as diabetes mellitus, the risk of developing and progressing periodontal pathology, as well as the severity and possibility of complications of this pathological condition, is much higher. However, the level of risk may be underestimated in patients who, in addition to severe somatic diseases, may have additional pathological conditions, such as chronic stress or distress, excessive weight, bruxism, and/or unhealthy life-style habits that can synergistically increase health risks. To this end, a comprehensive health risk assessment considering all modifiable and non-modifiable risk factors is instrumental for individualized patient profiling, robust predictive diagnostics and treatment algorithms tailored to the person. Contextually, per accumulated scientific evidence, an excessive BMI is a modifiable risk factor which creates strong predisposition to inflammatory and destructive lesions of the periodontium with cascading associated pathologies. Therefore, underestimation by patients and specialists of this risk factor leads to poor individual outcomes under the periodontal therapy and causes severe complication in implantology and orthopedic rehabilitation frequently observed in this patient cohort.

The relevance of investigating and mitigating health risks problem associated with excessive BMI in the formation of inflammatory-destructive lesions of the periodontium is primarily associated with its intensive growth, a high risk of developing concomitant diseases [7–10], a high frequency of severe complications and is directly related to insufficiently effective both non-drug and medicinal and surgical methods of treatment [2]. Contextually, the paradigm shifts from reactive medical services to predictive diagnostics, targeted prevention and treatment algorithms tailored to personalized patient profiles is in focus of multi-professional efforts to maintain periodontal health in primary (defined as suboptimal health conditions and protection against the transition from health-to-disease) and secondary (defined as protection against the disease progression and clinical manifestation of comorbidities) care [11, 12].

## 3 Study Design

A single-center, prospective, blind study was conducted at the Department of Therapeutic Dentistry and Periodontology of the St. Petersburg State Medical University. acad. I.P. Pavlov, Research Institute of ChLH and Dentistry and the City Periodontal Center PAKS. The study was approved by the institutional ethics committee.

The study involved 83 patients with type 1 diabetes mellitus (T1DM) aged 25 to 45 years, who made up two groups of comparison: group 1—patients with normal BMI (58 patients) and group 2—patients with excessive BMI (25 patients). The criterion for inclusion of patients in the first group was the value of the BMI ranging from 18.5 to 24.9 kg/m$^2$. The criterion for inclusion of patients in the second group was the excessive BMI ranging from 25 to 30 kg/m$^2$ (defined as pre-obesity). The dental criterion for inclusion in the study was the presence of chronic generalized periodontitis of mild to moderate severity (periodontitis I/II, class C) in accordance with clinical and radiological criteria. All patients were diagnosed with stable T1DM without complications. All patients were under dispensary observation at the St. Petersburg Regional Diabetes Center, their participation in the study was voluntary, in connection with which they filled out informed voluntary consent to participate in the study.

All patients included into the study underwent a comprehensive dental examination, namely a generalized survey, comprehensive clinical examination, determination of hygienic and periodontal indices (caries intensity index—KPU, simplified Green-Vermillion hygiene index—OHI-S, plaque index of proximal surfaces—API, papillary-marginal-alveolar index—PMA, bleeding index of gingival papillae—BOP), pH-metry of the oral fluid, microbiological examination of the contents of periodontal pockets.

All patients were offered a questionnaire containing tests for Korach's dental anxiety, Spielberger-Khanin's situational and personal anxiety, a compliance test (according to S.V. Davydov), a sheet of voluntary confidential information from the doctor to the patient (determining the level of PSAF-ADA).

After finalizing the clinical examination, patients in both groups of comparison underwent the first stage of active periodontal treatment—professional oral hygiene, including the removal of mineralized supra- and subgingival dental deposits using an ultrasonic scaler, air-abrasive treatment of the air-flow tooth surface using an air-abrasive mixture based on glycine, polishing of the crown and visualized root parts of the teeth with brushes and paste.

Further, a training conversation was performed with the patients on the rules and features of the implementation of individual hygienic dental measures, the tasks of which included the correction of individual theoretical and manual skills, as well as motivating the patient to comply with all treatment and preventive recommendations.

The re-examination of all parameters involved was performed after 1 month.

## 4 Data Analysis and Interpretation

According to the results of the examination in patients with T1DM with excessive versus normal BMI, the index of caries intensity of the KPU was similar: 11.12 ± 1.06 and 11.52 ± 1.17 units.

Green-Vermillion hygiene indices in both groups corresponded to satisfactory values (1.45 ± 0.12 points and 1.26 ± 0.08 points, respectively); however, the values of the plaque index on the approximate API surfaces corresponded to poor oral hygiene (72.68 ± 5.77% and 68.60 ± 3.94%).

The values of the papillary-marginal-alveolar index in both groups indicated the moderate severity of inflammation of the gingival margin (32.55 ± 3.23% and 35.48 ± 2.23%).

The bleeding index of the gingival papillae BOP indicated a high risk of progression of periodontitis (33.96 ± 6.56% and 30.80 ± 4.40%).

The pH of the oral fluid in the group of patients with T1DM and excessive BMI differed significantly from the pH level in the group of comparison with normal BMI (6.75 ± 0.12 units and 7.01 ± 0.09 units).

As summarized with Table 1, 1 month after the professional oral hygiene was performed, hygiene indicators improved.

The values of the Green-Vermillion indices and the plaque index on the approximal surfaces decreased in both groups of comparison. However, in the group of patients with normal BMI these changes were more pronounced.

The value of the papillary-marginal-alveolar index significantly decreased (by 24.28%) in the T1DM group with normal BMI indicating a decreased manifestation of an inflamed reaction in periodontal tissues after professional hygiene. In contrast, T1DM with excessive BMI these changes were insignificant (by 1%), apparently

**Table 1** A comparative analysis of dental indices values among the groups of comparison (T1DM overweight versus normal BMI) before and after professional hygiene performance

| | Overweight patients ($n$ = 25) | | Normal weight patients ($n$ = 58) | |
|---|---|---|---|---|
| | Before | After | Before | After |
| OHI-S (points) | 1.45 ± 0.12 | 1.28 ± 0.09 | 1.26 ± 0.08 | 0.97 ± 0.06 |
| API (%) | 72.68 ± 5.77 | 63.08 ± 4.55 | 68.6 ± 3.94 | 57.67 ± 3.41 |
| PMA (%) | 32.55 ± 3.23 | 31.64 ± 3.47 | 35.48 ± 2.23 | 24.28 ± 2.63 |
| BOP (%) | 33.96 ± 6.56 | 26.12 ± 6.49 | 30.80 ± 4.40 | 23.30 ± 3.94 |
| pH (units) | 6.75 ± 0.12 | 6.79 ± 0.07 | 7.01 ± 0.09 | 7.05 ± 0.09 |

due to the more severe course of periodontal diseases and the need to supplement the stage of professional oral hygiene with systemic antibacterial and anti-inflammatory drug therapy.

The degree of bleeding according to the results of the BOP test decreased in both groups of comparison, close to being equal.

The pH values of the oral fluid increased equally in both groups of comparison: in the group of patients with normal BMI, this indicator approached the normal values in contrast to the group with overweight T1DM patients.

The health status of the oral cavity improved in both groups. However, corresponding parameters (the hygienic status, the degree of inflammation of the periodontal tissues and the acid-base state of the oral cavity) demonstrated better lever of improvement in the group with normal BMI compared to the overweight patients that may be associated with a more severe initial impairments to the periodontium in the group of overweight T1DM, as well as with their evidently weaker response to treatments.

Overall microbiologic parameters were similar in both groups. However, in the overweight T1DM patients, microorganisms responsible for a more aggressive course of periodontitis were more prevalent such as Candida spp. and Prevotella intermedia; their prevalence remained higher in this group of comparison even after professional oral hygiene—see Table 2 and Fig. 1.

Fasting glucose levels remained the same in the T1DM group with normal BMI, namely 7.11 mmol/L and 7.10 mmol/L before and after professional hygiene performed, respectively. In contrast, in the T1DM group with excessive BMI, corresponding glucose level increased from 7.56 mmol/L (before) to 8.19 mmol/L (after)—see Fig. 2. The latter can be explained by inadequate stress reaction towards even a slight injury to the soft tissues of the oral mucosa in this group and a high level of anxiety in patients before dental treatment, which must be taken into account when performing invasive interventions to these patients.

The diabetes duration was similar in both groups (16.58 and 17.18 years, respectively). Diets were adhered to by 46.5% of patients of the first group and 40% of patients of the second group.

The level of glycated hemoglobin in the overweight T1DM group was slightly higher than in the normal BMI T1DM group, namely 7.97% and 7.59%, respectively.

**Table 2** Qualitative and quantitative composition of periodontal microflora in the groups of comparison—T1DM with normal BMI versus T1DM with excessive BMI; comparative analysis was carried out before and after professional hygiene performed

| Name of microorganism | Overweight patients ($n = 25$) | | Normal weight patients ($n = 58$) | |
|---|---|---|---|---|
| | Microflora quantity upon initial examination | Microflora quantity upon initial re-examination | Microflora quantity upon initial examination | Microflora quantity upon initial re-examination |
| Staphylococcus aureus | $2000*10^3$ | $400*10^3$ | $1000*10^3$ | $30*10^3$ |
| Staphylococcus haemolyticis | $50*10^3$ | $4*10^3$ | $60*10^3$ | $3*10^3$ |
| Streptococcus sanguis | $2*10^3$ | $0.4*10^2$ | $3*10^3$ | $0.5*10^3$ |
| Streptococcus intermedius | $1*10^3$ | $1*10^3$ | $2*10^3$ | $0.1*10^3$ |
| Streptococcus mutans | $2*10^3$ | $10*10^3$ | $3*10^3$ | $0.4*10^3$ |
| Neisseria sicca | $20*10^3$ | $1*10^3$ | $2*10^3$ | $2*10^3$ |
| Neisseria lactamica | $0.2*10^3$ | $0.1*10^3$ | $0.1*10^3$ | $0.1*10^3$ |
| Rothia mucilaginosa | $3*10^3$ | $0.4*10^3$ | $5*10^3$ | $0.1*10^3$ |
| Moraxella catarrhalis | $0.4*10^3$ | 0 | 0 | 0 |
| Corynebacterium xerosis | $0.4*10^3$ | $0.3*10^3$ | $0.05*10^3$ | $0.02*10^3$ |
| Veillonella parvula | $5*10^3$ | $2*10^3$ | $3*10^3$ | $1*10^3$ |
| Prevotella intermedia | $100*10^3$ | $10*10^3$ | $0.3*10^3$ | 0 |
| Aggregatibacter actinomycetemcomitans | $1*10^3$ | $0.3*10^3$ | $0.2*10^3$ | $0.1*10^3$ |
| Candida albicans | $40*10^3$ | $4*10^3$ | $0.1*10^3$ | 0 |
| Candida dubliniensis | $40*10^3$ | $0.2*10^3$ | $0.5*10^3$ | 0 |

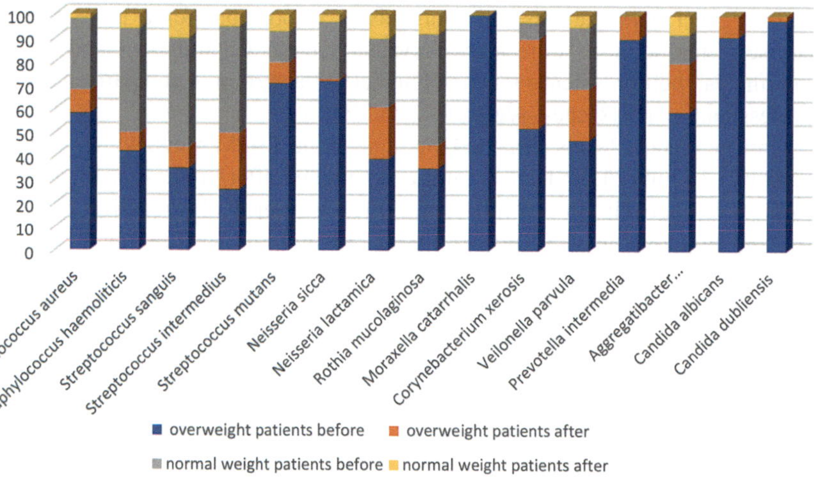


**Fig. 1** Qualitative and quantitative composition of periodontal microflora in the groups of comparison before and after professional hygiene performed

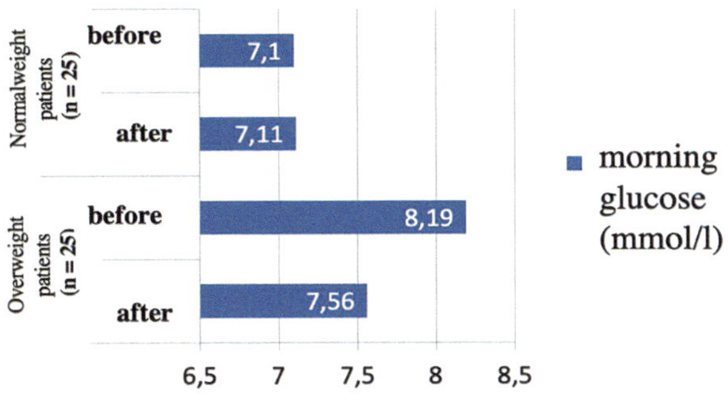


**Fig. 2** Fasting glucose levels in both groups of comparison before and after professional hygiene performed

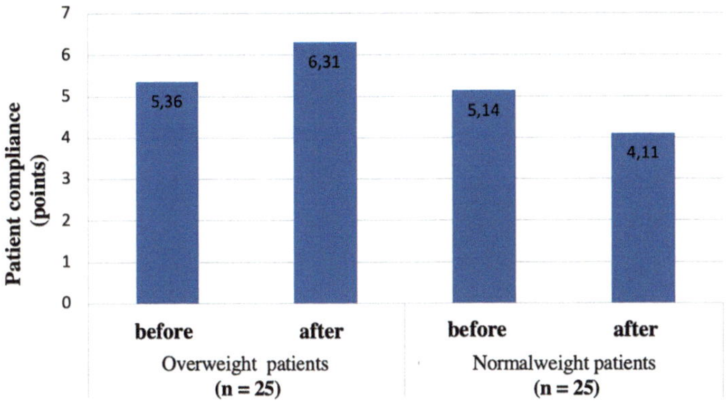


**Fig. 3** Compliance evaluation in the groups of comparison before and after professional hygiene performed

Psychological survey revealed moderately positive initial levels of compliance in both groups of comparison, namely in group 1—5.14 points and in group 2—5.36 points. However, 1 month after conservative treatment of inflammatory periodontal diseases applied, in the second group, it worsened and became weakly positive—4.11 points, whereas in the first group it increased by 6.31 points as summarized in Fig. 3. To this end, no direct correlation between objective clinical improvement and subjective level of compliance was monitored demonstrating a discrepancy between the objective and subjective assessments.

Initially, the dental anxiety level in the T1DM group with normal and excessive BMI was 8.12 and 7.76 units (considered as a mild level of anxiety). After the therapy performed, corresponding levels slightly decreased in both groups, namely to 7.98 and 7.08 points, respectively.

Initially, situational anxiety in both groups was at low levels for both groups of comparison (first group—1.95 and second group—1.89), whereas personal anxiety was at an average level in both groups (first group—2.36, second group—2.2). After occupational hygiene performed, situational and personal anxiety in the first group decreased whereas in the second group of patients it increased as summarized in Fig. 4. This is considered as the group-specific phenomenon of T1DM overweight patients.

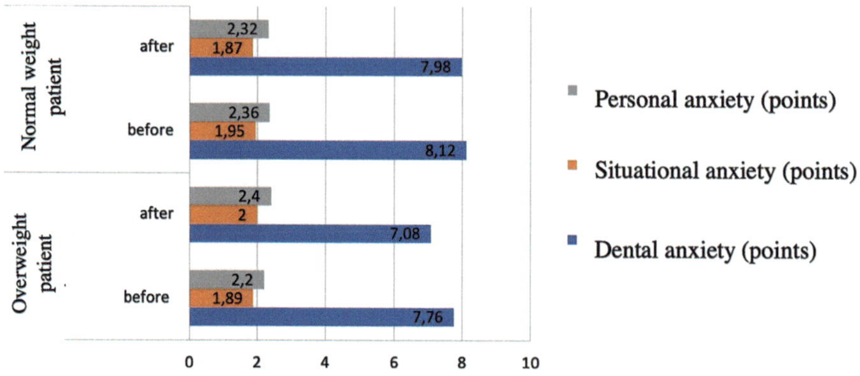


**Fig. 4** Values of dental, situational, and personal anxiety recorded in groups of comparison before and after professional oral hygiene

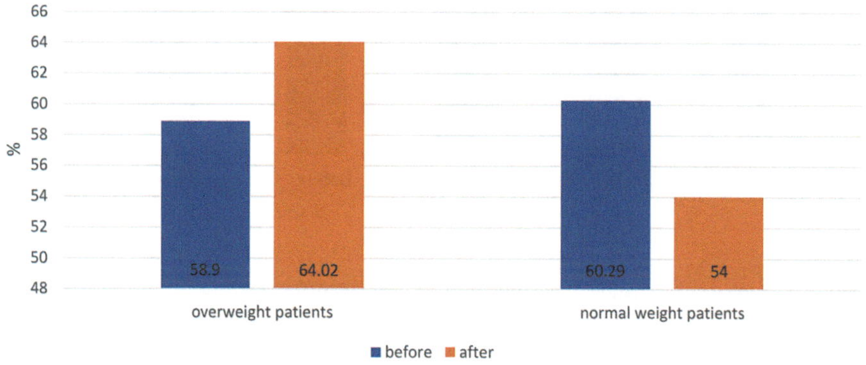


**Fig. 5** Values of the level of PSAF-autodeadaptation recorded for the groups of comparison before and after a complex of professional oral hygiene

The level of PSAF-autodeadaptation in the first group was 60.29%, and in the second group—58.9%, which indicates minor maladaptation. Noteworthy, 1 month after the interventions, the level of autodeadaptation in the first group decreased, whereas it increased in the second group—see Fig. 5.

## 5 Conclusions and Expert Recommendations in the Framework of 3PM

Excessive BMI in patients with periodontal disease and diabetic history has been recorded as being indicative for more severe manifestations of pro/inflammatory reactions and for an increased risk of progressive periodontitis.

Excessive BMI can be considered as an independent risk factor of a more aggressive course of periodontitis, due to more prevalent pathogenic microflora composition such as Candida spp., Aggregatibacter actinomycetemcomitans and Prevotella intermedia responsible for less positive dynamics after professional oral hygiene performed.

Due to the aggravation of the course of periodontitis, T1DM history and excessive BMI affected patients experience more pronounced psychological distress accompanied with higher levels of autodeadaptation. Noteworthy, application of reasonable elements of participatory medicine such as an explanatory and motivating conversation increased the adherence of patients to the treatments planned in the group with excessive BMI more significantly compared to the group with the normal BMI that again promotes the concept of individualized approach adapted to the needs of stratified patient cohorts.

Excessive BMI and T1DM history are risk factors to be considered providing periodontal services as likely to cause potential stress-related complications such as increased fasting glucose after occupational hygiene and manipulations such as the removal of dental deposits. Contextually, to inform relevant care-givers (dentist-therapists, periodontists, dental hygienists) is strongly recommended to adapt treatment measures to the individual risk profiles.

Finally, modifiable risk factors should be taken into consideration to apply mitigation measures prior to providing periodontal/dental care to individuals at increased risk. Patient phenotyping and stratification as well as predictive diagnostics are highly instrumental for these purposes [13–18].

## References


1. Orekhova LY, Grinenko EV, Loboda ES, Musaeva RS (2020) Evaluation of the effectiveness of a professional oral hygiene complex in patients with type 1 diabetes mellitus and chronic generalized periodontitis. Dentist 1(36):46–51. https://doi.org/10.32993/stomatologist.2020.1(36).5
2. Sycheva YA, Popov DA, Gorbacheva IA, Orekhova LY, Shabak-Spassky PS (2016) Changes in the microcirculation of the oral mucosa and disorders of regional hemodynamics in patients with heart failure. Scientific Notes of St. Petersburg State Medical University 3:60–64. https://doi.org/10.24884/1607-4181-2016-23-3-60-64
3. Fominykh YA, Gorbacheva IA, Uspenskii YP, Gulunov ZK (2019) Psychological status and quality of life of patients with metabolic syndrome. Med Alphabet 3(20):46–50. https://doi.org/10.33667/2078-5631-2019-2-20(395)-46-50
4. Schwartz V (2009) Inflammation of adipose tissue. Part 3. Pathogenetic role in the development of atherosclerosis. Problems Endocrinol 55(6):40–45. https://doi.org/10.14341/probl200955640-45
5. Orekhova LY, Musaeva RS, Barmasheva AA (2013) The significance of the components of the metabolic syndrome in the occurrence of microcirculatory disorders in periodontal tissues. Mod Dent 2:131–133
6. Soloviev MM, Kadyrov MB, Magradze GN, Pimenov KP (2017) The severity and structure of psycho-sensory-anatomical-functional autodeadaptation in patients with acute inflammatory diseases of the maxillofacial localization, vol 4. Scientific Notes of St. Petersburg State Medical University, 68–74. https://doi.org/10.24884/1607-4181-2017-24-4-68-74

7. Slazhneva ES, Atrushkevich VG, Orekhova LY, Loboda ES (2022) The prevalence of periodontal disease in patients with different body mass index. Periodontology 27(3):202–208. https://doi.org/10.33925/1683-3759-2022-27-3-202-208
8. Uspensky YP, Fominykh YA, Gorbacheva IA, Vovk AV, Balukova EV, Ivanov SV, Gulunov ZK (2020) Gastroenterological manifestations of the metabolic syndrome. In: Shabrov AV (ed) Metabolic syndrome. St. Petersburg State Pediatric Medical University, 281–320
9. Thomas G, Khunti K, Curcin V, Molokhia M, Millett C, Majeed A, Paul S (2014) Obesity paradox in people newly diagnosed with type 2 diabetes with and without prior cardiovascular disease. Diab Obes Metab 16(4):317–325. https://doi.org/10.1111/dom.12217
10. Strelitz J, Ahern AL, Long GH, Hare MJL, Irving G, Boothby CE, Wareham NJ, Griffin SJ (2019) Moderate weight change following diabetes diagnosis and 10 year incidence of cardiovascular disease and mortality. Diabetologia 62(8):1391–1402. https://doi.org/10.1007/s00125-019-4886-1
11. Sitkina EV, Tachalov VV, Isaeva ER, Orekhova LY, Kudryavtseva TV (2017) Psychological characteristics of patients influencing adherence to the recommendations of a dentist. Scientific notes of St. Petersburg State Medical University 1:62–67. https://doi.org/10.24884/1607-4181-2017-24-1-62-67
12. Timmerman MF, van der Weijden GA (2008) Risk factors for periodontitis. Int J Dent Hyg 4(1):2–7. https://doi.org/10.1111/j.1601-5037.2006.00168.x
13. Thoppay J, Desai B (2019) Oral burning: local and systemic connection for a patient-centric approach. EPMA J 10(1):1–11. https://doi.org/10.1007/s13167-018-0157-3
14. Yu JC, Khodadadi H, Baban B (2019) Innate immunity and oral microbiome: a personalized, predictive, and preventive approach to the management of oral diseases. EPMA J 10(1):43–50. https://doi.org/10.1007/s13167-019-00163-4
15. Tachalov VV, Orekhova LY, Kudryavtseva TV, Isaeva ER, Loboda ES (2016) Manifestations of personal characteristics in individual oral care. EPMA J 7(1):8. https://doi.org/10.1186/s13167-016-0058-2
16. Tachalov VV, Orekhova LY, Kudryavtseva TV, Loboda ES, Pachkoriia MG, Berezkina IV, Golubnitschaja O (2021) Making a complex dental care tailored to the person: population health in focus of predictive, preventive and personalised (3P) medical approach. EPMA J 12(2):129–140. https://doi.org/10.1007/s13167-021-00240-7
17. Ma X, Wang Y, Wu H, Li F, Feng X, Xie Y, Xie D, Wang W, Lo ECM, Lu H (2021) Periodontal health related-inflammatory and metabolic profiles of patients with end-stage renal disease: potential strategy for predictive, preventive, and personalized medicine. EPMA J 12(2):117–128. https://doi.org/10.1007/s13167-021-00239-0
18. Kunin A, Polivka J Jr, Moiseeva N, Golubnitschaja O (2018) "Dry mouth" and "Flammer" syndromes-neglected risks in adolescents and new concepts by predictive, preventive and personalised approach. EPMA J 9(3):307–317. https://doi.org/10.1007/s13167-018-0145-7

# Systemic Inflammation as the Health-Related Communication Tool Between the Human Host and Gut Microbiota in the Framework of Predictive, Preventive, and Personalized Medicine

**Payam Behzadi, Veronica I. Dodero, and Olga Golubnitschaja**

**Preamble**

The level of synergies between the human host and gut microbiota is frequently underestimated. Previous research efforts were focused on correlations between the gut microbiota composition and severe medical conditions of the host. However, recent discoveries clearly demonstrated that there are much most aspects involved in this multi-faceted interplay including the health status stability of the host, their quality of life, disease-predisposition, health-to-disease transition, disease severity grad, therapy-resistance, and individual outcomes—all under direct influence of the gut microbiota quantity and quality setup. Moreover, a powerful instrument has been established in cross-talk between both partners, namely an inflammation which is systemically activated in the host (gastrointestinal tract, immune, neuro- and cardiovascular systems, etc.) as soon as the synergies between the partners

P. Behzadi
Department of Microbiology, Islamic Azad University, Tehran, Iran
e-mail: behzadipayam@yahoo.com

V. I. Dodero
Faculty of Chemistry, Bielefeld University, Bielefeld, Germany
e-mail: veronica.dodero@uni-bielefeld.de

O. Golubnitschaja (✉)
3P medicine research unit, University Hospital, Rheinische Friedrich-Wilhelms Universität Bonn, Bonn, Germany

European Association for Predictive, Preventive and Personalised Medicine, Brussels, Belgium
e-mail: olga.golubnitschaja@ukbonn.de



W. Wang (ed.), *All Around Suboptimal Health*, Advances in Predictive, Preventive and Personalised Medicine 18,
https://doi.org/10.1007/978-3-031-46891-9_15

becomes suboptimal. Therefore, a detailed understanding of mechanisms underlying systemic inflammation as the key-tool to regulate the quality and stability of cooperation between both partners is crucial for cost-effective screening programs and targeted disease prevention in primary and secondary care following the principles of 3P Medicine [1, 2].

The term "human gut microbiota" comprises all microorganisms inhabiting the human gastrointestinal tract. This dynamic population of microflora encompasses both—the microbiome and virome consisting mainly of the prokaryotic domain and to a lesser extent, also of fungi, parasites, archaea, and viruses. Taken together, in the human body there is an approximate parity between the overall number of own cells and bacterial ones [3] that gives a clue to the high level of reciprocity between both cellular populations at the local and organismal levels. There is a multi-factorial influence on the gut microbial ecosystem resulting in the inter-individual variation with great impacts on the individual health status.

The gut microbiota develops during infancy starting with the mode of the birth: via a vaginal delivery, the neonate is exposed to maternal vaginal bacterial environment with a strong predominance of Lactobacillus, Prevotella, and Sneathia genera in the microflora. A caesarean section predisposes a newborn to the maternal skin flora with the less diverse microbiotas and high prevalence of Staphylococcus, Corynebacterium, and Propionibacterium and concomitant risks of chronic infections and allergies and, therefore, a systemic inflammation developed later on in life [4–8].

Further, there is an evidence-based difference in gut microflora of breastfed babies compared to those fed with formula milk, due to a milk-composition which differs in bacterial, nutrients, and bioactive compounds profiles. Consequently, more diverse microbiota and predominant Bifidobacterium species are typical for breastfed-individuals, whereas mono-flora with predominant Enterobacteriaceae species are characteristic for the gut microbiota of the formula milk-fed infants with consequent impacts on their gut microbiota and associated effects such as systemic inflammation and related disorders developed later on in life [9]. Microorganisms perform a large spectrum of functions complementary to the host such as digesting specific components of dietary fiber exemplified with some carbohydrates indigestible for humans, which thanks certain micro-species undergo a fermentation into absorbable forms such as short-chain fatty acids (SCFAs). In turn, SCFAs demonstrate anti-inflammatory and immunomodulatory effects [10]. In a similar way, gut microbiota is capable of producing vitamins and other bio-compounds valuable for the host immune system to defend against pathogenic invasion and to protect the host against systemic inflammation and associated pathologies such as metabolic syndrome, cardiovascular disease, and malignant transformation.

## 1 Gut Microbiome and Systemic Inflammation

Results reported from previous investigations show, the human host gut microbiome constructs a huge microbial community within the stomach area (with a bacterial cell concentration between 10 and 10,000 per mL or g), the small intestine region (with a bacterial cell concentration between 10,000 and 100,000,000 per mL or g), and the large intestine area (with a bacterial cell concentration between 10,000,000,000 and 1000,000,000,000 per mL or g) [11, 12].

Before the innovation of advanced high-throughput sequencing methods (such as molecular diagnostic techniques based on the 16 small ribosomal subunit RNA (16S rRNA) gene (16S rDNA) for prokaryotes and 18S rRNA gene (18S rDNA) for eukaryotes), metagenomic approaches and progression of bio-informatics software tools (in silico studies), the most portion of our microbiome (~80%) were unidentifiable through the application of standard traditional wet lab techniques like culture media. In recent years with the help of new molecular and bioinformatic technologies and software tools in dry labs, we can find out about microbial populations associated with the human microbiome, particularly the gut microbiome [13–20]. It is estimated that the ratio of microbiome cells to human cells is 1.3, it means that the number of microbiome cells is 1.3 times more than the constitutive cells of the human body. Hence, $>10^6$ of human genes involving more than 99% of the human host genomic pool are recognized as microbial genes [21].

As previous studies show, *Firmicutes* (~65%) (e.g., *Bacillus*, *Clostridium, Enterococcus, Eubacterium*, *Lactobacillus*, and *Ruminococcus*), *Bacteroidetes* (23%) (e.g., *Prevotella* and *Bacteroides*), *Actinobacteria* (5%) (e.g., *Bifidobacterium*), and *Proteobacteria* (including lipopolysaccharide bearing Gram-negative bacteria, for example, *Escherichia* and *Helicobacter*) are identified as dominated bacterial phyla among gut microbiota and ~ 99% of the bacterial populations of the gut human host microbiome are detected as anaerobes [22–27]. *Escherichia coli* is an opportunistic pathogen that can be recognized as a bacterial causative agent of different infectious diseases, for example, urinary tract infections (UTIs) [28–35].

These bacterial phyla cover ~90% of the human host's normal flora. Indeed, an individual's microbiome is pretty stable for a long time; however, a collection of factors such as age, birth condition, diet, lifestyle, genetics, medication, and social contacts may alter the composition of the human host microbiome [22, 36–40].

## 2 An Interplay Between the Inflammation-Associated Gut Microbiota and Corresponding Host Phenotypes

The presence of a microbiome in the body of healthy people protects the human host body from pathogens. This feature is achieved by producing a wide range of metabolites and postbiotic products. The microbiome community acts as microbial consortia been built by a variety of microbial populations with their specific functions and activities. Some populations contribute to the fermentation of herbal carbohydrate complexes and convert these polysaccharides into short-chain fatty acids (SCFAs) [16]. The SCAFs act as molecular energies that support the gut epithelial cells, particularly the epithelial cells living within the colon. In parallel with this effective activity, the SCFAs can bind to G-protein coupled receptors (GPRs) to inactivate the histone deacetylase enzymes. This feature results in beneficial outcomes such as triggering regulatory T cells ($T_{regs}$) or may suppress the expression of pro-inflammatory cytokines which are secreted via antigen-presenting cells (APCs) [41–45]. In addition to SCFAs, microbial macromolecules of polysaccharides such as *Bifidobacterium longum* subsp. *longum* 35,624 superficial exopolysaccharide reduces gut inflammatory responses [46, 47]. In some cases, any decrease in the number of effective microbial populations, for example, the Gram-positive and anaerobe bacterial cells of *Faecalibacterium prausnitzii* leads to the appearance of inflammatory immune responses in the gut. This feature can be seen in inflammatory bowel disease (IBD) patients. The main reason is associated with the secretion of bacterial metabolites, including N-acyl homoserine lactones (the molecules involved in the bacterial quorum-sensing system), salicylic acid, and peptides [48–51].

Furthermore, the gut microbiome is involved in the biosynthesis of some vital amino acids and vitamins, and the secretion of some small molecules which interact with the human host body, for example, to mature, activate, and develop the immune system. The attachment of segmented filamentous bacteria or some microbial agents (sometimes pathogenic microorganisms) such as *E. coli* O157, *Citrobacter rodentium*, and *Candida albicans* upon the small intestinal epithelial cells induces T helper 17 ($T_{helper17}$) cells. In turn, activated $T_{helper17}$ cells trigger neutrophils which may lead to the activation of intestinal epithelial cells. This process results in the activation of group 3 innate lymphoid cells (ILC3s) and plasma cells (which express IgA) promoting the omission of extracellular pathogenic microbial agents [52–56].

According to the importance of microbiome, eubiosis resulting from the residence of good bacteria in the human host body may lead to an effective and suitable homeostatic balance in different parts of the human body like the gut. In contrast, dysbiosis, which is resulted from the uncontrolled condition of harmful bacteria via good bacteria in the human host body, may lead to dysregulation of the human host normal condition, imbalanced homoeostatic and physiological status, and diverse disorders and diseases, for example, immunoinflammatory responses [57, 58]. Hence, the occurrence of different types of inflammatory and autoimmune diseases is related to dysbiosis for the most.

## 2.1 Gender as the Non-modifiable Risk Factor

Some published reports show that specifically the post-puberty period in both males and females is associated with changes in the gut microbiome. In this regard, after this period, sex hormones are actively expressed and secreted in males and females; therefore, the sex hormones in both genders affect the gut microbiome structures.

According to reports, the ratio of bacterial cells to human host cells is higher in females (2.2) than in males (1.3). The term "micro-genderome" depicts the related interactions between the gut microbiome and sex hormones in different genders [59–62].

Several studies confirm the close association between sex/gender and the gut microbiome. Indeed, sex and gender are important factors that differentiate the human host gut microbiome [63]. Moreover, the terms "genderome" or "gut micro-sex" depict the sexual dimorphism feature associated with the microbiome [64–66].

Estrogen, as a sex hormone which can be produced via adipose tissue, adrenal glands, and ovaries (or through diet), affects steroid receptors, for example, estrogen receptor-ß. This functional activity of estrogen regulates microbial metabolism [67, 68]. Bacterial strains in the gut microbiome express and secrete the enzyme of β-glucuronidase activity, do contribute to the deconjugation of conjugated estrogen molecules. Deconjugated estrogens will be reabsorbed into the blood circulation. The circulating deconjugated estrogen molecules interact with estrogen receptors located within different systems, including the central nervous, musculoskeletal, reproductive, cardiovascular, etc. So, bacterial strains of gut microbiome with the ability to produce ß-glucuronidases, ß-glucosidases, and hydrolytic enzymes participate in the process of estrogens deconjugation. This implies that because of the gut microbiome β-glucuronidase activities, the conjugated estrogen molecules, which are absorbed by the liver and delivered to the gut through the bile, get deconjugated [59, 64, 69, 70].

Indeed, the endogenous estrogens in females are recognized in five forms: (1) estrone which is the major form of estrogens in menopausal females (E1); (2) 17β-estradiol, the major form of estrogen in non-pregnant and pre-menopausal women (E2); (3) estriol that is highly recognized in pregnant females (E3); (4) sterol (E4) and (5) 27-hydroxycholesterol (27HC). The circulating estrogen molecules in blood can be in detached or attached forms. The attached form of estrogen is usually linked to proteins. Estrogen molecules and the related metabolites are capable of being conjugated via the processes of glucuronidation or also through sulfonation [59, 69, 71, 72]. The conjugated forms of estrogens are discharged in feces, urine, and bile. Following previous reports, the human host diet and gut microbiome are determinative factors that regulate the functional activity of ß-glucuronidase enzyme. In this regard, those with the healthy condition who use fibers in their diet experience reduced fecal functional activity of ß-glucuronidase enzyme while, highly consumption of proteins and fatty nutrition in healthy individuals leads to the promotion of fecal available activity of ß-glucuronidase enzyme [59, 69].

Other studies regarding the relationship between the sex hormones of androgen and testosterone and gut microbiome have been achieved. As previous studies show, the gut microbiome can modulate the systematic levels of testosterone. This goal is performed by reducing 17β associated with androgen [73]. Moreover, secretion of a high amount of estradiol (the main sex hormone in females) and testosterone (the main sex hormone in males) results in higher bacterial diversity associated with gut microbiome [74]. Thus, sex hormones are effective modulators of microbiome diversity, and this process may lead to the induction of inflammatory immune responses [64, 73].

The Lactobacilli pertaining to *Firmicutes* phylum is one of the main bacterial genera and constitutes a portion of the vagina microbiome. Estrogens affect the spread and expansion of Lactobacilli populations in the vaginal environment in women and their presence in the vagina is known as a biomarker of the host's health [75].

Previous studies that considered the gut microbiome show, on the one hand, that female neonates encompass higher populations of *Clostridiales* relating to *Firmicutes* phylum rather than male neonates. On the other hand, male neonates contain higher populations of *Enterobacterales* belonging to *Proteobacteria* phylum rather than female neonates [75].

## 2.2 Age as the Non-modifiable Risk Factor

The microbiota composition depends on the means of delivery, environmental factors, and nutrition. In this regard, cesarean or vaginal delivery affects the individual's microbiota composition. During the first half year after birth, the facultative aerobic bacteria, for example, *Proteobacteria* begin to colonize within the neonates' gut to form the early gut microbiome. In parallel with this feature, oxygen consumption by the facultative aerobic bacteria results in the appearance of an anaerobic condition. Obligatory anaerobic bacteria such as *Actinobacteria* phylum (such as *Bifidobacterium*), *Bacteroidetes* phylum (like *Bacteroides*), and *Firmicutes* phylum (e.g., *Clostridium*) create the secondary microbial communities as a part of the gut microbiome [22, 75, 76]. It seems that the gut microbiome in early infants involves a limited species of those that are contributed to human milk oligosaccharide metabolism and about 25–30% of the microbiome population in infants originates from breastmilk including *Bifidobacterium longum* (belonging to *Actinobacteria* phylum) and *Streptococcus thermophilus* (belonging to *Firmicutes* phylum) [75, 77, 78]. After the breastfeeding period in infants, which normally takes up to 6 months, a new period begins. During this new period which usually continues up to 2 years (from days of 450–2000) old, "solid nutrients may lead to an accelerated progression in infants" gut microbiome both in structures and functions. This feature maturates the "gut microbiome, and its condition resembles the adults" gut microbiome. By the maturation of the gut microbiome, microbial metabolites, for example, SCFAs will be produced through the degradation of a wide range of components, including complex carbohydrates, glycans, mucin, etc. [78].

However, it should be mentioned that those infants who were fed by their own "mothers" breastmilk had higher levels of *Clostridiales* and *Lactobacillales* in their gut microbiome compared to those infants who were not fed by their own mothers' breastmilk [79].

In accordance with previous reports, the bacterial genera of *Bifidobacterium* and *Lactobacillus* can be transmitted via mother's breastmilk to neonates. This bacterial transmission from mother to neonate results in positive outcomes associated with cognitive development, neuro-behavior, and reduction in infectious diseases. In this regard, *Lactobacilli,* as a bacterial community of the infants' gut microbiome participate in carbohydrate metabolism in which a highly amount of acetic acid and lactic acid are produced. The carbohydrate metabolism recruits different metabolic pathways, including the phosphor-ketolase pathway, pentose-phosphate pathway, and Embden-Meyerhof pathway, which leads to the release of high levels of adenosine tri-phosphate (ATP) molecules to cover the infant's growth [75, 80]. On the other hand, the *Bifidobacteria*, as a bacterial community of the infants' gut microbiome, contributes to the fermentation of breast milk oligosaccharides, production of SCFAs, etc., which are necessary for the infants' growth. The SCFAs, as high caloric compounds, are metabolized by colonic- and hepatocytes to release ATP molecules [81–83]. In the age range of two to five, gut microbiome construction gets more stability than before by the presence of butyrate-producing species of *Bacteroidetes* and *Firmicutes* [84]. In the age range of 7–12, known as the pre-adolescent period, the gut microbiome is composed of microbial communities that contribute to development through the biosynthesis of effective compounds, for example, vitamin $B_{12}$ and folate [85]. As previous investigations show, the gut microbiome in adolescent individuals aged 11 to 18, the dominant bacterial genera are *Bifidobacterium* and *Clostridium*. These bacterial genera are considerably higher compared to adults. The gut microbiome's function and structure differ in individuals older than 65. These changes are directly correlated to physiological changes, lifestyle changes, diet changes, promotion of inflammatory factors, etc.; all in all, the composition of the gut microbiome in old individuals gets significant changes such as a high level of *Enterobacteriaceae*, a reduced ratio of *Bacteroidetes* to *Firmicutes* compared to younger adults [86–88].

## 2.3 *Imbalanced Stress Overload is Highly Relevant for Pro/ Inflammatory Cross-Talk*

There is a wide range of stresses which has different resources such as daily problems and arguments, life events, traumas, and adversities. Following previous studies, we now know that early life stresses, for example, sexual abuse, physical, emotional, and trauma in individual's childhood, set the related physiologic conditions in both body and brain to respond to the stressors in the future. This programming mechanism leads to negative feedback and dysregulation in the neuroendocrine-neuroimmune axis during adulthood [89–93]. On the other hand, the functional gut-microbiome-brain axis is active through an effective interaction between the gut microbiome and the central nervous system (CNS). Therefore, this process is bidirectional and several significant pathways participate in the communication between the brain and gut microbiome. According to currently accumulated knowledge, the hypothalamic pituitary adrenal [94] axis, neurotransmitters, vagus nerve, immune-inflammatory mechanisms, bacterial metabolites, and other unknown pathways contribute to this communication [89, 95–100].

In one investigation, a healthy pregnant female participated in the Trier Social Stress Test (TSST), in which her stool was evaluated. The results from evaluations associated with the individual's stool sample showed that diverse gut microbial taxa reacted to the acute stressor via the expression of cytokines and induction of cortisol secretion. In this regard, interleukin-6 (IL-6), C-reactive protein (CRP), serum cortisol, and tumor necrosis factor-α (TNF-α) response were recognized as positive overgrowth inductions for *Bacteroides*; *Megasphaera* and *Ruminococcaceae*; *Dialister* and *Rikenellaceae*; and *Bacteroides*, *Provotella*, and *Megasphaera*, respectively [89, 100]. In contrast, IL-6, C-reactive protein (CRP), serum cortisol, and TNF-α response were negatively correlated with Clostridiales, Lachnospiraceae, Dialister, and Enterobacteriaceae; and none; *Bacteroides*; and *Ruminococcaceae*, respectively [89, 100].

In other studies, the effects of chronic stresses on the gut microbiota were evaluated. In this regard, an investigation showed that a 1-month-length stress on 3-month-old infants in a childcare center had no considerable effect on the "infants" gut microbiota composition versus animal models with maternal separation [101]. The results obtained from another survey show that the preparing period for national examinations with a duration of about 6 months led to a reduction of *Bifidobacterium* spp. and promotion of *Streptococcus* spp. populations in the gut microbiome composition among 60 Japanese medical students [102]. Moreover, academic examinations as naturalistic stressors affecting the cortisol amount within the human body may reduce the lactic acid bacteria portion of the gut microbiome [102, 103]. Michels et al. [104] have shown that apart from nutrition intake, stressors both in children and adolescents cross-sectionally affect gut microbiome composition. The occurrence of high stress may lead to a reduction of *Firmicutes* phylum and the *Phascolarctobacterium* genus levels. It may simultaneously lead to promoting *Bacteroides*, *Methanobrevibacter*, *Parabacteroides*, *Rhodococcus*, and *Roseburia* [104]. Some effective surveys have been performed to detect the correlation between childhood adversities and the gut microbiome in humans. D'Agata et al. [105] performed their study in the neonatal intensive care unit (NICU) involving the infants' first 6 weeks as the earliest stages of their life time. In NICU, effective stresses may occur for the participating infants, such as medical procedures (e.g., pain) and infants' separation from their parents. The stress was measured via the Neonatal Infant Stressor Scale [45] as a related criterion. D'Agata et al. [105] have shown that considerable changes have occurred in bacterial communities at the genera level of the infants' gut microbiome composition. In this regard, the γ-Proteobacteria was recognized as the dominated bacterial taxon. The parameters of antibiotic consumption, birth weight, gender, stress exposure, and sampling time had particular effects on different bacterial genera. For example, stress exposure had an influent impact on the bacterial genera of *Proteus* and *Veillonella* [105]. Moreover, the consumption of antibiotics was another influential parameter that effectively affected *Clostridium perfringens* and *Proteus*. For those infants who consumed antibiotics and encompassed *Proteus* in their gut microbiome, the population of *Proteus* bacterial cells was considerably lower, while the populations of *C. perfringens* and *Citrobacter* bacterial cells were significantly higher. Furthermore, the population of *Proteus* bacterial cells was considerably lower in female infants. Interestingly, the week of sampling was important item for evaluation of the stress impact associated with *Bifidobacterium*, *C. butyricum*, *C. perfringens*, *Enterococcus*, *Escherichia*, *Proteus*, *Staphylococcus*, and *Streptococcus* [105].

## 2.4 Behavioral Patterns Relevant for Inflammatory Risks

The hypothalamo-pituitary axis [94] is part of the limbic system, which is the most critical system that contributes to the coordination of adaptive responses in exposure to different stressors; therefore, it has a crucial role in the modulation of the main brain activities, for example, emotions and memory [106]. Stressors like environmental factors and any promotion of proinflammatory cytokines may lead to the activation of HPA. This process may lead to hypothalamus induction through corticotropin-releasing factor (CRF) production. The release of CRF results in the induction of pituitary gland which may lead to adrenocorticotrophic hormone (ACTH) expression. Production of ACTH triggers the adrenal cortex and leads to the secretion of cortisol. Cortisol, and an effective stress hormone, influences different body parts, for example, the human host brain. As a result, hormones and nerves determine the brain's coordinative role in gastrointestinal tract activities [106]. Therefore, different types of stresses and stressors, whether physical or psychological ones, may directly affect the HPA-gut (microbiome) axis as it can be seen in post-infectious irritable bowel syndrome [107]—known as a type of post-infectious gastrointestinal disorders—which may result in a wide range of gut-brain axis disorders, for example, anxiety and depression [108, 109].

On the other hand, the human host gut microbiome is composed of neurotransmitter-producing bacteria. The produced bacterial neurotransmitters are likewise those neurotransmitters that are detectable in the human host brain. Bacterial neurotransmitters' functions are limited to the gut and act as enteric nervous system regulators. In this regard, *Bacillus* spp. secrete dopamine and noradrenaline, *Escherichia* spp. produce noradrenaline and serotonin, while *Lactobacillus* spp. release acetylcholine and $\gamma$-aminobutyric acid (GABA). *Bifidobacterium* spp. are GABA producers, too. The yeasts of *Saccharomyces* spp. and *Candida* spp. biosynthesize noradrenaline and serotonin, respectively. In addition, the Gram-positive bacterial cells of *Enterococcus* spp. and *Streptococcus* spp. are serotonin producers [108, 110, 111]. This mechanism is one of the multiple microbial mechanisms that affect the CNS. The good bacteria of Bifidobacteria affects the CNS by promoting the level of tryptophan amino acid which is known as the precursor of serotonin. Simultaneously, a portion of Lactobacilli can change the metabolism, which can alter the metabolism GABA. This feature leads to alteration in the production of GABA receptors and their activities [112].

According to recorded reports, the vagus nerve, neurotransmitters, immune-, enteric nervous-, and autonomic nervous systems link the brain and gut microbiome showing effective communication pathways between them [21].

As previous investigations show, the frequency of the immune cells within the gastrointestinal tract is the highest compared with the other parts of the human host body. Furthermore, several types of immune cells are co-evolved with microbiome. These features explain the sensitive and complicated communications between the immune cells and the gut microbiome [113]. The Goblet cells, which are differentiated epithelial cells, can produce and secrete mucosal barriers within airways and intestines. This mucosal barrier separates the intestinal cells and the related microbial components. In addition, the secretion of the mucosal barrier by Goblet cells and the activity of this mucosal boundary is associated with the presence of the microbiome; the lack of this barrier is observed in germ-free mice and those mice which consumed antibiotics. A reported investigation shows that the microbiome in the small intestine triggers the secretion of meprin β, a zinc-dependent metalloprotease enzyme by the enterocytes. The meprin β acts as a mucin cleaver which may result in the mucin unfolding and entire expansion [114–116]. Indeed, mucus is constructed by different components, including MUC2 mucin, the main structural molecule in mucus. As previous investigations show, the spaces among villi and the top of villi situated in the small intestine are protected via the mucus. This protective mucosal layer is mobile and not joint to the villi; therefore, the movable layer of the mucus can easily be transferred by the intestinal peristaltic waves and other physical factors. The floating mucus appears to act as a bacterial trap which may move those bacteria away. This functional activity protects the intestinal epithelial cells against bacterial populations; the immobile mucosal layer is the influential environmental factor for bacterial overgrowth [116].

## 2.5 *Nutrition is Pivotal for Pro- and Anti-Inflammatory Regulation Pathways*

In parallel with the nutrient program and diet, which are recognized as the most influential factors that directly affect the construction of the human host gut microbiome and, in consequence, the immune system, the lifestyle items such as circadian clocks (circadian rhythmicity) and exercise (physical activity) are important items, too [23, 117–119]. Following recorded reports, the effect of diet on gut microbiome structure is fast and quick. In other words, the diet directly affects the microbial growth rate. Hence, a particular nutrient may lead to an increase in the growth of a category of bacterial populations. Normally, a diet involves both micronutrients including bioactive compounds, vitamins, and minerals (e.g., selenium and zinc)), and macro-nutrients such as lipids, carbohydrates, fibers, and proteins, which support human host body to have continuous development and growth through feeding [23, 120–122].

This process is achieved in parallel with some environmental factors comprising the pH and the permeability of the intestine. In this regard, some changes may occur in bacterial metabolites, leading to the occurrence or inhibition of the inflammation feature [23].

As known, the macro-nutrients are related to energy production and strengthening of the human host body structure. At the same time, the micro-nutrients contribute to the modulation of vital biochemical processes and keep the human host body healthy against various diseases. A wide range of micro-nutrient molecules is neutralizing free radicals, such as vitamins A, C, and E, and copper, zinc, and selenium minerals. Therefore, these types of micro-nutrients are known as antioxidants which can neutralize effectively free radicals such as reactive nitrogen species (RON) and reactive oxygen species (ROS) [120]. As previous studies show, insufficient consumption of antioxidants, for example, ascorbic acid, carotenoids, selenium, polyphenols, zinc, and tocopherols (vitamin E) through the diet leads to the occurrence of a wide range of chronic diseases. These diseases are associated with oxidative stress-related diseases including cancers and diabetes among others [120, 123–127].

Now it is well-established that the gut microbiome is pivotal to facilitate an effective absorption of a wide range of vital biomolecules such as macro- and micro-nutrients in human host body and simultaneously, protect the body from pathogens. As the results of previous studies indicate, the antioxidants are bi-functional molecules which on the one hand neutralize the free radicals and, on the other hand, support the human host's health through their positive effects on the gut microbiome composition [120, 128, 129]. Due to this evidence, the occurrence of any changes and functional dysbiosis in human host gut microbiome composition, which can be the result of environmental exposures, is directly correlated with a wide range of chronic disorders and diseases, for example, from enteric infectious diseases and respiratory diseases to IBD and colorectal cancer [130, 131]. It should be mentioned that the gut microbiome composition is known as a significant treasure for bacterial enzymes because the microbiome bacterial populations produce and secret a wide range of enzymes such as $\alpha$-rhamnosidase, $\beta$-glucuronidase, $\beta$-glucosidase, sulfatase, and esterase(s) which target different types of molecules including glycosides, glucuronides, sulfates, amides, esters, lactones, etc. through the hydrolyzation mechanism. Moreover, further bacterial enzymatic reactions are achieved by bacterial populations pertaining to gut microbiome composition via the cleavage of biomolecule's aromatic rings. These enzymes involve decarboxylases, dehydroxylases, demethylases, isomerases, hydrogenases, reductases, etc. This vast treasure trove of enzymes enables gut bacterial populations to break down the eaten food by the human into its constituents for example, vitamins, amino acids, etc. These biomolecules participate in metabolic pathways (e.g., energy metabolism) and the immune system, known as human host physiological activities. So, the production and secretion of bacterial enzymes within the human host gut environment may lead to valuable and effective microbial metabolites including fatty acids such as linoleic acid and essential vitamins such as vitamins K and B group (like $B_2$, $B_9$, $B_{12}$) or hurtful and detrimental products [120, 132–134]. Simultaneously, the gut microbiome contributes to stimulation of the intestinal immune system, promoting the production of gut antimicrobial antibodies [113].

Although different factors, including clinical, environmental, feeding and maternal items, form the human host gut microbiota composition, the architecture of the individual's gut microbiome is established during the prepartum (pregnancy period) and postpartum (lactation period) periods. Because a mother shares her microbiome and the related metabolites with her fetus and infant during her pregnancy and after delivery [135, 136]. And the mother's gut microbiome composition is determined through her diet. Hence, maternal diet directly affects the future fetus's gut microbiome composition. Furthermore, any significant alternation in mother's diet during the pregnancy period leads to alternation in mother's gut microbiome composition and consequently, in the fetal gut microbiome composition. The mother's breastmilk composition is a determinative factor in infant gut microbiome composition. As we know, colostrum, which is the mother's postpartum first milk is quantitively low but high in quality. It contains effective components like antibodies and growth factors contributing to infant's immunity and growth, respectively. Although the composition of the maternal milk gets changes during the lactation period, vital nutrient components, and bioactive factors, for example, macro- and micronutrients, together with other compositions including pre- and probiotics and immunoglobulins still can be recognized during the alternation [137–140]. Cereals, fruits, legumes, and vegetables are essential sources for fibers with a high level of carbohydrates; olive oil and nuts have significant nourishing characteristics such as anti-inflammatory and antiatherogenic activities because of the presence of adequate nutrients containing unsaturated (poly) fatty acids; antioxidants such as polyphenols, phytosterols, terpenes, and flavonoids are known as bioactive nourish compounds. On the other hand, enriched food containing natural micro-nutrients such as minerals and vitamins protects the human host consumer against immunodeficiencies and malnutrition. Nutrient-rich foods support the human body's disorders, such as inflammations caused by poor diet or consumption of foods with high calories [141–144].

The gut microbiome composition is an effective biomarker for a healthy diet and human host health condition [145]. Due to this fact, consumption of the Mediterranean diet—which is introduced as a healthy diet—may lead to an increase in *Bacteroidetes* abundance and a reduction in *Firmicutes* abundance in the human host gut microbiome composition [145, 146]. Nutrients, food components, natural sources, and their effects on the gut microbiome composition are summarized in Table 1.

## 2.6 Abnormal Body Mass Index (BMI) as an Indicator of Potential Health Risks

BMI is calculated through the weight (kg)/height ($m^2$) formula. In this regard, the BMI can be categorized into five groups (1) underweight ($\leq$19.9 kg/$m^2$), (2) (normal (<25 kg/$m^2$), (3) overweight ($\geq$25 kg/$m^2$ to <30 kg/$m^2$), (4) obese ($\geq$30 kg/$m^2$), and morbid obese (> 35 kg/$m^2$) [174–176].

In parallel with changing microbiome composition by age variation, microbiome composition differs in individuals with different BMI. An abnormal weight in individuals either obesity/overweight or underweight shows the presence of a microbiome composition that does not belong to a healthy individual [147]. Furthermore, the microbiome composition is an effective biomarker for the recognition of balanced or imbalanced metabolisms.

As previous studies show, mothers with high BMI deliver infants who are predisposed to diabetes and obesity during their lives. Mothers with higher BMI and obesity have high levels of *Bacteroides*, *Staphylococcus*, and *Clostridium* and low levels of *Bifidobacterium* in their stool samples [135, 177–180].

**Table 1** Nutrients, food components, natural sources, and their effects on the gut microbiome composition

| Nutrient | Components | Food sources | Positive effects | Negative effects | Physiologic microflora | Pathologic microflora | References |
|---|---|---|---|---|---|---|---|
| Digestible carbohydrates | Mono-, di-, and polysaccharides, for example, fructose, galactose, glucose, lactose, maltodextrin, starch | Cereals, tuberous plants, etc. | Easily degrades into glucose | Non-communicable diseases, for example, asthma. Risk of metabolic disorders | – | Dysbiosis via an increase in *E.coli* and *C.albicans* abundances in mice; the increase of the gut inflammation through TLR4 signaling pathway; increase in systematic low-grade inflammation, colon inflammation in mice, mucus degradation via the increase in *Akkermansia muciniphila* abundance, increase in colitis through the decrease in the production of SCFAs and promotion of gut permeability | [147–150] |

(continued)

**Table 1** (continued)

| Nutrient | Components | Food sources | Positive effects | Negative effects | Physiologic microflora | Pathologic microflora | References |
|---|---|---|---|---|---|---|---|
| Resistant carbohydrates (dietary fibers) | Lignin, non-digestible oligo- and non-starch polysaccharides, for example, cellulose, glucans, gums, hemicellulose, inulin, oligofructose, pectin, raffinose | Cereals, vegetables, some groups of fruits and human milk (in breast-feeding period) | Essential for gut eubiosis, they act as prebiotics and an effective source for the growth and proliferation of a wide range of microbial populations which may lead to the production and secretion of beneficial microbial metabolites, including carbon dioxide and methane gases, SCFAs, for example, acetate, butyrate, propionate, and monosaccharides.<br>Insulin sensitivity increases and improves the activities of the gut barrier and the profile of the fats.<br>The microbiota-accessible carbohydrates (MACs) in mice reduce the growth of pathogens like *Clostridium difficile*, which is known as an opportunistic pathogen that causes diarrhea | – | *Lactobacillus* spp. *Faecalibacterium prausnitzii*, and *Akkermansia muciniphila*, a mucin-degrading bacterium, have both been associated with beneficial health effects, including reduced inflammation and improved gut barrier function, respectively | – | [147, 151–156] |

| Nutrient | Components | Food sources | Positive effects | Negative effects | Physiologic microflora | Pathologic microflora | References |
|---|---|---|---|---|---|---|---|
| Proteins | Amino acids | Animals such as red meat and plants such as pulses, for example, beans, lentils, and peas | Bacterial proteolytic degradation in the distal colon and fermentation to produce SCFAs, for example, 2-methyl butyrate, isovalerate, and isobutyrate. Plant proteins, for example, glycated pea proteins, increase good bacteria and decrease harmful bacteria like *Bacteroides fragilis* and *Clostridium perfringens;* Increase in SCFAs such as acetate and butyrate led to a reduction of gut inflammation-associated proteins; the presence of resistant starches and bioactive compounds in plant proteins increases the gut microbial homeostasis | High risk of cardiovascular diseases (CVD), increase in amino acid L-carnitine and converting into γ-butyrobetaine and crotonobetaine and then into trimethyl amine<br>Production of potentially toxic substrates such as nitrosamines, ammonia, and trimethylamine N-oxide<br>Consumption of animal proteins has a high risk of CVD by increasing sulfate-reducing bacteria (SRB) increase in hydrogen sulfide and increase the risk of gut inflammation | *Plant protein consumption increases the amount of Bifidobacterium* and *Lactobacillus*, *Faecalibacterium*, *Clostridium*, *Eubacterium*, and *Roseburia* | *Consumption of* red meat and dairy products of animal origin, increase in *Alistipes*, *Bacteroides*, *Bilophila*, an increase of SRB bacteria, for example, *Desulfovibrio* spp., (high risk of CVD, and gut inflammation) | [39, 147, 157–165] |

(continued)

**Table 1** (continued)

| Nutrient | Components | Food sources | Positive effects | Negative effects | Physiologic microflora | Pathologic microflora | References |
|---|---|---|---|---|---|---|---|
| Fats | Various types of fatty acids | Multi-saturated fatty acids. Mono-saturated fatty acids (MUFAs) such as eicosanoid palmitoleic and oleic in extra virgin olive oil, peanuts, and sesame. Medium chain fatty acids (MCFAs) in human milk and virgin coconut oil. Polyunsaturated fatty acids (PUFAs) in e.g., nuts, sunflower oil, fatty fish, etc. | Enriched foods with MUFAs positively affect gut microbiome composition in healthy and unhealthy human host bodies<br>PUFAs are not biosynthesized by the human body and it should be taken from the diet | Correlation of saturated fatty acids (e.g., long-chain saturated fatty acids) and dysbiosis, increasing in *Firmicutes* and *Proteobacteria* and reduction in *Bacterioidetes*, rising inflammation in adipose tissue, promotion of insulin-resistance feature, and increase in gut permeability. Enriched diets by coconut oil enhance the bacterial abundances of *Clostridium*, *Staphylococcus*, *Lactobacillus*, *Allobacullum,* and the *Firmicutes/Bacteroidetes* ratio may lead to the occurrence of inflammation in adipose tissue and metabolic disorders. MUFAs may lead to enhance bacterial abundances of *Parabacteroides*, *Prevotella*, *Turicibacter* genera, and the *Enterobacteriaceae* family; the use of a diet with a high Ω-6/Ω-3 PUFA ratio may lead to enhancement of permeability in the gut barrier, dysbiosis, and appearance of metabolic disorders, for example, endotoxemiass | MAFs increase *Bifidobacterium* and *Lactobacillus*, improving cognitive and metabolic activities. The Ω-3 PUFAs re-establish *Firmicutes/ bacteroidetes* ratio and enhance the beneficial bacterial producers of butyrate from *Lachnospiraceae* | High-fat nutrients, for example, milk fat with high content of sulfide, provide a suitable condition for SRB growth which may lead to a decrease in mucosal sulfide bonds and mucosal layer, leading to an increase in gut inflammation | [147, 166–173] |

Recorded results depict high maternal BMI in pregnant mothers can be recognized as effective indicator for pregnancy complications; furthermore, this problem may affect their infants, too. For example, high BMI in pregnant women can be presumed as an alarm of risk for a wide range of chronic diseases, for example, diabetes, hypertension, and heart disease. These disorders include asthma, coronary heart disease, diabetes, hypertension, obesity, and stroke can also be seen in their infants during their lives [174, 181].

Although the underweight maternal BMI may lead to some limited complications, including low enhancement in premature birth and low decrease in birthweight in their infants, the occurrence of usual pregnancy complications such as gestational diabetes mellitus, pre-eclampsia, and obstetric interventions decreases.

## 2.7 Gut Microbiota-Associated Pregnancy Complications

Preterm birth is usually related to dysbiosis in vaginal microbiome composition [182–184]. The fetus is directly in contact with the mother's vagina during the birth. Hence the mother's vaginal health directly affects the infant's microbiome composition. The former studies show that the vaginal microbiome includes *Bacteroidales*, *Clostridiales*, and *Lactobacillales* [135, 177]. *Lactobacillus* is an influent bacterial member of the healthy vaginal microbiome composition because it keeps the pH of the vagina low and secretes bacteriocin, which may support the health of the vagina through the prevention of pathogens growth. However, the diversity of the microbiome composition decreases during pregnancy. In this regard, the prevalence of *Ureoplasma* and *Mycoplasma* abundances decreases in vaginal microbiome composition in pregnant women [185, 186]. Some investigations show that in healthy pregnant women, there is an abundance of four species of *Lactobacillus* comprising *L. jensenii*, *L. crispatus*, *L. vaginalis*, and *L. gasseri* in vaginal microbiome that increases while the abundance of bacterial causative agents of vaginosis involving *Parvimonas*, *Sneathia*, *Atopobium*, *Prevotella*, *Ruminococcaceae*, *Gardnerella*, and *Mobiluncus* decreases [187, 188].

Consumption of antibiotics in pregnant women considerably affects both mother and her infant's microbiome composition. Streptococci get domination in mother's gut microbiome composition and *Enterococcus faecalis* predominate the infants' microbiome composition. Moreover, administering antibiotics in normal vaginal delivery may promote Clostridium bacterial cells and decrease *Bifidobacterium* abundance [189–191].

Smoking in pregnant mothers has a direct effect on infants. In this regard, the infants exposed to environmental tobacco smoke compared to those not exposed to smoke encompass higher populations of *Ruminococcus* and *Akkermansia* in their gut microbiome composition. Moreover, tobacco-exposed infants between 3 and 6 months of age bear higher *Firmicutes*; and *Staphylococcus* and *Bacteroides* in their gut microbiome composition, respectively. The presence of Firmicutes may lead to obesity or overweight in children between the age of 1 and 3 months [192].

## 3 Conclusions and Expert Recommendations in the Framework of 3PM

The level of synergies the human host and gut microbiota have developed to satisfy needs of both cooperation partners to maintain their health is frequently underestimated. Research group with multi-professional expertise demonstrated an evidence-based interplay between the human host and gut microbiota including the health status stability of the host, their quality of life, disease-predisposition, health-to-disease transition, disease severity grad, therapy-resistance, and individual outcomes—all under direct influence of the gut microbiota quantity and quality setup. Thereby specifically pro- and anti-inflammatory mechanisms are the key-tool to regulate the quality and stability of cooperation between both partners. The multi-faceted aspects of the pro- and anti-inflammation are crucial for implementing the principles of 3P Medicine in the area, the main pillars of which are the predictive approach, targeted prevention of the health-to-disease transition, patient stratification, and treatments tailored to individualized patient profiles [1, 2]. To this end, depending on the individual composition, the gut microflora profiles may be associated with both pro- and anti-inflammatory systemic processes relevant for primary and secondary care considering

- Individuals in suboptimal health conditions, for example, with family predisposition to severe pathologies, with abnormal BMI (both underweight and overweight), living in toxic environment, affected by non-compensated stress overload, carriers of relevant phenotypes, etc. [193–195].
- Individuals affected by chronic multisystem medical conditions such as metabolic syndromes and inflammation-related disorders [196, 197].

Pro- and anti-inflammatory pathways may be triggered by structural components of certain bacterial populations of the gut microflora: interleukins and other cytokines belong to the cascade of inflammatory pathways, whereas by-products of metabolic processes such as short-chain fatty acids possess a power to inhibit inflammation [2]. Pre- and probiotics application is a cost-effective treatment approach to be implemented based on the individualized patient profile and accompanying therapy monitoring at molecular and sub/cellular levels in a holistic manner [195]. In Table 2, probiotics application is exemplified for clinically relevant health and medical conditions.

**Table 2** Probiotics exemplified for treatment of severe medical conditions associated with inflammation

| Medical Condition | Known preventive effects and successful treatment | Strains | References |
|---|---|---|---|
| Oxidative stress overload | Yes | *Bifidobacterium animalis* subsp. infantis BLI-02, *Bifidobacterium breve* Bv889, *Bifidobacterium bifidum* VDD088, *B. animalis subsp. lactis* CP-9, and *Lactobacillus plantarum* PL-02 | [198] |
| | | *Lactococcus lactis* MG5125, *Bifidobacterium bifidum* MG731, and *Bifidobacterium animalis* subsp. *lactis* MG74 | [199] |
| | | *Lactococcus lactis* CLFP 100, *Leuconostoc mesenteroides* CLFP 196, and *L. sakei* CLFP 202 | [200] |
| | | *Bifidobacterium breve*, *B. longum*, *B. infantis*, *Lactobacillus plantarum*, *L. acidophilus*, *L. casei*, *L. delbrueckii* subsp. *bulgaricus*, and *Streptococcus thermophilus* | [201] |
| | | *L. acidophilus, L .casei, L. rhamnosus*, *L. bulgaricus, B. breve, B. longum, S. thermophilus*, Fructo-oligosaccharide | [202] |
| | | *Bifidobacterium animalis*, *Lactobacillus rhamnosus*, and *Bacillus* LBP32 | [203, 204] |
| | | *Bacillus* SC06 | [205] |
| | | *B. animalis* subsp. *lactis* MG741; *B. breve* MG729; *L. reuteri* MG505; *L. rhamnosus* MG316 | [206] |
| | | *Streptococcus thermophilus* DSM 32245, *Bifidobacterium lactis* DSM 32246, *Bifidobacterium lactis* DSM 32247, *Lactobacillus acidophilus* DSM 32241, *Lactobacillus helveticus* DSM 32242, *Lactobacillus paracasei* DSM 32243, *Lactobacillus plantarum* DSM 32244, and *Lactobacillus brevis* DSM 27961 | [207] |

(continued)

**Table 2** (continued)

| Medical Condition | Known preventive effects and successful treatment | Strains | References |
|---|---|---|---|
| Impaired wound healing | Yes | Nanoparticle *Bifidobacterium bifidum*, *Lactobacillus acidophilus* and *Bacillus amyloliquefaciens* | [208] |
| | | *Lactobacillus fermentum* and *Lactobacillus delbruekii* | [209, 210] |
| | | *Lactobacillus rhamnosus* GG (ATCC 53103) | [211, 212] |
| | | *Lactobacillus acidophilus*, *lactobacillus casei*, *Lactobacillus fermentum*, and *Bifidobacterium bifidum* | [213] |
| | | *Lactobacillus acidophilus* LA-5, *Bifidobacterium* BB-12, *Streptococcus thermophilus* STY-31, and *Lactobacillus delbrueckii ssp. bulgaricus* LBY-27 | [209] |
| | | *L. plantarum; S. thermophiles* | [214] |
| | Insufficient evidence | *Lactobacillus reuteri* (DSM 17938 and ATCC PTA 5289) | [215, 216] |
| | | *Saccharomyces boulardii* | [217] |
| Diabetes mellitus type II | Yes | *Lactobacillus acidophilus*, *Bifidobacterium bifidum*, *Bifidobacterium lactis*, and *Bifidobacterium longum* | [218, 219] |
| | | *Lactobacillus acidophilus* La-5 and *Bifidobacterium animalis* subsp. *lactis* BB-12 | [219, 220] |
| | | *L. acidophilus, L.casei, L. rhamnosus, L. bulgaricus, B. breve, B. longum, S. thermophilus, Fructo-oligosaccharide* | [202] |
| | | *Bacillus subtilis* | [221] |
| | | *Lactobacillus plantarum* | [222–224] |
| | | *Akkermansia muciniphila* | [225–227] |
| | | *Akkermansia muciniphila, Clostridium beijerinckii, Clostridium butyricum, Bifidobacterium infantis* and *Anaerobutyricum hallii,* inulin | [228] |
| | | *Lactobacillus acidophilus* La5 and *Bifidobacterium lactis* Bb12 | [229] |
| | | *B. bifidum, L. casei, L. acidophilus* | [230, 231] |
| | | *Lactobacillus casei* | [232] |
| | Subset of study participants | *Lactobacillus reuteri* DSM 17938 | [219, 233] |
| | Insufficient evidence | *Lactobacillus casei Shirota* | [234] |

**Table 2** (continued)

| Medical Condition | Known preventive effects and successful treatment | Strains | References |
|---|---|---|---|
| Hyperhomocysteinemia | Yes | *Bifidobacterium bifidum* W23, *Bifidobacterium lactis* W51, *Bifidobacterium lactis* W52, *lactobacillus acidophilus* W37, *Lactobacillus brevis* W63, *Lactobacillus casei* W56, *Lactobacillus salivarius* W24, *Lactococcus lactis* W19 and *Lactococcus lactis* W58 | [235] |
| | | *B. Infantis* DSM24737, *B. Longum* DSM24736, *B. Breve* DSM24732, *L. acidophilus* DSM24735, *L. delbrueckii ssp. bulgaricus* DSM24734, *L. paracasei* DSM24733, *L. plantarum* DSM24730, *S. Thermophilus* DSM24731 | [236] |
| | | *L. plantarum* | [219, 222] |
| Multiple sclerosis | Yes | *L. acidophilus, L. casei, B. bifidum* and *L. fermentum* | [237, 238] |
| | | *B. infantis, B. lactis, L. reuteri, L. casei, L. plantarum,* and *L. fermentum* | [237, 239] |
| Colorectal carcinoma | Yes | *Bifidobacterium lactis* Bb12, *Lactobacillus rhamnosus* GG, oligofructose-enriched inulin | [240, 241] |
| | | *Bifidobacterium longum, Lactobacillus acidophilus, Enterococcus faecalis* | [240, 242] |
| | | *Bacillus natto, Lactobacillus acidophilus* | [240, 243] |
| | | *Lactobacillus plantarum* CGMMCC No 1258, *Lactobacillus acidophilus* LA-11, *Bifidobacterium longum* BL-88 | [240, 244, 245] |
| | | *Lactobacillus rhamnosus GG* | [240, 246] |
| | | *Streptococcus thermophilus* and *Lactobacillus delbruckii subsp. bulgaricus* | [240, 247, 248] |
| | | *Lactobacillus gasseri* OLL2716 (LG21) | [240, 249] |
| | | *Lactobacillus acidophilus, Lactobacillus plantarum, Bifidobacterium lactis, Saccharomyces boulardii* | [240, 250] |
| | | *Bifidobacterium longum* | [240, 251] |
| Liver cancer | Yes | *Lactobacillus rhamnosus* LC705, *Propionibacterium freudenreichii subsp. shermanii* | [240, 252] |
| Gastric cancer | Yes | *Lactobacillus reuteri* PTCC 1655 | [240, 253] |
| | | *Lactobacillus kefiri* P-IF | [240, 254] |
| Cervical cancer | Yes | *Lactobacillus acidophilus, Bifidobacterium bifidum* | [240, 255] |

(continued)

**Table 2** (continued)

| Medical Condition | Known preventive effects and successful treatment | Strains | References |
|---|---|---|---|
| Bladder cancer | Yes | *Lactobacillus casei* strain Shirota | [240, 256] |
| Breast cancer | Yes | Lactobacillus casei Shirota (LcS) and isoflavones from soy product | [240, 257] |
| | Ongoing clinical trial (NCT03358511) | *Laccharomyces boulardii, Lactobacillus plantarum, Bacillus subtilis, Bifidobacterium lactis, Bifidobacterium bifidum, Lactobacillus rhamnosus, Bifidobacterium breve, lactobacillus casei, Lactobacillus salivarius, Lactobacillus acidophilus, Lactobacillus brevis, Bifidobacterium longum*, and *Lactobacillus paracasei* | [248, 258] |
| Prostate cancer | Insufficient evidence | – | [259, 260] |
| Brain cancer | Glioblastoma cancer cell | Kefir drink supernatant (LAB) | [261] |
| Chronic fatigue | Insufficient evidence | – | [262, 263] |
| Rheumatoid arthritis | Yes | *Lactobacillus casei* (ATCC334) | [264, 265] |
| Musculoskeletal inflammation | Yes | *Lactobacillus casei* strain Shirota | [266] |
| | | *Lactobacillus rhamnosus PB01, DSM14870* | [267] |
| Mitochondrial impairments | Yes | *Lactobacillus salivarius* subsp. *salicinius* AP-32 | [268] |
| | | *Bifidobacterium infantis, Bifidobacterium animalis*, and *Lactobacillus acidophilus* | [269] |
| CVD | ***Yes*** | ***Bifidobacterium lactis HN019*** | [270] |
| | | ***B. bifidum, L. casei, L. acidophilus*** | [230, 231, 271] |
| | | ***L. plantarum 299v (Lp299v)*** | [224, 271–274] |
| | | ***L. rhamnosus GG (LGG)*** | [271, 275, 276] |
| | | ***Lactobacilli. Biola, L. acidophilus LA-5, B. lactis Bb12, and L. rhamnosus GG, L. acidophilus LA-5 and B. lactis Bb12*** | [224, 277] |
| | | ***Lactobacillus reuteri*** | [224, 278, 279] |
| | | *Lactobacillus Casei* | [232] |
| | Insufficient evidence | *Lactobacillus casei* strain Shirota | [234] |

**Table 2** (continued)

| Medical Condition | Known preventive effects and successful treatment | Strains | References |
|---|---|---|---|
| Allergies (dermatitis, eczema) | Yes | *Lactobacillus* GG | [280] |
| | | *Bifidobacterium lactis* Bb-12 and *Lactobacillus rhamnosus* GG (LGG) | [280, 281] |
| | | *Lactobacillus rhamnosus* 19,070–2 and *Lactobacillus reuteri* DSM 122460 | [280, 282] |
| | | LGG, *L. rhamnosus* LC705, B. breve Bb99 and *Propionibacterium freudenreichii* ssp. shermanii JS | [280, 283] |
| | | *Lactobacillus fermentum* VRI-033 PCC | [280, 284] |
| | | *L. plantarum* IS-10506 | [280, 285] |
| | | Mixture of *Lactobacillus casei, L. rhamnosus, L. plantarum, and Bifidobacterium lactis* | [280, 286] |
| | In children | *L. rhamnosus* and *Bifidobateria lactis* | [287] |
| | Insufficient evidence | *B. longum* BL999 and *L. rhamnosus* LPR | [288] |
| | | *Lactobacillus rhamnosus* or *Lactobacillus GG* | [289] |
| | | *Lactobacillus acidophilus* LAVRI-A1 | [290] |
| Asthma | Yes | *Bifidobacterium bifidum, B. lactis, and Lc. lactis* | [291, 292] |
| | Insufficient evidence | *Lactobacillus reuteri, Lactobacillus rhamnosus* GG (LGG), *Lactobacillus paracasei* ssp *paracasei* | [284, 291, 293, 294] |
| Celiac disease/ gluten-sensitive patients | Yes (with gluten-free diet) | *Consortia I: Lactobacillus (Lp.) plantarum, (Lc.) paracasei, Bacillus subtilis, Bacillus pumilus, and consortia II: Lp. plantarum, Lc. Paracasei, Limosilactobacillusreuteri, Bacillus megaterium, B. pumilus* | [295] |
| | | *Lactobacillus helveticus* R0052 and *Bifidobacterium longum* R0175 | [296] |
| | | *Bifidobacterium longum* | [297] |
| | | *Bifidobacterium breve* | [298–300] |
| | | *Bifidobacterium breve, B. longum, B. infantis, Lactobacillus plantarum, L. acidophilus, L. casei, L. delbrueckii* subsp. *bulgaricus*, and *Streptococcus thermophilus* | [301] |

## References


1. Golubnitschaja O, Baban B, Boniolo G, Wang W, Bubnov R, Kapalla M, Krapfenbauer K, Mozaffari MS, Costigliola V (2016) Medicine in the early twenty-first century: paradigm and anticipation-EPMA position paper 2016. EPMA J 7:23
2. Boyko N, Costigliola V, Golubnitschaja O. Microbiome in the Framework of Predictive, Preventive and Personalised Medicine. In Microbiome in 3P Medicine Strategies: The First Exploitation Guide; Springer 2023, V. 16. https://doi.org/10.1007/978-3-031-19564-8
3. Sender R, Fuchs S, Milo R (2016) Are we really vastly outnumbered? Revisiting the ratio of bacterial to host cells in humans. Cell 164:337–340
4. Negele K, Heinrich J, Borte M, Von Berg A, Schaaf B, Lehmann I, Wichmann HE, Bolte G, LISA Study Group (2004) Mode of delivery and development of atopic disease during the first 2 years of life. Pediatr Allergy Immunol 15:48–54
5. Dominguez-Bello MG, Costello EK, Contreras M, Magris M, Hidalgo G, Fierer N, Knight R (2010) Delivery mode shapes the acquisition and structure of the initial microbiota across multiple body habitats in newborns. Proc Natl Acad Sci 107:11971–11975
6. Bäckhed F, Roswall J, Peng Y, Feng Q, Jia H, Kovatcheva-Datchary P, Li Y, Xia Y, Xie H, Zhong H (2015) Dynamics and stabilization of the human gut microbiome during the first year of life. Cell Host Microbe 17:690–703
7. Chu DM, Ma J, Prince AL, Antony KM, Seferovic MD, Aagaard KM (2017) Maturation of the infant microbiome community structure and function across multiple body sites and in relation to mode of delivery. Nat Med 23:314–326
8. Wampach L, Heintz-Buschart A, Fritz JV, Ramiro-Garcia J, Habier J, Herold M, Narayanasamy S, Kaysen A, Hogan AH, Bindl L (2018) Birth mode is associated with earliest strain-conferred gut microbiome functions and immunostimulatory potential. Nat Commun 9:5091
9. Matamoros S, Gras-Leguen C, Le Vacon F, Potel G, de La Cochetiere M-F (2013) Development of intestinal microbiota in infants and its impact on health. Trends Microbiol 21:167–173
10. Tan J, McKenzie C, Potamitis M, Thorburn AN, Mackay CR, Macia L (2014) The role of short-chain fatty acids in health and disease. Adv Immunol 121:91–119
11. O'Hara AM, Shanahan F (2006) The gut flora as a forgotten organ. EMBO Rep 7:688–693
12. Derrien M, van Hylckama Vlieg JE (2015) Fate, activity, and impact of ingested bacteria within the human gut microbiota. Trends Microbiol 23:354–366
13. Weisburg WG, Barns SM, Pelletier DA, Lane DJ (1991) 16S ribosomal DNA amplification for phylogenetic study. J Bacteriol 173:697–703
14. Hugerth LW, Muller EE, Hu YO, Lebrun LA, Roume H, Lundin D, Wilmes P, Andersson AF (2014) Systematic design of 18S rRNA gene primers for determining eukaryotic diversity in microbial consortia. PLoS One 9:e95567
15. Tringe SG, Rubin EM (2005) Metagenomics: DNA sequencing of environmental samples. Nat Rev Genet 6:805–814
16. Clemente JC, Manasson J, Scher JU (2018) The role of the gut microbiome in systemic inflammatory disease. BMJ 360:j5145
17. Behzadi P, Ranjbar R (2019) DNA microarray technology and bioinformatic web services. Acta Microbiol Immunol Hung 66:19–30
18. Ranjbar R, Behzadi P, Najafi A, Roudi R (2017) DNA microarray for rapid detection and identification of food and water borne bacteria: from dry to wet lab. Open Microbiology J 11:330–338
19. Behzadi P, Ranjbar R, Alavian SM (2015) Nucleic acid-based approaches for detection of viral hepatitis. *Jundishapur*. J Microbiol 8:8
20. Behzadi P, Behzadi E, Alavian SM (2017) DNA microarray technology in HBV genotyping. Minerva Med 108:473–476
21. Karakan T, Ozkul C, Küpeli Akkol E, Bilici S, Sobarzo-Sánchez E, Capasso R (2021) Gut-brain-microbiota axis: antibiotics and functional gastrointestinal disorders. Nutrients 13:389

22. Gomaa EZ (2020) Human gut microbiota/microbiome in health and diseases: a review. Antonie Van Leeuwenhoek 113:2019–2040
23. García-Montero C, Fraile-Martínez O, Gómez-Lahoz AM, Pekarek L, Castellanos AJ, Noguerales-Fraguas F, Coca S, Guijarro LG, García-Honduvilla N, Asúnsolo A (2021) Nutritional components in Western diet versus Mediterranean diet at the gut microbiota–immune system interplay. Implications for health and disease. *Nutrients* 13:699
24. Adak A, Khan MR (2019) An insight into gut microbiota and its functionalities. Cell Mol Life Sci 76:473–493
25. Rinninella E, Raoul P, Cintoni M, Franceschi F, Miggiano GAD, Gasbarrini A, Mele MC (2019) What is the healthy gut microbiota composition? A changing ecosystem across age, environment, diet, and diseases. Microorganisms 7:14
26. Rizzatti G, Lopetuso L, Gibiino G, Binda C, Gasbarrini A (2017) Proteobacteria: a common factor in human diseases. Biomed Res Int 2017:9351507
27. Ranjbar R, Behzadi P, Farshad S (2017) Advances in diagnosis and treatment of helicobacter pylori infection. Acta Microbiol Immunol Hung 64:273–292
28. Behzadi P, Najafi A, Behzadi E, Ranjbar R (2016) Microarray long oligo probe designing for Escherichia coli: an in-silico DNA marker extraction. CEJU 69:105–111
29. Behzadi P, Behzadi E (2008) The microbial agents of urinary tract infections at central laboratory of Dr. Shariati hospital, Tehran, Iran. Turk Klin Tip Bilim 28:445–449
30. Khonsari MS, Behzadi P, Foroohi F (2021) The prevalence of type 3 fimbriae in Uropathogenic Escherichia coli isolated from clinical urine samples. Meta Gene 28:100881
31. Behzadi P, Behzadi E (2017) Uropathogenic Escherichia coli: An ideal resource for DNA microarray probe designing. In: Proceedings of the bioinformatics and biomedical engineering: 5th International Work-Conference, IWBBIO 2017, Granada, Spain, April 26–28, 2017, proceedings, Part II 5. Springer International Publishing, pp 12–19
32. Behzadi P, García-Perdomo HA, Gómez AMA, Pinheiro M, Sarshar M (2023) Uropathogens, urinary tract infections, the host-pathogen interactions and treatment. Front Microbiol 14:937
33. Behzadi P, Urbán E, Matuz M, Benkő R, Gajdács M (2021) The role of gram-negative bacteria in urinary tract infections: current concepts and therapeutic options. Adv Exp Med Biol 15:35–69
34. Hozzari A, Behzadi P, Kerishchi Khiabani P, Sholeh M, Sabokroo N (2020) Clinical cases, drug resistance, and virulence genes profiling in Uropathogenic Escherichia coli. J Appl Genet 61:265–273
35. Behzadi P (2020) Classical chaperone-usher (CU) adhesive fimbriome: uropathogenic Escherichia coli (UPEC) and urinary tract infections (UTIs). Folia Microbiol 65:45–65
36. Ghosh TS, Shanahan F, O'Toole PW (2022) The gut microbiome as a modulator of healthy ageing. Nat Rev Gastroenterol Hepatol 19:1–20
37. Nagpal R, Tsuji H, Takahashi T, Nomoto K, Kawashima K, Nagata S, Yamashiro Y (2017) Ontogenesis of the gut microbiota composition in healthy, full-term, vaginally born and breast-fed infants over the first 3 years of life: a quantitative bird's-eye view. Front Microbiol 8:1388
38. Hasan N, Yang H (2019) Factors affecting the composition of the gut microbiota, and its modulation. Peer J 7:e7502
39. David LA, Maurice CF, Carmody RN, Gootenberg DB, Button JE, Wolfe BE, Ling AV, Devlin AS, Varma Y, Fischbach MA (2014) Diet rapidly and reproducibly alters the human gut microbiome. Nature 505:559–563
40. Behzadi P, Gajdács M (2021) Writing a strong scientific paper in medicine and the biomedical sciences: a checklist and recommendations for early career researchers. Biol Futur 72:395–407
41. Berer K, Krishnamoorthy G (2014) Microbial view of central nervous system autoimmunity. FEBS Lett 588:4207–4213

42. Arpaia N, Campbell C, Fan X, Dikiy S, Van Der Veeken J, Deroos P, Liu H, Cross JR, Pfeffer K, Coffer PJ (2013) Metabolites produced by commensal bacteria promote peripheral regulatory T-cell generation. Nature 504:451–455
43. Smith PM, Howitt MR, Panikov N, Michaud M, Gallini CA, Bohlooly-y M, Glickman JN, Garrett WS (2013) The microbial metabolites, short-chain fatty acids, regulate colonic Treg cell homeostasis. Science 341:569–573
44. Chang PV, Hao L, Offermanns S, Medzhitov R (2014) The microbial metabolite butyrate regulates intestinal macrophage function via histone deacetylase inhibition. Proc Natl Acad Sci 111:2247–2252
45. Behzadi P, Sameer AS, Nissar S, Banday MZ, Gajdács M, García-Perdomo HA, Akhtar K, Pinheiro M, Magnusson P, Sarshar M (2022) The Interleukin-1 (IL-1) superfamily cytokines and their single nucleotide polymorphisms (SNPs). J Immunol Res 2022:2054431
46. Lebeer S, Bron PA, Marco ML, Van Pijkeren J-P, Motherway MOC, Hill C, Pot B, Roos S, Klaenhammer T (2018) Identification of probiotic effector molecules: present state and future perspectives. Curr Opin Biotechnol 49:217–223
47. Schiavi E, Gleinser M, Molloy E, Groeger D, Frei R, Ferstl R, Rodriguez-Perez N, Ziegler M, Grant R, Moriarty TF (2016) The surface-associated exopolysaccharide of Bifidobacterium longum 35624 plays an essential role in dampening host proinflammatory responses and repressing local TH17 responses. Appl Environ Microbiol 82:7185–7196
48. Sokol H, Pigneur B, Watterlot L, Lakhdari O, Bermúdez-Humarán LG, Gratadoux J-J, Blugeon S, Bridonneau C, Furet J-P, Corthier G (2008) Faecalibacterium prausnitzii is an anti-inflammatory commensal bacterium identified by gut microbiota analysis of Crohn disease patients. Proc Natl Acad Sci 105:16731–16736
49. Quévrain E, Maubert M, Michon C, Chain F, Marquant R, Tailhades J, Miquel S, Carlier L, Bermúdez-Humarán L, Pigneur B (2016) Identification of an anti-inflammatory protein from Faecalibacterium prausnitzii, a commensal bacterium deficient in Crohn's disease. Gut 65:415–425
50. Miquel S, Leclerc M, Martin R, Chain F, Lenoir M, Raguideau S, Hudault S, Bridonneau C, Northen T, Bowen B (2015) Identification of metabolic signatures linked to anti-inflammatory effects of Faecalibacterium prausnitzii. MBio 6:e00300–e00315
51. Landman C, Grill J-P, Mallet J-M, Marteau P, Humbert L, Le Balch E, Maubert M-A, Perez K, Chaara W, Brot L (2018) Inter-kingdom effect on epithelial cells of the N-acyl homoserine lactone 3-oxo-C12: 2, a major quorum-sensing molecule from gut microbiota. PLoS One 13:e0202587
52. Blander JM, Longman RS, Iliev ID, Sonnenberg GF, Artis D (2017) Regulation of inflammation by microbiota interactions with the host. Nat Immunol 18:851–860
53. Gensollen T, Iyer SS, Kasper DL, Blumberg RS (2016) How colonization by microbiota in early life shapes the immune system. Science 352:539–544
54. Atarashi K, Tanoue T, Ando M, Kamada N, Nagano Y, Narushima S, Suda W, Imaoka A, Setoyama H, Nagamori T (2015) Th17 cell induction by adhesion of microbes to intestinal epithelial cells. Cell 163:367–380
55. Behzadi P, Behzadi E, Ranjbar R (2015) Urinary tract infections and Candida albicans. CEJU 68:96–101
56. Behzadi P, Behzadi E (2012) Evaluation of UVB light efficacy for inducing apoptosis in Candida albicans cultures. Roum Arch Microbiol Immunol 71:39–42
57. Iebba V, Totino V, Gagliardi A, Santangelo F, Cacciotti F, Trancassini M, Mancini C, Cicerone C, Corazziari E, Pantanella F (2016) Eubiosis and dysbiosis: the two sides of the microbiota. New Microbiol 39:1–12
58. Hooks KB, O'Malley MA (2017) Dysbiosis and its discontents. *MBio* 8:e01492–e01417
59. Yoon K, Kim N (2021) Roles of sex hormones and gender in the gut microbiota. J Neurogastroenterol Motil 27:314
60. Kim Y, Unno T, Kim B, Park M (2020) Sex differences in gut microbiota. World J Mens Health 38:48–60

61. Sender R, Fuchs S, Milo R (2016) Revised estimates for the number of human and bacteria cells in the body. PLoS Biol 14:e1002533
62. Mulak A, Taché Y, Larauche M (2014) Sex hormones in the modulation of irritable bowel syndrome. World J Gastroenterol: WJG 20:2433
63. Sisk-Hackworth L, Kelley ST, Thackray VG (2023) Sex, puberty, and the gut microbiome. Reproduction 165:R61–R74
64. Stefanaki C, Bacopoulou F, Chrousos GP (2022) Gut microsex/Genderome, immunity and the stress response in the sexes: an updated review. Theol Sex 3:533–545
65. Mulak A, Larauche M, Taché Y (2022) Sexual dimorphism in the gut microbiome: Microgenderome or Microsexome? J Neurogastroenterol Motil 28:332–333
66. Kim N (2022) Sexual dimorphism in the gut microbiome: Microgenderome or Microsexome? Author's reply. J Neurogastroenterol Motil 28:334–334
67. Chen KL, Madak-Erdogan Z (2016) Estrogen and microbiota crosstalk: should we pay attention? Trends Endocrinol Metab 27:752–755
68. Menon R, Watson SE, Thomas LN, Allred CD, Dabney A, Azcarate-Peril MA, Sturino JM (2013) Diet complexity and estrogen receptor β status affect the composition of the murine intestinal microbiota. Appl Environ Microbiol 79:5763–5773
69. Kwa M, Plottel CS, Blaser MJ, Adams S (2016) The intestinal microbiome and estrogen receptor–positive female breast cancer. J Natl Cancer Inst 108(3):djw029
70. Paterni I, Bertini S, Granchi C, Macchia M, Minutolo F (2013) Estrogen receptor ligands: a patent review update. Expert Opin Ther Pat 23:1247–1271
71. Arterburn JB, Prossnitz ER (2023) G Protein–Coupled Estrogen Receptor GPER: Molecular Pharmacology and Therapeutic Applications. Annu Rev Pharmacol Toxicol 63:295–320
72. Chakraborty B, Byemerwa J, Krebs T, Lim F, Chang C-Y, McDonnell DP (2023) Estrogen receptor signaling in the immune system. Endocr Rev 44:117–141
73. He S, Li H, Yu Z, Zhang F, Liang S, Liu H, Chen H, Lü M (2021) The gut microbiome and sex hormone-related diseases. Front Microbiol 12:711137
74. Shin J-H, Park Y-H, Sim M, Kim S-A, Joung H, Shin D-M (2019) Serum level of sex steroid hormone is associated with diversity and profiles of human gut microbiome. Res Microbiol 170:192–201
75. Valeri F, Endres K (2021) How biological sex of the host shapes its gut microbiota. Front Neuroendocrinol 61:100912
76. Del Chierico F, Vernocchi P, Petrucca A, Paci P, Fuentes S, Pratico G, Capuani G, Masotti A, Reddel S, Russo A (2015) Phylogenetic and metabolic tracking of gut microbiota during perinatal development. PLoS One 10:e0137347
77. Pannaraj PS, Li F, Cerini C, Bender JM, Yang S, Rollie A, Adisetiyo H, Zabih S, Lincez PJ, Bittinger K (2017) Association between breast milk bacterial communities and establishment and development of the infant gut microbiome. JAMA Pediatr 171:647–654
78. Robertson RC, Manges AR, Finlay BB, Prendergast AJ (2019) The human microbiome and child growth–first 1000 days and beyond. Trends Microbiol 27:131–147
79. Kozyrskyj A, Kalu R, Koleva P, Bridgman S (2016) Fetal programming of overweight through the microbiome: boys are disproportionately affected. J Dev Orig Health Dis 7:25–34
80. Gänzle MG (2015) Lactic metabolism revisited: metabolism of lactic acid bacteria in food fermentations and food spoilage. Curr Opin Food Sci 2:106–117
81. Sela DA, Chapman J, Adeuya A, Kim JH, Chen F, Whitehead TR, Lapidus A, Rokhsar D, Lebrilla C, German JB (2008) The genome sequence of Bifidobacterium longum subsp. infantis reveals adaptations for milk utilization within the infant microbiome. Proc Natl Acad Sci U S A 105:18964–18969
82. Turroni F, Peano C, Pass DA, Foroni E, Severgnini M, Claesson MJ, Kerr C, Hourihane J, Murray D, Fuligni F (2012) Diversity of bifidobacteria within the infant gut microbiota. PLoS One 7:e36957
83. Pokusaeva K, Fitzgerald GF, van Sinderen D (2011) Carbohydrate metabolism in Bifidobacteria. Genes Nutr 6:285–306

84. Fouhy F, Watkins C, Hill CJ, O'Shea C-A, Nagle B, Dempsey EM, O'Toole PW, Ross RP, Ryan CA, Stanton C (2019) Perinatal factors affect the gut microbiota up to four years after birth. Nat Commun 10:1517
85. Hollister EB, Riehle K, Luna RA, Weidler EM, Rubio-Gonzales M, Mistretta T-A, Raza S, Doddapaneni HV, Metcalf GA, Muzny DM (2015) Structure and function of the healthy pre-adolescent pediatric gut microbiome. Microbiome 3:1–13
86. Agans R, Rigsbee L, Kenche H, Michail S, Khamis HJ, Paliy O (2011) Distal gut microbiota of adolescent children is different from that of adults. FEMS Microbiol Ecol 77:404–412
87. Biagi E, Rampelli S, Turroni S, Quercia S, Candela M, Brigidi P (2017) The gut microbiota of centenarians: signatures of longevity in the gut microbiota profile. Mech Ageing Dev 165:180–184
88. Voreades N, Kozil A, Weir TL (2014) Diet and the development of the human intestinal microbiome. Front Microbiol 5:494
89. Hantsoo L, Zemel BS (2021) Stress gets into the belly: early life stress and the gut microbiome. Behav Brain Res 414:113474
90. McEwen BS (2012) Brain on stress: how the social environment gets under the skin. Proc Natl Acad Sci 109:17180–17185
91. Danese A, Pariante CM, Caspi A, Taylor A, Poulton R (2007) Childhood maltreatment predicts adult inflammation in a life-course study. Proc Natl Acad Sci 104:1319–1324
92. Miller GE, Chen E, Parker KJ (2011) Psychological stress in childhood and susceptibility to the chronic diseases of aging: moving toward a model of behavioral and biological mechanisms. Psychol Bull 137:959
93. Carpenter LL, Gawuga CE, Tyrka AR, Lee JK, Anderson GM, Price LH (2010) Association between plasma IL-6 response to acute stress and early-life adversity in healthy adults. Neuropsychopharmacology 35:2617–2623
94. Dhama K, Khan S, Tiwari R, Sircar S, Bhat S, Malik YS, Singh KP, Chaicumpa W, Bonilla-Aldana DK, Rodriguez-Morales AJ (2020) Coronavirus disease 2019–COVID-19. Clin Microbiol Rev 33:e00028–e00020
95. Cryan JF, O'Riordan KJ, Cowan CS, Sandhu KV, Bastiaanssen TF, Boehme M, Codagnone MG, Cussotto S, Fulling C, Golubeva AV (2019) The microbiota-gut-brain axis. Physiol Rev 99:1877
96. Ávila PRM, Fiorot M, Michels M, Dominguini D, Abatti M, Vieira A, de Moura AB, Behenck JP, Borba LA, Botelho MEM (2020) Effects of microbiota transplantation and the role of the vagus nerve in gut–brain axis in animals subjected to chronic mild stress. J Affect Disord 277:410–416
97. Doney E, Cadoret A, Dion-Albert L, Lebel M, Menard C (2022) Inflammation-driven brain and gut barrier dysfunction in stress and mood disorders. Eur J Neurosci 55:2851–2894
98. Maltz RM, Keirsey J, Kim SC, Mackos AR, Gharaibeh RZ, Moore CC, Xu J, Somogyi A, Bailey MT (2019) Social stress affects colonic inflammation, the gut microbiome, and short chain fatty acid levels and receptors. J Pediatr Gastroenterol Nutr 68:533
99. Wiley NC, Cryan JF, Dinan TG, Ross RP, Stanton C (2021) Production of psychoactive metabolites by gut bacteria. Mod Trends Psychiatry 32:74–99
100. Hantsoo L, Jašarević E, Criniti S, McGeehan B, Tanes C, Sammel MD, Elovitz MA, Compher C, Wu G, Epperson CN (2019) Childhood adversity impact on gut microbiota and inflammatory response to stress during pregnancy. Brain Behav Immun 75:240–250
101. Hermes GD, Eckermann HA, de Vos WM, de Weerth C (2020) Does entry to center-based childcare affect gut microbial colonization in young infants? Sci Rep 10:1–13
102. Nishida K, Sawada D, Kuwano Y, Tanaka H, Rokutan K (1859) Health benefits of lactobacillus gasseri CP2305 tablets in young adults exposed to chronic stress: a randomized, double-blind, placebo-controlled study. Nutrients 2019:11
103. Knowles SR, Nelson EA, Palombo EA (2008) Investigating the role of perceived stress on bacterial flora activity and salivary cortisol secretion: a possible mechanism underlying susceptibility to illness. Biol Psychol 77:132–137

104. Michels N, Van de Wiele T, Fouhy F, O'Mahony S, Clarke G, Keane J (2019) Gut microbiome patterns depending on children's psychosocial stress: reports versus biomarkers. Brain Behav Immun 80:751–762
105. D'Agata AL, Wu J, Welandawe MK, Dutra SV, Kane B, Groer MW (2019) Effects of early life NICU stress on the developing gut microbiome. Dev Psychobiol 61:650–660
106. Jang S-H, Woo YS, Lee S-Y, Bahk W-M (2020) The brain–gut–microbiome axis in psychiatry. Int J Mol Sci 21:7122
107. Maturo MG, Soligo M, Gibson G, Manni L, Nardini C (2020) The greater inflammatory pathway—high clinical potential by innovative predictive, preventive, and personalized medical approach. EPMA J 11:1–16
108. Cryan JF, Dinan TG (2012) Mind-altering microorganisms: the impact of the gut microbiota on brain and behaviour. Nat Rev Neurosci 13:701–712
109. Lee YY, Annamalai C, Rao SS (2017) Post-infectious irritable bowel syndrome. Curr Gastroenterol Rep 19:1–10
110. Galland L (2014) The gut microbiome and the brain. J Med Food 17:1261–1272
111. Lyte M (2013) Microbial endocrinology in the microbiome-gut-brain axis: how bacterial production and utilization of neurochemicals influence behavior. PLoS Pathog 9:e1003726
112. Forsythe P, Bienenstock J, Kunze WA (2014) Vagal pathways for microbiome-brain-gut axis communication. Adv Exp Med Biol 817:115–133
113. Wu H-J, Wu E (2012) The role of gut microbiota in immune homeostasis and autoimmunity. Gut Microbes 3:4–14
114. Cortez V, Schultz-Cherry S (2021) The role of goblet cells in viral pathogenesis. FEBS J 288:7060–7072
115. Ganal-Vonarburg SC, Duerr CU (2020) The interaction of intestinal microbiota and innate lymphoid cells in health and disease throughout life. Immunology 159:39–51
116. Schütte A, Ermund A, Becker-Pauly C, Johansson ME, Rodriguez-Pineiro AM, Bäckhed F, Müller S, Lottaz D, Bond JS, Hansson GC (2014) Microbial-induced meprin β cleavage in MUC2 mucin and a functional CFTR channel are required to release anchored small intestinal mucus. Proc Natl Acad Sci 111:12396–12401
117. Codella R, Luzi L, Terruzzi I (2018) Exercise has the guts: how physical activity may positively modulate gut microbiota in chronic and immune-based diseases. Dig Liver Dis 50:331–341
118. Aragón-Vela J, Solis-Urra P, Ruiz-Ojeda FJ, Álvarez-Mercado AI, Olivares-Arancibia J, Plaza-Diaz J (2021) Impact of exercise on gut microbiota in obesity. Nutrients 13:3999
119. Zheng D, Ratiner K, Elinav E (2020) Circadian influences of diet on the microbiome and immunity. Trends Immunol 41:512–530
120. Naliyadhara N, Kumar A, Gangwar SK, Devanarayanan TN, Hegde M, Alqahtani MS, Abbas M, Sethi G, Kunnumakara A (2023) Interplay of dietary antioxidants and gut microbiome in human health: what has been learnt thus far? J Funct Foods 100:105365
121. Gentile CL, Weir TL (2018) The gut microbiota at the intersection of diet and human health. Science 362:776–780
122. Payling L, Fraser K, Loveday S, Sims I, Roy N, McNabb W (2020) The effects of carbohydrate structure on the composition and functionality of the human gut microbiota. Trends Food Sci Technol 97:233–248
123. Babakanrad E, Mohammadian T, Esmaeili D, Behzadi P (2023) Cervical cancer: a review of epidemiology, treatments, and anticancer drugs. Curr Cancer Ther Rev 19:1–15. https://doi.org/10.2174/1573394719666230207101655
124. Kheirollahzadeh F, Eftekhari E, Ghollasi M, Behzadi P (2022) Anti-hyperglycemic effects of Eryngium billardierei F. Delaroche extract on insulin-resistance HepG2 cells in vitro. Mol Biol Rep 49:3401–3411
125. Behzadi P (2022) Toll-like receptor (TLR) polymorphisms in prostate cancer. In: Genetic polymorphism and disease. CRC Press, pp 379–399

126. Behzadi P (2021) The role of toll-like receptor (TLR) polymorphisms in urinary bladder cancer. In: Genetic polymorphism and cancer susceptibility, pp 281–317
127. Demir M, Demir C (2022) Oxidative stress has a negative effect on the development and progression of bladder cancer. Turk J Oncol/Türk Onkoloji Dergisi 37(2):158–162
128. Lyu Y, Wu L, Wang F, Shen X, Lin D (2018) Carotenoid supplementation and retinoic acid in immunoglobulin a regulation of the gut microbiota dysbiosis. Exp Biol Med 243:613–620
129. Riaz Rajoka MS, Thirumdas R, Mehwish HM, Umair M, Khurshid M, Hayat HF, Phimolsiripol Y, Pallarés N, Martí-Quijal FJ, Barba FJ (2021) Role of food antioxidants in modulating gut microbial communities: novel understandings in intestinal oxidative stress damage and their impact on host health. Antioxidants 10:1563
130. Vijay A, Valdes AM (2022) Role of the gut microbiome in chronic diseases: a narrative review. Eur J Clin Nutr 76:489–501
131. Khan MF, Wang H (2020) Environmental exposures and autoimmune diseases: contribution of gut microbiome. Front Immunol 10:3094
132. Duda-Chodak A, Tarko T, Satora P, Sroka P (2015) Interaction of dietary compounds, especially polyphenols, with the intestinal microbiota: a review. Eur J Nutr 54:325–341
133. Rowland I, Gibson G, Heinken A, Scott K, Swann J, Thiele I, Tuohy K (2018) Gut microbiota functions: metabolism of nutrients and other food components. Eur J Nutr 57:1–24
134. Heiss CN, Olofsson LE (2018) Gut microbiota-dependent modulation of energy metabolism. J Innate Immun 10:163–171
135. Sarkar A, Yoo JY, Valeria Ozorio Dutra S, Morgan KH, Groer M (2021) The association between early-life gut microbiota and long-term health and diseases. *Journal of.* Clin Med 10:459
136. Alcazar CG-M, Paes VM, Shao Y, Oesser C, Miltz A, Lawley TD, Brocklehurst P, Rodger A, Field N (2022) The association between early-life gut microbiota and childhood respiratory diseases: a systematic review. *The lancet.* Microbe 3:e867
137. Zhou L, Xiao X (2018) The role of gut microbiota in the effects of maternal obesity during pregnancy on offspring metabolism. Biosci Rep 38:BSR20171234
138. Radford-Smith DE, Anthony DC (2023) Mechanisms of maternal diet-induced obesity affecting the offspring brain and development of affective disorders. Meta 13:455
139. Ballard O, Morrow AL (2013) Human milk composition: nutrients and bioactive factors. Pediatr Clin 60:49–74
140. Zhang Y, Zhang X, Mi L, Li C, Zhang Y, Bi R, Pang J, Li Y (2022) Comparative proteomic analysis of proteins in breast Milk during different lactation periods. Nutrients 14:3648
141. Serra-Majem L, Roman-Vinas B, Sanchez-Villegas A, Guasch-Ferre M, Corella D, La Vecchia C (2019) Benefits of the Mediterranean diet: epidemiological and molecular aspects. Mol Asp Med 67:1–55
142. Pecora F, Persico F, Argentiero A, Neglia C, Esposito S (2020) The role of micronutrients in support of the immune response against viral infections. Nutrients 12:3198
143. Barrea L, Muscogiuri G, Frias-Toral E, Laudisio D, Pugliese G, Castellucci B, Garcia-Velasquez E, Savastano S, Colao A (2021) Nutrition and immune system: from the Mediterranean diet to dietary supplementary through the microbiota. Crit Rev Food Sci Nutr 61:3066–3090
144. Esposito K, Maiorino MI, Bellastella G, Panagiotakos DB, Giugliano D (2017) Mediterranean diet for type 2 diabetes: cardiometabolic benefits. Endocrine 56:27–32
145. Krznaric Ž, Bender DV, Meštrovic T (2019) The Mediterranean diet and its association with selected gut bacteria. Curr Opin Clin Nutr Metab Care 22:401–406
146. Gutiérrez-Díaz I, Fernández-Navarro T, Sánchez B, Margolles A, González S (2016) Mediterranean diet and faecal microbiota: a transversal study. Food Funct 7:2347–2356
147. Rinninella E, Tohumcu E, Raoul P, Fiorani M, Cintoni M, Mele MC, Cammarota G, Gasbarrini A, Ianiro G (2023) The role of diet in shaping human gut microbiota. *Best Practice & Research Clinical.* Gastroenterology 62-63:101828

148. Fajstova A, Galanova N, Coufal S, Malkova J, Kostovcik M, Cermakova M, Pelantova H, Kuzma M, Sediva B, Hudcovic T (2020) Diet rich in simple sugars promotes pro-inflammatory response via gut microbiota alteration and TLR4 signaling. Cell 9:2701
149. Khan S, Waliullah S, Godfrey V, Khan MAW, Ramachandran RA, Cantarel BL, Behrendt C, Peng L, Hooper LV, Zaki H (2020) Dietary simple sugars alter microbial ecology in the gut and promote colitis in mice. Sci Transl Med 12:eaay6218
150. Laffin M, Fedorak R, Zalasky A, Park H, Gill A, Agrawal A, Keshteli A, Hotte N, Madsen KL (2019) A high-sugar diet rapidly enhances susceptibility to colitis via depletion of luminal short-chain fatty acids in mice. Sci Rep 9:12294
151. Mudgil D, Barak S (2013) Composition, properties and health benefits of indigestible carbohydrate polymers as dietary fiber: a review. Int J Biol Macromol 61:1–6
152. Levy M, Thaiss CA, Elinav E (2016) Metabolites: messengers between the microbiota and the immune system. Genes Dev 30:1589–1597
153. Maukonen J, Saarela M (2015) Human gut microbiota: does diet matter? Proc Nutr Soc 74:23–36
154. Holscher HD (2017) Dietary fiber and prebiotics and the gastrointestinal microbiota. Gut Microbes 8:172–184
155. Hughes RL, Alvarado DA, Swanson KS, Holscher HD (2022) The prebiotic potential of inulin-type fructans: a systematic review. Adv Nutr 13:492–529
156. Hryckowian AJ, Van Treuren W, Smits SA, Davis NM, Gardner JO, Bouley DM, Sonnenburg JL (2018) Microbiota-accessible carbohydrates suppress Clostridium difficile infection in a murine model. Nat Microbiol 3:662–669
157. Scott KP, Gratz SW, Sheridan PO, Flint HJ, Duncan SH (2013) The influence of diet on the gut microbiota. Pharmacol Res 69:52–60
158. Barrea L, Annunziata G, Muscogiuri G, Laudisio D, Di Somma C, Maisto M, Tenore GC, Colao A, Savastano S (2019) Trimethylamine N-oxide, Mediterranean diet, and nutrition in healthy, normal-weight adults: also a matter of sex? Nutrition 62:7–17
159. Zhang X, Gérard P (2022) Diet-gut microbiota interactions on cardiovascular disease. *Computational and structural*. Biotechnol J 20:1528
160. Dostal Webster A, Staley C, Hamilton MJ, Huang M, Fryxell K, Erickson R, Kabage AJ, Sadowsky MJ, Khoruts A (2019) Influence of short-term changes in dietary sulfur on the relative abundances of intestinal sulfate-reducing bacteria. Gut Microbes 10:447–457
161. Dominika Ś, Arjan N, Karyn RP, Henryk K (2011) The study on the impact of glycated pea proteins on human intestinal bacteria. Int J Food Microbiol 145:267–272
162. Graf D, Monk JM, Lepp D, Wu W, McGillis L, Roberton K, Brummer Y, Tosh SM, Power KA (1853) Cooked red lentils dose-dependently modulate the colonic microenvironment in healthy C57Bl/6 male mice. Nutrients 2019:11
163. Gullón P, Gullón B, Tavaria F, Vasconcelos M, Gomes AM (2015) In vitro fermentation of lupin seeds (Lupinus albus) and broad beans (Vicia faba): dynamic modulation of the intestinal microbiota and metabolomic output. Food Funct 6:3316–3322
164. Kadyan S, Sharma A, Arjmandi BH, Singh P, Nagpal R (2022) Prebiotic potential of dietary beans and pulses and their resistant starch for aging-associated gut and metabolic health. Nutrients 14:1726
165. Hidalgo M, Oruna-Concha MJ, Kolida S, Walton GE, Kallithraka S, Spencer JP, de Pascual-Teresa S (2012) Metabolism of anthocyanins by human gut microflora and their influence on gut bacterial growth. J Agric Food Chem 60:3882–3890
166. Malesza IJ, Malesza M, Walkowiak J, Mussin N, Walkowiak D, Aringazina R, Bartkowiak-Wieczorek J, Mądry E (2021) High-fat, western-style diet, systemic inflammation, and gut microbiota: a narrative review. Cell 10:3164
167. Zhang C, Zhang M, Pang X, Zhao Y, Wang L, Zhao L (2012) Structural resilience of the gut microbiota in adult mice under high-fat dietary perturbations. ISME J 6:1848–1857

168. Devkota S, Wang Y, Musch MW, Leone V, Fehlner-Peach H, Nadimpalli A, Antonopoulos DA, Jabri B, Chang EB (2012) Dietary-fat-induced taurocholic acid promotes pathobiont expansion and colitis in Il10−/− mice. Nature 487:104–108
169. Wolters M, Ahrens J, Romaní-Pérez M, Watkins C, Sanz Y, Benítez-Páez A, Stanton C, Günther K (2019) Dietary fat, the gut microbiota, and metabolic health–a systematic review conducted within the MyNewGut project. Clin Nutr 38:2504–2520
170. Roopashree P, Shetty SS, Kumari NS (2021) Effect of medium chain fatty acid in human health and disease. J Funct Foods 87:104724
171. e Dias MDM, Siqueira NP, da Conceição LL, dos Reis SA, Valente FX, dos Santos Dias MM, Rosa CDOB, de Paula SO, da Matta SLP, de Oliveira LL (2018) Consumption of virgin coconut oil in Wistar rats increases saturated fatty acids in the liver and adipose tissue, as well as adipose tissue inflammation. J Funct Foods 48:472–480
172. Noriega BS, Sanchez-Gonzalez MA, Salyakina D, Coffman J (2016) Understanding the impact of omega-3 rich diet on the gut microbiota. Case Rep Med 2016:3089303
173. Chaplin A, Parra P, Serra F, Palou A (2015) Conjugated linoleic acid supplementation under a high-fat diet modulates stomach protein expression and intestinal microbiota in adult mice. PLoS One 10:e0125091
174. Doi L, Williams AJ, Marryat L, Frank J (2020) Cohort study of high maternal body mass index and the risk of adverse pregnancy and delivery outcomes in Scotland. BMJ Open 10:e026168
175. Yazdani S, Yosofniyapasha Y, Nasab BH, Mojaveri MH, Bouzari Z (2012) Effect of maternal body mass index on pregnancy outcome and newborn weight. BMC Res Notes 5:1–4
176. van Hoorn F, de Wit L, van Rossem L, Jambroes M, Groenendaal F, Kwee A, Lamain-de Ruiter M, Franx A, van Rijn BB, Koster MP (2021) A prospective population-based multicentre study on the impact of maternal body mass index on adverse pregnancy outcomes: focus on normal weight. PLoS One 16:e0257722
177. Kumbhare SV, Patangia DV, Patil RH, Shouche YS, Patil NP (2019) Factors influencing the gut microbiome in children: from infancy to childhood. J Biosci 44:1–19
178. Vitoratou D-I, Mavrogianni C, Karatzi K, Cardon G, Iotova V, Tsochev K, Lindström J, Wikström K, González-Gil EM, Moreno L (2023) Do parental risk factors for type 2 diabetes predict offspring risk of overweight and obesity? The Feel4Diabetes study. Nutrition 107:111900
179. Yang J, Qian J, Qu Y, Zhan Y, Yue H, Ma H, Li X, Man D, Wu H, Huang P (2023) Pre-pregnancy body mass index and risk of maternal or infant complications with gestational diabetes mellitus as a mediator: a multicenter, longitudinal cohort study in China. Diabetes Res Clin Pract 110619:110619
180. Mehta SH, Kruger M, Sokol RJ (2012) Is maternal diabetes a risk factor for childhood obesity? J Matern Fetal Neonatal Med 25:41–44
181. Godfrey KM, Reynolds RM, Prescott SL, Nyirenda M, Jaddoe VW, Eriksson JG, Broekman BF (2017) Influence of maternal obesity on the long-term health of offspring. Lancet Diabetes Endocrinol 5:53–64
182. Sebire N, Jolly M, Harris J, Regan L, Robinson S (2001) Is maternal underweight really a risk factor for adverse pregnancy outcome? A population-based study in London. Br J Obstet Gynaecol 108:61–66
183. Brown RG, Marchesi JR, Lee YS, Smith A, Lehne B, Kindinger LM, Terzidou V, Holmes E, Nicholson JK, Bennett PR (2018) Vaginal dysbiosis increases risk of preterm fetal membrane rupture, neonatal sepsis and is exacerbated by erythromycin. BMC Med 16:1–15
184. MacIntyre DA, Chandiramani M, Lee YS, Kindinger L, Smith A, Angelopoulos N, Lehne B, Arulkumaran S, Brown R, Teoh TG (2015) The vaginal microbiome during pregnancy and the postpartum period in a European population. Sci Rep 5:1–9
185. O'Hanlon DE, Moench TR, Cone RA (2013) Vaginal pH and microbicidal lactic acid when lactobacilli dominate the microbiota. PLoS One 8:e80074

186. Freitas AC, Chaban B, Bocking A, Rocco M, Yang S, Hill JE, Money DM (2017) The vaginal microbiome of pregnant women is less rich and diverse, with lower prevalence of Mollicutes, compared to non-pregnant women. Sci Rep 7:1–16
187. Romero R, Hassan SS, Gajer P, Tarca AL, Fadrosh DW, Nikita L, Galuppi M, Lamont RF, Chaemsaithong P, Miranda J (2014) The composition and stability of the vaginal microbiota of normal pregnant women is different from that of non-pregnant women. Microbiome 2:1–19
188. Mesa MD, Loureiro B, Iglesia I, Fernandez Gonzalez S, Llurba Olivé E, Garcia Algar O, Solana MJ, Cabero Perez MJ, Sainz T, Martinez L (2020) The evolving microbiome from pregnancy to early infancy: a comprehensive review. Nutrients 12:133
189. Gonzalez-Perez G, Hicks AL, Tekieli TM, Radens CM, Williams BL, Lamousé-Smith ES (2016) Maternal antibiotic treatment impacts development of the neonatal intestinal microbiome and antiviral immunity. J Immunol 196:3768–3779
190. Nyangahu DD, Lennard KS, Brown BP, Darby MG, Wendoh JM, Havyarimana E, Smith P, Butcher J, Stintzi A, Mulder N (2018) Disruption of maternal gut microbiota during gestation alters offspring microbiota and immunity. Microbiome 6:1–10
191. Kim H, Sitarik AR, Woodcroft K, Johnson CC, Zoratti E (2019) Birth mode, breastfeeding, pet exposure, and antibiotic use: associations with the gut microbiome and sensitization in children. Curr Allergy Asthma Rep 19:1–9
192. McLean C, Jun S, Kozyrskyj A (2019) Impact of maternal smoking on the infant gut microbiota and its association with child overweight: a scoping review. World J Pediatr 15:341–349
193. Golubnitschaja O, Liskova A, Koklesova L, Samec M, Biringer K, Büsselberg D, Podbielska H, Kunin AA, Evsevyeva ME, Shapira N (**2021**) Caution,"normal" BMI: health risks associated with potentially masked individual underweight—EPMA Position Paper 2021. EPMA J 12:243–264
194. Wang W, Yan Y, Guo Z, Hou H, Garcia M, Tan X, Anto EO, Mahara G, Zheng Y, Li B (2021) All around suboptimal health—a joint position paper of the suboptimal health study consortium and European Association for Predictive, preventive and personalised medicine. *EPMA J* 12:403–433
195. Koklesova L, Mazurakova A, Samec M, Kudela E, Biringer K, Kubatka P, Golubnitschaja O (2022) Mitochondrial health quality control: measurements and interpretation in the framework of predictive, preventive, and personalized medicine. EPMA J 13:177–193
196. Kropp M, Golubnitschaja O, Mazurakova A, Koklesova L, Sargheini N, Vo T-TKS, de Clerck E, Polivka J Jr, Potuznik P, Polivka J (2023) Diabetic retinopathy as the leading cause of blindness and early predictor of cascading complications—risks and mitigation. EPMA J 14:21–42
197. Mazurakova A, Samec M, Koklesova L, Biringer K, Kudela E, Al-Ishaq RK, Pec M, Giordano FA, Büsselberg D, Kubatka P (2022) Anti-prostate cancer protection and therapy in the framework of predictive, preventive and personalised medicine—comprehensive effects of phytochemicals in primary, secondary and tertiary care. EPMA J 13:461–486
198. Lin W-Y, Lin J-H, Kuo Y-W, Chiang P-FR, Ho H-H (2022) Probiotics and their metabolites reduce oxidative stress in middle-aged mice. Curr Microbiol 79:104
199. Lee JY, Kang C-H (2022) Probiotics alleviate oxidative stress in H2O2-exposed hepatocytes and t-BHP-induced C57BL/6 mice. Microorganisms 10:234
200. Balcázar JL, De Blas I, Ruiz-Zarzuela I, Vendrell D, Gironés O, Muzquiz JL (2007) Enhancement of the immune response and protection induced by probiotic lactic acid bacteria against furunculosis in rainbow trout (Oncorhynchus mykiss). FEMS Immunol Med Microbiol 51:185–193
201. Rashid SK, Khodja NI, Auger C, Alhosin M, Boehm N, Oswald-Mammosser M, Schini-Kerth VB (2014) Probiotics (VSL# 3) prevent endothelial dysfunction in rats with portal hypertension: role of the angiotensin system. PLoS One 9:e97458
202. Asemi Z, Zare Z, Shakeri H, Sabihi S-S, Esmaillzadeh A (2013) Effect of multispecies probiotic supplements on metabolic profiles, hs-CRP, and oxidative stress in patients with type 2 diabetes. Ann Nutr Metab 63:1–9

203. Amaretti A, Di Nunzio M, Pompei A, Raimondi S, Rossi M, Bordoni A (2013) Antioxidant properties of potentially probiotic bacteria: in vitro and in vivo activities. Appl Microbiol Biotechnol 97:809–817
204. Singh RK, Chang H-W, Yan D, Lee KM, Ucmak D, Wong K, Abrouk M, Farahnik B, Nakamura M, Zhu TH (2017) Influence of diet on the gut microbiome and implications for human health. J Transl Med 15:1–17
205. Wu Y, Wang B, Xu H, Tang L, Li Y, Gong L, Wang Y, Li W (2019) Probiotic bacillus attenuates oxidative stress-induced intestinal injury via p38-mediated autophagy. Front Microbiol 10:2185
206. Kim H, Kim J-S, Kim Y, Jeong Y, Kim J-E, Paek N-S, Kang C-H (2020) Antioxidant and probiotic properties of lactobacilli and Bifidobacteria of human origins. Biotechnol Bioprocess Eng 25:421–430
207. Zheng Y, Zhang L, Bonfili L, de Vivo L, Eleuteri AM, Bellesi M (2023) Probiotics supplementation attenuates inflammation and oxidative stress induced by chronic sleep restriction. Nutrients 15:1518
208. Alkushi AG, Elazab ST, Abdelfattah-Hassan A, Mahfouz H, Salem GA, Sheraiba NI, Mohamed EA, Attia MS, El-Shetry ES, Saleh AA (2022) Multi-strain-probiotic-loaded nanoparticles reduced colon inflammation and orchestrated the expressions of tight junction, NLRP3 Inflammasome and Caspase-1 genes in DSS-induced colitis model. Pharmaceutics 14:1183
209. El-Ghazely M, Mahmoud W, Atia M, Eldip E (2016) Effect of probiotic administration in the therapy of pediatric thermal burn. Ann Burns Fire Disasters 29:268
210. Togo C, Zidorio AP, Gonçalves V, Botelho P, de Carvalho K, Dutra E (2022) Does probiotic consumption enhance wound healing? A systematic review. Nutrients 14:111
211. Esposito C, Roberti A, Turrà F, Cerulo M, Severino G, Settimi A, Escolino M (2018) Frequency of antibiotic-associated diarrhea and related complications in pediatric patients who underwent hypospadias repair: a comparative study using probiotics vs placebo. Probiotics Antimicrob Proteins 10:323–328
212. Mayes T, Gottschlich MM, James LE, Allgeier C, Weitz J, Kagan RJ (2015) Clinical safety and efficacy of probiotic administration following burn injury. J Burn Care Res 36:92–99
213. Mohseni S, Bayani M, Bahmani F, Tajabadi-Ebrahimi M, Bayani MA, Jafari P, Asemi Z (2018) The beneficial effects of probiotic administration on wound healing and metabolic status in patients with diabetic foot ulcer: a randomized, double-blind, placebo-controlled trial. Diabetes Metab Res Rev 34:e2970
214. Knackstedt R, Knackstedt T, Gatherwright J (2020) The role of topical probiotics on wound healing: a review of animal and human studies. Int Wound J 17:1687–1694
215. Twetman S, Pedersen AML, Yucel-Lindberg T (2018) Probiotic supplements containing lactobacillus reuteri does not affect the levels of matrix metalloproteinases and interferons in oral wound healing. BMC Res Notes 11:1–5
216. Wälivaara D-Å, Sjögren I, Gerasimcik N, Yucel-Lindberg T, Twetman S, Abrahamsson P (2019) Effects of lactobacillus reuteri-containing lozenges on healing after surgical removal of mandibular third molars: a randomised controlled trial. Benefic Microbes 10:653–659
217. Partlow J, Blikslager A, Matthews C, Law M, Daniels J, Baker R, Labens R (2016) Effect of topically applied saccharomyces boulardii on the healing of acute porcine wounds: a preliminary study. BMC Res Notes 9:1–7
218. Kassaian N, Feizi A, Aminorroaya A, Ebrahimi MT, Norouzi A, Amini M (2019) Effects of probiotics and synbiotic on lipid profiles in adults at risk of type 2 diabetes: a double-blind randomized controlled clinical trial. Funct Food Health Dis 9:494–507
219. Rittiphairoj T, Pongpirul K, Janchot K, Mueller NT, Li T (2021) Probiotics contribute to glycemic control in patients with type 2 diabetes mellitus: a systematic review and meta-analysis. Adv Nutr 12:722–734

220. Tonucci LB, Dos Santos KMO, de Oliveira LL, Ribeiro SMR, Martino HSD (2017) Clinical application of probiotics in type 2 diabetes mellitus: a randomized, double-blind, placebo-controlled study. Clin Nutr 36:85–92
221. Cardinali N, Bauman C, Rodriguez Ayala F, Grau R (2020) Two cases of type 2 diabetes mellitus successfully treated with probiotics. Clin Case Rep 8:3119–3124
222. Barreto FM, Simão ANC, Morimoto HK, Lozovoy MAB, Dichi I, da Silva Miglioranza LH (2014) Beneficial effects of lactobacillus plantarum on glycemia and homocysteine levels in postmenopausal women with metabolic syndrome. Nutrition 30:939–942
223. Hariri M, Salehi R, Feizi A, Mirlohi M, Ghiasvand R, Habibi N (2015) A randomized, double-blind, placebo-controlled, clinical trial on probiotic soy milk and soy milk: effects on epigenetics and oxidative stress in patients with type II diabetes. Genes Nutr 10:1–8
224. Pavlidou E, Fasoulas A, Mantzorou M, Giaginis C (2022) Clinical evidence on the potential beneficial effects of probiotics and prebiotics in cardiovascular disease. Int J Mol Sci 23:15898
225. Ding L-N, Ding W-Y, Ning J, Wang Y, Yan Y, Wang Z-B (2021) Effects of probiotic supplementation on inflammatory markers and glucose homeostasis in adults with type 2 diabetes mellitus: a systematic review and meta-analysis. Front Pharmacol 12:770861
226. Corb Aron RA, Abid A, Vesa CM, Nechifor AC, Behl T, Ghitea TC, Munteanu MA, Fratila O, Andronie-Cioara FL, Toma MM (2021) Recognizing the benefits of pre–/probiotics in metabolic syndrome and type 2 diabetes mellitus considering the influence of akkermansia muciniphila as a key gut bacterium. Microorganisms 9:618
227. Plovier H, Everard A, Druart C, Depommier C, Van Hul M, Geurts L, Chilloux J, Ottman N, Duparc T, Lichtenstein L (2017) A purified membrane protein from Akkermansia muciniphila or the pasteurized bacterium improves metabolism in obese and diabetic mice. Nat Med 23:107–113
228. Perraudeau F, McMurdie P, Bullard J, Cheng A, Cutcliffe C, Deo A, Eid J, Gines J, Iyer M, Justice N (2020) Improvements to postprandial glucose control in subjects with type 2 diabetes: a multicenter, double blind, randomized placebo-controlled trial of a novel probiotic formulation. BMJ Open Diabetes Res Care 8:e001319
229. Ejtahed H, Mohtadi-Nia J, Homayouni-Rad A, Niafar M, Asghari-Jafarabadi M, Mofid V, Akbarian-Moghari A (2011) Effect of probiotic yogurt containing lactobacillus acidophilus and Bifidobacterium lactis on lipid profile in individuals with type 2 diabetes mellitus. J Dairy Sci 94:3288–3294
230. Raygan F, Rezavandi Z, Bahmani F, Ostadmohammadi V, Mansournia MA, Tajabadi-Ebrahimi M, Borzabadi S, Asemi Z (2018) The effects of probiotic supplementation on metabolic status in type 2 diabetic patients with coronary heart disease. Diabetol Metab Syndr 10:1–7
231. Tajabadi-Ebrahimi M, Sharifi N, Farrokhian A, Raygan F, Karamali F, Razzaghi R, Taheri S, Asemi Z (2017) A randomized controlled clinical trial investigating the effect of synbiotic administration on markers of insulin metabolism and lipid profiles in overweight type 2 diabetic patients with coronary heart disease. Exp Clin Endocrinol Diabetes 125:21–27
232. Nakajima K, Hata Y, Osono Y, Hamura M, Kobayashi S, Watanuki M (1995) Antihypertensive effect of extracts of lactobacillus casei in patients with hypertension. J Clin Biochem Nutr 18:181–187
233. Mobini R, Tremaroli V, Ståhlman M, Karlsson F, Levin M, Ljungberg M, Sohlin M, Bertéus Forslund H, Perkins R, Bäckhed F (2017) Metabolic effects of L actobacillus reuteri DSM 17938 in people with type 2 diabetes: a randomized controlled trial. Diabetes Obes Metab 19:579–589
234. Tripolt N, Leber B, Blattl D, Eder M, Wonisch W, Scharnagl H, Stojakovic T, Obermayer-Pietsch B, Wascher T, Pieber T (2013) Effect of supplementation with lactobacillus casei Shirota on insulin sensitivity, β-cell function, and markers of endothelial function and inflammation in subjects with metabolic syndrome—a pilot study. J Dairy Sci 96:89–95

235. Majewska K, Kręgielska-Narożna M, Jakubowski H, Szulińska M, Bogdański P (2020) The multispecies probiotic effectively reduces homocysteine concentration in obese women: a randomized double-blind placebo-controlled study. J Clin Med 9:998
236. Valentini L, Pinto A, Bourdel-Marchasson I, Ostan R, Brigidi P, Turroni S, Hrelia S, Hrelia P, Bereswill S, Fischer A (2015) Impact of personalized diet and probiotic supplementation on inflammation, nutritional parameters and intestinal microbiota–the "RISTOMED project": randomized controlled trial in healthy older people. Clin Nutr 34:593–602
237. Morshedi M, Hashemi R, Moazzen S, Sahebkar A, Hosseinifard E-S (2019) Immunomodulatory and anti-inflammatory effects of probiotics in multiple sclerosis: a systematic review. J Neuroinflammation 16:1–11
238. Kouchaki E, Tamtaji OR, Salami M, Bahmani F, Kakhaki RD, Akbari E, Tajabadi-Ebrahimi M, Jafari P, Asemi Z (2017) Clinical and metabolic response to probiotic supplementation in patients with multiple sclerosis: a randomized, double-blind, placebo-controlled trial. Clin Nutr 36:1245–1249
239. Salami M, Kouchaki E, Asemi Z, Tamtaji OR (2019) How probiotic bacteria influence the motor and mental behaviors as well as immunological and oxidative biomarkers in multiple sclerosis? A double blind clinical trial. J Funct Foods 52:8–13
240. Śliżewska K, Markowiak-Kopeć P, Śliżewska W (2021) The role of probiotics in cancer prevention. Cancer 13:20
241. Rafter J, Bennett M, Caderni G, Clune Y, Hughes R, Karlsson PC, Klinder A, O'Riordan M, O'Sullivan GC, Pool-Zobel B (2007) Dietary synbiotics reduce cancer risk factors in polypectomized and colon cancer patients. Am J Clin Nutr 85:488–496
242. Zhong L, Zhang X, Covasa M (2014) Emerging roles of lactic acid bacteria in protection against colorectal cancer. World J Gastroenterol: WJG 20:7878
243. Ohigashi S, Hoshino Y, Ohde S, Onodera H (2011) Functional outcome, quality of life, and efficacy of probiotics in postoperative patients with colorectal cancer. Surg Today 41:1200–1206
244. Liu Z, Qin H, Yang Z, Xia Y, Liu W, Yang J, Jiang Y, Zhang H, Yang Z, Wang Y (2011) Randomised clinical trial: the effects of perioperative probiotic treatment on barrier function and post-operative infectious complications in colorectal cancer surgery–a double-blind study. Aliment Pharmacol Ther 33:50–63
245. Liu Z-H, Huang M-J, Zhang X-W, Wang L, Huang N-Q, Peng H, Lan P, Peng J-S, Yang Z, Xia Y (2013) The effects of perioperative probiotic treatment on serum zonulin concentration and subsequent postoperative infectious complications after colorectal cancer surgery: a double-center and double-blind randomized clinical trial. Am J Clin Nutr 97:117–126
246. Österlund P, Ruotsalainen T, Korpela R, Saxelin M, Ollus A, Valta P, Kouri M, Elomaa I, Joensuu H (2007) Lactobacillus supplementation for diarrhoea related to chemotherapy of colorectal cancer: a randomised study. Br J Cancer 97:1028–1034
247. Pala V, Sieri S, Berrino F, Vineis P, Sacerdote C, Palli D, Masala G, Panico S, Mattiello A, Tumino R (2011) Yogurt consumption and risk of colorectal cancer in the Italian European prospective investigation into cancer and nutrition cohort. Int J Cancer 129:2712–2719
248. Lu K, Dong S, Wu X, Jin R, Chen H et al (2021) Front Oncol 11:638148
249. Ohara T, Yoshino K, Kitajima M (2010) Possibility of preventing colorectal carcinogenesis with probiotics. Hepato-Gastroenterology 57:1411–1415
250. Kotzampassi K, Stavrou G, Damoraki G, Tsaousi G (2015) A four-probiotics regimen reduces postoperative complications after colorectal surgery: a randomized, vol 39, p 2776
251. Zhang J-W, Du P, Yang B-R, Gao J, Fang W-J, Ying C-M (2012) Preoperative probiotics decrease postoperative infectious complications of colorectal cancer. Am J Med Sci 343:199–205
252. El-Nezami HS, Polychronaki NN, Ma J, Zhu H, Ling W, Salminen EK, Juvonen RO, Salminen SJ, Poussa T, Mykkänen HM (2006) Probiotic supplementation reduces a biomarker for increased risk of liver cancer in young men from southern China. Am J Clin Nutr 83:1199–1203

253. Rasouli BS, Ghadimi-Darsajini A, Nekouian R, Iragian G-R (2017) In vitro activity of probiotic lactobacillus reuteri against gastric cancer progression by downregulation of urokinase plasminogen activator/urokinase plasminogen activator receptor gene expression. J Cancer Res Ther 13:246–251
254. Ghoneum M, Felo N (2015) Selective induction of apoptosis in human gastric cancer cells by lactobacillus kefiri (PFT), a novel kefir product. Oncol Rep 34:1659–1666
255. Chitapanarux I, Chitapanarux T, Traisathit P, Kudumpee S, Tharavichitkul E, Lorvidhaya V (2010) Randomized controlled trial of live lactobacillus acidophilus plus bifidobacterium bifidum in prophylaxis of diarrhea during radiotherapy in cervical cancer patients. Radiat Oncol 5:1–6
256. Ohashi Y, Nakai S, Tsukamoto T, Masumori N, Akaza H, Miyanaga N, Kitamura T, Kawabe K, Kotake T, Kuroda M (2002) Habitual intake of lactic acid bacteria and risk reduction of bladder cancer. Urol Int 68:273–280
257. Toi M, Hirota S, Tomotaki A, Sato N, Hozumi Y, Anan K, Nagashima T, Tokuda Y, Masuda N, Ohsumi S (2013) Probiotic beverage with soy isoflavone consumption for breast cancer prevention: a case-control study. Curr Nutr Food Sci 9:194–200
258. Mendoza L (2019) Potential effect of probiotics in the treatment of breast cancer. Oncol Rev 13:13
259. Che B, Zhang W, Xu S, Yin J, He J, Huang T, Li W, Yu Y, Tang K (2021) Prostate microbiota and prostate cancer: a new trend in treatment. *Frontiers*. Oncology 11:5260
260. Fujita K, Matsushita M, De Velasco MA, Hatano K, Minami T, Nonomura N, Uemura H (2023) The gut-prostate Axis: a new perspective of prostate cancer biology through the gut microbiome. Cancer 15:1375
261. Fatahi A, Soleimani N, Afrough P (2021) Anticancer activity of kefir on glioblastoma cancer cell as a new treatment. Int J Food Sci 2021:1
262. König RS, Albrich WC, Kahlert CR, Bahr LS, Löber U, Vernazza P, Scheibenbogen C, Forslund SK (2022) The gut microbiome in myalgic encephalomyelitis (ME)/chronic fatigue syndrome (CFS). Front Immunol 12:628741
263. Corbitt M, Campagnolo N, Staines D, Marshall-Gradisnik S (2018) A systematic review of probiotic interventions for gastrointestinal symptoms and irritable bowel syndrome in chronic fatigue syndrome/myalgic encephalomyelitis (CFS/ME). Probiotics Antimicrob Proteins 10:466–477
264. Mohammed AT, Khattab M, Ahmed AM, Turk T, Sakr N, Khalil AM, Abdelhalim M, Sawaf B, Hirayama K, Huy NT (2017) The therapeutic effect of probiotics on rheumatoid arthritis: a systematic review and meta-analysis of randomized control trials. Clin Rheumatol 36:2697–2707
265. Pan H, Guo R, Ju Y, Wang Q, Zhu J, Xie Y, Zheng Y, Li T, Liu Z, Lu L (2019) A single bacterium restores the microbiome dysbiosis to protect bones from destruction in a rat model of rheumatoid arthritis. Microbiome 7:1–11
266. Lei M, Guo C, Wang D, Zhang C, Hua L (2017) The effect of probiotic lactobacillus casei Shirota on knee osteoarthritis: a randomised double-blind, placebo-controlled clinical trial. Benefic Microbes 8:697–703
267. Alipour H, Gazerani P, Heidari M, Dardmeh F (2021) Modulatory effect of probiotic lactobacillus rhamnosus PB01 on mechanical sensitivity in a female diet-induced obesity model. Pain Res Manag 2021:1
268. Nurrahma BA, Tsao S-P, Wu C-H, Yeh T-H, Hsieh P-S, Panunggal B, Huang H-Y (2021) Probiotic supplementation facilitates recovery of 6-OHDA-induced motor deficit via improving mitochondrial function and energy metabolism. Front Aging Neurosci 13:668775
269. Ren T, Zhu L, Shen Y, Mou Q, Lin T, Feng H (2019) Protection of hepatocyte mitochondrial function by blueberry juice and probiotics via SIRT1 regulation in non-alcoholic fatty liver disease. Food Funct 10:1540–1551

270. Bernini LJ, Simão ANC, Alfieri DF, Lozovoy MAB, Mari NL, de Souza CHB, Dichi I, Costa GN (2016) Beneficial effects of Bifidobacterium lactis on lipid profile and cytokines in patients with metabolic syndrome: a randomized trial. Effects of probiotics on metabolic syndrome. Nutrition 32:716–719
271. Wu H, Chiou J (2021) Potential benefits of probiotics and prebiotics for coronary heart disease and stroke. Nutrients 13:2878
272. Malik M, Suboc TM, Tyagi S, Salzman N, Wang J, Ying R, Tanner MJ, Kakarla M, Baker JE, Widlansky ME (2018) Lactobacillus plantarum 299v supplementation improves vascular endothelial function and reduces inflammatory biomarkers in men with stable coronary artery disease. Circ Res 123:1091–1102
273. Hofeld BC, Puppala VK, Tyagi S, Ahn KW, Anger A, Jia S, Salzman NH, Hessner MJ, Widlansky ME (2021) Lactobacillus plantarum 299v probiotic supplementation in men with stable coronary artery disease suppresses systemic inflammation. Sci Rep 11:1–11
274. Naruszewicz M, Johansson M-L, Zapolska-Downar D, Bukowska H (2002) Effect of lactobacillus plantarum 299v on cardiovascular disease risk factors in smokers. Am J Clin Nutr 76:1249–1255
275. Moludi J, Kafil HS, Qaisar SA, Gholizadeh P, Alizadeh M, Vayghyan HJ (2021) Effect of probiotic supplementation along with calorie restriction on metabolic endotoxemia, and inflammation markers in coronary artery disease patients: a double blind placebo controlled randomized clinical trial. Nutr J 20:1–10
276. Moludi J, Khedmatgozar H, Nachvak SM, Abdollahzad H, Moradinazar M, Sadeghpour Tabaei A (2022) The effects of co-administration of probiotics and prebiotics on chronic inflammation, and depression symptoms in patients with coronary artery diseases: a randomized clinical trial. Nutr Neurosci 25:1659–1668
277. Brantsæter AL, Myhre R, Haugen M, Myking S, Sengpiel V, Magnus P, Jacobsson B, Meltzer HM (2011) Intake of probiotic food and risk of preeclampsia in primiparous women: the Norwegian mother and child cohort study. Am J Epidemiol 174:807–815
278. Jones ML, Martoni CJ, Di Pietro E, Simon RR, Prakash S (2012) Evaluation of clinical safety and tolerance of a lactobacillus reuteri NCIMB 30242 supplement capsule: a randomized control trial. Regul Toxicol Pharmacol 63:313–320
279. Khalesi S, Sun J, Buys N, Jayasinghe R (2014) Effect of probiotics on blood pressure: a systematic review and meta-analysis of randomized, controlled trials. Hypertension 64:897–903
280. Lopez-Santamarina A, Gonzalez EG, Lamas A, Mondragon ADC, Regal P, Miranda JM (2021) Probiotics as a possible strategy for the prevention and treatment of allergies. A narrative review. Foods 10:701
281. Isolauri E, Arvola T, Sütas Y, Moilanen E, Salminen S (2000) Probiotics in the management of atopic eczema. Clin Exp Allergy 30:1605–1610
282. Rosenfeldt V, Benfeldt E, Nielsen SD, Michaelsen KF, Jeppesen DL, Valerius NH, Paerregaard A (2003) Effect of probiotic lactobacillus strains in children with atopic dermatitis. J Allergy Clin Immunol 111:389–395
283. Viljanen M, Savilahti E, Haahtela T, Juntunen-Backman K, Korpela R, Poussa T, Tuure T, Kuitunen M (2005) Probiotics in the treatment of atopic eczema/dermatitis syndrome in infants: a double-blind placebo-controlled trial. Allergy 60:494–500
284. Weston S, Halbert A, Richmond P, Prescott SL (2005) Effects of probiotics on atopic dermatitis: a randomised controlled trial. Arch Dis Child 90:892–897
285. Prakoeswa C, Herwanto N, Prameswari R, Astari L, Sawitri S, Hidayati A, Indramaya D, Kusumowidagdo E, Surono I (2017) Lactobacillus plantarum IS-10506 supplementation reduced SCORAD in children with atopic dermatitis. Benefic Microbes 8:833–840
286. Yang H-J, Min TK, Lee HW, Pyun BY (2014) Efficacy of probiotic therapy on atopic dermatitis in children: a randomized, double-blind, placebo-controlled trial. Allergy, Asthma Immunol Res 6:208–215
287. Sistek D, Kelly R, Wickens K, Stanley T, Fitzharris P, Crane J (2006) Is the effect of probiotics on atopic dermatitis confined to food sensitized children? Clin Exp Allergy 36:629–633

288. Soh S, Aw M, Gerez I, Chong Y, Rauff M, Ng Y, Wong H, Pai N, Lee B, Shek LC (2009) Probiotic supplementation in the first 6 months of life in at risk Asian infants–effects on eczema and atopic sensitization at the age of 1 year. Clin Exp Allergy 39:571–578
289. Brouwer M, Wolt-Plompen S, Dubois A, Van Der Heide S, Jansen D, Hoijer M, Kauffman H, Duiverman E (2006) No effects of probiotics on atopic dermatitis in infancy: a randomized placebo-controlled trial. Clin Exp Allergy 36:899–906
290. Taylor AL, Dunstan JA, Prescott SL (2007) Probiotic supplementation for the first 6 months of life fails to reduce the risk of atopic dermatitis and increases the risk of allergen sensitization in high-risk children: a randomized controlled trial. J Allergy Clin Immunol 119:184–191
291. Mennini M, Dahdah L, Artesani MC, Fiocchi A, Martelli A (2017) Probiotics in asthma and allergy prevention. Front Pediatr 5:165
292. Gorissen D, Rutten N, Oostermeijer C, Niers L, Hoekstra M, Rijkers G, Van Der Ent C (2014) Preventive effects of selected probiotic strains on the development of asthma and allergic rhinitis in childhood. The panda study. Clin Exp Allergy 44:1431–1433
293. Abrahamsson TR, Jakobsson T, Björksten B, Oldaeus G, Jenmalm MC (2013) No effect of probiotics on respiratory allergies: a seven-year follow-up of a randomized controlled trial in infancy. Pediatr Allergy Immunol 24:556–561
294. Cabana MD, McKean M, Caughey AB, Fong L, Lynch S, Wong A, Leong R, Boushey HA, Hilton JF (2017) Early probiotic supplementation for eczema and asthma prevention: a randomized controlled trial. Pediatrics 140(3):e20163000
295. De Angelis M, Siragusa S, Vacca M, Di Cagno R, Cristofori F, Schwarm M, Pelzer S, Flügel M, Speckmann B, Francavilla R (2021) Selection of gut-resistant bacteria and construction of microbial consortia for improving gluten digestion under simulated gastrointestinal conditions. Nutrients 13:992
296. Karakula-Juchnowicz H, Rog J, Juchnowicz D, Łoniewski I, Skonieczna-Żydecka K, Krukow P, Futyma-Jedrzejewska M, Kaczmarczyk M (2019) The study evaluating the effect of probiotic supplementation on the mental status, inflammation, and intestinal barrier in major depressive disorder patients using gluten-free or gluten-containing diet (SANGUT study): a 12-week, randomized, double-blind, and placebo-controlled clinical study protocol. Nutr J 18:1–13
297. Olivares M, Castillejo G, Varea V, Sanz Y (2014) Double-blind, randomised, placebo-controlled intervention trial to evaluate the effects of Bifidobacterium longum CECT 7347 in children with newly diagnosed coeliac disease. Br J Nutr 112:30–40
298. Klemenak M, Dolinšek J, Langerholc T, Di Gioia D, Mičetić-Turk D (2015) Administration of Bifidobacterium breve decreases the production of TNF-α in children with celiac disease. Dig Dis Sci 60:3386–3392
299. Wagh SK, Lammers KM, Padul MV, Rodriguez-Herrera A, Dodero VI (2022) Celiac disease and possible dietary interventions: from enzymes and probiotics to Postbiotics and viruses. Int J Mol Sci 23:11748
300. Primec M, Klemenak M, Di Gioia D, Aloisio I, Cionci NB, Quagliariello A, Gorenjak M, Mičetić-Turk D, Langerholc T (2019) Clinical intervention using Bifidobacterium strains in celiac disease children reveals novel microbial modulators of TNF-α and short-chain fatty acids. Clin Nutr 38:1373–1381
301. De Angelis M, Rizzello CG, Fasano A, Clemente MG, De Simone C, Silano M, De Vincenzi M, Losito I, Gobbetti M (2006) VSL# 3 probiotic preparation has the capacity to hydrolyze gliadin polypeptides responsible for celiac sprue probiotics and gluten intolerance. Biochim Biophys Acta 1762:80–93

# Conventional and Traditional Medicine: A "Hand-in-Hand" Collaboration Benefiting the Patient and Healthcare at Large

**Yulu Zheng, Zheng Guo, and Xiuhua Guo**

## Abbreviations

| | |
|---|---|
| NCDs | Non-communicable chronic diseases |
| PPPM/3PM | Predictive, preventive, and personalized medicine |
| SHS | Suboptimal health status |
| SHSQ-25 | Suboptimal health status questionnaire-25 |
| TCM | Traditional Chinese medicine |

## 1 Modern Western Medicine

Modern western medicine, which can be stretched back to Greek medicine thousands of years ago and is the foundation of many of the modern health systems in the world [1]. Western medicine is defined as "A system in which medical doctors and other healthcare professionals (such as nurses, pharmacists, and therapists) treat symptoms and diseases using drugs, radiation, or surgery". The focus of modern Western medicine is symptomatic treatment. Related principles mainly included physical examinations based on the patient's symptoms and evidence-based diagnosis of a disease with clinically proven therapy [1]. With the rapid

Y. Zheng (✉) · Z. Guo
Centre for Precision Health, Edith Cowan University, Joondalup, WA, Australia
e-mail: yuluz@our.ecu.edu.au; zguo0@our.ecu.edu.au

X. Guo
Beijing Key Laboratory of Clinical Epidemiology, School of Public Health, Capital Medical University, Beijing, China
e-mail: statguo@ccmu.edu.cn



W. Wang (ed.), *All Around Suboptimal Health*, Advances in Predictive, Preventive and Personalised Medicine 18,
https://doi.org/10.1007/978-3-031-46891-9_16

progress in industrialization, modern Western medicine has become the dominant stream in the medical field. It achieved a significant milestone in fighting infectious diseases with targeted therapies [2–4]. With this comes a longer life expectancy, and we realize that single-molecule medications cannot cope with more complicated diseases or disorders, such as age-related chronic diseases, immune diseases, and psychological illnesses. Moreover, most Western medicine is reactive medicine that diagnoses the disease after the onset, which is a late response from the perspective of preventative medicine [5]. Therefore, it is imperative to solve complicated health issues by applying comprehensive medical practices. Traditional Chinese medicine, which is a representative form of Eastern medicine, is a more personalized medicine that can provide more preventative care compared with Western medicine [5].

## 2 Eastern Medicine

Eastern medicine, occasionally referred to as "Traditional and Complementary Medicine", "Oriental medicine" or "alternative medicine", is the most ancient codified system of medicine that can be traced back more than 2000 years [6]. Traditional and complementary medicine has been playing an essential role in lifelong improvements in well-being and health [7]. According to the "Regional Framework for Harnessing Traditional and Complementary Medicine for Achieving Health and Well-being in the Western Pacific" reported by the World Health Organization, traditional and complementary medicine is suggested to have a supportive effect on the disease prevention and the management of long-term chronic conditions in primary healthcare settings [8]. The disease progress is generally complicated or accompanied by psychosomatic disturbances, and the prognosis of the disease is often affected by the environmental, social, and mental conditions of the patient. To improve public health interventions regarding health outcomes, a variety of efforts have been made. Related evidence-based interventions or therapies have been widely reported, and the summarized approaches are indicated in Fig. 1.

The basic philosophy of traditional and complementary medicine practitioners is to maximize the effectiveness and quality for the promotion of overall health status and well-being. Some traditional and complementary medicine, such as traditional Chinese medicine (TCM), Ayurveda [9], Bush medicine [6, 10], and Unani Tibb ("Greek Medicine" in Arabic) [11], are seeking, invoking, and restoring the balance of body elements. Taking the TCM as an example, the balance of "Yin" and "Yang" is a prerequisite for maintaining an overall health status for an individual [12]. Such framework usually relates to the whole person and applies complex patterns of disharmony or imbalance within the body for the disease diagnosis [12, 13]. Thus, TCM specifies the "disharmony pattern" and collects and compiles all the information about the physical and mental health conditions, i.e. the presented signs, functional and adaptive deficits, and other general characteristics of the patient [14]. The goal of TCM treatment is then to restore the individual's harmony by bringing

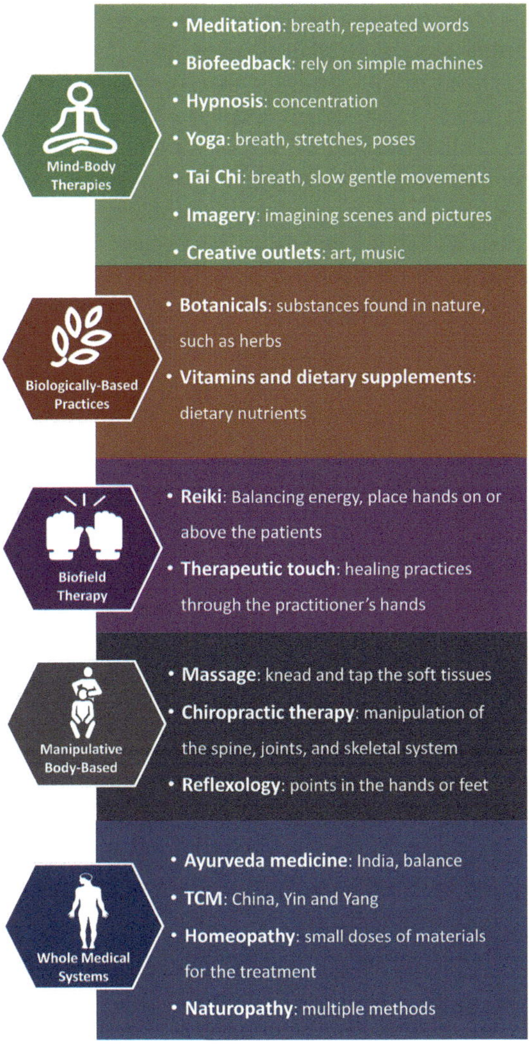


**Fig. 1** Main categories and example of traditional and complementary medicine

the organism back into balance [6]. However, TCM lacks knowledge of molecular mechanisms in the aetiology of the disease, as well as scientific proof of the effectiveness of treatment for patients.

## 3 Integrative Medicine—Western Medicine Meets Eastern Medicine

Integrative medicine, the combination of both modern western and traditional eastern complementary medicine practices, has been proven scientifically to be both reliable and efficient [15]. Integrative medicine tends to emphasize the patient's preferences and attempts to address the physical, mental, and spiritual aspects of health status [16]. Main types or therapies of integrative medicine involves modern medicine practices such as advanced diagnostic approaches and surgical treatments, as well as traditional complementary medicine practices like herbs, acupuncture, and food treatment [17]. As a result, multimodal interventions—treatments that include at least two interventions, such as physical rehabilitation, psychotherapy, healthy lifestyles, and complementary health technologies—are prioritized in integrative medicine. This in turn explains why integrative medicine places more of an emphasis on treating the whole person rather than, say, a particular organ system (Fig. 2).

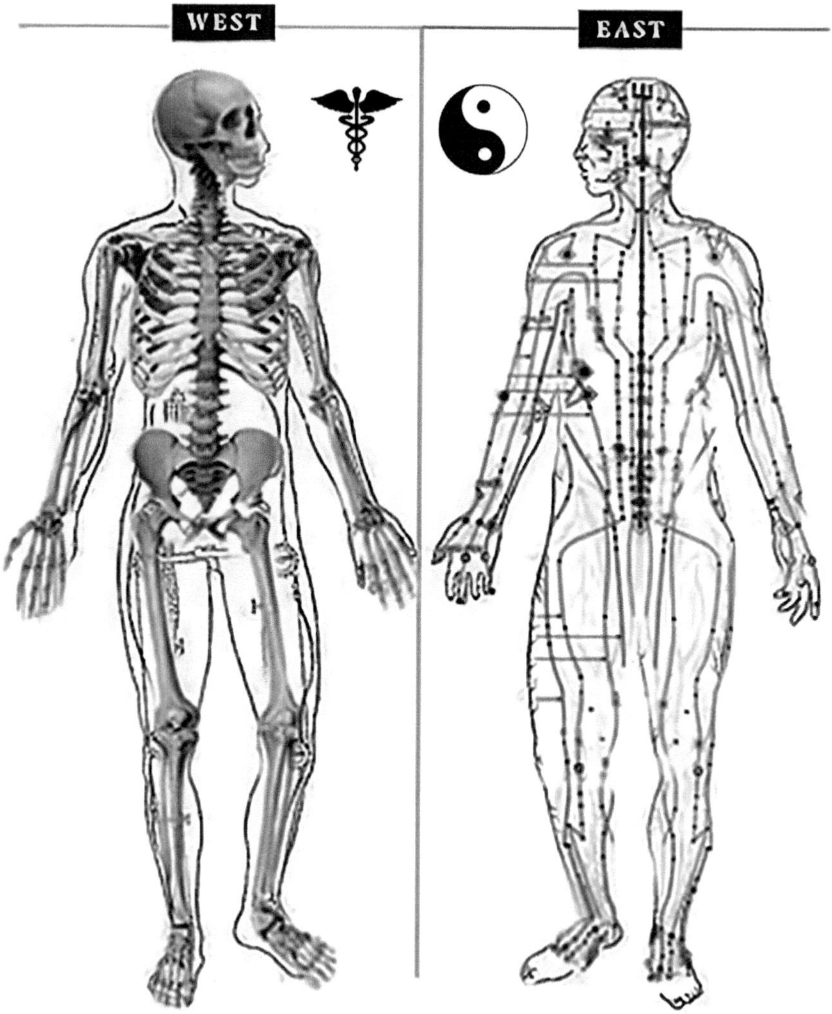


**Fig. 2** The hand-in-hand, modern-traditional, Western-Eastern strategy within the framework of predictive, preventive, and personalized medicine (PPPM/3PM)

## 4 Suboptimal Health Status: A Bridge Between Western and Eastern Medicine

In order to assess the physical condition between health and disease from the perspective of predictive, preventive, and personalized medicine (PPPM/3PM), our team proposed the concept of "Suboptimal Health Status" (SHS) from the unique expertise aspect of TCM, allowing a strong bridge between modern medicine and traditional medicine [14, 18]. At the same time, by fusing the benefits of modern medicine and TCM principles, our team has established a solid, efficient, and trustworthy tool called the "SHSQ-25" for assessing SHS and promoting greater personalization of preventive care [19, 20]. In addition, we have implemented multilingual translations of SHSQ-25, including Chinese, English, Russian, Korean, Arabic, Japanese, Portuguese, Thai, and Slovakian. This can support us overcome language barriers and enhance the usefulness of the tool, which will be helpful for further expanding its application to a wider range of people. The novel hybrid strategy combines the benefits of both modern medicine and TCM. In addition, the fusion of the two fields benefits patients and improves the resources and collective knowledge of a committed professional community, ensuring the reproducibility of TCM methods and results [21].

Practical application of SHSQ-25 in the general population makes SHS a new dimension of health in translational medicine [18]. According to the prior research, SHS has been associated with a variety of diseases, disorders, and pathological alterations, including the changes of intestinal microbiota [22], telomere length [23], mRNA expression level of glucocorticoid receptor $\alpha$ (GR$\alpha$) [24], cardiovascular health metrics [25], plasma cortisol [26], plasma catechol-amines [24], oxidative stress [27], blood transcriptome profiling [28], metabolites [5], plasma N-glycans profiling [29], and biological ageing [23], with an increased incidence of cardiovascular diseases [30], type 2 diabetes mellitus [31], metabolic syndrome [29], Parkinson's disease [32], systemic lupus erythematosus [33], rheumatoid arthritis [34], dyslipidemia [35], stroke [36], and preeclampsia [37]. Therefore, SHS has an essential role in predicting the pathogenesis and progression of non-communicable diseases.

Investigations in the past years have indicated that SHS is primarily influenced by the lifestyle-related factors [38]. With the rapid development of industrialization in modern society, the current social living environment and lifestyles of individuals have changed dramatically, for example, the diversification of transportation has reduced the level of physical activity, which has led to the increased risk of SHS. Additionally, people are facing stress in numerous aspects, which involves personal, family, and social pressures, changes in life circumstances, overwork, complex interpersonal relationships, and psychological stress [39]. Given the multiple risk factors described above, the early intervention of SHS within the framework of PPPM/3PM are thus necessary before the onset of the diseases. Correspondingly, many early-stage interventions in the TCM are widely acknowledged, such as traditional physical exercise (e.g. Baduanjin, Chinese martial arts,

Tai Chi, and Health Qigong Wu Qin Xi), moxibustion, cupping, massage, herbal medicine, and acupuncture [40, 41].

In more detail, for example, as one of the most common forms of qigong, Baduanjin exercise consists of eight separate and subtle movements [42]. While Wu Qin Xi is another type of traditional Chinese Qigong and also widely practiced, and it imitates the action and breathing movements of the five animals (deer, tiger, monkey, bear, and crane) and focuses on the unified regulation of body, mind, and breathing [43]. Other examples, such as moxibustion and cupping, are well-recognized complementary therapies. Moxibustion is one form of heat therapies involving burning plant materials named "moxa" on acupoints [44]. Cupping is one application of suction on the skin of the body to influence the fluid circulation and blood [45]. As a result, from the perspective of PPPM/3PM, it will be more crucial to prevent SHS using interventions from the TCM.

## 5 Conclusion, Expert Recommendations, and Future Perspective

In summary, both early detection and prevention of SHS can minimize the potential risk factors for SHS. This could potentially not only to improve individuals' health outcomes and quality of life, but also could help to reduce the economic burden of NCDs on the global healthcare system. As the PPPM/3PM concept achieves, this successful hand-in-hand, modern-traditional, Western-Eastern strategy of healthcare will provide a holistic and comprehensive way that benefits both the individual and the global healthcare system.

**Declaration of Interest Statement** Declarations of interest: none.

## References

1. Medibank. The origins of western and eastern medicine 2019. from https://www.medibank.com.au/livebetter/health-brief/health-insights/the-origins-of-western-and-eastern-medicine/#:~:text=Western%20(or%20'conventional'),continue%20to%20influence%20practice%20today
2. Doblhammer G, Kreft D, Dethloff A (2012) Life years gained. Long-term trends in mortality by causes of death in Germany and in an international perspective. Bundesgesundheitsbl Gesundheitsforsch Gesundheitsschutz 55(4):448–458
3. Yang G, Kong L, Zhao W, Wan X, Zhai Y, Chen LC, Koplan JP (2008) Emergence of chronic non-communicable diseases in China. Lancet 372(9650):1697–1705
4. Huicho L, Trelles M, Gonzales F, Mendoza W, Miranda J (2009) Mortality profiles in a country facing epidemiological transition: an analysis of registered data. BMC Public Health 9(1):1–13
5. Wang H, Tian Q, Zhang J, Liu H, Zhang X, Cao W, Zhang J, Anto EO, Li X, Wang X, Liu D, Zheng Y, Guo Z, Wu L, Song M, Wang Y, Wang W (2020) Population-based case-control study revealed metabolomic biomarkers of suboptimal health status in Chinese population-potential utility for innovative approach by predictive, preventive, and personalized medicine. EPMA J 11(2):147–160

6. Kaptchuk T (1982) The holistic logic of Chinese medicine. Sci Dig 90(11):32–34
7. Zhang M, Moalin M, Haenen G (2019) Connecting west and east. Int J Mol Sci 20(9):2333
8. WHO. Regional framework for harnessing traditional and complementary medicine for achieving health and well-being in the Western Pacific Regional Office for the Western Pacific. 2022, from: Regional framework for harnessing traditional and complementary medicine for achieving health and well-being in the Western Pacific
9. Nair PP, Nair PG, Pratap Shankar KM (2022) An Ayurvedic personalized prophylactic protocol in COVID-19. J Ayurved Integr Med 13(1):100351
10. Clarke P (2008) Aboriginal healing practices and Australian bush medicine. J Anthropol 33(1):3–38
11. Sheehan HE, Hussain S (2002) Unani Tibb: history, theory, and contemporary practice in South Asia. Ann Am Acad Pol Soc Sci 583(1):122–135
12. Kung Y-Y, Kuo TB, Lai C-T, Shen Y-C, Su Y-C, Yang CC (2021) Disclosure of suboptimal health status through traditional Chinese medicine-based body constitution and pulse patterns. Complement Ther Med 56:102607
13. Yun H, Hou L, Song M, Wang Y, Zakus D, Wu L, Wang W (2012) Genomics and traditional Chinese medicine: a new driver for novel molecular-targeted personalized medicine? Curr Pharmacogenomics Pers Med 10(1):16–21
14. Wang W, Russell A, Yan Y (2014) Traditional Chinese medicine and new concepts of predictive, preventive and personalized medicine in diagnosis and treatment of suboptimal health. EPMA J 5(1):4
15. Woods R. Eastern vs Western: history of medical practices 2021, from https://www.powerofprevention.com/eastern-vs-western-medicine/
16. NIH. Complementary and alternative medicine 2022, from https://www.cancer.gov/about-cancer/treatment/cam
17. Boehme K. Western, Eastern, Holistic and Integrative Medicine: What's the Difference? 2022, from: https://www.thedrakecenter.com/resources/materials/general/western-eastern-holistic-and-integrative-medicine-whats-difference
18. Wang W, Yan Y (2012) Suboptimal health: a new health dimension for translational medicine. Clin Transl Med 1(1):28
19. Yan YX, Dong J, Liu YQ, Yang XH, Li M, Shia G, Wang W (2012) Association of suboptimal health status and cardiovascular risk factors in urban Chinese workers. J Urban Health 89(2):329–338
20. Wang Y, Ge S, Yan Y, Wang A, Zhao Z, Yu X, Qiu J, Alzain MA, Wang H, Fang H, Gao Q, Song M, Zhang J, Zhou Y, Wang W (2016) China suboptimal health cohort study: rationale, design and baseline characteristics. J Transl Med 14(1):1–12
21. Golubnitschaja O, Baban B, Boniolo G, Wang W, Bubnov R, Kapalla M, Krapfenbauer K, Mozaffari MS, Costigliola V (2016) Medicine in the early twenty-first century: paradigm and anticipation—EPMA position paper 2016. EPMA J 7(1):23
22. Sun Q, Xu X, Zhang J, Sun M, Tian Q, Li Q, Cao W, Zhang X, Wang H, Liu J, Zhang J, Meng X, Wu L, Song M, Liu H, Wang W, Wang Y (2020) Association of suboptimal health status with intestinal microbiota in Chinese youths. J Cell Mol Med 24(2):1837–1847
23. Alzain MA, Asweto CO, Zhang J, Fang H, Zhao Z, Guo X, Song M, Zhou Y, Chang N, Wang Y, Wang W (2017) Telomere length and accelerated biological aging in the china suboptimal health cohort: a Case–Control Study. OMICS 21(6):333–339
24. Yan YX, Wu LJ, Xiao HB, Wang S, Dong J, Wang W (2018) Latent class analysis to evaluate performance of plasma cortisol, plasma catecholamines, and SHSQ-25 for early recognition of suboptimal health status. EPMA J 9(3):299–305
25. Wang Y, Liu X, Qiu J, Wang H, Liu D, Zhao Z, Song M, Song Q, Wang X, Zhou Y, Wang W (2017) Association between ideal cardiovascular health metrics and suboptimal health status in Chinese population. Sci Rep 7(1):1–6
26. Zhu J, Ying W, Zhang L, Peng G, Chen W, Anto EO, Wang X, Lu N, Gao S, Wu G, Yan J, Ye J, Wu S, Yu C, Yue M, Huang X, Xu N, Ying P, Chen Y, Tan X, Wang W (2020) Psychological symptoms in Chinese nurses may be associated with predisposition to chronic disease: a cross-sectional study of suboptimal health status. EPMA J 11(4):1–13

27. Anto EO, Roberts P, Coall DA, Adua E, Turpin CA, Tawiah A, Wang Y, Wang W (2020) Suboptimal health pregnant women are associated with increased oxidative stress and unbalanced pro- and antiangiogenic growth mediators: a cross-sectional study in a Ghanaian population. Free Radic Res 54(1):27–42
28. Wang H, Tian Q, Zhang J, Liu H, Zhang J, Cao W, Zhang X, Li X, Wu L, Song M, Kong Y, Wang W, Wang Y (2021) Blood transcriptome profiling as potential biomarkers of suboptimal health status: potential utility of novel biomarkers for predictive, preventive, and personalized medicine strategy. EPMA J 12(2):103–115
29. Adua E, Memarian E, Russell A, Trbojević-Akmačić I, Gudelj I, Jurić J, Roberts P, Lauc G, Wang W (2019) Utilization of N-glycosylation profiles as risk stratification biomarkers for suboptimal health status and metabolic syndrome in a Ghanaian population. Biomark Med 13(15):1273–1287
30. Wu Z, Guo Z, Zheng Y, Wang Y, Zhang H, Pan H, Li Z, Balmer L, Li X, Tao, L, Guo, X, Wang W (2023) IgG N-glycosylation cardiovascular age tracks cardiovascular risk beyond calendar age. Engineering 26:99–107
31. Ge S, Xu X, Zhang J, Hou H, Wang H, Liu D, Zhang X, Song M, Li D, Zhou Y, Wang Y, Wang W (2019) Suboptimal health status as an independent risk factor for type 2 diabetes mellitus in a community-based cohort: the China suboptimal health cohort study. EPMA J 10(1):65–72
32. Russell A, Drozdova A, Wang W, Thomas M (2014) The impact of dementia development concurrent with Parkinson's disease: a new perspective. CNS Neurol Disord Drug Targets 13(7):1160–1168
33. Vučković F, Krištić J, Gudelj I, Teruel M, Keser T, Pezer M, Pučić-Baković M, Štambuk J, Trbojević-Akmačić I, Barrios C, Pavić T, Menni C, Wang Y, Zhou Y, Cui L, Song H, Zeng Q, Guo X, Pons-Estel BA, McKeigue P, Leslie Patrick A, Gornik O, Spector TD, Harjaček M, Alarcon-Riquelme M, Molokhia M, Wang W, Lauc G (2015) Association of systemic lupus erythematosus with decreased immunosuppressive potential of the IgG glycome. Arthritis Rheum 67(11):2978–2989
34. Sebastian A, Alzain MA, Asweto CO, Song H, Cui L, Yu X, Ge S, Dong H, Rao P, Wang H, Fang H, Gao Q, Zhang J, He D, Guo X, Song M, Wang Y, Wang W (2016) Glycan biomarkers for rheumatoid arthritis and its remission status in Han Chinese patients. OMICS 20(6):343–351
35. Liu D, Chu X, Wang H, Dong J, Ge SQ, Zhao ZY, Peng HL, Sun M, Wu LJ, Song MS, Guo XH, Meng Q, Wang YX, Lauc G, Wang W (2018) The changes of immunoglobulin G N-glycosylation in blood lipids and dyslipidaemia. J Transl Med 16(1):1–10
36. Liu D, Zhao Z, Wang A, Ge S, Wang H, Zhang X, Sun Q, Cao W, Sun M, Wu L, Song M, Zhou Y, Wang W, Wang Y (2018) Ischemic stroke is associated with the pro-inflammatory potential of N-glycosylated immunoglobulin G. J Neuroinflammation 15(1):1–10
37. Anto EO, Roberts P, Coall D, Turpin CA, Adua E, Wang Y, Wang W (2019) Integration of suboptimal health status evaluation as a criterion for prediction of preeclampsia is strongly recommended for healthcare management in pregnancy: a prospective cohort study in a Ghanaian population. EPMA J 10(3):211–226
38. Ma C, Xu W, Zhou L, Ma S, Wang Y (2018) Association between lifestyle factors and suboptimal health status among Chinese college freshmen: a cross-sectional study. BMC Public Health 18(1):1–9
39. Li G, Xie F, Yan S, Hu X, Jin B, Wang J, Wu J, Yin D, Xie Q (2013) Subhealth: definition, criteria for diagnosis and potential prevalence in the central region of China. BMC Public Health 13:1–8
40. Fokunang CN, Ndikum V, Tabi OY, Jiofack RB, Ngameni B, Guedje NM, Tembe-Fokunang EA, Tomkins P, Barkwan S, Kechia F, Asongalem E, Ngoupayou J, Torimiro NJ, Gonsu KH, Sielinou V, Ngadjui BT, Angwafor F 3rd, Nkongmeneck A, Abena OM, Ngogang J, Asonganyi T, Colizzi V, Lohoue J, Kamsu-Kom (2011) Traditional medicine: past, present and future research and development prospects and integration in the National Health System of Cameroon. Afr J Tradit Complement Altern Med 8(3):284–295

41. Zheng S, Du J, Lu X, Zhang Y, Hu L, Wang W (2010) Quality of randomized controlled trials in acupuncture treatment of hepatitis B virus infection--a systematic review. Acupunct Electrother Res 35(3–4):119–131
42. Liao Y, Lin Y, Zhang C, Xue XL, Mao QX, Zhang Y, Dai JG, Wang TF (2015) Intervention effect of Baduanjin exercise on the fatigue state in people with fatigue-predominant subhealth: a cohort study. J Altern Complement Med 21(9):554–562
43. Guo Y, Xu M, Wei Z, Hu Q, Chen Y, Yan J, Wei Y (2018) Beneficial effects of qigong wuqinxi in the improvement of health condition, prevention, and treatment of chronic diseases: evidence from a systematic review. Evid Based Complement Alternat Med 2018:3235950
44. Shen J, Ai B, Shen M (2018) Effectiveness of mild moxibustion for sub-health conditions in pre- and post-menopausal women: a randomized controlled clinical trial. Med Sci Monit 24:2907–2911
45. Yang Y, Ma LX, Niu TL, Niu X, Yang XZ, Wang JX, Lu Y, Gao LJ, Chen TY, Zhang YJ, Wu YJ, Song Y (2018) Effects of pulsatile cupping on body pain and quality of life in people with suboptimal health: a randomized controlled exploratory trial. Med Acupunct 30(6):326–335

# Tourism, Suboptimal Health Status, and Dementia

**Fangli Hu, Jun Wen, Danni Zheng, and Wei Wang**

F. Hu
Centre for Precision Health, Edith Cowan University, Joondalup, WA, Australia
e-mail: fanglih@our.ecu.edu.au

J. Wen (✉)
School of Business and Law, Edith Cowan University, Joondalup, WA, Australia
e-mail: j.wen@ecu.edu.au

D. Zheng
Department of Tourism, Fudan University, Shanghai, China
e-mail: zdn@fudan.edu.cn

W. Wang
First Affiliated Hospital, Shantou University Medical College, Shantou, China

Beijing Key Laboratory of Clinical Epidemiology, Capital Medical University, Beijing, China

School of Public Health, Shandong First Medical University and Shandong Academy of Medical Sciences, Jinan, China

Centre for Precision Health, Edith Cowan University, Perth, Australia

Suboptimal Health Study Consortium, Kumasi, Ghana

Suboptimal Health Study Consortium, Perth, Australia

Suboptimal Health Study Consortium, Beijing, China

Suboptimal Health Study Consortium, Bonn, Germany

European Association for Predictive, Preventive and Personalised Medicine, EPMA, Brussels, Belgium
e-mail: wei.wang@ecu.edu.au



W. Wang (ed.), *All Around Suboptimal Health*, Advances in Predictive, Preventive and Personalised Medicine 18,
https://doi.org/10.1007/978-3-031-46891-9_17

## Abbreviations

| | |
|---|---|
| mRNA | Messenger RNA |
| NCDs | Non-communicable chronic diseases |
| PPPM/3PM | Predictive, preventive, and personalised medicine |
| SHS | Suboptimal health status |
| SHSC | Suboptimal Health Study Consortium |
| SHSQ-25 | Suboptimal Health Status Suestionnaire-25 |

# 1 Introduction

With a faster pace of life and increased social pressure, a growing number of people are experiencing unhealthy lifestyles and the ensuing suboptimal health status (SHS) [1]. They often feel unwell but have no overtly diagnosable conditions [2]. According to the World Health Organization, only 5% of the world's population is truly healthy; that is, few are in "a state of complete physical, mental, and social well-being and not merely the absence of disease or infirmity". The remaining 75% are in an intermediate state between health and disease, while 20% suffer from non-communicable chronic diseases (NCDs) such as diabetes, heart disease, cancer, and mental disorders [3, 4]. SHS tends to cause fatigue and can affect one's mental state, immune system, cardiovascular system, and digestive system. SHS often prompts hospital visits and poor quality of life [5]. NCDs kill 41 million people annually, accounting for 71% of the world's total deaths and representing a major threat—especially in an increasingly ageing society [6]. Despite remarkable medical investment, these diseases remain challenging to prevent [7]. Dementia, a neurological disorder, is a particular public health priority. It currently affects about 55 million people worldwide but is expected to afflict 78 million by 2030 and 139 million by 2050 [8, 9]. Unfortunately, as of now, dementia has no cure or powerful disease-modifying approaches. SHS and NCDs are caused by complex interactions among one's genes, age, environment, and lifestyle along with other factors. Their aetiologies are similarly complicated and have yet to be elucidated [10, 11]. In contrast to difficulties in modifying risk factors such as genes and age, one's environment and lifestyle can be altered to help prevent and relieve symptoms of SHS and NCDs [1, 12]. The philosophy of predictive, preventive, and personalised medicine (PPPM) involves forecasting individuals' predisposition to disease, providing targeted preventive measures, and creating personalised treatment algorithms. Bearing these principles in mind, SHS presents a window of opportunity to discover timely interventions for NCDs [13].

Travel is the most popular leisure and vacation activity of the twentieth century and offers many health benefits [14]. However, its positive impacts on SHS and NCDs (e.g. dementia) have gone overlooked thus far [15, 16]. As a promising non-pharmacological intervention, travel is part of a healthy lifestyle and involves environmental change [16]. It can contribute to health promotion, as well as disease prevention and treatment, in several ways (e.g. via cognitive, affective, conative, and sensorial dimensions), thanks to positive travel experiences [17]. Health issues generally fall within the medical science realm, while tourism is a social science. These domains seem disparate at first glance but are in fact related [18]. On the one hand, the high mobility of travel can exacerbate the spread of infectious diseases and lead to public health crises, such as SARS and COVID-19. On the other hand, it can improve individuals' physical and psychological health and partially alleviate public health concerns, such as population ageing and NCDs [16, 19]. Interdisciplinary collaboration between tourism and medical science is therefore warranted to address complex social issues [18]. This chapter summarises current knowledge about SHS and dementia and proposes that tourism can play a role in their management, creatively bridging the social and medical sciences. Potential research avenues are suggested accordingly.

## 2 Suboptimal Health Status

SHS refers to "an overall physical status between health and illness characterised by the perception of health complaints, chronic fatigue, and a constellation of physical symptoms such as the cardiovascular system, the digestive system, the immune system, and mental status; lasting for at least 3 months" [1]. Traditional Chinese medicine uncovered this intermediate state thousands of years ago and put forward preventive treatment theory in *The Emperor's Classic of Internal Medicine* [20]. SHS manifests in various ways, including reduced vitality, decreased function, and lower adaptive capacity of the organism [21]. Environmental pollution, social stress, and an unhealthy lifestyle are key risk factors for SHS [2]. This status usually causes dysfunction in multiple physiological systems along with other negative health outcomes; it can even deteriorate into chronic disease. A majority of NCDs progress from a reversible subclinical state to an irreversible disease state with obvious symptoms over a mere several years, placing a heavy burden on individuals, caregivers, and society [22]. Put simply, SHS is a critical risk factor for NCDs and typically precedes their onset. Early identification and intervention of SHS will provide new insight into NCD control and management, thus minimizing negative consequences [21]. Yet it is arduous to identify and assess SHS because its manifestations do not meet clinical diagnostic criteria in modern medicine. This condition can hence be easily ignored in the medical field [23]. Our team, the Suboptimal Health Study Consortium (SHSC), seeks to better understand SHS and encourage innovative clinical practices. We have explored validated SHS measures (Fig. 1), such as the Suboptimal Health Status Questionnaire-25 (SHSQ-25) and objective biological indicators [1, 5, 20]. These instruments are useful for recognizing high-risk groups to avoid under-diagnosis, enabling physicians to adopt targeted preventive responses

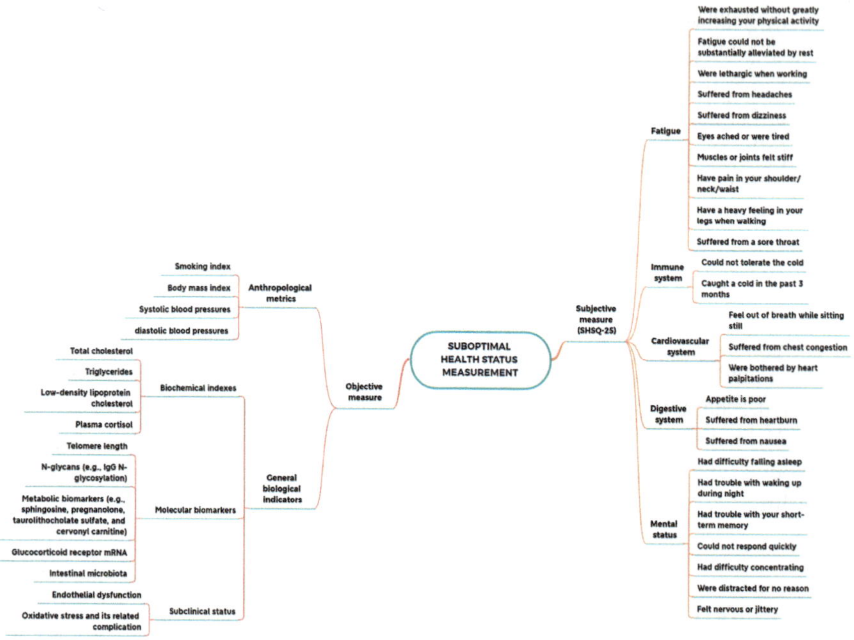


**Fig. 1** Suboptimal health status measurement

before NCDs occur. Such measures are also helpful for excluding low-risk populations to obviate over-diagnosis and wasted medical resources [24].

The SHSQ-25, a self-report tool, was developed in 2009 to facilitate self-assessment [2]. It includes five domains—fatigue, the cardiovascular system, the digestive system, the immune system, and mental status—and 25 items. Respondents are required to score their discomfort experienced in the past 3 months. Each item is rated on a 5-point Likert-type scale with a total possible score of 100. Scores greater than 35 are considered SHS; the higher one's score, the more severe their SHS. As a simple, free, and convenient health measurement tool, this questionnaire is applicable to a wide range of surveys among the general population in clinical and community contexts. From a PPPM perspective, the SHSQ-25 provides an accessible way to evaluate health status and inform health judgements and public health operations [5, 23]. It has been translated into multiple languages (e.g. Chinese, English, Korean, and Russian) and has been used in multi-ethnic populations, including Asians, Africans, and Caucasians [1]. In addition, the instrument has been applied extensively to demonstrate the correlation between SHS and NCDs [3]. The China Suboptimal Health Cohort Study revealed that people with higher SHSQ-25 scores have a greater risk of cardiovascular and metabolic diseases [21, 23, 25]. Several studies in Ghana showed a high association of SHS with type 2 diabetes and preeclampsia [26, 27]. With the help of this measure, the concept of SHS should overcome the confines of traditional health evaluations to encourage proactive healthcare. Advances may include predictive diagnosis as well as targeted prevention and treatment [28].

To compensate for subjective deficiencies of the SHSQ-25, we have examined biometric signs of SHS—both anthropological metrics and general biological indicators [1, 29]. First, SHS is typically associated with changes in common anthropological metrics such as smoking index, body mass index, systolic blood pressure, and diastolic blood pressure [20, 22]. Second, because SHS affects several mental and physical systems, a number of biological indicators can guide assessment [30–32]. Three categories of interest are biochemical indices (e.g. total cholesterol, triglycerides, low-density lipoprotein cholesterol, plasma cortisol) [20], molecular biomarkers (e.g. telomere length, N-glycans, metabolic biomarkers, glucocorticoid receptor mRNA, intestinal microbiota) [22, 33–36], and subclinical status (e.g. endothelial dysfunction, oxidative stress, and associated complications) [26, 37]. These objective indicators are important for evaluating health and predicting disease progression. They can additionally contribute to a well-rounded view of the intricacies of SHS [38, 39].

## 3 Dementia

As a common NCD, dementia is "not a specific disease but is rather a general term for the impaired ability to remember, think, or make decisions that interferes with doing everyday activities" [40]. It consists of two primary symptom classes: cognitive degeneration (e.g. confusion, memory loss, reduced concentration, poor judgement) and psychological and behavioural symptoms (e.g. psychosis, aggression, agitation, sleep problems, depression) [41, 42]. There are many kinds of dementia, such as Alzheimer's disease, vascular dementia, and Lewy body dementia, each of which has varying symptoms. Of these, Alzheimer's disease is most prevalent, accounting for 60–80% of cases [8, 43]. The underlying causes of dementia are exceedingly complex: its aetiology is uncertain despite decades of research, and only a few risk factors have been identified. Prominent elements include age, genes, the environment, and lifestyle [44, 45]. The elderly population is most frequently diagnosed with dementia—roughly 80% of people with dementia are over age 75 [46]. The number of people with dementia will only continue to grow as ageing increases [47]. Worryingly, the onset of dementia is trending younger, and early-onset dementia cannot be ignored [48]. In addition to its constellation of effects, the depth of dementia's impact is staggering. It is the fifth largest contributor to worldwide disease burden. Its estimated yearly financial cost to the global economy exceeded $1 trillion in 2018 and is set to double by 2030 [49]. As such, dementia sits high on the medical agenda [50].

Dementia is also a twenty-first-century social health challenge [8]. Even though a multitude of medical resources have been devoted to its prevention and treatment, little encouraging progress has been made [51]. Theoretically, effective prevention can decrease the incidence of dementia. The medical community employs pharmacological and non-pharmacological interventions targeting a variety of risk factors (e.g. lifestyle-based aspects) to prevent dementia [47, 52, 53]. Yet pharmacological prevention strategies aimed at treating chronic diseases (e.g. diabetes, hypertension, hearing loss) in high-risk populations have significant side effects and limited effectiveness [54, 55]. Although benefits need to be observed in the long-term, non-pharmacological interventions including healthy lifestyle behaviours do not have adverse consequences and are widely recommended [56, 57]. Dementia treatment outcomes remain largely unsatisfactory: symptoms can be partly alleviated, but the disease cannot be cured [50]. More than 100 therapies have been eliminated in the past 10 years, and the failure rate of new drug development is 99.6%—far higher than the 81% failure rate of new drugs designed for cancer [58]. For decades, only five new drugs (i.e. donepezil, rivastigmine, galantamine, memantine, and namzaric) have been routinely used following approval from the U.S. Food and Drug Administration [50, 59]. However, their clinical efficacy and safety are controversial [51].

To make matters worse, academic misconduct has severely hampered dementia research. The journal *Science* recently claimed to have found strong evidence that images in a much-cited study underpinning a reigning theory of Alzheimer's disease, published 16 years ago in *Nature*, might have been fabricated. This alleged fraud is more than an academic scandal that has rocked the medical world; it may have misled 16 years of Alzheimer's studies, wasted billions of dollars in funding and made the dismal state of Alzheimer's research even sadder [60]. Numerous non-pharmacological approaches exist for dementia treatment, such as those targeting cognition, behaviour, emotions, and the senses [61, 62]. Such options are traditionally cost-effective and are strongly recommended as first-line interventions to relieve dementia symptoms [63, 64]. A range of non-pharmacological interventions have hence been suggested to prevent and treat dementia [65]. Travel is well worth trying as a recreational activity conducive to physical and psychological well-being [17].

## 4 Travel Therapy: An Emerging Health Intervention Embracing the Principles of PPPM

Tourism encompasses "the activities of persons traveling to and staying in places outside their usual environment for not more than one consecutive year for leisure, business, and other purposes not related to the exercise of an activity remunerated from within the place visited" [66]. It has brought substantial positive effects to the economy, culture, ecology, and social life [67]. The health benefits of travel have long been recognised [14]. For example, productive travel experiences improve the flexibility of bones and joints and lower the risk of cardiovascular disease, inflammation, headaches, and congestion, thereby enhancing physical health [68]. Travel can also contribute to psychological restoration and well-being by evoking positive emotions and memories that reduce stress, enhance cognition, and mitigate health issues [69]. Even with the proliferation of related studies, scholars have rarely pushed the boundaries of social science to investigate the more far-reaching health outcomes of tourism [16, 70]. The COVID-19 outbreak has highlighted a link between tourism and public health although these areas seem intuitively unrelated. Importantly, even as tourism can fuel public health crises by transmitting infectious diseases, it can contribute positively to public health by elevating people's physical and mental states [16].

Tourism involves food, accommodation, travel, visits, shopping, and entertainment [71]. It therefore has multiple functions to foster tourists' health and well-being [17]. Specifically, tourism allows people to escape from the everyday, embrace nature, and breathe fresh air to relieve stress [66]. Tourism can also enable people to better fit in socially, thus alleviating loneliness and social isolation [72]. Tourists who exercise can strengthen their bodies through physical exertion as well [73]. In an effort to creatively leverage these health benefits, we put forth travel therapy as "a therapeutic approach that enhances people's physical and psychological health and well-being through positive travel experiences and engagement" [70]. This form of therapy is an interdisciplinary concept integrating tourism and medical science. Through physical activity, socialisation, positive emotions, and healthy eating, travel therapy can serve as an effective non-pharmacological intervention for many health issues, similar to music therapy, art therapy, and other techniques [16, 17]. In addition to health enhancement and disease prevention among general tourists, travel therapy can aid tourists with SHS and NCDs (e.g. dementia, depression, cardiovascular problems). Travel can boost the physical and mental capacities of people with SHS to promote healthy states and prevent negative progression to NCDs. For tourists with NCDs, travel may ease symptoms and pain. This non-pharmacological intervention usually cannot cure disease [74]; however, it can act as a complementary intervention to slow disease progression and to maintain and improve patients' abilities to perform daily activities. These effects can promote one's quality of life and reduce societal health burdens [16]. Overall, travel should occupy a prominent position in disease management, especially for dementia where medications have limited success but noticeable side effects (Fig. 2) [17]. Travel therapy embraces the principles of PPPM by providing tailored experiences suited to people's characteristics. This approach promotes personalised prevention and treatment. For example, by gaining an in-depth understanding of tourists' needs and health status, travel experiences can be customised to include specialised physical activities, healthy eating choices, mind–body relaxation techniques, and wellness services [16, 70]. Such individualised measures can help maintain health, manage disease, and provide long-term wellness benefits.

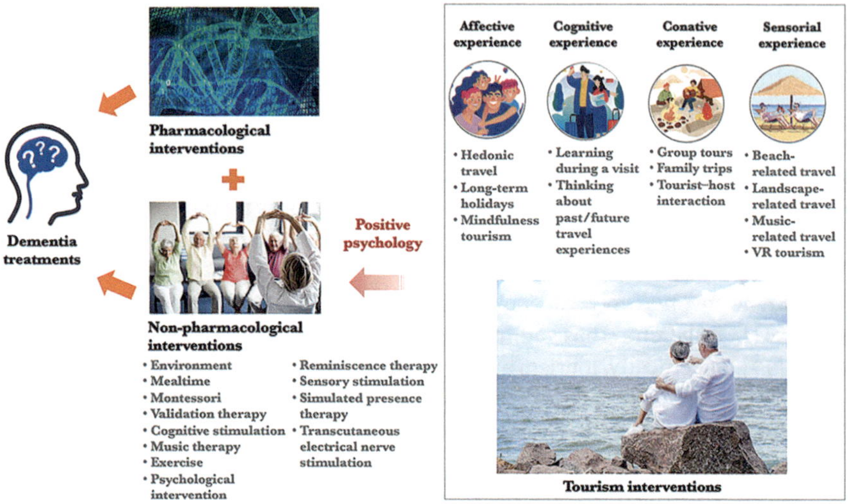


**Fig. 2** Tourism as a dementia treatment based on positive psychology. (Source: Wen et al. (2022) [17])

## 5 Conclusions and Recommendations

In response to scientific and societal progress, interdisciplinary research—especially between the natural and social sciences—has emerged as a trend in academia to address social concerns. This chapter links apparently unrelated fields of tourism, SHS, and dementia through the interdisciplinary concept of travel therapy. Travel, as one component of a healthy and active lifestyle, represents a promising non-pharmacological intervention for SHS and NCDs (e.g. dementia). Travel therapy is an emerging intervention that embodies PPPM guidelines and can help resolve public health issues. Interdisciplinary studies linking tourism and medical science hold meaningful implications for stakeholders. Such work can help protect the rights (e.g. health equality, service equality) of people with health conditions by presenting a disease management option. Practitioners in medicine and tourism/hospitality can benefit from practical guidance to promote industry recovery and transformation, ultimately reducing burdens on society while fostering sustainable development. Relevant research may address diverse topics. First, because people with health conditions are an under-investigated tourist group, little is known about their travel behaviour (e.g. motivations, experiences, expectations, constraints). An in-depth understanding of their actions is essential. Second, more robust empirical research using multidisciplinary methods (e.g. interviews, randomised controlled trials, case–control designs) and biomarkers are strongly recommended. Such work can test the clinical efficacy of travel therapy, develop personalised tourism interventions in line with PPPM tenets, and maximise travel therapy's promise for public health [75].

**Declaration of Interest Statement** Declarations of interest: none.

## References


1. Wang W, Yan Y, Guo Z, Hou H, Garcia M, Tan X, Anto EO, Mahara G, Zheng Y, Li B, Kang T, Zhong Z, Wang Y, Guo X, Golubnitschaja O; Suboptimal Health Study Consortium and European Association for Predictive, Preventive and Personalised Medicine (2021) All around suboptimal health - a joint position paper of the Suboptimal Health Study Consortium and European Association for Predictive, Preventive and Personalised Medicine. EPMA J 12:403–433. https://doi.org/10.1007/s13167-021-00253-2
2. Yan YX, Liu YQ, Li M, Hu PF, Guo AM, Yang XH, Qiu JJ, Yang SS, Shen J, Zhang LP, Wang W (2009) Development and evaluation of a questionnaire for measuring suboptimal health status in urban Chinese. J Epidemiol 19:333–341. https://doi.org/10.2188/jea.je20080086
3. Wang W, Tan X (2019) Suboptimal health status and cardiovascular deficits. In: Golubnitschaja O (ed) Flammer syndrome: from phenotype to associated pathologies, prediction, prevention and personalisation, pp 287–315. https://doi.org/10.1007/978-3-030-13550-8_17
4. Guo Z, Meng R, Zheng Y, Li X, Zhou Z, Yu L, Tang Q, Zhao Y, Garcia M, Yan Y, Song M, Balmer L, Wen J, Hou H, Tan X, Wang W; Suboptimal Health Study Consortium (SHSC) and the Global Health Epidemiology Research Group (GHERG) (2022) Translation and cross-cultural validation of a precision health tool, the Suboptimal Health Status Questionnaire-25, in Korean. J Glob Health 12:04077. https://doi.org/10.7189/jogh.12.04077
5. Ge S, Xu X, Zhang J, Hou H, Wang H, Liu D, Zhang X, Song M, Li D, Zhou Y, Wang Y, Wang W (2019) Suboptimal health status as an independent risk factor for type 2 diabetes mellitus in a community-based cohort: the China suboptimal health cohort study. EPMA J 10:65–72. https://doi.org/10.1007/s13167-019-0159-9
6. WHO. Non communicable diseases. 2021, from https://www.who.int/news-room/fact-sheets/detail/noncommunicable-diseases
7. Di Cesare M, Khang YH, Asaria P, Blakely T, Cowan MJ, Farzadfar F, Guerrero R, Ikeda N, Kyobutungi C, Msyamboza KP, Oum S, Lynch JW, Marmot MG, Ezzati M; Lancet NCD Action Group (2013) Inequalities in non-communicable diseases and effective responses. Lancet 381:585–597. https://doi.org/10.1016/s0140-6736(12)61851-0
8. Chan KY, Wang W, Wu JJ, Liu L, Theodoratou E, Car J, Middleton L, Russ TC, Deary IJ, Campbell H, Wang W, Rudan I; Global Health Epidemiology Reference Group (GHERG) (2013) Epidemiology of Alzheimer's disease and other forms of dementia in China, 1990-2010: a systematic review and analysis. Lancet 381:2016–2023. https://doi.org/10.1016/s0140-6736(13)60221-4
9. WHO. Dementia. 2021. , from https://www.who.int/news-room/fact-sheets/detail/dementia
10. Wang W, Yan Y (2012) Suboptimal health: a new health dimension for translational medicine. Clin Transl Med 1:28. https://doi.org/10.1186/2001-1326-1-28
11. Kluge HHP, Wickramasinghe K, Rippin HL, Mendes R, Peters DH, Kontsevaya A, Breda J (2020) Prevention and control of non-communicable diseases in the COVID-19 response. Lancet 395:1678–1680. https://doi.org/10.1016/s0140-6736(20)31067-9
12. Schmidt MI, Duncan BB, Azevedo e Silva G, Menezes AM, Monteiro CA, Barreto SM, Chor D, Menezes PR (2011) Chronic non-communicable diseases in Brazil: burden and current challenges. Lancet 377:1949–1961. https://doi.org/10.1016/s0140-6736(11)60135-9
13. Wang W (2012) Suboptimal health: a potential preventive instrument for non-communicable disease control and management. J Transl Med 10:1. https://doi.org/10.1186/1479-5876-10-S2-A45
14. Godovykh M, Ridderstaat J (2020) Health outcomes of tourism development: A longitudinal study of the impact of tourism arrivals on residents' health. J Destin Mark Manag 17:100462. https://doi.org/10.1016/j.jdmm.2020.100462
15. Guo Z, Wen J, Zheng D, Yulu Z, Hou H, Wang W (2022) Proposing an avenue for suboptimal health research through the lens of tourism. J Glob Health 12:03058. https://doi.org/10.7189/jogh.12.03058

16. Hu F, Wen J, Zheng D, Wang W (2023) Travel medicine in hospitality: An interdisciplinary perspective. Int J Contemp Hosp 35(9):ahead-of-print. https://doi.org/10.1108/IJCHM-05-2022-0574
17. Wen J, Zheng D, Hou H, Phau I, Wang W (2022) Tourism as a dementia treatment based on positive psychology. Tour Manag 92:104556. https://doi.org/10.1016/j.tourman.2022.104556
18. Wen J, Wang W, Kozak M, Liu X, H. H. (2021) Many brains are better than one: The importance of interdisciplinary studies on Covid-19 in and beyond tourism. Tour Recreat Res 46:2310–2313. https://doi.org/10.1080/02508281.2020.1761120
19. Jiang Y, Wen J, Zheng D, Phau I, Wang W (2022) Pandemic prevention via tourism: A conceptual framework. Ann Tour Res 96:103463. https://doi.org/10.1016/j.annals.2022.103463
20. Wang W, Russell A, Yan Y (2014) Traditional Chinese medicine and new concepts of predictive, preventive and personalized medicine in diagnosis and treatment of suboptimal health. EPMA J 5:4. https://doi.org/10.1186/1878-5085-5-4
21. Yan YX, Dong J, Liu YQ, Yang XH, Li M, Shia G, Wang W (2012) Association of suboptimal health status and cardiovascular risk factors in urban Chinese workers. J Urban Health 89:329–338. https://doi.org/10.1007/s11524-011-9636-8
22. Yan YX, Dong J, Liu YQ, Zhang J, Song MS, He Y, Wang W (2015) Association of suboptimal health status with psychosocial stress, plasma cortisol and mRNA expression of glucocorticoid receptor $\alpha/\beta$ in lymphocyte. Stress 18:29–34. https://doi.org/10.3109/10253890.2014.999233
23. Wang Y, Ge S, Yan Y, Wang A, Zhao Z, Yu X, Qiu J, Alzain MA, Wang H, Fang H, Gao Q, Song M, Zhang J, Zhou Y, Wang W (2016) China suboptimal health cohort study: rationale, design and baseline characteristics. J Transl Med 14:291. https://doi.org/10.1186/s12967-016-1046-y
24. Hou H, Feng X, Li Y, Meng Z, Guo D, Wang F, Guo Z, Zheng Y, Peng Z, Zhang W, Li D, Ding G, Wang W (2018) Suboptimal health status and psychological symptoms among Chinese college students: a perspective of predictive, preventive and personalised health. EPMA J 9:367–377. https://doi.org/10.1007/s13167-018-0148-4
25. Adua E, Roberts P, Wang W (2017) Incorporation of suboptimal health status as a potential risk assessment for type II diabetes mellitus: a case-control study in a Ghanaian population. EPMA J 8:345–355. https://doi.org/10.1007/s13167-017-0119-1
26. Anto EO, Coall DA, Addai-Mensah O, Wiafe YA, Owiredu WKBA, Obirikorang C, Annani-Akollor ME, Adua E, Tawiah A, Acheampong E, Asamoah EA, Wang X, Opoku S, Boakye DK, Hou H, Wang Y, Wang W; Suboptimal Health Study Consortium (SHSC) (2021) Early gestational profiling of oxidative stress and angiogenic growth mediators as predictive, preventive and personalised (3P) medical approach to identify suboptimal health pregnant mothers likely to develop preeclampsia. EPMA J 12:517–534. https://doi.org/10.1007/s13167-021-00258-x
27. Kupaev V, Borisov O, Marutina E, Yan YX, Wang W (2016) Integration of suboptimal health status and endothelial dysfunction as a new aspect for risk evaluation of cardiovascular disease. EPMA J 7:19. https://doi.org/10.1186/s13167-016-0068-0
28. Meng X, Wang B, Xu X, Song M, Hou H, Wang W, Wang Y (2022) Glycomic biomarkers are instrumental for suboptimal health status management in the context of predictive, preventive, and personalized medicine. EPMA J 13:195–207. https://doi.org/10.1007/s13167-022-00278-1
29. Wang H, Tian Q, Zhang J, Liu H, Zhang J, Cao W, Zhang X, Li X, Wu L, Song M, Kong Y, Wang W, Wang Y (2021) Blood transcriptome profiling as potential biomarkers of suboptimal health status: potential utility of novel biomarkers for predictive, preventive, and personalized medicine strategy. EPMA J 12:103–115. https://doi.org/10.1007/s13167-021-00238-1
30. Anto EO, Roberts P, Coall DA, Adua E, Turpin CA, Tawiah A, Wang Y, Wang W (2020) Suboptimal health pregnant women are associated with increased oxidative stress and unbalanced pro- and antiangiogenic growth mediators: a cross-sectional study in a Ghanaian population. Free Radic Res 54:27–42. https://doi.org/10.1080/10715762.2019.1685668
31. Ding G, Zhao X, Wang Y, Song D, Chen D, Deng Y, Xing W, Dong H, Zhou Y, Li D, Hou H (2020) Evaluation of the relationship between cognitive impairment and suboptimal health status in a northern Chinese population: a cross-sectional study. J Glob Health 10:010804. https://doi.org/10.7189/jogh.10.010804

32. Adua E, Afrifa-Yamoah E, Frimpong K, Adama E, Karthigesu SP, Anto EO, Aboagye E, Yan Y, Wang Y, Tan X, Wang W (2021) Construct validity of the Suboptimal Health Status Questionnaire-25 in a Ghanaian population. Health Qual Life Outcomes 19:180. https://doi.org/10.1186/s12955-021-01810-z
33. Alzain MA, Asweto CO, Zhang J, Fang H, Zhao Z, Guo X, Song M, Zhou Y, Chang N, Wang Y, Wang W (2017) Telomere Length and Accelerated Biological Aging in the China Suboptimal Health Cohort: A Case-Control Study. OMICS 21:333–339. https://doi.org/10.1089/omi.2017.0050
34. Adua E, Memarian E, Russell A, Trbojević-Akmačić I, Gudelj I, Jurić J, Roberts P, Lauc G, Wang W (2019) Utilization of N-glycosylation profiles as risk stratification biomarkers for suboptimal health status and metabolic syndrome in a Ghanaian population. Biomark Med 13:1273–1287. https://doi.org/10.2217/bmm-2019-0005
35. Wang H, Tian Q, Zhang J, Liu H, Zhang X, Cao W, Zhang J, Anto EO, Li X, Wang X, Liu D, Zheng Y, Guo Z, Wu L, Song M, Wang Y, Wang W (2020) Population-based case-control study revealed metabolomic biomarkers of suboptimal health status in Chinese population-potential utility for innovative approach by predictive, preventive, and personalized medicine. EPMA J 11:147–160. https://doi.org/10.1007/s13167-020-00200-7
36. Sun Q, Xu X, Zhang J, Sun M, Tian Q, Li Q, Cao W, Zhang X, Wang H, Liu J, Zhang J, Meng X, Wu L, Song M, Liu H, Wang W, Wang Y (2020) Association of suboptimal health status with intestinal microbiota in Chinese youths. J Cell Mol Med 24:1837–1847. https://doi.org/10.1111/jcmm.14880
37. Anto EO, Coall DA, Asiamah EA, Afriyie OO, Addai-Mensah O, Wiafe YA, Owiredu W, Obirikorang C, Annani-Akollor ME, Titiloye NA, Adua E, Acheampong E, Adu EA, Opoku S, Anto AO, Tawiah A, Wang Y, Wang W (2022) Placental lesions and differential expression of pro-and anti-angiogenic growth mediators and oxidative DNA damage marker in placentae of Ghanaian suboptimal and optimal health status pregnant women who later developed pre-eclampsia. PLoS One 17:e0265717. https://doi.org/10.1371/journal.pone.0265717
38. Yan YX, Wu LJ, Xiao HB, Wang S, Dong J, Wang W (2018) Latent class analysis to evaluate performance of plasma cortisol, plasma catecholamines, and SHSQ-25 for early recognition of suboptimal health status. EPMA J 9:299–305. https://doi.org/10.1007/s13167-018-0144-8
39. Zhu J, Ying W, Zhang L, Peng G, Chen W, Anto EO, Wang X, Lu N, Gao S, Wu G, Yan J, Ye J, Wu S, Yu C, Yue M, Huang X, Xu N, Ying P, Chen Y, Tan X, Wang W (2020) Psychological symptoms in Chinese nurses may be associated with predisposition to chronic disease: a cross-sectional study of suboptimal health status. EPMA J 11:551–563. https://doi.org/10.1007/s13167-020-00225-y
40. (CDC) CfDCaP. About Dementia. 2019. , from https://www.cdc.gov/aging/dementia/index.html
41. Kales HC, Gitlin LN, Lyketsos CG (2015) Assessment and management of behavioral and psychological symptoms of dementia. BMJ 350:h369. https://doi.org/10.1136/bmj.h369
42. Langa KM, Larson EB, Crimmins EM, Faul JD, Levine DA, Kabeto MU, Weir DR (2017) A Comparison of the Prevalence of Dementia in the United States in 2000 and 2012. JAMA Intern Med 177:51–58. https://doi.org/10.1001/jamainternmed.2016.6807
43. Bessey LJ, Walaszek A (2019) Management of Behavioral and Psychological Symptoms of Dementia. Curr Psychiatry Rep 21:66. https://doi.org/10.1007/s11920-019-1049-5
44. Lourida I, Hannon E, Littlejohns TJ, Langa KM, Hyppönen E, Kuzma E, Llewellyn DJ (2019) Association of Lifestyle and Genetic Risk With Incidence of Dementia. JAMA 322:430–437. https://doi.org/10.1001/jama.2019.9879
45. Licher S, Ahmad S, Karamujić-Čomić H, Voortman T, Leening MJG, Ikram MA, Ikram MK (2019) Genetic predisposition, modifiable-risk-factor profile and long-term dementia risk in the general population. Nat Med 25:1364–1369. https://doi.org/10.1038/s41591-019-0547-7
46. Hukins D, Macleod U, Boland JW (2019) Identifying potentially inappropriate prescribing in older people with dementia: a systematic review. Eur J Clin Pharmacol 75:467–481. https://doi.org/10.1007/s00228-018-02612-x

47. Grande G, Qiu C, Fratiglioni L (2020) Prevention of dementia in an ageing world: Evidence and biological rationale. Ageing Res Rev 64:101045. https://doi.org/10.1016/j.arr.2020.101045
48. Hendriks S, Peetoom K, Bakker C, van der Flier WM, Papma JM, Koopmans R, Verhey FRJ, de Vugt M, Köhler S; Young-Onset Dementia Epidemiology Study Group; Withall A, Parlevliet JL, Uysal-Bozkir Ö, Gibson RC, Neita SM, Nielsen TR, Salem LC, Nyberg J, Lopes MA, Dominguez JC, De Guzman MF, Egeberg A, Radford K, Broe T, Subramaniam M, Abdin E, Bruni AC, Di Lorenzo R, Smith K, Flicker L, Mol MO, Basta M, Yu D, Masika G, Petersen MS, Ruano L (2021) Global Prevalence of Young-Onset Dementia: A Systematic Review and Meta-analysis. JAMA Neurol 78:1080–1090. https://doi.org/10.1001/jamaneurol.2021.2161
49. GBD 2019 Dementia Forecasting Collaborators (2022) Estimation of the global prevalence of dementia in 2019 and forecasted prevalence in 2050: an analysis for the Global Burden of Disease Study 2019. Lancet Public Health 7:e105–ee25. https://doi.org/10.1016/S2468-2667(21)00249-8
50. Livingston G, Huntley J, Sommerlad A, Ames D, Ballard C, Banerjee S, Brayne C, Burns A, Cohen-Mansfield J, Cooper C, Costafreda SG, Dias A, Fox N, Gitlin LN, Howard R, Kales HC, Kivimäki M, Larson EB, Ogunniyi A, Orgeta V, Ritchie K, Rockwood K, Sampson EL, Samus Q, Schneider LS, Selbæk G, Teri L, Mukadam N (2020) Dementia prevention, intervention, and care: 2020 report of the Lancet Commission. Lancet 396:413–446. https://doi.org/10.1016/s0140-6736(20)30367-6
51. Livingston G, Sommerlad A, Orgeta V, Costafreda SG, Huntley J, Ames D, Ballard C, Banerjee S, Burns A, Cohen-Mansfield J, Cooper C, Fox N, Gitlin LN, Howard R, Kales HC, Larson EB, Ritchie K, Rockwood K, Sampson EL, Samus Q, Schneider LS, Selbæk G, Teri L, Mukadam N (2017) Dementia prevention, intervention, and care. Lancet 390:2673–2734. https://doi.org/10.1016/s0140-6736(17)31363-6
52. Horstkötter D, Deckers K, Köhler S (2021) Primary Prevention of Dementia: An Ethical Review. J Alzheimers Dis 79:467–476. https://doi.org/10.3233/jad-201104
53. Fong TG, Inouye SK (2022) The inter-relationship between delirium and dementia: the importance of delirium prevention. Nat Rev Neurol 18:579–596. https://doi.org/10.1038/s41582-022-00698-7
54. Tariq S, Barber PA (2018) Dementia risk and prevention by targeting modifiable vascular risk factors. J Neurochem 144:565–581. https://doi.org/10.1111/jnc.14132
55. Cunningham EL, Todd SA, Passmore P, Bullock R, McGuinness B (2021) Pharmacological treatment of hypertension in people without prior cerebrovascular disease for the prevention of cognitive impairment and dementia. Cochrane Database Syst Rev 5:Cd004034. https://doi.org/10.1002/14651858.CD004034.pub4
56. Tipton PW, Graff-Radford NR (2018) Prevention of late-life dementia: what works and what does not. Pol Arch Intern Med 128:310–316. https://doi.org/10.20452/pamw.4263
57. Rosenberg A, Mangialasche F, Ngandu T, Solomon A, Kivipelto M (2020) Multidomain Interventions to Prevent Cognitive Impairment, Alzheimer's Disease, and Dementia: From FINGER to World-Wide FINGERS. J Prev Alzheimers Dis 7:29–36. https://doi.org/10.14283/jpad.2019.41
58. Cummings J, Lee G, Ritter A, Sabbagh M, Zhong K (2019) Alzheimer's disease drug development pipeline: 2019. Alzheimers Dement (N Y) 5:272–293. https://doi.org/10.1016/j.trci.2019.05.008
59. Dyer SM, Harrison SL, Laver K, Whitehead C, Crotty M (2018) An overview of systematic reviews of pharmacological and non-pharmacological interventions for the treatment of behavioral and psychological symptoms of dementia. Int Psychogeriatr 30:295–309. https://doi.org/10.1017/s1041610217002344
60. Piller C (2022) Blots on a field? Science 377(6604):358–363. https://doi.org/10.1126/science.ade0209
61. Liao YJ, Parajuli J, Jao YL, Kitko L, Berish D (2021) Non-pharmacological interventions for pain in people with dementia: A systematic review. Int J Nurs Stud 124:104082. https://doi.org/10.1016/j.ijnurstu.2021.104082

62. Koch J, Amos JG, Beattie E, Lautenschlager NT, Doyle C, Anstey KJ, Mortby ME (2022) Non-pharmacological interventions for neuropsychiatric symptoms of dementia in residential aged care settings: An umbrella review. Int J Nurs Stud 128:104187. https://doi.org/10.1016/j.ijnurstu.2022.104187
63. Chancellor B, Duncan A, Chatterjee A (2014) Art therapy for Alzheimer's disease and other dementias. J Alzheimers Dis 39:1–11. https://doi.org/10.3233/jad-131295
64. Gómez-Romero M, Jiménez-Palomares M, Rodríguez-Mansilla J, Flores-Nieto A, Garrido-Ardila EM, González López-Arza MV (2017) Benefits of music therapy on behaviour disorders in subjects diagnosed with dementia: a systematic review. Neurologia 32:253–263. https://doi.org/10.1016/j.nrl.2014.11.001
65. Meyer C, O'Keefe F (2020) Non-pharmacological interventions for people with dementia: A review of reviews. Dementia (London) 19:1927–1954. https://doi.org/10.1177/1471301218813234
66. Govers R, Van Hecke E, Cabus P (2008) Delineating tourism: Defining the usual environment. Ann Tour Res 35:1053–1073. https://doi.org/10.1016/j.annals.2008.09.001
67. Jordan E, Spencer D, Prayag G (2019) Tourism impacts, emotions and stress. Ann Tour Res 75:213–226. https://doi.org/10.1016/j.annals.2019.01.011
68. Fredrickson BL, Cohn MA, Coffey KA, Pek J, Finkel SM (2008) Open hearts build lives: positive emotions, induced through loving-kindness meditation, build consequential personal resources. J Pers Soc Psychol 95:1045–1062. https://doi.org/10.1037/a0013262
69. Pressman SD, Cohen S (2005) Does positive affect influence health? Psychol Bull 131:925–971. https://doi.org/10.1037/0033-2909.131.6.925
70. Wen J, Zheng D, Hu F (2022) The emerging concept of travel therapy in health science: Will it be applied to tourists visiting sub-frigid climate zones? Frigid Zone Med 2(4):200–203. https://doi.org/10.2478/fzm-2022-00042
71. Park S, Woo M, Nicolau J (2020) Determinant factors of tourist expenses. J Travel Res 59:267–280. https://doi.org/10.1177/0047287519829257
72. Buckley R (2019) Therapeutic mental health effects perceived by outdoor tourists: A large-scale, multi-decade, qualitative analysis. Ann Tour Res 77:164–167. https://doi.org/10.1016/j.annals.2018.12.017
73. Fromel K, Kudlacek M, Groffik D (2020) Tourism and physical activity preferences: Development and sustainability strategy. Sustainablity 12:8824. https://doi.org/10.3390/su12218824
74. Abraha I, Rimland JM, Trotta FM, Dell'Aquila G, Cruz-Jentoft A, Petrovic M, Gudmundsson A, Soiza R, O'Mahony D, Guaita A, Cherubini A (2017) Systematic review of systematic reviews of non-pharmacological interventions to treat behavioural disturbances in older patients with dementia. The SENATOR-OnTop series The SENATOR-OnTop series. BMJ Open 7:e012759. https://doi.org/10.1136/bmjopen-2016-012759
75. Zheng D, Wen J, Kozak M, Phau I, Hou H, Wang W (2023) Vulnerable populations with psychological disorders in tourism: Methodological challenges and recommended solutions for empirical research. Tour Manag 98:104760. https://doi.org/10.1016/j.tourman.2023.104760

# Appendix



W. Wang (ed.), *All Around Suboptimal Health*, Advances in Predictive, Preventive and Personalised Medicine 18,
https://doi.org/10.1007/978-3-031-46891-9

# Arabic Version of SHSQ-25

أسئلة الإستبيان:

| 1 | 2 | 3 | 4 | 5 |
|---|---|---|---|---|
| أبداً | من حين الى آخر | غالباً | غالباً جداً | دائماً |

| 1 | 2 | 3 | 4 | 5 | ما مدى تكرار شعورك/ي بألعراض التالية؟ |
|---|---|---|---|---|---|
| □ | □ | □ | □ | □ | 1. إرهاق من غير زيادة ملحوضة في نشاطك البدني. |
| □ | □ | □ | □ | □ | 2. إعياء ال يمكن تخفيفه بشكل كبيرعن طريق الراحة. |
| □ | □ | □ | □ | □ | 3. الخمول أثناء العمل. |
| □ | □ | □ | □ | □ | 4. صداع الرأس. |
| □ | □ | □ | □ | □ | 5. دوار الرأس. |
| □ | □ | □ | □ | □ | 6. تعب أو إرهاق في العينين. |
| □ | □ | □ | □ | □ | 7. التهاب الحلق. |
| □ | □ | □ | □ | □ | 8. تصلب العضالت أو المفاصل. |
| □ | □ | □ | □ | □ | 9. ألم في الكتف, الرقبة أو منطقة الخصر. |
| □ | □ | □ | □ | □ | 10. شعورك بثقل في الساقين عند المشي. |
| □ | □ | □ | □ | □ | 11. شعورك بضيق في التنفس أثناء الجلوس. |
| □ | □ | □ | □ | □ | 12. إحتقان في الصدر. |
| □ | □ | □ | □ | □ | 13. خفقان في القلب. |
| □ | □ | □ | □ | □ | 14. فقدان الشهية لألكل. |
| □ | □ | □ | □ | □ | 15. حرقة في المعدة. |
| □ | □ | □ | □ | □ | 16. الغثيان. |
| □ | □ | □ | □ | □ | 17. عدم القدرة على تحمل البرد. |
| □ | □ | □ | □ | □ | 18- صعوبة في النوم. |
| □ | □ | □ | □ | □ | 19. عدم القدرة على النوم المتواصل أثناء اليل. |
| □ | □ | □ | □ | □ | 20. صعوبة في تذكر ألشياء على المدى القصير. |
| □ | □ | □ | □ | □ | 21. عدم إإلستجابة للمؤثرات بسرعة. |
| □ | □ | □ | □ | □ | 22. الصعوبة في التركيز. |
| □ | □ | □ | □ | □ | 23. تشتت ذهني من دون سبب. |
| □ | □ | □ | □ | □ | 24. شعور بالتوتر. |
| □ | □ | □ | □ | □ | 25. إصابة بنزلة برد في الثالث أشهر الماضية. |

## Chinese Version of SHSQ-25

| | 对于下表中所列的问题，在过去的三个月内，这些症状在您身上发生的频率是怎样的? | 1<br>完全没有 | 2<br>很少有 | 3<br>有 | 4<br>多数有 | 5<br>几乎总是 |
|---|---|---|---|---|---|---|
| 1 | 您觉得疲劳吗(在运动量没有明显增加的情况下)? | | | | | |
| 2 | 您的疲劳在休息后能缓解吗? | | | | | |
| 3 | 在工作时您有困倦或倦怠的现象吗? | | | | | |
| 4 | 感觉头痛 | | | | | |
| 5 | 感觉头晕 | | | | | |
| 6 | 眼睛酸胀 | | | | | |
| 7 | 咽喉疼痛 | | | | | |
| 8 | 肌肉和关节经常感到发僵或僵硬 | | | | | |
| 9 | 肩、颈或腰部酸痛 | | | | | |
| 10 | 走路时感到双腿沉重 | | | | | |
| 11 | 静息时感到气短 | | | | | |
| 12 | 胸闷 | | | | | |
| 13 | 心悸 | | | | | |
| 14 | 食欲减退 | | | | | |
| 15 | 胃部不适 | | | | | |
| 16 | 消化不良 | | | | | |
| 17 | 低热或怕冷 | | | | | |
| 18 | 入睡有困难 | | | | | |
| 19 | 多梦或易惊醒的情形 | | | | | |
| 20 | 记忆力减退 | | | | | |
| 21 | 反应能力下降 | | | | | |
| 22 | 注意力不集中 | | | | | |
| 23 | 没有原因的心烦意乱 | | | | | |
| 24 | 紧张、焦虑现象 | | | | | |
| 25 | 您是否患过感冒 | | | | | |

## Dutch Version of SHSQ-25

**Dotazník SHSQ-25**

| | Hoe vaak was het in de afgelopen 3 maand dat u (uw) | 1<br>Nooit of bijna nooit | 2<br>Soms | 3<br>Vaak | 4<br>Heel vaak | 5<br>Altijd |
|---|---|---|---|---|---|---|
| 1 | uitgeput was zonder uw fysieke activiteit aanzienlijk te verhogen? | | | | | |
| 2 | vermoeidheid ervaarde die niet substantieel kon worden verlicht door rust? | | | | | |
| 3 | lusteloos was tijdens het werk? | | | | | |
| 4 | leed aan hoofdpijn? | | | | | |
| 5 | last had van duizeligheid? | | | | | |
| 6 | ogen vermoeid waren of pijn deden? | | | | | |
| 7 | last had van keelpijn? | | | | | |
| 8 | spieren of gewrichten stijf aanvoelden? | | | | | |
| 9 | pijn had in uw schouder / nek / taille? | | | | | |
| 10 | u een zwaar gevoel in uw benen had tijdens het lopen? | | | | | |
| 11 | zich buiten adem voelde terwijl u stil zat? | | | | | |
| 12 | last had van een verstopte borstkas? | | | | | |
| 13 | last had van hartkloppingen? | | | | | |
| 14 | een verminderde eetlust had? | | | | | |
| 15 | last had van brandend maagzuur? | | | | | |
| 16 | last had van misselijkheid? | | | | | |
| 17 | koude omgevingen niet kon verdragen? | | | | | |
| 18 | moeite had om in slaap te vallen? | | | | | |
| 19 | 's nachts meerdere keren wakker werd? | | | | | |
| 20 | problemen had met uw kortetermijngeheugen? | | | | | |
| 21 | niet snel kon reageren? | | | | | |
| 22 | moeite had te concentreren? | | | | | |
| 23 | zonder reden werd afgeleid? | | | | | |
| 24 | zich nerveus of zenuwachtig gevoeld? | | | | | |
| 25 | een verkoudheid had in de afgelopen 3 maanden? | | | | | |

## English Version of SHSQ-25

| | How often is it, that you (your) | 1<br>Never or almost never | 2<br>Occasionally | 3<br>Often | 4<br>Very often | 5<br>Always |
|---|---|---|---|---|---|---|
| 1 | were exhausted without greatly increasing your physical activity | | | | | |
| 2 | fatigue could not be substantially alleviated by rest | | | | | |
| 3 | were lethargic when working | | | | | |
| 4 | were lethargic when working | | | | | |
| 5 | suffered from dizziness | | | | | |
| 6 | eyes ached or were tired | | | | | |
| 7 | suffered from a sore throat | | | | | |
| 8 | muscles or joints felt stiff | | | | | |
| 9 | have pain in your shoulder/neck/waist | | | | | |
| 10 | have a heavy feeling in your legs when walking | | | | | |
| 11 | feel out of breath while sitting still | | | | | |
| 12 | suffered from chest congestion | | | | | |
| 13 | were bothered by heart palpitations | | | | | |
| 14 | appetite is poor | | | | | |
| 15 | suffered from heartburn | | | | | |
| 16 | suffered from nausea | | | | | |
| 17 | could not tolerate the cold | | | | | |
| 18 | had difficulty falling asleep | | | | | |
| 19 | had trouble with waking up during night | | | | | |
| 20 | had trouble with your short-term memory | | | | | |
| 21 | could not respond quickly | | | | | |
| 22 | had difficulty concentrating | | | | | |
| 23 | were distracted for no reason | | | | | |
| 24 | felt nervous or jittery | | | | | |
| 25 | caught a cold in the past 3 months | | | | | |

## Japanese Version of SHSQ-25

| | 3か月以内でのあなたの頻度で: | 1<br>全くないまたはほとんどない | 2<br>時々ある | 3<br>よくある | 4<br>頻繁によくある | 5<br>毎回ある |
|---|---|---|---|---|---|---|
| 1 | 運動をあまりしてなくても疲れを感じましたか? | | | | | |
| 2 | 休んでも疲れが取れなかった経験はありますか? | | | | | |
| 3 | 仕事中、疲れや眠気を感じましたか? | | | | | |
| 4 | 頭痛はありましたか? | | | | | |
| 5 | めまいはありましたか? | | | | | |
| 6 | 目の疲れや痛みはありましたか? | | | | | |
| 7 | のどの痛みはありましたか? | | | | | |
| 8 | 筋肉や関節が固くなりましたか? | | | | | |
| 9 | 腰、肩、首に痛みを感じましたか? | | | | | |
| 10 | 歩いている途中、足に重みを感じましたか? | | | | | |
| 11 | 座っているとき、息苦しく感じましたか? | | | | | |
| 12 | 肺が圧迫されてる感じはしますか? | | | | | |
| 13 | 動悸を感じましたか? | | | | | |
| 14 | 食欲がないと感じましたか? | | | | | |
| 15 | 胸やけを感じましたか? | | | | | |
| 16 | 吐き気を感じましたか? | | | | | |
| 17 | 寒い場所にたえられないときがありましたか? | | | | | |
| 18 | 眠りにつくのが難しいときはありましたか? | | | | | |
| 19 | 夜中に起きることがありましたか? | | | | | |
| 20 | 短期記憶に問題はありましたか? | | | | | |
| 21 | 質問に対し、早く答えれないときがありましたか? | | | | | |
| 22 | 集中力に問題がありましたか? | | | | | |
| 23 | 理由もなく集中力が途切れたことはありましたか? | | | | | |

| | 3か月以内でのあなたの頻度で: | 1<br>全くないまたはほとんどない | 2<br>時々ある | 3<br>よくある | 4<br>頻繁によくある | 5<br>毎回ある |
|---|---|---|---|---|---|---|
| 24 | 興奮や緊張を感じたことはありましたか? | | | | | |
| 25 | 3か月以内に風邪をひきましたか? | | | | | |

## Korean Version of SHSQ-25

| 증상 | 전혀 없었다 | 거의 없었다 | 그렇다 | 자주 그렇다 | 거의 항상 그렇다 |
|---|---|---|---|---|---|
| B1. 귀하는 피곤하십니까(운동량이 현저히 증가되지 않는 경우) | 1 | 2 | 3 | 4 | 5 |
| B2. 귀하는 휴식 후 피로가 풀릴 수 있습니까 | 1 | 2 | 3 | 4 | 5 |
| B3. 귀하는 일할 때 졸리거나 권태로운 현상이 있습니까 | 1 | 2 | 3 | 4 | 5 |
| B4. 두통 | 1 | 2 | 3 | 4 | 5 |
| B5. 머리가 어지럽다 | 1 | 2 | 3 | 4 | 5 |
| B6. 눈이 쓰리고 탱탱하다 | 1 | 2 | 3 | 4 | 5 |
| B7. 인후통 | 1 | 2 | 3 | 4 | 5 |
| B8. 근육과 관절은 항상 경직되거나 뻣뻣함을 느낀다 | 1 | 2 | 3 | 4 | 5 |
| B9. 어깨, 목 또는 허리가 시큰거리다 | 1 | 2 | 3 | 4 | 5 |
| B10. 걸을 때 다리가 무겁다 | 1 | 2 | 3 | 4 | 5 |
| B11. 숨을 죽일 때 숨이 가쁘다 | 1 | 2 | 3 | 4 | 5 |
| B12. 가슴이 답답하다. | 1 | 2 | 3 | 4 | 5 |
| B13. 속이 떨리다 | 1 | 2 | 3 | 4 | 5 |
| B14. 식욕 감퇴 | 1 | 2 | 3 | 4 | 5 |
| B15. 속이 안 좋다 | 1 | 2 | 3 | 4 | 5 |
| B16. 소화 불량 | 1 | 2 | 3 | 4 | 5 |
| B17. 저열 혹은 추위를 탄다 | 1 | 2 | 3 | 4 | 5 |
| B18. 잠들기 힘들다 | 1 | 2 | 3 | 4 | 5 |
| B19. 꿈이 많거나 놀라 깨기 쉽다 | 1 | 2 | 3 | 4 | 5 |
| B20. 기억력이 감퇴하다 | 1 | 2 | 3 | 4 | 5 |
| B21. 순발력이 떨어지다 | 1 | 2 | 3 | 4 | 5 |
| B22. 집중력이 떨어지다 | 1 | 2 | 3 | 4 | 5 |
| B23. 이유 없이 정신이 사납다 | 1 | 2 | 3 | 4 | 5 |
| B24. 긴장, 불안 | 1 | 2 | 3 | 4 | 5 |
| B25. 귀하는 최근 1년 동안 감기에 걸린 적이 있습니까 | 1 | 2 | 3 | 4 | 5 |

## Portuguese Version of SHSQ-25

| | Nos últimos 3 meses, o quão frequentemente você | 1<br>Nunca ou quase nunca | 2<br>Às vezes | 3<br>Frequentemente | 4<br>Muito frequentemente | 5<br>Sempre |
|---|---|---|---|---|---|---|
| 1 | Esteve exausto mesmo sem ter aumentado muito a sua atividade física? | | | | | |
| 2 | Experienciou fadiga que não pode ser substancialmente aliviada com descanso? | | | | | |
| 3 | Esteve sonolento e apático (letárgico) no trabalho? | | | | | |
| 4 | Sentiu dores de cabeça? | | | | | |
| 5 | Sentiu tonturas? | | | | | |
| 6 | Ficou com os olhos doendo ou cansados? | | | | | |
| 7 | Sentiu dor de garganta? | | | | | |
| 8 | Sentiu rigidez nas articulações ou músculos? | | | | | |
| 9 | Esteve com dores no pescoço/cintura/ombro? | | | | | |
| 10 | Sentiu suas pernas pesadas enquanto caminhava? | | | | | |
| 11 | Se sentiu com falta de ar enquanto estava sentado? | | | | | |
| 12 | Sentiu os seus pulmões congestionados? | | | | | |
| 13 | Se incomodou com palpitações no coração? | | | | | |
| 14 | Teve falta de apetite? | | | | | |
| 15 | Sentiu queimação no peito/ estômago (azia)? | | | | | |
| 16 | Sentiu náuseas? | | | | | |
| 17 | Não conseguiu tolerar ambientes frios? | | | | | |
| 18 | Teve dificuldades para dormir? | | | | | |
| 19 | Ficou acordando durante a noite? | | | | | |
| 20 | Teve problemas com a sua memoria de curta duração? | | | | | |
| 21 | Não conseguia responder rápido a perguntas? | | | | | |
| 22 | Teve dificuldade de concentração? | | | | | |

| | Nos últimos 3 meses, o quão frequentemente você | 1 Nunca ou quase nunca | 2 Às vezes | 3 Frequentemente | 4 Muito frequentemente | 5 Sempre |
|---|---|---|---|---|---|---|
| 23 | Ficou distraído por nenhuma razão aparente? | | | | | |
| 24 | Se sentiu nervosa(a) ou ansioso(a)? | | | | | |
| 25 | Teve uma gripe nos últimos 3 meses? | | | | | |

## Russian Version of SHSQ-25

| | Как часто это происходит с Вами? | 1 никогда или почти никогда | 2 редко | 3 часто | 4 очень часто | 5 всегда |
|---|---|---|---|---|---|---|
| 1 | Испытываете ли Вы усталость, не связанную с увеличением физической активности | | | | | |
| 2 | Испытываете усталость, сохраняющуюся после отдыха | | | | | |
| 3 | Испытываете ли Вы сонливость во время работы | | | | | |
| 4 | Беспокоит ли Вас головная боль | | | | | |
| 5 | Бывает ли у Вас головокружение | | | | | |
| 6 | Чувствуете ли Вы боль или усталость в глазах | | | | | |
| 7 | Болит ли у Вас горло | | | | | |
| 8 | Беспокоит ли Вас скованность, дискомфорт в мышцах или суставах | | | | | |
| 9 | Беспокоят ли Вас боли в шее, плечах, пояснице | | | | | |
| 10 | Ощущаете ли Вы чувство тяжести в ногах при ходьбе | | | | | |
| 11 | Испытываете ли Вы одышку в покое | | | | | |
| 12 | Чувствуете ли Вы стеснение в груди | | | | | |
| 13 | Бывает ли у Вас учащенное сердцебиение | | | | | |
| 14 | Бывает ли у Вас сниженные аппетит | | | | | |
| 15 | Беспокоит ли Вас изжога | | | | | |
| 16 | Испытываете ли Вы тошноту | | | | | |
| 17 | Болеете ли Вы простудными заболеваниями | | | | | |
| 18 | Беспокоит ли Вас бессонница | | | | | |

| | | 1 | 2 | 3 | 4 | 5 |
|---|---|---|---|---|---|---|
| | Как часто это происходит с Вами? | никогда или почти никогда | редко | часто | очень часто | всегда |
| 19 | Просыпаетесь ли Вы среди ночи | | | | | |
| 20 | Испытываете ли Вы затруднения с кратковременной памятью | | | | | |
| 21 | Чувствуете ли Вы снижение скорости реакции | | | | | |
| 22 | Испытываете ли Вы трудности с концентрацией внимания | | | | | |
| 23 | Отвлекаетесь ли Вы без причины | | | | | |
| 24 | Нервничаете ли Вы или впадаете в панику | | | | | |
| 25 | Страдали ли Вы простудой за последние 3 месяца | | | | | |

# Sinahla Version of SHSQ-25

| පූර්ව මාස 03 තුල ඔබ කොපමණ වරයක් | 1 | 2 | 3 | 4 | 5 | ලකුණු |
|---|---|---|---|---|---|---|
| | කවදාවත් නැතහොත් කවදාවත් නැති තරම් | ඉඳහිට | බොහෝ විට | නිතරම | සෑම විටම | සෞඛ්‍ය සේවකයන් විසින් සම්පූර්ණ කිරීමට |
| 1. ඔබේ ශාරීරික ක්‍රියාකාරකම් වැඩිමනත් ලෙස ඉහල දැමීමකින් තොරව වෙහෙසට පත් වී ඇත්ද? | | | | | | |
| 2.විවේකය මඟින් සලකිය යුතු ලෙස අඩු කළ නොහැකි තෙහෙට්ටුව අත් විඳ ඇත්ද? | | | | | | |
| 3.වැඩ කරන විට උදාසීන වී ඇත්ද? | | | | | | |
| 4.හිසරදයෙන් පීඩා විඳ ඇත්ද? | | | | | | |
| 5.කරකැවිල්ලෙන් පීඩා විඳ ඇත්ද? | | | | | | |
| 6.ඇස් රිදීම හෝ ඇස් වෙහෙසට පත් වී ඇත්ද? | | | | | | |
| 7.උගුරේ අමාරුවෙන් පීඩා වින්දා ද? | | | | | | |
| 8.මාංශ පේශී හෝ සන්ධි දැඩි බවක් දැනුනාද? | | | | | | |
| 9.ඔබේ උරහිසේ/බෙල්ලේ/ඉඟටියෙහි වේදනාවක් තිබේද? | | | | | | |
| 10.ඇවිදින විට ඔබේ කකුල් වල තද ගතියක් තියනවද? | | | | | | |
| 11නිශ්චලව හිඳින විට හුස්ම හිර වීමක් දැනුනාද? | | | | | | |
| 12.පපුවේ තද වීමෙන් පීඩා වින්දා ද? | | | | | | |
| 13.හෘද ස්පන්දනය/ගැස්සීම නිසා පීඩාවට පත් උනාද? | | | | | | |
| 14.ආහාර රුචිය දුර්වලද? | | | | | | |
| 15.පපුව දැවිල්ලෙන් පීඩා වින්දාද? | | | | | | |
| 16.ඔක්කාරයෙන් පීඩා වින්දාද? | | | | | | |
| 17.සීතල පරිසරය ඉවසිය නොහැකිද? | | | | | | |
| 18.නිදාගැනීමට අපහසු වූවාද ? | | | | | | |
| 19.රාත්‍රී කාලය තුල අවදි වීමේ ගැටළුවක් තිබුණාද? උදා:රෑට නින්දෙන් අවදි වීම. | | | | | | |
| 20.ඔබේ කෙටි කාලීන මතකය සමඟ ගැටළු ඇතිව තිබුණාද? | | | | | | |
| 21.යමකට ඉක්මනින් ප්‍රතිචාර දක්වීට නොහැකි වුනාද? | | | | | | |
| 22.අවධානය යොමු කිරීමේ අපහසුවක් ඇති වුනාද? | | | | | | |
| 23. හේතුවක් නොමැතිව අවධානය වෙනතකට යොමු වුණාද? | | | | | | |
| 24.කෝන්තියක් හෝ ව්‍යාකූල බවක් දැනුනාද? | | | | | | |
| 25.පසුගිය මාස තුන තුල සෙම්ප්‍රතිශ්‍යාව වැළඳී තිබේද? | | | | | | |

## Slovak Version of SHSQ-25

**Dotazník SHSQ-25**

| | Odpovedzte, prosím, na všetky otázky tak, že zapíšete X pod frekvenciu (1-5), ktorá, podľa Vás, najviac zodpovedá skutočnosti vo Vašom prípade. | 1 | 2 | 3 | 4 | 5 |
|---|---|---|---|---|---|---|
| | Ako často ste:/Ako často sa stáva, že: | Nikdy alebo skoro nikdy | Zriedka | Často | Veľmi často | Stále |
| 1 | unavený, aj keď nevykonávate výrazne zvýšenú fyzickú aktivitu? | | | | | |
| 2 | neviete zmierniť únavú tým, že si oddýchnete? | | | | | |
| 3 | malátny pri vykonávaní práce? | | | | | |
| 4 | trpíte bolesťami hlavy? | | | | | |
| 5 | trpíte závratmi alebo nevoľnosťou? | | | | | |
| 6 | trpíte bolesťou očí alebo únavou? | | | | | |
| 7 | trpíte zápalom hrdla? | | | | | |
| 8 | máte stuhnuté svaly alebo kĺby? | | | | | |
| 9 | máte bolesti v ramenách, krku, drieku? | | | | | |
| 10 | cítite, že vaše nohy sú akoby ťažké pri chôdzi? | | | | | |
| 11 | lapáte po dychu napriek tomu, že kľudne sedíte? | | | | | |
| 12 | trpíte sťaženým dýchaním? | | | | | |
| 13 | Vás rozruší tzv. „búšenie srdca“? | | | | | |
| 14 | máte slabú chuť do jedla? | | | | | |
| 15 | trpíte pálením záhy? | | | | | |
| 16 | trpíte nevoľnosťou s nutkaním na zvaracaie? | | | | | |
| 17 | nedokážete tolerovať chlad? | | | | | |
| 18 | máte ťažkosti so zaspávaním? | | | | | |
| 19 | trpíte zobúdzaním sa počas noci? | | | | | |
| 20 | máte problém s krátkodobou pamäťou?. | | | | | |
| 21 | nedokážete rýchlo reagovať? | | | | | |
| 22 | máte problém sústrediť sa? | | | | | |
| 23 | ste bezdôvodne roztržitý alebo zmätený/á? | | | | | |
| 24 | cítite nervozitu alebo paniku? | | | | | |
| 25 | ste mali nádchu v posledných troch mesiacoch? | | | | | |

## Spanish Version of SHSQ-25

| | ¿Con qué frecuencia es que usted (su/sus) | 1<br>Nunca o casi nunca | 2<br>Ocasionalmente | 3<br>A menudo | 4<br>Muy a menudo | 5<br>Siempre |
|---|---|---|---|---|---|---|
| 1 | estuvo exhausto sin aumentar significativament su actividad física? | | | | | |
| 2 | fatiga no pudo ser aliviada sustancialmente por el descanso? | | | | | |
| 3 | estuvo letárgico cuando trabajaba? | | | | | |
| 4 | sufrió de dolores de cabeza? | | | | | |
| 5 | sufrió de mareos? | | | | | |
| 6 | ojos dolían o estaban cansados? | | | | | |
| 7 | sufrió de dolor de garganta? | | | | | |
| 8 | músculos o articulaciones se sentían rígidos/as? | | | | | |
| 9 | tiene dolor en su hombro/ cuello/cintura? | | | | | |
| 10 | tiene una sensación de pesadez en sus piernas cuando camina? | | | | | |
| 11 | siente falta de aire mientras está sentado/a? | | | | | |
| 12 | sufrió de congestion en el pecho? | | | | | |
| 13 | fue molestado por palpitaciones en el corazón? | | | | | |
| 14 | tiene poco apetito? | | | | | |
| 15 | sufrió de acidez estomacal? | | | | | |
| 16 | sufrió de nauseas? | | | | | |
| 17 | no pudo tolerar el frío? | | | | | |
| 18 | tuvo dificultad para conciliar el sueño? | | | | | |
| 19 | tuvo problemas para despertarse en la noche? | | | | | |
| 20 | tuvo problemas con su memoria a corto plazo? | | | | | |
| 21 | no pudo responder rápidamente? | | | | | |
| 22 | tuvo dificultad para concentrarse? | | | | | |
| 23 | se distrajo sin razón aparente? | | | | | |

| | ¿Con qué frecuencia es que usted (su/sus) | 1 Nunca o casi nunca | 2 Ocasionalmente | 3 A menudo | 4 Muy a menudo | 5 Siempre |
|---|---|---|---|---|---|---|
| 24 | sintió nervioso/a o tembloroso/a? | | | | | |
| 25 | se resfrió en los últimos 3 meses? | | | | | |

# Thai Version of SHSQ-25

| | สำหรับคำถามทีแสดงในตารางด้านล่างอาการเหล่านีเกิดขึนกับคุณบ่อยเพียงใดในช่วงสามเดือนทีผ่านมา? (ตัวเลือกเดียวต่อบรรทัด) | 1 ไม่เคย | 2 มีบ้าง | 3 มี | 4 บ่อยครัง | 5 เป็นประจำ |
|---|---|---|---|---|---|---|
| 1 | คุณรู้สึกเหนือยไหม (ในกรณีทีไม่มีการออกกำลังกายเพิมขึนอย่างมีนัยสำคัญ) | | | | | |
| 2 | ความเหนือยล้าของคุณดีขึนหลังจากพักผ่อนได้หรือไม | | | | | |
| 3 | คุณรู้สึกง่วงนอนหรือเหนือยจากการทำงานหรือไม | | | | | |
| 4 | รู้สึกปวดหัว | | | | | |
| 5 | รู้สึกวิงเวียน | | | | | |
| 6 | เจ็บตา | | | | | |
| 7 | เจ็บคอ | | | | | |
| 8 | กล้ามเนือและข้อต่อมักรู้สึกตึงหรือแข็ง | | | | | |
| 9 | เจ็บไหล่คอหรือเอว | | | | | |
| 10 | รู้สึกหนักขาเมือเดิน | | | | | |
| 11 | หายใจถีขณะพัก | | | | | |
| 12 | แน่นหน้าอก | | | | | |
| 13 | ใจสัน | | | | | |
| 14 | ไม่อยากอาหาร | | | | | |
| 15 | ไม่สบายท้อง | | | | | |
| 16 | อาหารไม่ย่อย | | | | | |
| 17 | ร้อนๆหนาวๆ | | | | | |
| 18 | นอนหลับยาก | | | | | |
| 19 | ฝันหรือตืนได้ง่าย | | | | | |
| 20 | ลืมง่าย | | | | | |
| 21 | การตอบสนองลดลง | | | | | |
| 22 | ไม่มีสมาธิ | | | | | |
| 23 | หงุดหงิดโดยไม่มีสาเหตุ | | | | | |
| 24 | วิตกกังวล | | | | | |
| 25 | ในปีทีผ่านมาคุณเคยเป็นหวัดหรือไม่ | | | | | |

GPSR Compliance

*The European Union's (EU) General Product Safety Regulation (GPSR) is a set of rules that requires consumer products to be safe and our obligations to ensure this.*

*If you have any concerns about our products, you can contact us on ProductSafety@springernature.com*

In case Publisher is established outside the EU, the EU authorized representative is:

Springer Nature Customer Service Center GmbH
Europaplatz 3
69115 Heidelberg, Germany

**Batch number: 10732044**

Printed by Printforce, the Netherlands